Nurturing the Nation

Nurturing
the Nation

The Family Politics of Modernizing,
Colonizing, and Liberating Egypt,
1805–1923

Lisa Pollard

UNIVERSITY OF CALIFORNIA PRESS
Berkeley / *Los Angeles* / *London*

University of California Press
Berkeley and Los Angeles, California

University of California Press, Ltd.
London, England

© 2005 by the Regents of the University of California

Library of Congress Cataloging-in-Publication Data

Pollard, Lisa.
　　Nurturing the nation : the family politics of modernizing, colonizing,
and liberating Egypt (1805–1923) / Lisa Pollard.
　　　　p.　cm.
　　Includes bibliographical references and index.
　　ISBN 0-520-24022-7 (cloth : alk. paper) — ISBN 0-520-24023-5 (pbk. : alk.
paper)
　　　1. Family — Egypt — History.　2. Family policy — Egypt — Cross-
cultural studies — History.　3. Egypt — History — 19th century.
4. Egypt — History — 20th century.　I. Title.

HQ691.7.P65　2005
306.85'0962 — dc22　　　　　　　　　　　　　　　　　　　　　2004005280

Manufactured in the United States of America
14　13　12　11　10　09　08　07　06　05
10　9　8　7　6　5　4　3　2　1

To my parents, Bob, Evelyn, and LaNelle,
with love and gratitude

Contents

Illustrations

Acknowledgments

This book is the result of many years of work in California, Egypt, and North Carolina. It has benefited wholly from the guidance of various people to whom thanks are owed. My professors at Berkeley — Ira Lapidus, Barbara Daly Metcalf, and Thomas Metcalf — provided me with friendship as well as the example of their fine scholarship. I hope that both are reflected in these pages. My very first college history professor, Jack McCune, has been my mentor and friend for many years, supporting this book in a number of ways.

In Cairo, Amira al-Azhary Sonbol of Georgetown University took me under her wing and helped me to navigate Egypt's archives. At the American University in Cairo, I was helped and encouraged to read, write, and speak Arabic by an amazing faculty, foremost among whom were Nadia Harb and 'Azza Waked. They of course are not responsible for my translations and interpretations of texts and documents, but they are wholly credited for providing me with the Arabic skills without which this book would not exist. Raghda el-'Essawi, 'Emad al-Din Rushdie, Zeinab Ibrahim, Kristen Brustad, and Mahmoud al-Batal have kept me from forgetting the really important things over the years, not the least of which is Arabic.

The research for this project was carried out in archives in Egypt, Great Britain, and the United States. My great thanks to the staffs at Dar al-Kuttub al-Misriyya, Dar al-Watha'iq al-Misriyya, the Museum of Education at the Egyptian Ministry of Education, l'Institut d'Égypte in Cairo, and the Creswell Library at the American University of Cairo. In Great

Britain, I received tremendous help and support at the Bodelian Library at Oxford, the archives and library of St. Antony's College, Oxford, and the Public Records Office at Kew Gardens. In the United States I was graciously assisted by the archivists and librarians at the University of California, Berkeley, and the Presbyterian Historical Society in Philadelphia. Sherman Hayes and Sue Cody at the University of North Carolina, Wilmington, have kept the materials flowing into our small collection.

International research is expensive, and I am indebted to the American Research Center in Egypt, the Social Science Research Council, the Mellon Foundation, and the University of North Carolina, Wilmington. I am twice indebted to the Center for Arabic Studies Abroad at the American University in Cairo.

A number of friends and colleagues have read all or parts of this manuscript simply because they wanted to. I thank Preeti Chopra, Patricia Coughlin (who read it twice!), Bruce Kinzer, Elizabeth Oram, Mona Russell, Virginia Stewart, and Christopher Toensing for their time and their many suggestions, all of which added to the quality of this book. The two anonymous readers from the University of California Press set examples of the finest scholarship and collegiality in their comments and critiques.

Camron Amin and Ellen Fleischman have enriched this manuscript with their work on women and the state in Iran and Palestine. Mona Russell, the mother of research on consumerism among women in early-twentieth-century Egypt, shared this project with me from its beginning, endowing it with her amazing friendship and scholarship. The late Mine Ener nurtured my early forays into research in Cairo, and I wish to remember her generosity and spirit here. Great thanks to Lynne Haney and the contributors to *Families of a New World* for sharing their work on states and families all over the globe. Thanks to Laura Bier and Hossam Bahgat for their help and friendship on my research trip to Cairo in the summer of 2001.

Thanks to Lynne Withey, Kate Warne, and Julie Brand at the University of California Press for their encouragement and commitment to *Nurturing the Nation*. Huge thanks to Matt Stevens, the ever-accomplished copy editor, for his hard work and patience.

Friends from places as far-flung as Santa Rosa, California, and Beni Suef, Egypt, have loved and supported me at critical moments in the production of this book. If I tried to name them all I would surely leave someone out. But I must mention the Dewidar-'Effat clan, especially the

inimitable Madame Zuzu, who has included me in all of her "family politics" and taught me more about Egypt than I could ever learn in the
archives.

My parents, Bob and Evelyn Pollard, have been constant sources of
love and support, and I thank them both.

The final drafts of this book were written in Wilmington, North
Carolina, my home since 1997. My students and colleagues at UNC-
Wilmington have been ever stimulating, supportive, and encouraging.
Thanks to my graduate students Scott Huntley and Matt Parnell for their
interest in 1919. The members of the Southeast Regional Middle East and
Islamic Studies Seminar (SERMEISS) and the Carolina Seminar on
Islam welcomed me into their communities and nurtured this project. I
wish to thank Sarah Shields and Hager el-Hadidi, in particular, for sharing their endless enthusiasm for the Middle East, as well as their friendship with me. Jane Lowe, Katya Campbell, Jackie Jenkins, and Peggy
Canady helped me make the transition from San Francisco to a small
town in the American South. LaNelle Clontz adopted me into her great
southern family for absolutely no reason, picking up the pieces more than
once, and providing me with enough laughter and joy to finish this
book and, I hope, others. It is to her, and to my mother and father, that
Nurturing the Nation is dedicated.

Note on Translation
and Transliteration

For the convenience of the nonspecialist, I have omitted Arabic diacritical marks, except for the *'ayn* (') and the *hamza* ('). I have transliterated Arabic and anglicized names according to the system used by the *International Journal of Middle East Studies*. The Egyptian letter *gim* has been translated as *j*, except in those cases where the Egyptian rendering is more familiar (for example, Giza).

All translations, unless otherwise indicated, are my own. In places where my translations needed additional clarification, I have indicated such changes in brackets.

Introduction

In May 1919, Egypt's acting consul general, Sir Milne Cheetham (1869–1938), sent an intelligence report to the Foreign Office in an attempt to explain why Egypt had erupted in a series of violent uprisings. Having perused the Egyptian political press, Cheetham reported to British foreign secretary Lord Curzon (1859–1925) that he found the Egyptian peasants, workers, and bourgeois nationalists (the *effendiyya*) to be largely uninterested in politics. The contagions of Bolshevism, Turkish nationalism, and general Egyptian unruliness — not desires for independence and self-rule — were at the heart of the uprisings.[1] His comments, designed as much to explain away the causes of the 1919 Revolution as to uncover them, were meant to persuade Curzon to maintain Egypt as a British protectorate state. Cheetham wrote:

> More significant than what appeared in the Press were often the things which were entirely ignored. There were endless general expressions of admiration for the noble hospitality of the Egyptian people, and for its wonderful success in proving its political solidarity by demonstrations, modified only by a repudiation on behalf of the intellectuals of any responsibility for the excesses of the mob . . . the resignation of the . . . ministry passed almost without comment, and henceforth references to Zaghloul Pasha's delegation were comparatively few and far between. Attention was henceforth diverted mainly to such matters as the necessity of more interest on the part of Egyptians in trade, the uses of trade unionism, and the *necessity of charity on the part of the rich towards the poor.*[2]

In explaining away the revolution, the British missed a number of crucial points about Egyptian politics and the ways that they were shaped.

I

→ Brits do not see the importance

Acts such as hospitality and charity — "nurturing the nation" — were potent political symbols throughout the turbulent years of 1919–22. Caring for the nation as a family had become the sine qua non of modern Egyptian politics by 1919. A preoccupation with charity during the 1919 Revolution was symbolic of political acumen, not apathy.

The iconography of the revolution suggests that regard for the nation's children and dedication to improving domestic life connoted a real concern for the nation's progress and welfare. It also demonstrates that such stereotypically female behavior was not reserved for women: The household and its activities, central to which was a kind of maternalism practiced by both sexes, was the arena where Egyptians created new sexual and social relationships, demonstrated political acumen, and defined a new bourgeois culture.

Household relations

Indeed, during the revolution, bourgeois male nationalists exalted for themselves behavior that can readily be referred to as "maternal."[3] Great political significance was attached to acts such as tending to the nation's children, its poor, sick, and homeless. Men's marital behavior and domestic habits appeared central to demonstrating Egypt's readiness for self-rule. That the British missed this dimension of Egyptian nationalism in their analysis of Egyptian revolutionary activities represents a potent historical irony. Indeed, conflating charity and domesticity with politics was an Egyptian response to the politics of the British protectorate state in their country. In 1919, as in the decades leading up to it, Egyptian nationalists responded to a basic premise of British colonial policy in Egypt: The inability of the Egyptian nation to govern itself stemmed from the domestic and marital habits of the Egyptian governing elite. Upon the British invasion and subsequent occupation of Egypt in 1882, British officials had to legitimize an expensive and seemingly unwanted extension of their overseas rule. They faced the task of shaping policies to rule Egypt without making it an outright colony. By claiming that Egyptians had to be reformed before they could take charge of their own government, the British could both justify and afford an open-ended stay in Egypt. Under British supervision, the Egyptian ruling elite would be allowed to work within their own political institutions until they could prove to their overseers that they had been transformed into modern, competent rulers.[4]

Sir Evelyn Baring (r. 1883–1907; Lord Cromer after 1892), Egypt's consul general and architect of the protectorate, claimed that such reform had to start with the transformation of Egyptians' domestic affairs. Cromer and his contemporaries conflated the political and economic aptitude of Egypt's khedives and their ministers with the practice of

→ B Egypt reforms to in rel to Brit power

polygamy and the keeping of harems. For the British, Egyptian politics were synonymous with the familial habits — marital practices, living arrangements, relations between parents and children — of Egyptian rulers. Because the connubial relations of the Egyptian elite did not match the Victorian ideals of monogamy, the British claimed that Egyptian political and economic institutions were morally unsound. The realpolitik of British foreign policy was thus undergirded by the *moralpolitik* of domestic affairs, turning familial practices into family politics — in essence, domestic mores as measures of the ability of the nation-state to govern itself.

The British use of domestic images to classify non-Western subjects and to justify and shape colonial policy for ruling them was not at all limited to Egypt. In India, the British claimed to be horrified by such customs as widow burning (suttee), child marriage, and regulations against widow remarriage.[5] Vitriol against such practices, as well as laws limiting their usage, served to divide "modern, moral" Englishmen from Indians. It was seemingly easy for the British to justify colonial rule over a "backward, immoral" populace that engaged in such appalling (and, later, illegal) traditions. Easier yet was locking Indians out of governmental positions because of their family politics: Effeminate Indian men who could not protect their wives and daughters from the funeral pyre were deemed inadequate to the task of governing their own country.[6]

Likewise, in colonial Africa, where British colonial policy was largely carried out with the assistance of Christian missionaries and white settlers, domestic and sexual practices served to separate Europeans from Africans, Christian from pagan, modern from traditional. In Kenya, from the turn of the twentieth century onward, Christian missionaries of all denominations waged campaigns to eradicate the practice of the clitoridectomy, or female circumcision, labeling it a "brutal," "pagan ritual" and combating it both as a means of Christianizing Kenyans and cutting them off from their "traditional" practices.[7] The ensuing controversy reached its peak in the 1920s when some denominations threatened excommunication to Kenyan Christians, both male and female, who supported the practice.

The British government entered the debate over the clitoridectomy in the late 1920s out of anxiety over increased tension between the missionaries and Kenyans in the Kikuyu province who were "engaged in a widespread campaign for the revival of the most brutal form of female circumcision, which they declare to be necessary to true Kikuyu nationality."[8] Parliamentary debates over how to curtail the practice appear, on the surface, to have been geared toward protecting African women from a "barbaric" act. The Duchess of Atholl, the House's most prominent female Conservative, stated, "I regard this custom of the mutilation of girls as practiced in Kenya among the Kikuyu as even more injurious to the race than suttee."[9] Ultimately, however, debates about the clitoridectomy reflected on African men and served to separate those Kenyans who were "reformable" from those who were not. While the Labour government was committed to the gradual diminishing of British settlers' privileges and a concomitant extension of self-government to Africans, it was apprehensive about granting such a rule to those natives who supported the mutilation of their wives and daughters.[10]

Like Indians, Africans like the Kikuyu used British campaigns against their "traditional" practices to shape nationalist platforms. Nineteenth-century Indian intelligentsia had championed discussions and debates over household practices and marital customs as a means of separating themselves from the British and of exerting in their private lives the kind of control that they had lost in the public arena.[11] In a similar fashion, Kikuyu nationalists claimed rituals such as the clitoridectomy as a "deeply ingrained" Kikuyu custom and as holding a central place in the tribe's history.[12] When in the early 1930s British officials encouraged members of the nationalist Kikuyu Central Association to distance their platforms from the defense of the practice, the result was "a question of Kikuyu patriotism."[13] For the Kikuyu and Indians, defining and controlling marital, sexual, and domestic issues was intrinsic to self-definition and delineating tradition and modernity. Participation in debates about the domestic order was an opportunity to contest colonial claims about their alleged barbarism and backwardness.

In Egypt, the British did not pass laws against polygamy or child marriage. They did, however, construct a pseudocolonial state in which Egyptians were limited from participation in politics. The vague, open-ended nature of the protectorate state, as well as the power given to colonial officials to appoint and dismiss Egyptian officials at will, reflected the belief that Egyptians needed reform before they could govern themselves. The British did very little to ameliorate those things that they found lacking in the newest additions to their empire.

Egyptian nationalists did, however, attend to the transformation of the arenas in which the British characterized them as "wanting." As in India and Africa, the Egyptian intelligentsia appropriated the marital and domestic relationships that seemed to horrify the British and engaged in heated debates about them. The relationship between the future of the nation and the transformation of the household became a topic in the press, in the classroom, and, later, in political parties, where otherwise disenfranchised nationalists could address the future of their nation.

This book addresses the ascendance of the image of the monogamous couple, their children, and the reformed, modernized domicile as templates for discussing political transformation from the middle of the nineteenth century through the Egyptian 1919 Revolution.[14] As the result of political and economic transformations that took place in Egypt prior to the British occupation in 1882, and later as a response to British colonial discourse, the Victorian family came to symbolize modernity, economic solvency, and the rise and success of the nation-state.[15] The result was the association of monogamy with political maturity; claiming citizenship in a modern, independent nation-state required adherence to a set of new, sometimes imported, domestic traditions. While the Egyptian middle classes never became fully "European," they came to define national character in terms of domestic behavior.[16]

Indeed, from the 1890s onward, the Egyptian press was full of columns, articles, and advertisements attesting to the relationship between the condition of the family and the shape and function of the state, past and present. Bourgeois men and women alike prescribed the kind of marital and domestic behavior suitable to transforming Egypt into a liberal, constitutional state along European lines, or, by contrast, to returning it to the greatness of its past. In either case, the logic inherent to discussions about the household dictated that political transformation of any sort must stem from a thorough examination of domestic mores and required replacing some customs with new ones.

Central to such conversations and debates were Egyptian women, both real and ideal. In both the male- and female-authored press, uneducated, superstitious Egyptian women were commonly evoked as symbolic of the sins of Egypt's past, while refined, competent wives and mothers heralded a new era. "The woman question," or debates about women's education and emancipation, seemed to accompany the rise of nationalist aspirations and to dominate political commentary about the condition and the future of the nation in the decades preceding the 1919 Revolution.

The centrality of women and their reform to discussions about the household has led historians to believe that debates about domestic reform were wholly about creating a new Egyptian womanhood. Such conclusions overlook the extent to which debates about "women" were part of a larger project of remaking men and women alike. Leila Ahmed, in her *Women and Gender in Islam* (1992), for example, places the rise of male nationalist discourse about women in the context of an environment in which changes in such issues as education, governmental structures, and the world economy led Egyptian men to think about themselves and the world around them differently.[17] In what she calls the "discourse of the veil," reformers of both religious and secular orientations endeavored to improve the condition of Egypt's women. Both groups tended to argue that the position of women in Islamic societies in general and Egyptian society in particular had decayed but could be restored through a careful interrogation of the past. Men's domination of women, they argued, most clearly manifested in veiling and seclusion, had led to Egypt's social, intellectual, and political retardation. Reform of domestic practices and the abolition of the veil were tantamount to liberating Egypt from the chains of an oppressive past. As men "woke up" to the decay of their political institutions, as signaled, above all, by the occupation of Egypt in 1882, they began to take action. Their determination to create a new generation of educated homemakers, morally sound mothers, and suitable marital partners reflected a symbolic concern to rectify past injustices and assure a promising future for all Egyptians.[18]

Ahmed's analysis perpetuates the tendency of historians who study turn-of-the-twentieth-century Egypt to attribute change, particularly changes in the status and the condition of women, to a handful of enlightened elite.[19] It also underplays the environment — intellectual and otherwise — into which the woman question seemingly "appeared." Ahmed's text was one of the first to place the position of women in Islamic societies in historical context. But left unclear in her text are the historical processes that led to a vocabulary of reform in which domesticity came to be responsible for the sins of the past and the potential of the future.[20] Were male reformers unaffected by the institutions and ideologies that surrounded them, or did their discourse about reform reveal the strategies and subtleties of modernization and the British occupation? There is no doubt that certain turn-of-the-century (male) reformers wished to emancipate women, or, by contrast, to confine and circumscribe their roles in Egyptian society. At the same time, however, images of the "woman," "female," and "feminine" belied far greater debates about Egyptian manhood, the role and position of a colonized nation, and the ascendance of European political and economic institutions over traditional, Islamic ones.[21]

In their determination to record women's exit from the domicile in the early twentieth century, as well as women's increased knowledge of, and interest in, the world outside of the home, scholars of the feminist movement in Egypt have likewise overlooked the extent to which domestic life was actually critical to shaping women's connection to the political arena. Margot Badran, for example, whose work on Egypt's most famous feminist, Huda Sha'rawi (1879–1947), has pioneered a generation of scholarship on feminism in Egypt, also places the earliest articulations of feminism within the context of the great awakenings that are characterized as having taken place throughout the Middle East in the late nineteenth century. Women, she claims, began to take notice of the differences between them and men, to interrogate discrepancies in their powers and privileges, and to formulate solutions to their problems. She writes, "The earliest manifestations of upper- and middle-class women's nascent 'feminist consciousness' surfaced as a new culture of modernity was being shaped in nineteenth-century Egypt. . . . Upper- and middle-class women observed how men in their families were freer to innovate while they were more restricted. As women expanded their female circles, they discovered different ways that they *as women* — across lines of class, religion and ethnicity — were controlled. As they imagined new lives, women began to withhold complicity in their own subordination."[22]

In a process that appears to have paralleled the "awakenings" of male Egyptian reformers, secular nationalists and Islamic modernists alike, women "woke up" to the powers that oppressed them, according to Badran, and began to articulate ways to empower themselves. Beginning with a rising "feminist consciousness" in the press in the latter decades of the nineteenth century, the feminist movement was later transformed into "individual and collective forms of political action." Nationalism for men and women alike, Badran argues, was a collective self-review through which the position of individuals and the nation would be rectified. Similarly, in *The Women's Awakening in Egypt*, historian Beth Baron argues that the rise of the women's press in Egypt corresponded with a growing awareness of the problem plaguing turn-of-the-century Egyptians. She illustrates that during the 1890s, the women's press became an arena in which "female intellectuals were active agents, shifting and weighing various ideas, absorbing some and reacting against others, and shaping their own programs." She suggests that women were "compelled" to take pen in hand in support of nationalism in both its immediate and far-reaching goals.[23] But as nationalism gave women greater access to the public realm, Badran suggests that they had to leave the domestic realm behind. Domesticity was thus reduced to a kind of "cult" toward which some women were drawn, while others set their sights on politics and the public sphere. It is quite a contradiction, then, according to Badran, "that just as the pioneers of the women's press were transcending the confines of domesticity and laying claim to a new occupation, they employed their pens to exalt the very domesticity they were escaping."[24]

This study does not view the domestic realm as the mere target of men's intellectual activities or, by contrast, that which men (and some women) explicitly singled out in order to keep women out of public roles. Rather, it illustrates the extent to which nineteenth-century discourse about the relationship between the state of the nation and that of the home ultimately confined debates and discussions about Egyptian nationalism to a rather limited field. Domestic debates, familial activities, and connubial relations formed a basic framework through which abstract concepts such as nation and, along with it, loyalty and citizenship were imagined, articulated, and debated by Egyptians from the inception of the modern Egyptian nation-state in the early nineteenth-century. Men and women did not champion the home (or, by contrast, denounce it) in order to be nationalists. Rather, it was home life that shaped modern, bourgeois debates about nationalism for both sexes.[25]

The domestic nature of nineteenth- and early twentieth-century bourgeois nationalist discourse, however, had enormously different consequences for men and women. Displaying the extent to which they had reformed their family politics allowed Egyptian men to claim that they were acquiring political maturity and purging the nation of its political ills. In other words, subjecting themselves and their homes to reform seemed to guarantee that men would become active in independent Egypt's political realm. By subjecting themselves to the terms of the nineteenth-century equation between the home and the political realm, however, male nationalists created a political realm that depended on the existence of a sound, domestic order. Were women to leave the domestic realm, the political realm could not function. Thus, while nationalist discourse written by men and women alike often championed women's emancipation and political enfranchisement, nationalism actually created a vision of an independent Egypt in which mothers had to remain at home.[26]

While the family fully appeared in the years after the British occupation as a metaphor for political commentary and critique, political and economic transformations throughout the nineteenth century were reflected in discussions about the domestic realm and familial practices. Egypt is distinguished from India and Africa in the colonial period by the nascent nation-state's role in political and economic transformations that

[handwritten margin note: Egypt already in process of reform by Brits arrive.]

were taking place there prior to the British occupation. While the British brought with them a discourse in which Egyptian marital and domestic practices signaled despotism and political backwardness, Egyptians had already begun to view changes in household arrangements as heralding political and economic centralization and modernization. At the same time, they had begun to use domestic practices as a means of distinguishing themselves as distinctly Egyptian as opposed to European or Ottoman.

In making the Egyptian state more efficient, loyal, and distinct from the Ottoman rule that preceded it, Viceroy Mohammad 'Ali (r. 1805–48), founder of the dynasty that ruled Egypt until 1952, exposed Egyptians to a whole host of new ideas and practices. The gradual centralization of the Egyptian state over the nineteenth century, for example, began to displace the "household" as a coalition of military, political, and economic alliances and to replace it with kin-based households. As the eighteenth century gave way to the nineteenth, membership in a household was characterized by relationships of blood or marriage rather than military, economic, or political alliances.[27] As a means of consolidating his power, Mohammad 'Ali discontinued the architectural style of the Mamluks who preceded him. He discouraged the use of houses that could hold many people and mandated the construction of smaller-family dwellings along European lines, therefore discouraging the formation of coalitions that might rival his authority.[28] New building styles and living arrangements thus signaled changes in political structures.

[handwritten margin note: Mehmet Ali reforms]

[handwritten margin note: In effort to secure power, he encourages familial, small households.]

The transformation of Egypt's economy, bureaucracy, and educational system under Mohammad 'Ali also gave rise to a class of Egyptians whose taste and habits differed from the generation that preceded it.[29] Mohammad 'Ali's policy of granting state-held lands to government officials, family, and relatives in exchange for loyalty led to the growth of a new cadre of landed wealthy Egyptians. The children of this new elite were among those targeted by the viceroy's limited forays into the establishment of a national educational system designed to produce civil servants for the new state bureaucracy. Such students were exposed not only to traditional forms of learning but to the Western sciences that the viceroy deemed necessary to the construction of a centralized state. Through the study of European languages and literature, this generation of educated Egyptians was exposed to Western institutions, ideologies, habits, and customs, including those pertaining to familial structures and domestic arrangements. Domestic practices appeared as part of the vocabulary with which a new generation of Egyptians learned about European

[handwritten margin note: Ali creates new tastes w/i society.]

[handwritten note at bottom: Western Education aids in the adoption of Western domestic ideas.]

politics, and through which they began to fit themselves into a new cosmology of modern nations. State servants — fathers as well as sons — were exposed to new marital and domestic mores.

This new class of Egyptians was further transformed by exposure to Western domestic practices in the two decades prior to the British occupation. Mohammad 'Ali's grandson Isma'il (r. 1863–79), in his determination to transform Egypt along Western lines, promoted European investment in Egypt. The growth of European expatriate merchant communities in Cairo and Alexandria gave rise to new models of behavior and consumption for bourgeois, urban Egyptians. Isma'il himself was determined to transform his household into a mirror of European aristocracy, and, as historian Mona Russell has shown, his consumption habits at home served as a model for bourgeois Egyptians, especially those who aspired to positions within Isma'il's government. For Egypt's governing elite, buying homes in Cairene districts planned especially for them, and furnishing those homes in both Oriental and European fashions, served both to distinguish them from their Ottoman predecessors and to demonstrate their loyalty to Isma'il and his programs.[30]

Likewise, due to economic changes and as a means of distinguishing themselves from Ottoman Turks, many bourgeois Egyptians began to practice monogamy rather than polygamy in the years surrounding the British occupation.[31] Tawfiq (r. 1879–92), under whose reign the occupation took place, distinguished himself from his father, Isma'il, by taking only one wife. It is not clear whether or not his marital practices served as a model for Egyptians, but his reign did see an increase in the number of elite Egyptians who married similarly. While such changes in marital customs were not attached to official state blueprints for modernization and central rule (in other words, polygamy was not officially discouraged or made illegal), changes in political and economic structures brought about variations not only in home furnishings but in Egyptian domestic mores.

Thus in the years prior to the occupation, changes in the home and the family accompanied economic and political transformations. Domestic behavior became a means of distinguishing oneself as a member of a new, elite class and as "Egyptian" rather than "Ottoman." Whether or not commentary on personal habits became linked to political critique in turn-of-the-century Egypt because of the occupation or simply due to Egypt's own process of political and economic reform is a matter of historical conjecture. What is clear, however, is that British discourse about the role of Egyptian domestic practices in necessitating the veiled protectorate met

Egypt will use Brit criticism to strengthen bourgeois affiliation.

head on with the changing ideas and practices of a bourgeois, educated Egyptian elite that was already in the process of reacting to changes precipitated by internal reforms and by Egypt's increased contact with Europe.

The occupation of 1882 thus did not serve as a defining moment after which unwitting Egyptians were subjected to a colonial discourse and simply swayed by its messages. At the same time, however, British notions about the relationship between politics and familial structures did not take root in wholly foreign soil. Rather, the rise and subsequent prevalence of the familial-political metaphor in bourgeois Egyptian culture illustrate the complex ways in which ideas are circulated in societies under foreign occupation as well as the opaque boundaries between colonial and indigenous discourses. While this study does not examine the effects of the colonial experience in Egypt on British culture in England, it does illustrate the ways in which familial images and tropes were circulated between Egyptians and the British and how family politics came to signify so much more than its intended justification for colonial subjugation.[32] As such, *Nurturing the Nation* is a case study of what happens to the tropes of colonial discourse once subject populations are exposed to them. In using the familial-political metaphor to address modernity, "Egyptian-ness," and the place of their country in a hierarchy of modern nations, Egyptians rejected British notions of their backwardness and inability. At the same time, by answering "the Egypt question" in the same language with which it was constructed, Egyptians signaled to the British that such familial metaphors resonated within their culture. When nationalists used the family to announce their readiness for self-rule in 1919, they alluded both to the success of the political and economic reform programs that had begun prior to 1882 and to their unwillingness to tolerate further hindrances to those programs by an outside power.

Summary

Chapter 1 examines "travel literature" written by servants of the state who traveled to Europe to learn foreign languages from the 1820s to the 1840s and who translated European texts into Turkish and Arabic for the state's use. These state servants, members of the new family of officials created by Mohammad 'Ali to work within an increasingly large government apparatus, paid enormous attention to European domiciles and to the practices of their inhabitants when they chronicled their activities in Europe. These government officials cum travel writers used domestic practices as a means of measuring the modernity of their destination countries.[33] At the same time, state-produced translations of texts on

Travel Lit.

European history and world geography exposed new generations of Egyptians to a positivist view of history in which the rise and success of the Western nation-state was attributed to the private habits and customs of European rulers and citizens. While the Egyptians who traveled to Europe did not focus exclusively on European women and their status, state-produced travel literature made clear connections between modernity and very particular kinds of domiciles. In this view of nineteenth-century Egypt, domestic habits were responsible for the rise and success of nation-states and their citizens.

Chapter 2 investigates travel literature produced by Europeans who visited Egypt when Egyptian state-modernizing programs were taking place. The nineteenth century witnessed the Europeans' thorough penetration of the inner realms of Egyptians' homes, monuments, and edifices and the creation of a seamless distinction between what allegedly went on inside them and the very nature and structure of Egypt itself. The result of such imagery was the creation, in both the Western imagination and, later, the British colonial administration, of a gendered feminine territorial and historical entity known as Egypt. Egyptians were "known" to the Europeans through the activities that took place in their homes. Despite the fact that Egyptian society was in the process of substantial transformation over the course of the nineteenth century, European travel literature depicted Egypt and its traditions as timeless. Two "Egypts" thus existed: the territory in which a modern nation-state and its servants were establishing themselves and an imaginary Egypt created by Europeans. Which of the two did the British colonize?

Chapter 3 addresses the extent to which the frequently erroneous legacies of travel literature and European scholarship about the Middle East shaped British colonial policy.[34] The chapter illustrates the role played by the alleged domestic practices of Isma'il Pasha and his ministers in the creation and administration of the British protectorate state in the early 1880s. Official correspondence between the Foreign Office and officials on the ground in Egypt, as well as the papers and memoirs of the officials who formulated and implemented British policy in Egypt, reveal that Egyptian domestic practices — both real and imagined — were used not only to fashion the policies through which the British ruled Egypt but to justify their open-ended tenure there. The images that appear in such correspondence do not capture the transformations that were taking place among the ruling classes but instead favor depictions of Egypt that appear to be out of *A Thousand and One Nights*. While territorial and financial crises were responsible for the British decision to invade Egypt in 1882, what lay at the heart of British relations with the Egyptians once the occupation was a *fait accompli,* was a vision of Egypt and its institutions that had little to do with monetary or territorial concerns. If "the Egypt question" was shaped by the impetus of crown and capital, its solution was shaped through the imagination of travelers and the often fictitious images of art and scholarship.

Chapter 4 examines the educational system in which new domestic relations were learned and practiced, both prior to the occupation and after its establishment. Children's textbooks, teachers' guides, and syllabi from the nineteenth and early twentieth centuries illustrate the extent to which the turn-of-the-century home had become politicized. The nascent nation-state, both Egyptian and colonial, extended its hand into the private lives of its citizens by normalizing their home life and by connecting their domestic practices to political success.

Chapter 5 examines the role that the Egyptian press played from the 1870s through the beginning of World War I in defining Egyptian-ness and in contesting and subverting colonial discourse. By the turn of the twentieth century, Egyptian journalists used images of Egyptian homes and families to address British critiques about their society. At the same time, however, domestic imagery was used to attack British discourse and to propose strategies for resisting it. Seemingly innocuous columns on home economics and table manners often contained scathing critiques of the British, lessons in Egyptian history, and recipes for rebellion. The chapter argues that the rise of "the woman question" in the Egyptian press around 1900 was not really about women at all but was rather part of a larger attempt to liberate and remake the colonized nation. "Lifting the veil" on Egypt's domestic practices exposed the habits and customs of men as well as those of their wives and daughters.

Chapter 6 recounts the demonstrations of 1919 to illustrate that by the time the revolution broke out, the reformed family had become a concrete symbol of bourgeois Egyptians' quest for independence. Poetry, fiction, and biographies written by the *effendiyya* — notables, their Western-educated sons, bureaucrats, and professionals with degrees from state schools — during the revolutionary years reveal that nurturing the nation had become a political ideal for both sexes. Political caricatures, which depicted the nation in many feminine forms, show that the breast milk of mothers infused the nation and gave it the greatest strength.[35] But the nation was not, as Deniz Kandiyoti has correctly claimed, represented as a woman simply to be protected or sexually and morally policed.[36] Rather, "women" and the virtues attributed to them and their domestic activities embodied the nation, gave birth to it, and guaranteed its success. Nurturing the nation, for men and women alike, meant not only giving birth to a modern, independent nation-state but also practicing the ideals of modern motherhood both inside and outside of the home in order to assure that nation's success.

The family politics of the Egyptian 1919 Revolution, however, had vastly different consequences for men and women. Putting the reformed, bourgeois Egyptian family on display allowed male nationalists to demonstrate the extent to which they had transformed the nation. By displaying their family politics, a class of Egyptian men showed off their values, virtues, and, most importantly, their readiness to govern themselves. Their exposition of reformed family politics allowed them to create and demonstrate a new kind of paternalism toward the classes of Egyptians they would soon govern: The *effendiyya* class could claim a fully privileged position in Egyptian society because they demonstrated that they had learned and practiced the personal lessons of modernity and nationalist struggle. They could claim to have given birth to a new kind of Egyptian identity, and they promised to nurture the governed classes into a new era.

For women, however, the discourse of the revolutionary period and the decades leading up to it had deleterious consequences. "Playing house" allowed men to respond to colonial discourse and, in so doing, gave them an active roll in the political realm in which they had been theretofore sidelined. Meanwhile, the discourse of the revolution and the decades leading up to it cemented the relationship between the reformed political realm and the presence inside the home of Egyptian women who were both reformed and reformers. While real women with political aspirations appeared in the revolutionary demonstrations, they were overshadowed by images of and discussions about a second Egyptian woman — an image of mother Egypt and her attendant set of attributes — without which independent Egypt could not stand. When the revolution was over and men set about creating a nation-state, real women were asked to play the role of mother Egypt — this time from their homes.

CHAPTER I

My House and Yours

Egyptian State Servants and the New Geography
of Nationalism

In the early decades of the nineteenth century, the nascent Egyptian state's
quest to modernize and strengthen its institutions and create new ones
produced a kind of "travel literature" about the world outside Egypt's
borders. Through the creation of the student missions abroad and a corps
of translators, the state institutionalized, sanctioned, and funded the practice of knowing the West. While state-produced knowledge was not
designed to dominate Europe, it exposed and analyzed the arenas in
which Europeans excelled.

The nineteenth century was obviously not the first time that Egyptians
had ventured outside their borders, nor was it the first time that travel
chronicles had appeared as a literary genre.[1] What was distinct about this
new travel literature, however, was not only its intended utility as part of
the state's mission to transform itself but the ways in which it was ultimately used by the state and its servants to locate Egypt in the Valhalla of
modern, reformed nation-states.

Mohammad 'Ali's campaign ranked the world's "nations" scientifically
and placed Egypt vis-à-vis other nations in a hierarchy of development,
at the apex of which sat "modernity." Knowledge that was useful to the
state created a cartography of modernity in which the intimate details of
domestic activities stood out as prominent features and were used as units
of measurement. Nineteenth-century travel literature, written by and for
the state, produced the world as a modern map, on which Egypt was
placed — both by Europeans and by Egyptians themselves — according to
the Egyptians' institutions, practices, and relationships.[2] Such travel lit-

erature suggested that Egypt would claim its place in the cosmology of modern nation-states when Egyptian habits, including those of the domicile, were transformed.

Part of Mohammad 'Ali's initial drive to reform the state included defining modernity and its sociopolitical structures and articulating how those institutions could be constructed in Egypt. At the same time, building a modern Egypt required isolating institutions and ideologies that did not meet the criteria for modernity and subjecting them to reform. In both cases, the very act of refashioning Egypt was undergirded by the state's active production of knowledge about the sciences and structures that it wished to construct and emulate or dismantle and reject. Much like the kinds of discourses produced about Egypt by Europeans, state-sponsored knowledge in early-nineteenth-century Egypt put the domicile and its inhabitants on display, linking familial behavior in Egypt and elsewhere to Western science, progress, and political reform.[3] In Egyptian-produced literature about the domestic realm and its activities, the habits and customs of the upper classes were not linked to the past but, rather, connected Egypt with modernity and the West.

For the Egyptian state, mastery of the ideologies and institutions of the modern nation-state led to explorations of Western institutions that were often as penetrating as European travelogues. As the result of projects designed to capture the West and its institutions for the state, civil servants became unwitting voyagers to hitherto unexplored terrains. Many of them thus "journeyed" without leaving Egypt. Others actually ventured abroad in search of new fields of knowledge through which modern Egypt would later be constructed.

Indeed, from the 1820s onward, as more ships carried Western tourists and would-be Egyptologists to Alexandria, more ships also carried Egyptians to Europe. The Egyptians who embarked on journeys westward were not holiday makers setting off on a grand tour, aging or ailing members of the middle and upper classes seeking cures in the warm, winter sun, or archeologists in search of artifacts. Rather, the Egyptians who set sail from Alexandria were students and servants of the state, sent off to learn the "sciences" of European statehood, the secrets of Europe's military prowess, the mechanics of industrial development, and the languages through which to know them. Unlike the nineteenth-century Europeans who journeyed to Egypt in search of the ancient, the exotic, and the fantastic, the Egyptians who left Alexandria for Europe were sent out in search of practical knowledge. While European tours to Egypt usually had as their leitmotif a quest for a rediscovery of the past — the way the world once was — Egyptians in Europe set sail in search of Egypt's future — a future that they themselves would later construct.

While the packaging of such voyages differed, the project of venturing abroad was markedly similar for both groups. Both European tours to Egypt and Egyptian educational missions to Europe had as their goal an intimate knowledge of the way other nations worked — how things were ordered or not; how the state functioned or, by contrast, did not function; how institutions were structured; how people behaved. The task of the Egyptian student, like the European tourist, was to observe, chronicle, make sense of the world, and reproduce it for an enthusiastic audience. While there was a distinct power differential inherent to the two projects (knowledge produced by the Egyptian state about Europe was not ultimately designed to conquer Europe or to colonize it), both "travel" ventures were crucial to understanding the appearance of the reformed domicile as symbolic of modernity and of the ascendance of the modern nation-state.

Two state-sponsored institutions were instrumental in the production of knowledge about the world outside of Egypt during the first half of the nineteenth century: Dar al-Alsun, or the School of Translation (known initially as Madrasat al-Tarjama [the School of Translation] and then as Dar al-Alsun [literally, the House of Tongues]), and the student missions abroad. Both institutions were crucial to Mohammad 'Ali's project of building a bigger state. Dar al-Alsun and the student missions also illustrate, however, the viceroy's concomitant need for a growing number of civil servants. Mohammad 'Ali's original tendency to appoint family members and Europeans to crucial administrative positions could not support the demands of the growing state apparatus. By the 1820s, Mohammad 'Ali's schools consequently became filled with the sons of Egyptian notables. Graduates of these schools ascended to important administrative positions in Cairo and the provinces in the 1850s and played important roles in further state expansion and development projects. They took positions in translation, civil administration, finance, education (diwan al-madaris), and in various forms of industry.[4] The sons of men whose allegiance to the state had first been won by gifts of land and high administrative posts were made loyal servants through the education that allowed them to rise through the administrative ranks.

The School of Translation opened in the early 1830s. It was created by Mohammad 'Ali to produce bureaucrats who were competent in European languages and versed in the European sciences. Ultimately, the school's main business was the translation and publication of texts in order to circulate knowledge about Western ideologies, institutions, and innovations to the state and Egypt's literate elite.[5]

The practice of sending student missions to Europe started in the early years of Mohammad 'Ali's reign but gained real strength and momentum when the first large, organized mission left Egypt on April 13, 1826. (The student missions continued through the first few decades of the twentieth century.) Like Dar al-Alsun, the missions had the goal of amassing and producing knowledge about the world outside of Egypt; students abroad studied not only Europe's languages but also all the institutions through which Europe defined itself as "modern."

The tropes for modernity that were produced by these institutions did not have their most forceful effects on large numbers of Egyptians until the last third of the nineteenth century. Likewise, the most heated debates over what it meant to be modern did not surface until the nineteenth century was drawing to a close. However, the roots of the shape and structure of a "modern" Egypt and, in it, "modern Egyptians" — central to which was the reformed family — are found in these early attempts by the state to expose Europe. Prior to the advent of the British occupation and of the colonial discourse that conflated family politics with the failure of the Egyptian political realm, state-produced knowledge about the home and its habits shaped a generation of Egyptian bureaucrats and was used by them as a means of knowing and measuring themselves and others. Reformed institutions, such as the household, became crucial markers on the landscape of modern Egypt.

Egyptian elites were not solely responsible for producing cultural and intellectual change in nineteenth-century Egypt, nor were European institutions the only institutions that served as the models by which the Egyptian state underwent reform. In order to explain why Egyptians and Europeans alike made Egyptian homes and families the target of reform, however, the roots of the household's role as a geographic and historical "marker" must be exhumed and analyzed. The landscape of modernity that such elite institutions produced was instrumental in forging a link between family politics and the shape and function of the nation-state.

The House of Mohammad 'Ali and the Making of a Modern State

Mohammad 'Ali ruled Egypt through innovation and imitation. From the Mamluks who preceded him he adopted the practice of state centralization. He departed from Mamluk rule, however, in his agricultural and industrial projects, the building of a modern military, and the creation of a nascent system of state-sponsored, secular education.[6] Mohammad 'Ali also established a cadre of civil servants who, over the course of the twentieth century, became increasingly loyal to the Egyptian state and vested in its success. While the viceroy ruled absolutely, he did so "with the help of nobles and technocrats he called into being."[7] While under Mohammad 'Ali, Egypt remained a part of the Ottoman Empire, Sultan 'Abd al-Majid (r. 1839–61) granted Egypt to the viceroy as a hereditary domain in 1841, and his descendants ruled over the state that he founded until 1952.

Mohammad 'Ali arrived in Egypt in 1801 as a deputy commander in the Ottoman military. The breakdown of law and order that accompanied the departure of the French expedition from Egypt that year afforded the Ottomans an opportunity to rid the region of the Mamluks who had rivaled Istanbul for power since 1517. While Egypt in the eighteenth century had formally been ruled by the Ottomans, in fact it was a powerful military cast of freed Turco-Circassian slaves who held actual power there. Because the Mamluks controlled Egypt militarily, they were the ones to whom Egyptians paid taxes. Thus there were two classes of rulers in Egypt between 1517 and the rise of Mohammad 'Ali to power: the Ottomans, who held de jure rule over Egypt, and the Mamluks, without whom the Ottomans had little military or economic sway over the native Egyptian population.

One of the reasons for the Ottoman failure to regain supremacy in Egypt in 1801 was the presence of a contingent of Albanian troops in the Ottoman service known for their fierceness and rebellious behavior.[8] Mohammad 'Ali used these troops (he was originally their second in command) to establish himself as the most powerful force in Egypt. By July of 1805, he succeeded in having himself appointed governor (wali) of Egypt, then one of the empire's wealthiest provinces. To secure his rule, he invited his relatives from Kavalla, Albania, to take up residence in Egypt, placing them in important positions within the military and the civil administration.[9] In contrast to the structure of the Mamluk dynasties that had previously ruled Egypt, political power after 1805 was embodied in one man and one household.[10] Unlike the houses of the Mamluks who preceded him, Mohammad 'Ali's household was able to command hegemony over Egypt by 1811.[11]

To further consolidate his power, Mohammad 'Ali took land from Mamluk families and from the local religious elite — the 'ulama — and placed it under state control. Land acquisition served the viceroy in two fundamental ways. To begin with, it allowed him to inaugurate a series of economic reforms. Not only did Mohammad 'Ali bolster Egypt's agricultural output through state-supported irrigation projects, he mandated what would be grown on Egyptian soil and to whom it would be sold. State-mandated production and export of cash crops such as long-staple cotton, sugarcane, indigo, and flax brought money into Mohammad 'Ali's coffers — funds that were then used to continue state expansion projects. A new system of direct taxation and the establishment of state-run industry also provided the viceroy with revenue.

At the same time, land allowed Mohammad 'Ali to create a loyal elite. He gave tracts of lands to members of his family, who, while never learning Arabic, became at least in part Egyptian as the result of their acquisition of Egyptian real estate. He also meted out land to the Ottoman elite who had developed ties to Egypt through service to the Ottoman state. To break their old attachments, Mohammad 'Ali appointed former Ottoman officials as landlords. Land also served as a means of cultivating the loyalty of Egyptian notables, who through the acquisition of large parcels of land became invested in Mohammad 'Ali and his projects. The production of cash crops made these men increasingly wealthy and, therefore, increasingly indebted to the state. While conflicts later arose between the Arabophone Egyptian notables and their Ottoman Turkish-speaking counterparts over parity within governing institutions (up to the British occupation of 1882 the Ottoman elite still maintained an edge over the Arabophone Egyptians within the government hierarchy), these new notables remained loyal state servants throughout the nineteenth century.

Mohammad 'Ali also used his fledgling state-run educational system to cultivate loyalty in the sons of this new, landed nobility. In its early days, Mohammad 'Ali's state resembled a Mamluk household, as the viceroy placed a substantial amount of power in the hands of his family members. In 1807, for example, he made his son Ibrahim governor of Cairo, setting a trend of appointing immediate family members to important civilian and administrative positions in Cairo and the provinces. He also employed a goodly number of family members in the military. But, as the state grew and expanded, so too did its need for functionaries. Hence, a second avenue into Mohammad 'Ali's "family" of military and administrative officials became the nascent educational system.

The roots of the Egyptian state educational system lie in the viceroy's desire to reform the military and make it fully loyal to him. Mohammad

'Ali replaced the Mamluk system through the conscription of ordinary Egyptians into his military and through the establishment of a European-trained officers' corps. Immediately after securing his power, the viceroy began relying on Europeans to train his new military elite. Egyptians' lack of acquaintance with European languages made it necessary for Mohammad 'Ali to send Egyptians to Europe and to bring Europeans to Egypt to teach foreign languages. Language instruction led to the establishment of a small number of military schools for the sons of the notable class; a Western, secular education replaced traditional Qur'anic learning. Graduates of these schools took jobs in the military or became members of the fledgling corps of civil servants who provided the foundation for an expanding administration. Between 1809 and 1849, eleven thousand Egyptians passed through Mohammad 'Ali's schools.[12]

The creation of a cadre of state-trained civil servants contributed to the beginnings of an Egyptian identity among those who worked for the state.[13] The acquisition of land by Mohammad 'Ali and his descendants, and by the notables and state servants to whom land was granted over the course of the nineteenth century, did much to cement the relationship between the ruling dynasty and the territory known as Egypt. But the creation of an administrative culture, shaped by the state and circulated by the movement of landowning notables and their sons between Cairo and the provinces, led to the rise of a rank of Egyptians with increasingly common interests. Additionally, a new, professional class of state-trained bureaucrats and technocrats who did not necessarily own land — the *effendiyya* — came to share in this new culture. As the century progressed, the culture that was shaped by land and vested interests in running the state began to lessen the distinction between Arabophone Egyptians and their Ottoman-Turkish-speaking counterparts.[14]

By the 1850s, graduates of Mohammad 'Ali's schools held substantial positions within the Egyptian administration. Under his successor 'Abbas I (1848–54), the Egyptian government continued to grow and become more "Egyptianized." 'Abbas himself spoke Arabic and tended to appoint Arabic-speaking graduates of state schools and of the student missions abroad to middle- and low-ranking government positions. Despite 'Abbas's apparent contempt for Arabophone Egyptians, he promoted them within the government ranks because of their scientific training. Furthermore, the ever declining number of Turks in Egypt made reliance on native Egyptians a necessity.[15] While 'Abbas clamped down on education by shutting down many of Mohammad 'Ali's schools (important exceptions were the school of translation and the student missions), he did create new governing bodies in which he placed educated Ottoman-Turkish-speaking and Arabo-phone Egyptians.

Like 'Abbas, Sa'id (1854–63) did little to promote education but much to increase the size of Egypt's government, necessitating an increase in the number of bureaucrats in his service. Sa'id, who was European educated and who spoke French as well as Arabic, referred to himself as an Egyptian and spoke of the need to educate Egyptians in order to end the practice of allowing foreigners to run the government. He claimed that foreigners had enslaved Egyptians for centuries. Under Sa'id, the number of Ottoman-Turkish-speaking Egyptians was declining while the size of the adminis-tration was not. Hence, Sa'id favored the practice of promoting the rural notables and their sons to good positions in the civil and military admin-istrations, appointing a few of them as provincial governors.[16]

Isma'il went further still in promoting Arabophone Egyptians to prominent positions within the government. During his reign, the num-ber of bureaucrats rose from twenty thousand to fifty thousand.[17] The size of the government apparatus also increased: Isma'il created new admin-istrative councils and new *diwans* (ministries), including a ministry of public works in 1864 and a ministry of justice in 1872. He established new councils to study and debate matters ranging from taxes to the structure of the government. More Egyptians were promoted to governerships in the provinces; further, numbers of them were given positions in councils. To cement the loyalty of the rural notables, Isma'il created an elected Chamber of Deputies (Majlis shura al-nawwab) in 1866. Its seventy-five elected members, most of whom came "from families long associated with the administration," sat for three-to four-year terms and passed res-olutions on a variety of matters.[18]

By the 1870s, Egyptians were thus found at all levels of government in the provinces as well as Cairo. Arabic had "triumphed over Turkish as the language of administration."[19] Additionally, grants to administrators of land in the countryside and in Cairo led to an increased number of landed elites, made wealthy by the boom in Egyptian cotton produced in the 1860s and by increased trade with Europe into the 1870s.

During Isma'il's reign, the bureaucracy had become the mainstay of the state, and its growth led to the emergence of Egyptian state hegemony.[20] But the growth of the state also led to the creation of a new culture of Egyptian state bureaucrats who were educated by the state, dependent on the state, and increasingly desirous of more power within it.[21] Beginning under Mohammad 'Ali, land grants tied elites to rulers. But as the size of the bureaucracy increased, and as the administrative apparatus extended further into the countryside, Egypt's rulers became increasingly dependent upon the ranks of state functionaries. Mohammad 'Ali may well have given birth to modern Egypt, but his household and its descendants came to depend on their state-educated "family members" to run their household government.

Speaking (Modernity) in Tongues: The School of Translation and the Science of Knowing Nations

While 'Abbas and Sa'id gave little support to state-sponsored education, they did retain Mohammad 'Ali's School of Translation and continued to send missions of Egyptian students abroad. By the 1850s, a goodly number of Arabophone Egyptians who held positions within the administration were graduates of these institutions.

Mohammad 'Ali is credited with having said that translation, including the printing of translated books, was the best means of carrying out his goal of modernizing Egypt and exposing it to Western sciences and culture.[22] Historian Ahmad 'Izzat 'Abd al-Karim refers to the era of Mohammad 'Ali's rule as that of "translation and Arabization" ('asr al-tarjama wal-ta'rib). Al-Karim claims that Mohammad 'Ali believed that "modernity" and all its useful devices had been written about by those who invented them; through his translation project, he would be able to apply those devices to his own country.[23] When Mohammad 'Ali turned his attention toward modernizing Egypt in the 1820s, he found himself with a dearth of books in Turkish and Arabic. At first he borrowed books from Istanbul but found that they did not address his needs.[24] Dar al-Alsun gave the viceroy access to the kinds of texts he deemed necessary for modernizing Egypt.[25] Additionally, translations produced by Dar al-Alsun over the decades of its existence and published by state-controlled presses in Bulaq and Alexandria formed the staple diet of Egypt's literate classes and were instrumental in the formation of a new Egyptian intellectual elite.[26] By the time of Mohammad 'Ali's death in 1848, approximately one thousand texts had been translated from European languages into Turkish and Arabic.[27]

The School of Translation was first opened as part of Madrasat al-idara al-malakiyya (the Royal School of Administration), which was created in the 1820s in order to produce bureaucrats versed in the European languages and sciences. Students in the madrasa learned French in addition to the "arts" of civil administration, accounting, engineering, and geography. The original goal of translation was the production of a new cadre of civil servants from which the state would benefit; in the early stages of the school's development, students learned to translate in order to pursue careers within the administration.

A separate school of translation known as Dar al-Alsun opened in 1835 on the recommendation of one of the most prominent teachers in the Royal School of Administration, Rifaʿa Rafiʿ al-Tahtawi (1801–73), who himself began a long career as a state administrator as the result of his prowess as a translator. The curriculum at Dar al-Alsun consisted of a five-year program in which students studied Ottoman Turkish, Farsi, Italian, French, and, later, English. Students also took courses in accounting, history, geography, *adab* (belles lettres), and the shariʿa.

Students for the school were chosen from the student body at al-Azhar and from among the more promising students of the *kuttabs* in the provinces, largely by al-Tahtawi, who was made director of the school in 1837. The first students to finish the program graduated in 1839 and were either appointed to positions within the various governmental ministries or as translators. Most of them translated European literature and history into Arabic; their translations were used to train future groups of students.[28]

From its early years, Dar al-Alsun produced translations on a wide variety of topics, which can be divided into the categories of medicine; the sciences, including accounting, algebra, and various kinds of engineering; the military sciences, including shipbuilding, arms building, military administration; and the social sciences, history, geography, philosophy, and logic.[29] Together, translations of these different sciences were used "in the service of producing modernity the way Mohammad ʿAli wanted it produced."[30]

Records of the school's activities attest to the kinds of knowledge that the state found useful and provide a means of understanding modernity as it was revealed to the state and its servants through the process of translation. Modernity thus chronicled may not have manifested itself the way "Mohammad ʿAli wanted it." The khedive certainly unleashed forces that were far beyond his intentions. The translated texts on medicine and the sciences of industry and engineering would make a fascinating study in their own right, as they reveal the many ways in which the internal machinery of modernity was designed and constructed, and provide an excellent insight into the ways in which new relationships between the state and the physical bodies of its citizens were being established.[31]

But it is texts on the social sciences, particularly history and geography, that are of interest here, for it is precisely within those translations that one finds "modernity" depicted and illustrated through elaborate, "scientific" discussions of the manners and customs found in the world's many "nations." Geography and history were not new to Egypt, and the translation of texts about them does not represent the introduction of "science" to the Egyptians. Translations of history and geography exposed Egyptians to a very specific, positivist teleology of historical and national development. In that teleology, the habits and customs of rulers and ruled alike were assumed to have produced a particular kind of "modernity." While the manners and morals of rulers and their subjects had previously been of concern to governments in the Islamic world, and, in fact, constituted an entire body of literature, behavior was subsumed through this new translation project into a new framework in which nations were "placed" vis-à-vis one another in accordance with the new science of geography.[32] This science tended to use the habits and customs of the world's peoples as a means of delineating "nations" and of illustrating the condition of each nation's body politic. The result was a kind of new "moral geography" in which manners and customs were linked to political and scientific progress.[33]

In the 1820s, when the Egyptian state relied on expatriate Syrians as well as the student missions abroad to provide it with translators, a selection of histories about men (and sometimes women) who had reformed their nations were the object of the state's interest.[34] Mohammad 'Ali is said to have told the story of a certain Frenchman, Colonel Duhamel, who informed the viceroy that the path to becoming a great man lay in reading history.[35] Accordingly, he ordered Turkish translations of texts such as biographies of the prophet Mohammad and rulers such as Alexander the Great, Catherine the Great, and Napoleon. Some of these texts were later published and circulated while others were not. In 1824, for example, Machiavelli's *The Prince* was published by Dar al-Kuttub al-Misriyya. (It was translated from Italian into Arabic as *al-Amir fi 'ilm al-tarikh wal-siyassa wal-tadbir,* or, *The Prince [as he is known through] the Science of History, Politics and Organization.*) Likewise, Castera's *Histoire de l'Impératrice Cathrine II de Russie* was published by the Bulaq Press and sold locally for fifteen Egyptian piasters.[36]

In the years after the founding of Dar al-Alsun, graduates of the school continued the process of making European history available in Turkish and Arabic. Among the catalogue of histories translated by the state were Napoleon's memoirs, written during his exile and translated from French into Turkish in 1832. In the 1840s, al-Tahtawi published

Tarikh dawlat italia, his translation of "A History of the Italian State." In the 1840s, the publishing house at Bulaq also produced translations of a number of histories about European rulers written by Voltaire, such as his *Lion of the North: A History of Charles XII of Sweden* and *Life of Peter the Great*, which was translated from French to Arabic in 1842.[37] Such texts depicted history as being driven by the wills of great men and the nation-state as the product of their reform programs.

The translation and production of such texts by civil servants in Egypt for other civil servants and for the consumption of a reading public placed Mohammad 'Ali and his projects in the company of other rulers whose greatness, personality, and very character were made manifest in their reform projects.[38] Such texts also attached successful reform programs to the private habits of great men and women, equating the ability to create a strong state with particular kinds of habits and behavior. The history of the formation of the modern nation-state was thus characterized as a kind of ethnography in which progress was known and charted along the variables of habits and customs, especially those of rulers.[39]

This ethnography qua history is well illustrated by al-Tahtawi's 1833 translation of Frenchman Georges-Bernard Depping's *Aperçu historique sur les moeurs et coutumes des nations*, which was a staple text in the Egyptian public school system for the next century.[40] Al-Tahtawi's translation of Depping was divided in two parts. The first, called "On the Needs of Humans, and the Way They Live with Their Families and Their Clans," catalogued nations in terms of their houses and the customs practiced in them. The topics covered their clothes, cleanliness, marriage and its various customs, women, offspring, old age, funerals, hunting on land and sea, commerce, and money.[41] Part 2, "On Morals and Customs in Relation to Nations and Their Mentalities," considered the effects of morals and habits on the shape of nations and on their progress. It contains chapters on such topics as games and sports, poetry and music, writing, literature and laws, dance, hospitality with guests, holidays and seasons, slavery, beliefs, and politics.

In a chapter from part 1 on "cleanliness," Depping compared the civilized to the uncivilized peoples:

In non-Islamic lands[42] there is a great preoccupation with the cleanliness of objects, especially with that of the domicile. The cleanest are the Dutch: in their cities you see that most streets are paved with cobblestones, ordered and clean. Their homes are beautiful on the outside, and their windows are washed. . . . One finds a certain amount of cleanliness among the English and some of the Americans. The French aren't very clean, nor are the Germans. . . .

The uncivilized peoples are filthy. Among them you find many who have lice, and many who eat their lice. They smear their bodies with lard. Lots of people in the Americas and Asia spend a good deal of the year underground, where the air is plenty unwholesome. The foul air combines with other putrid odors, like those of their food. These people live for long periods without cleaning anything . . . they eat meat with their hands, and never touch a fork, knife, or spoon.[43]

This hierarchy of cleanliness corresponded to a hierarchy of political organization and development. Depping claimed that kingship, which he categorized as going hand and hand with cleanliness, had progressed from a time in which there were no kings and during which men lived in tribes. Then, kingship developed so that rulers like Alexander the Great were able to conquer large territories and force the conquered to pay tribute. In Europe, there were a number of kings and sultans of varying strengths who had developed enough power to enforce their rule, direct the production of goods, and impose a sense of order, progress, and stability. These were modern nations, the nations that kept house. About his own country, Depping wrote: "If the French are given to the sciences . . . if they enjoy a prosperous economic life and continue to cultivate refined habits and morals, this is thanks to favorable political order."[44]

In Asia, one of the "filthy" regions, such political leadership had not really developed. There were often strong kings, but no order, especially not the kind of order that would lead to controlled agricultural and industrial production as it was found in parts of Europe. He said:

In Asia, one finds both strong kings [muluk] and sultans [salatin]. Most of them rule however they please; they spill the blood and spend the money of those over whom they rule in any way they like. Power is had through the gaining of favors from the ruler.

Most of the rulers only rarely leave their harems, so it is hard to get an audience with them. They never hear the petitions of those who have been poorly treated. . . . One of the habits of the citizens of Asia is to hide money from their rulers; it is the habit of the rulers, in their public addresses and their firmans [decrees], to compare themselves to the sun and the moon. . . . Such rulers never go out unaccompanied by their military, and their houses resemble small cities.[45]

Political and historical development were thus underscored by investigation into the various landscapes that made up "nations" (including, apparently, subterranean landscapes) and into the living conditions of both kings and subjects. While the text gives no indication of how nations transcended putrid-smelling living conditions, Depping's implicit message was that it was only in doing so that a society could assure central-

ization and industrial development. Such views of history not only reinforced the idea that domestic practices were somehow connected to the
shape and function of governments but produced a vision of modernity
in which it was the ruler who drove history and in which state and
monarch were synonymous. It was thus a top-heavy state, not a government of the people, that made a nation "modern."

In the 1830s, translations of texts on geography reinforced the notion
that the globe was divided into civilized and uncivilized, clean and
unclean nations. Geography was defined as being a science by which
nations could be ranked and ordered.[46] Al-Tahtawi translated Malte-
Brun's *Géographie universelle* from French into Arabic in 1838; European
texts on descriptive geography, cosmography, physical geography, religious, political, and historical geographies, as well as moral geographies
were all translated into Arabic at that time. Archival evidence suggests
that translations of texts on geography were influential in producing a
new corps of Egyptian geographers and in creating interest in geography as a new practice. Al-Tahtawi's students at Dar al-Alsun were examined in "descriptive geography, cosmography, physical geography, religious, political and historical geography."[47] A review of primary- and
secondary-school literature from 1901 shows that al-Tahtawi's translation
of Malte-Brun was a staple in Egyptian classrooms into the twentieth
century.[48]

The first twenty-three of the text's fifty "books" provide a general
account of Malte-Brun's theories of geography, including cosmography
and hydrography, physical and atmospheric geography, and mathemati-
cal geography.[49] It includes precise maps and drawings of planetary
spheres. Theoretical sections present geography as a literal system through
which the world is divided, measured, and ordered and through which
the reader "sees" the contents of the globe and locates the multitude of
nations by which he is surrounded. "Is not geography the sister and the
rival of history? If the one enjoys the empire of universal time, does not
the other rightfully claim that of place?"[50]

Malte-Brun's "precise science" also extended to empirical discussions
of the habits and customs — both public and private — of nations. The
sometimes intimate habits of the globe's inhabitants were added to the
criteria through which the "universal system" was applied. His general
"theory of geography" insisted that the world could be known through
a study of morals, political tendencies, and national "character," and
hence the last "book" in his theoretical overview was entitled "Of Man
Considered as a Moral and Political Being; or Principles of Political

Geography." Here Malte-Brun divided nations not by the natural phenomena that separated them but, rather, by the languages they spoke,
their religion, the forms of their government, the way they ate and
drank, and the homes they inhabited. He separated the parts of the world
governed by democracy from those of theocracy and absolute monarchy,
giving all kinds of evidence for the political proclivities of the inhabitants
of various regions. Malte-Brun's geography was thus intended to be a science that would cover the globe, from its outer crust to its very inner core.
Its task was to banish the monsters of the world outside Europe's border
and convert "space into place."[51]

We shall take a view of the leading features of nature; the mountains which diver-
sify the surface of the land, the seas which bound its outline, and the rivers and
the valleys by which it is intersected. We shall seek our way downward, through
caverns and through mines . . . and thus do our utmost to explore the structure
of the globe. After inquiring into the motions of the atmosphere and the laws of
temperature, we shall distribute into their native regions the animals, the plants,
and all the beings that are nourished in the exhaustless bosom of the earth. We
shall conclude the picture by considering man in his natural and in his political
condition. We shall classify the races of our species according to the varieties
which are marked in their bodily appearance and character — according to the languages which they speak — according to the creeds by which their minds are con-
soled, or degraded and enslaved — and according to the laws which mark the
progress of civilization, or the profound darkness of utter barbarism.[52]

Thus this new geography can be characterized as the science through
which nations were categorized according to the natural phenomena that
separated them and through which the barbaric peoples were distinguished from the civilized through an empirical, scientific analysis of
manners and morals, customs and proclivities. The behavior of a region's
inhabitants, both ruler and ruled, like its longitude and latitude, its
topography, and its flora and fauna, was crucial to a nation's placement —
its ranking — in Malte-Brun's ordered, universal system.

Malte-Brun subjected his reader to many hundreds of pages of "exact"
science — endless tables, graphs, and formulas — as a preface to the
scientific evidence that followed. In fact the section of the book dedicated
to applying his "exact science" to the world, "nation by nation," is a sub-
jective cataloguing of morals, habits, and customs — a long series of
"ethnographies." Afghanistan, for example, in a section entitled "Its
General Physical Geography," was not presented as the product of particular natural, physical formations or configurations. Nor were any of the
author's precise sciences — like cosmography, for example — used to pre-

sent Afghanistan's location to the reader. Rather, Afghanistan's *physical* geography was described as "a part of Persia, and distinguished by the appellation of Eastern Persia; but both in its physical, civil and political *character*, it is entitled to a separate description."[53]

It was only after Malte-Brun described Afghanistan's character that he gave its precise physical location (latitude and longitude) and boundaries: "On the north it is bounded by the range of Hindoo Coosh . . . separating it from Independent Tartary." This formula, according to the author, was a kind of concession in which science and subjectivity would collapse on one another when such an implosion was crucial to the process of *knowing*. Malte-Brun said, "We shall not even scrupulously deny ourselves and our readers the *pleasure* of occasionally mingling our topographical descriptions with . . . anecdotes to illustrate manners, often serving to fix in the memory names of localities, which otherwise it would be difficult to retain."[54]

Malte-Brun's theories of geography, and others like them, produced a universe of national boundaries that were both fixed and fluid. Nations would continue to be located by the natural phenomena by which they were bordered. They were placed, however, according to the habits of their inhabitants, habits that were subject to change. The implication is that Afghanistan would continue to be located next to the "Hindu Coosh" but would only be placed relative to Persia if its political and cultural mores developed in particular ways. Thus, the placing of a country rendered its borders fluid: Just as Afghanistan was arbitrarily Persian or not Persian according to its civil and political mores, it could also be placed relative to other nations were its character to change.

In addition to texts on the military sciences, engineering, agriculture, industry, and what might be considered the general "politics" of national development, the state had a preoccupation with nations' strengths and weaknesses vis-à-vis one another and with the intimate details of their inhabitants. In translating and publishing such texts, the state made itself into a kind of unwitting ethnographer, both of other nations and of its own citizens. Translation established a relationship among the politics of socioeconomic reform, the knowledge through which reform was undertaken, and the intimate activities of the people who would be subjected to it. Official knowledge about the "modern" world created clear connections among the men who worked in the state's employ, the "national character" that resulted from their behavior, and their place in the universal system of nations.[55]

The State Sent Abroad:
Student Missions and the Sizing Up of Europe

The curriculum of Mohammad 'Ali's student missions to Europe in the 1820s and 1830s included another of Depping's texts, *Evening Entertainment*.[56] *Evening Entertainment* was a fictitious *tour du monde* in which a father regales his children with accounts of his adventures as a world traveler. The purpose of the book was to expose students to the "precise sciences" of geography and history as they embraced the study of the whole globe. The text included biographies of figures like Peter the Great, histories of reform programs, and catalogues of each nation's habits and customs — both public and private.

Given the templates through which they were educated, it is not surprising that students who were sent to Europe by the Egyptian state throughout the nineteenth century were concerned with both the physical and moral location of both Europe and Egypt. Like Dar al-Alsun, the missions had the goal of amassing and producing knowledge about the world outside Egypt; students abroad studied not only Europe's languages but all the institutions through which Europe claimed its modernity.

Mohammad 'Ali's first step in educational reform, which was designed initially as military reform, was the importation of advisers and instructors from Europe. It quickly became more practical and less expensive, however, for the state to send students and young bureaucrats to Europe to learn the languages and sciences that had previously been taught by Europeans in Cairo. It became "typical" of Mohammad 'Ali "to send his own kind to Europe to see for themselves what was lacking in the country and what the Westerners had to give and teach."[57] As early as 1809, he began sending students to Italy to learn how to establish munitions factories and build military arsenals and other technical facilities so that they could teach other Egyptians to do the same. Milan, Rome, and Florence were among the cities where Egyptian students studied military science, shipbuilding, engineering, and printing. In 1818, a second group of approximately thirty students was sent to England to study shipbuilding and mechanics. There were no recorded missions between 1818 and 1826, when the mission that included al-Tahtawi left for France.[58] Because of its size and its superior organization, that mission is often referred to as the first real mission abroad. The mission of 1826 consisted of approximately forty men chosen by the state.[59] Over the five-year period during which they resided in France, the students engaged in a complex course of studies that began with coursework in French. Most of the members of the mission spoke Turkish or Arabic as their native tongue; while some of them had taken Italian in Cairo, none had studied French. According to al-Tahtawi, the students worked from seven in the morning until six in the evening while they were learning French and were subjected to constant drilling.[60]

Once the students were proficient enough to engage in higher education, they were trained in subjects such as administration, either civil or military. Engineering was designated as a specialty, as was mechanics. Military engineering, artillery, metal founding, arms making, and diplomacy constituted a program of study in the military sciences. Students could also take courses in printing, lithography, and engraving. Chemistry, surgery, anatomy, physiology, and hygiene made up a core curriculum in the field of medicine. Other students took hydraulics, agriculture, natural history, and mining. In addition to these programs, translation was offered as a special program of study.[61]

In France the students were kept under constant surveillance and were required to keep the rules of a strict military discipline. While they were still learning French, the students were all housed together in a hotel on the Rue de Clichy; once their program of study had become diversified, however, they were sent to various pensions and schools or housed with their instructors. While discipline was tight and students were allowed little time outside the company of their peers, they were later allowed to mingle with the French. They were taken on excursions to parks on Sundays and on visits to museums, bookstores, and cafés.

Statesman or Homebody?
Rifa'a al-Tahtawi and the Grand Tour of Paris

Historians have long assumed that Egyptian students were sent abroad with very narrowly defined agendas, and that their acquired knowledge of Europe and its institutions was designed only for application to the state's reform and development projects (namely, industrial and military infrastructures). Because the students were kept under rigorous discipline and surveillance while abroad, and because they were often isolated from their French peers, the few scholars who have examined the missions and their history have concluded that the state wanted little contact between its wards and Europeans. In other words, the missions were not designed to encourage contact between the two cultures. Thus, historians have generally concluded that inquiries into the habits, mores, and tendencies of the local populations lay outside of the boundaries of what the state considered "useful" to its projects or "instrumental" to the construction of a modern state and the production of servants to work within it.[62] Given the kinds of texts that the state had translated in the 1820s and 1830s, and the centrality of the habits and customs of "nations" to them, such conclusions appear to be rather shortsighted. While it would be impossible to argue that the state's primary interest in sending students abroad was for an assessment of the habits and customs of the modern Europeans, one should not exclude such inquiries of the state's endeavors abroad and the subsequent construction of modernity at home.

The most celebrated example of the state "set loose" in Paris to learn science in its many dimensions is that of al-Tahtawi. His recordings of his investigations into the "sciences of Paris" *('ulum bariz)*, including those of the domestic realm, became not only a celebrated piece of Arabic literature but a seminal work on "modernity" and what it might require of Egyptians. Al-Tahtawi was not, when he left for France, a student in the state's employ. Rather, as a graduate of al-Azhar, he had been appointed by Mohammad 'Ali to serve in the capacity of imam, or religious advisor, to the delegation and to supervise and counsel the students. Nonetheless, during his sojourn in France he acquired an admirable knowledge of the French language and of the problems inherent to translating it into Arabic. During his years in Paris, he spent a great deal of time reading the works of the *philosophes* — Voltaire and Rousseau, in particular — as well as fiction and poetry, history, and geography. Upon his return from France, al-Tahtawi employed the knowledge and the skills that he learned in France while in service to the state.[63]

Al-Tahtawi was a member of a land-owning family from the Sa'id, a family that is said to have been of prodigious wealth with a long tradition of scholarship. While Mohammad 'Ali's land reforms significantly deprived al-Tahtawi's family of their fortunes, decreases in the size of their land holdings did not put an end to the family's tradition of educating sons at al-Azhar; accordingly, al-Tahtawi left the Sa'id for Cairo in 1817 to begin his course of studies. At al-Azhar, according to Albert Hourani, al-Tahtawi studied the typical curriculum but was also exposed to the new "sciences of Europe" through his mentor Sheikh Hasan al-'Attar, who frequented Bonaparte's Institut d'Égypte and was a proponent of the "new" European sciences.[64] Al-'Attar secured for his student an appointment as imam of a regiment in the new Egyptian army, and then as imam of the educational mission that went to Paris in 1826.

Other than his many translations, al-Tahtawi's greatest literary contribution from his years in France was his *Takhlis al-ibriz fi talkhis bariz* (An extraction of gold in a summary of Paris.). Published by order of Mohammad 'Ali in 1834, *Takhlis al-ibriz* was apparently written to tell the Egyptians as much as possible about European society and its customs, and to give suggestions, albeit indirect, for how Egypt might shape its institutions in the French image.[65] Mohammad 'Ali provided free copies to his state functionaries as well as to students in the government schools.[66] The text is a detailed account of al-Tahtawi's experiences in France, of his impressions of French society, the French, of their government and their economy, and their habits and customs, and, perhaps most importantly, their sciences. He explained his reasons for writing the book: "By writing this I intend to exhort the Islamic countries to look into foreign sciences and research; it is well known that they have been perfected in Europe. . . . I wanted to see the things of which the Islamic world had been deprived."[67]

Literary critic Roger Allen places *Takhlis al-ibriz* in what he calls the Egyptian "grand tour" literature of the mid- and late nineteenth century.[68] Like 'Ali Mubarak's *'Alam al-din,* published later in the century, *Takhlis al-ibriz* was an entertaining and palatable account of a foreign country that showed Egyptians how a "modern" society was structured and how it worked. Unlike Mubarak's work, which was a fictional account of Europe and the Europeans written as a series of conversations between a sheikh from al-Azhar and an English Orientalist while they toured Europe, al-Tahtawi presented his work as a "factual" account of what he observed during his travels in France. In both cases, however, tours through Europe and its institutions, both real and imaginary, were the vehicle through which French society was "exposed"; both men used visits to European institutions and excursions through public offices, museums, public libraries, hospitals, banks, the Bourse, theaters, and, finally, private homes to let Egyptian readers "see" how Europe was organized and how the Europeans behaved.[69]

While a later generation of state functionaries, trained by the texts produced by al-Tahtawi and his cohort, made clear connections between their domestic habits and their own "Egyptian-ness," al-Tahtawi left no indication that he himself linked his own domestic behavior with the "nation" in which it was produced. The question of whether al-Tahtawi would have called himself an Egyptian or distinguished himself from Ottoman-Egyptian elites has been the source of great debate. He has been labeled a committed Ottomanist who claimed loyalty to Mohammad 'Ali and

Isma'il Pasha because they were representatives of the sultan.[70] Scholars have also claimed that al-Tahtawi blamed Ottoman rule for Egypt's political and economic decline and called for Egypt's evolution into a republic in which Egyptians would rule themselves.[71] For those who place him within the Ottoman camp, the facts that he spoke Arabic, owned large tracts of land in Egypt, and professed great loyalty to the rulers in whose administrations he worked do not add up to any sort of national identity. It is likely, however, that al-Tahtawi applied the "sciences of geography" to Egypt, or to his own relationship to it, linking the habits of his class of Egyptians with the shape and structure of Egypt's government. Even if he did maintain a sense of loyalty to the Ottoman Empire, his intellectual and professional output offered ways of thinking about both transnational and local identities.

Takhlis al-ibriz, is structured in six essays, or *maqalaat.* The first two take up al-Tahtawi's journey to France (first from Cairo to Alexandria, and then the journey from Alexandria to Marseilles). The third and fourth provide a general description of the French — their "sciences," religion, home life, and eating habits. The fifth *maqula* gave an account of the members of the educational mission in France, including their living conditions and subjects of interest. Finally, the last *maqala* took up the subject of France's political system and al-Tahtawi's impressions of the Revolution of 1830, which he witnessed firsthand.

While *Takhlis al-ibriz* was a personal account of al-Tahtawi's impressions and experiences in France, the work in many senses conforms to the conventions of "science" as they were reflected in works like those of Depping and Malte-Brun.[72] Like Depping and Malte-Brun, al-Tahtawi began his summary of France with a discussion of how France could be *located,* of how it fit into the "universal system"; the first section of the book's third *maqala,* "A Description of Paris and its Civilization," is called "On the Geographic Placement of Paris and the Customs of its People." France's exact location on the globe, its longitude and latitude, its distance from other parts of the world, including Egypt, and its resulting weather, all helped the reader understand France's location and what that placement produced in terms of "French" features. In the words of the author:

Paris is located at forty-nine degrees, fifty minutes latitude, which is to say far from the equator. Its distance from Alexandria is 769 parasangs,[73] and its distance from Cairo is 890 parasangs. Its distance from holy Mecca is 740 parasangs. . . . Paris is not far from the Mediterranean, and it is well known that France is a country of moderate people, for its climate is neither too hot, nor too cold. Paris is covered with many trees, as the result of its geographic location. . . . There are seventy-five parks where Parisians go to enjoy such natural beauty.[74]

Much like Malte-Brun's tendency to conflate the scientific with the personal, al-Tahtawi's quest to "scientifically" locate France quickly gave way to lengthy discussions of placement, or the habits and customs of its inhabitants. France's social and political institutions were thus uncovered and analyzed. Indeed, the third *maqala* included articles like "The Habits of the Parisians in their Homes," "Food and Drink of the Parisians," and "The Clothing that Parisians Wear." Al-Tahtawi also included a chapter on parks and places of diversion, such as cafés.

The chapters in which al-Tahtawi's attention is focused on French institutions and habits do not differ much from European travel accounts about Egypt in the nineteenth century. His discussion of Parisian homes, for example, begins with a general description of the order of Parisian streets, the kinds of houses occupied by the different classes, and the types of materials with which they were constructed.[75] With such an overview of a city, he stated, one could surmise whether a people was civilized or barbaric.[76] Like the work of many of his European contemporaries, however, al-Tahtawi's portrait of France was routinely undertaken from the inside out: His focus quickly shifts from the streets of Paris to the home of an upper-class Parisian, where al-Tahtawi positioned himself as a surveyor of the home's contents and as an observer of its activities. Like European travel literature produced in the same period, al-Tahtawi's accounts record the home and its contents in extraordinary detail: "In each room there is fireplace, made of marble, on the mantle [ledge] of which a clock is placed. On each side of the clock, one finds a vase made of marble or of faux marble, in which flowers [both real and fake] are placed. On either side of the vases sit candelabras. . . . In most rooms there is a musical instrument called a piano. . . . Most rooms have pictures in them."[77] Al-Tahtawi draws the reader's attention to the fact that bourgeois Parisian home decor was a means of displaying a family's history: "Most rooms have pictures in them, especially of [the owner's] parents. Often an office will contain marvelous displays of art and of interesting objects which might well have belonged to [the owner's] ancestors."[78]

Likewise, al-Tahtawi used the contents of the rooms that he surveyed to draw conclusions about the interests of the Parisians and their proclivities. He said, for example:

If the room is a workroom or a reading room there is a table on which writing implements are kept, such as paper. . . . In one room I believe I saw a table with different kinds of documents on it, and I think I also saw in the rooms of upper-class homes brilliant chandeliers, of the kind that are lighted up with candles. And I think I saw in rooms where guests are received, a table on which a pile of books and papers had been placed for the guests' perusal. . . . All these things lead me to believe that the French place great importance on reading.[79]

His peregrinations through a Parisian domicile also led him to believe that men and women did not sleep together in the same bedroom.

He remarked that French homes, in general, could be characterized by a remarkable degree of cleanliness and order (he compared them only to the peoples of the Low Countries, for example, saying that the latter were the cleanest and most orderly people in the world), and mentioned that Parisian homes got lots of light and air, contributing to the general well-being of their inhabitants.[80] Of the domestic habits of modern Parisians, al-Tahtawi seemed to be most compelled by table manners. While he was initially somewhat startled by the presence of tables and chairs in Parisian dining quarters, it was the order of the dining room table itself that seemed to catch his greatest attention. He said: "On tables are always placed a knife, fork and spoon of silver. For them [the French] it is a matter of cleanliness that one not touch the food with his hands. Each person thus has a plate in front of him, as well as a glass for drinking. . . . No one drinks out of another's glass. There are individual containers for salt and pepper. . . . Everything on the table is well ordered."[81]

Al-Tahtawi had little to say about women's position in the home, their activities and responsibilities, except that all the home's possessions and their display were made more beautiful by "the presence of the lady of the house, in other words, the wife of the house's owner."[82] To this he added that the "lady of the house" greeted guests when they entered a room, as did her spouse subsequently; he compared this to Egypt, where guests were greeted by servants.

On the habits of upper-class Parisians outside of their homes, al-Tahtawi reported that men and women attended the theater, danced at balls, and went to stroll together as couples in parks on Sundays after church. While all these activities required a commingling of the sexes — indeed, were based on it — the fact of men and women appearing together in public did not illicit any direct commentary from the author. Al-Tahtawi made few comments on the position of women in French society and even fewer comments on the causes of such customs as free interactions between men and women. At the beginning of the book, he did state that one of the deleterious characteristics of French society was the lack of virtue in its women. Al-Tahtawi left the reader, however, to draw his own conclusions about the relationship, if any, between fallen virtue and the habits and customs of French society, saying, "Among their bad qualities is the lack of virtue of many of their women. . . . Fornication among them is a secondary sin (especially among those who are not married), rather than a major one."[83]

Al-Tahtawi also noted the Parisians' concern with their health, describing their habitual visitation of bathhouses and remarking that baths could also be taken at home, in bathtubs that could be purchased. He also made mention of the bourgeois Parisians' habit of participating in *madaris* (schools) along the Seine, where men and women alike could learn to swim and therefore preserve their health.[84] He said that if caring for the body and its health represented wisdom, then the French were the wisest of all peoples.

After al-Tahtawi captured the habits and daily activities of the upperclass Parisians, he then took the reader on another kind of tour, that of the many institutions in Paris that had produced "science." He began with a general "tour" of Paris' libraries, noting what was in them, how they were laid out, and commenting on the high percentage of Frenchmen and women who could read. The Arsenal Bibliothèque, Académie Française, and Bibliothèque du Jardin des Plantes were admired, both inside and out, for their utility as well as the frequency of their use, both among scholars and ordinary Parisians. Likewise, readers "toured" through museums.

Schools — from primary schools through "les academies" — were noted by al-Tahtawi as being "common" to the daily life of middle- and upperclass Frenchmen and to a certain percentage of French women, and as having produced the miracles of science. "Conservatoires," where the "tools" of astronomy and engineering were housed, "académies," "institutes," and "lycées" all formed al-Tahtawi's tour of the institutions through which the sciences were produced and propagated. About the various "royal colleges" in Paris, he said, for example, "They are schools in which the important sciences are learned and applied. There are five of them, and in them one studies industry and writing, ancient and Western languages, math and engineering, history and geography, philosophy. . . . A large number of people matriculate each year."[85] Al-Tahtawi was impressed by the overwhelming availability of schools as well as by the financial commitment of the French government to education. The number of newspapers and journals — "papers printed each day" — through which the French were educated "outside of the classroom" was also of enormous interest to him, as were the many varieties of journals and the number of people who read them. The preoccupation of the Parisians with reading and education, according to al-Tahtawi, was the motor behind the extraordinary development of the sciences there. He said, "The sciences progress everyday in Paris . . . not a single day passes without the French making a new discovery. Some years, they even discover a number of new disciplines, a number of new industries, a number of new processes."[86]

After finishing his tour, al-Tahtawi paused to remind the reader what had been done, and what had been "seen," what had been included in his rendering of modernity. He had just visited the "sciences" of Paris, the basis of France's progress, the sources of its success. From those sciences, he claimed, had sprung a number of ideologies and practices:

And from the sum of the sciences of Paris can be had almanacs; new censuses, and corrected [lists of] marriages[87] as well as things of that nature.

Every year, there appear a number of almanacs which record new discoveries in the arts and sciences, and which record governmental matters, and which list France's elite by name, address and profession. If anyone needs the name of one of these families, or to find their house, he just looks at the almanac.

In Paris, people have special rooms in their homes for reading, and there are public reading rooms where people go to learn, where they read all the latest newspapers, journals and books. They borrow the books they need, read them and return them.[88]

Science, then, had produced a number of customs. It led to annual discoveries, which were compiled in new records of births and deaths and government-produced lists of married couples. State and citizen alike had access to the domestic affairs of other citizens; interested readers made inquiries into such affairs from inside their homes. The state — well organized and scientific — extended its hand into private and domestic affairs of its citizens and made knowledge about those affairs public.

It was with a discussion of the French state that al-Tahtawi closed his account of Paris. His chapter on "the organization of the French state" (tadbir al-dawla al-faransiyya) was written "in order for us to discover the way France is organized, so that we may fully benefit from most of its principles, and so that the remarkable things about it will be a lesson to whoever is seeking one."[89] In a kind of genealogy, al-Tahtawi connected organization in the political realm to education and domestic habits.

The Landscape of an Increasingly Modern Cairo

As state modernization projects continued, parts of Cairo's landscape began to resemble descriptions from al-Tahtawi's texts. While the most significant transformation of Cairo's terrain did not take place until the 1860s under Isma'il's reign, the rule of Mohammad 'Ali and his successors witnessed the appearance of the markers of modernity that al-Tahtawi described.

In 1808, Mohammad 'Ali began the construction of a European-style palace and gardens in Shubra, just north of Cairo's ancient walls. A wide avenue connected the palace with the city. To further mark his household's rise to power, the pasha turned his attention to the Citadel in 1812, ridding it of almost all the Mamluk buildings and replacing them with his own palace, army barracks, government buildings, and, later, a mosque. The viceroy's modernizing agendas were also reflected in the appearance of cotton, silk, and paper factories in Cairo, its surrounding villages, and the provinces, part of a boom in industry that lasted through the late 1820s.[90] Bulaq, also north of Cairo, saw the construction of textile factories as of 1818, an iron foundry in 1820, and the national press in 1822. Schools were also opened in Cairo and Bulaq; the School of Civil Engineering opened in Bulaq in 1821, becoming a polytechnic institute in 1834.[91] The Abu Za'bal Medical School and Hospital were opened in the north of Cairo in 1827. Dar al-Alsun opened in Azbakiyya in 1835.

In his later days in power, Mohammad 'Ali concerned himself with Cairo's public works. He issued laws to clean, clear, and widen the streets. One European reported that in 1832 Cairo's streets were cleaned three times a day and that garbage was collected and burned outside the city.[92] The viceroy banned the use of *mashrabiyya* (wooden lattice work) window covering in houses, which tended to hang out over the streets, and ordered them replaced with glass windowpanes.[93] Cairo's transformation was further marked in 1845 when Mohammad 'Ali formed a council responsible for ordering and organizing the city. He assigned the council the task of naming the streets and numbering the buildings on them.[94] The council proposed opening up the city through the demolition of certain old neighborhoods and the subsequent construction of two wide boulevards — a project that was only completed under Isma'il.

At the same time, Mohammad 'Ali and his elites — both Ottoman and Arabophone Egyptian — began to reside in new dwelling styles. The viceroy, his family members, and the elite he brought to power built houses and palaces all over Cairo.[95] But they did not build in the style of their predecessors. When Mohammad 'Ali eliminated the Mamluks by killing them off in 1811, he also eliminated their style of architecture. Mamluk houses, in which 150 to 200 people often resided, were not torn down; in fact, the viceroy presented former Mamluk residences as gifts to his family members. But new residential styles soon overtook the old forms, each housing one family rather than confederations of families. By 1850, an allegedly Greek-style home, called the Constantinopolitan, had become popular with Mohammad 'Ali's family and the new elite classes. According to 'Ali Mubarak, the new elites started building the Constantinopolitan in order to imitate the royals.⁹⁶ Mubarak himself lived in such a house. By the second half of the nineteenth century, the popularity of this fashion was eclipsed by neoclassical and rococo styles. All became symbols of the position and power of the new elite. The rise of Arabophone Egyptians to bureaucratic prominence in the 1850s, their acquisition of land, and their increasing desire to set themselves apart from civil servants with Turkish backgrounds gave rise to a new, Egyptian bureaucratic culture. "They [Arabophone Egyptians] felt obliged to live in a certain way, to buy the 'right kind' of home and furnish it appropriately."⁹⁷ Historian F. Robert Hunter argues that by the 1860s land ownership and living practices among the bureaucratic elite served to diminish the Ottoman-Turkish–Arabophone-Egyptian split, replacing it with a common set of interests and a common "Egyptian" bureaucratic culture. While animosities still existed between the two groups over who had the right to rule Egypt, and while Egyptians resented their practical exclusion from the highest echelons of military and civilian administrations, personal wealth gave rise to greater commonalities between them.⁹⁸

Changes in Cairo's appearance were obviously not the simple reaction to texts produced by Mohammad 'Ali's education and translation projects; change did not just happen "by the book." Khedival mandates for construction and development met with changes in the tastes and demands of a growing, increasingly prosperous Egyptian elite. Elites tended not to return their investments to their land. Rather, their wont was to spend profit on consumption and on a European style of living.⁹⁹

While these new domiciles were built all over Cairo, 'Abbas began the custom of building neighborhoods devoted to housing those who worked to run the state. Palace building was apparently a passion for 'Abbas Pasha, and he had seven built or rebuilt for himself.¹⁰⁰ One of his best known palaces was in the heart of a new suburb named after himself, 'Abbasiyya, which sat in the desert on Cairo's eastern flank. Around him members of the royal family were given land and ordered to build palaces.[101] 'Abbasiyya's landscape included military schools and barracks, 'Abbas's palace, and a hospital; the area gradually developed some commercial activity. 'Abbas improved the road between Cairo and 'Abbasiyya both to make travel easier for himself and his ministers and to make the suburb more attractive to the elite. Historians' and travelers' accounts of 'Abbasiyya claim that 'Abbas's palace "set an example for palace beauty" and that the royal princes, like 'Abbas himself, preferred to build in European fashions.[102] One European traveler left an account that was not wholly unlike that of al-Tahtawi's descriptions of Egyptian homes: "The interior contained magnificently paved halls. The furniture is sometimes magnificent, the style of which is mostly Louis XIV more than Moorish. . . . Everything came from Paris: cloth, doors, tables . . . everything."[103] 'Abbas also had a railway constructed between Cairo and Alexandria and began the construction of a line connecting the capital to Suez. Cairo was now a railway junction and, increasingly, accessible to a greater number of Egyptians. Out of hatred for 'Abbas, Sa'id let the suburb fall into neglect by discontinuing plans for the quarter's development. But the neighborhood began to flourish again under Isma'il, who built two palaces in 'Abbasiyya, and laid a water pipeline to the neighborhood in 1867.[104]

'Abbasiyya underwent another period of growth under Tawfiq (r. 1879–92), who resided nearby. When Cairo's tramway was opened in 1896, the neighborhood became a desirable residential area. On the eastern side of the neighborhood, villas and mansions housed Europeans and the most elite Egyptians; middle-class Egyptians lived in the western half. An increase in Cairo's population in the 1870s as well as the arrival of British officials and their families also contributed to 'Abbasiyya's continued growth and to that of Cairo's other middle-class suburbs, including al-Faggala, al-Dahir, and Sakakini.

The greatest transformations of Cairo's landscape took place under Isma'il's rule. Isma'il considered Egypt to be part of Europe, not Africa, and he therefore desired to make Cairo look like a European city. In 1864–65 he created a Ministry of Public Works to help put through plans for Cairo's transformation. He attended the 1867 Universal Exposition at Paris and witnessed the culmination of Hausmann's work in Paris firsthand. Once back at home, the Khedive was determined to transform Cairo along the lines of what he had seen in Europe. He assigned 'Ali Mubarak to the task of overseeing the Ministry of Public Works, entrusting him with Cairo's modernization. He presented Mubarak with three tasks: the construction of a suburb to be named after the khedive; the redevelopment of Azbakiyya, and the drafting of a master plan for the modernization of all of Cairo.[105]

Isma'il wanted to have Cairo ready to display to the foreign dignitaries who would attend the opening of the Suez Canal in 1869. Laws were promulgated to widen the streets, especially those in the quarters of Isma'iliyya and Azbakiyya. Azbakiyya was the heart of Isma'il's plan to Hausmannize Cairo; there, he ordered the demolition of old buildings, streets, and alleyways and replaced them with broad streets, mansions, and government buildings. New shops, places of entertainment, gardens, and an opera house appeared in the new neighborhood. Those who were willing to build a Constantinopolitan were given government land grants.

Isma'il began the development of the neighborhood named after him. He had the streets laid out in grid fashion and provided homes with the most modern amenities. By 1865, gas lamps dotted the streets, and two years later there was running water in elite homes. As in Azbakiyya, Isma'il encouraged development by offering free land to those who could afford to build showy, European houses. The khedive intended to make this a Europeanized neighborhood and to parade his foreign visitors through it.

As Mona Russell's study of the rise of consumerism among the new elites has illustrated, the Egyptian press gave the upper classes clear instructions for how to furnish these new homes.[106] By the 1880s, journals began advising readers about location (neighborhoods with modern amenities such as schools and hospitals were best), building materials, and selecting neighbors. In descriptions of model houses, school textbooks from the late 1880s onward gave precise details about the kinds of rooms in homes, advising readers that they should obtain a house with a library. Proper furnishings and decorations were as crucial to these new households as cleanliness, and journals were full of lengthy discussions about the hygienic practices and decor appropriate to modern, elite households.

Under Isma'il and Tawfiq, Cairo also witnessed the construction of a zoo, parks, restaurants, conservatories, libraries, museums, theaters, sporting clubs, and schools. A national theater was inaugurated in 1868; the opera house opened its doors in 1869. The first patrons of the Khedival Library were welcomed in 1870. In 1875, the members of the Khedival Geographic Society celebrated the building's inauguration.[107]

The habits and customs of the new elites also began to change. While some elites preferred traditional clothing, many Egyptian men and women began to dress in European clothing. Elite women wore fashions from Paris, fezes replaced turbans, and carriages became more common than horseback.[108] The Egyptian elite smoked their tobacco in the form of cigars and cigarettes rather than water pipes; Isma'il himself was a big fan of cigars.[109] Not all Western innovations were accepted. Indeed, the local press featured debates over the extent to which Western habits and customs should be adopted. Elements of both the Ottoman-Turkish and the Arabophone population tended to resist innovation, preferring to adhere to their traditional practices.[110]

Change was also evident in relationships between men and women. Until 1877, when the practice of white slavery was abolished, Egyptian elites tended to prefer Circassian women as wives and concubines. Outside of the ruling family, the keeping of multiple concubines in addition to a man's four legal wives was not common, even though there were no restrictions on the number of concubines a man could keep.[111] Girls brought in from the Caucasus and sold on the Egyptian slave market were status symbols for Arabophone and Ottoman-Turkish Muslim families. The girls were often acquired at a young age and raised as elites, in the harem, or women's quarters of a house. They were provided with a traditional, Islamic education or, as the century wore on, tutored by the wives and daughters of Europeans residing in Egypt.[112] Mohammad 'Ali and his successors each educated their daughters. Isma'il and Tawfiq's daughters were educated by European governesses, as were the slaves of the khedives and high-ranking officials who were often married off to their owner's sons once manumitted.[113]

The taking of white slave women as wives and concubines was a remnant of Mamluk days. To replenish their ranks, the Mamluks routinely brought in large supplies of slaves from outside Egypt (mostly from the Caucasus) and maintained large harems of wives and concubines. While concubines did not have the same formal rights as Mamluk wives, they were treated as part of the family and manumitted once they had produced a son for their master. Often a slave would be taken as wife once she gave birth to a male. Mamluks were also known to free their slaves and marry them off to other Mamluks or to high-ranking Egyptians.[114] White slaves were still being kept as concubines by some elite Egyptians, even after the practice of slavery was abolished. But monogamy, if not common, was increasingly practiced by government officials. While elites from the 1870s onward tended to marry more than once, they took only one wife at a time, a pattern that was followed by state servants such as 'Ali Mubarak.[115] Isma'il was polygamous, but Tawfiq was not. As more men became educated, they began to insist upon marrying educated women, and companionate marriages began to be fashionable.[116]

Thus, while much of Cairo remained unchanged by the time of the rise of Mohammad 'Ali and his descendants, small sections of the city's landscape were changing with the introduction of new architecture, new habits, and new fashions. A growing number of Cairo's inhabitants came to call themselves Egyptian, and to refer to their habits as "modern" Egyptian as the century progressed.

Conclusion

In comparing travel literature written by al-Tahtawi to that by Edward Lane, who was in Egypt at about the same time that his contemporary was in France, literary critic Sandra Naddaf noted similarities between the objects of both men's inquiries. She argues that the essential difference between the travel literature produced by al-Tahtawi and that produced by Lane is the degree to which each author attempted to situate himself in (or, by contrast, erase himself from) the landscape through which he traveled. Al-Tahtawi, she claims, was willing to look for similarities between his country and Europe, whereas Lane was simply fixated by difference. Naddaf argues that while Lane searched for and focused his attentions on the strange and the bizarre — the ultimately foreign — in order to distance himself from Egypt, al-Tahtawi attempted to see himself and his own society reflected in what he saw in France.[117]

Quoting from Lane, Naddaf points out that while the similarities between European cafés and those of Cairo were abundant, Lane's task was to establish Cairo's cafés as a "thing apart, an institution specific to the culture in which they are found . . . [with] no physical characteristics which suggest the possibility of comparison with their Western counterparts."[118] In his obsession with the hashish that was allegedly consumed in the cafés, and the musicians and storytellers who performed in them, Lane accomplished the Orientalist's task of distant observation, of knowing the Orient through detachment from it.

Al-Tahtawi, she suggests, was victim to a different obsession, that of seeing the West as a mirror of the East. Knowing, for al-Tahtawi, was a matter of "shuttling between" the poles of East and West, and of self-reflection. In the following quote from al-Tahtawi, she locates what she considers to be the "driving force" behind Eastern travel literature: "The first time I visited this coffee shop, I thought it was a bustling city because there were so many people there. If a group of people came in or went out, their reflections appeared on each of the mirrored walls, so that whether they were sitting, walking, or standing, their number seemed to increase. It seemed then that the café extended indefinitely, until I saw my own reflection in the mirror."[119]

Naddaf is certainly correct in seeing the mirror as central to the project in which Egyptian travel literature "placed" Egypt by seeing itself reflected in the landscapes and institutions of the "modern" nations. There is another point, however, about the atmosphere in which al-Tahtawi undertook his work. The mirrors in al-Tahtawi's description of the French coffeehouse are emblematic of the project that undergirded the production of *Takhlis al-ibriz* and of literature like it. By seeing itself reflected in Europe's mirror, Egypt had naturally to be placed and ranked in the hierarchy of nations whose institutions it attempted to emulate. The mirror represents not the willingness of an Egyptian to see similarities where Europeans could only see difference but rather reveals the exigencies that faced al-Tahtawi as a servant of Mohammad 'Ali's state.

The process of building the state in early nineteenth-century Egypt resulted in a particularly configured relationship among the state, its citizens, and the world outside of Egypt's borders. As an ethnographer — unwitting or otherwise — Mohammad 'Ali had produced, via a corps of civil servants, a body of literature and blueprints about modernity and its trappings. In that literature, produced and published for the purpose of expanding the state and its dominion, the domestic realm of the citizen both at home and abroad was penetrated, chronicled, and used as a yardstick for measuring modernity. Through "travel literature," the state began to see itself as modern and to envision for itself a position in the modern world.

It is clear that state-produced ethnographies and ethnographers made their way out of Dar al-Alsun and the classrooms of the student missions over the course of the nineteenth century. The texts produced by al-Tahtawi and 'Ali Mubarak were used in the state school system as it grew over the course of the twentieth century. Ahmed Hussein al-Rashidi, for example, translator of *Géographie universelle,* taught and translated in the School of Medicine in Cairo. Likewise, Ahmed 'Abid al-Tahtawi, who translated Voltaire's history of Peter the Great into Arabic, later became representative to Cairo's Council of Merchants (Wakil majlis al-tujar). 'Abdullah abu al-Sa'ud, responsible for the translation of *The Superlative Behavior of the Men who have Governed France,* was a prominent figure in the Bureau of Translations and taught at Dar al-'Ulum, a teachers' college founded later in the century, and later edited Isma'il Pasha's palace newspaper, *Wadi el-nil*.[120] From Dar al-'Ulum, lessons on modern "mapping" and geography made their way into primary- and secondary-school curricula, such that future generations of Egyptian school children became familiar with the relationship between domestic behavior and the location of their country.

CHAPTER 2

Inside Egypt

The Harem, the Hovel, and the Western Construction of an Egyptian National Landscape

At precisely the same time that monogamous, bourgeois couples and modern, single-family dwellings became the products of Egyptian modernization and centralization, European travelers were emphasizing Egypt's polygamy, extended families, timeless domestic practices, and bizarre sexual habits. While Egypt's upper classes assumed marital and domestic relationships that, in fact, separated them culturally from previous generations of Egyptian elites, European travel literature linked nineteenth-century Egyptians to a set of social, cultural, and political traditions that had little to do with the realities of contemporary reform programs. The struggle to "control" Egypt over the course of the nineteenth century was not only waged at the level of realpolitik but rather saw some of its fiercest battles at the level of discourse.[1] Elite Egyptians increasingly defined themselves in terms that would have been familiar to Victorian Europeans, while Western authors were determined to link the habits and customs of the Egyptian upper classes either to imaginary practices or to the traditions of bygone days.[2]

This chapter considers the role of travel literature in the construction of Western visions of Egypt in the nineteenth century and its role in shaping the British administration's subsequent understanding of "the Egypt question." While Europeans in art and travel literature from the nineteenth century depicted the region called Palestine as lacking in peoples and institutions, they reduced Egypt to stereotypes and generalizations.[3] Images of Egypt as a country defined by the domestic habits and the sexual politics of the upper-class harem and the squalor of the peasants' hovel were instrumental to the British understanding of the territory they occupied in 1882, to their plans for Egypt's reform, and to their articulation of the terms of their ultimate withdrawal.

In the century preceding the occupation, the territory known as Egypt was seldom described or depicted in travel literature and travel guides without reference to its domestic spaces. The quotidian habits of the upper-class harem and, by contrast, of the peasant hovel — while historically of interest to Western travelers — became objects of fixation during the mid- and late nineteenth century. To know Egypt and to understand its peculiar political and economic institutions was to have entered its homes, traveled through its inner spaces, seen its women. Over the course of the nineteenth century, Europeans came to understand Egypt's identity from inside the Egyptian domicile.

While tales of Oriental despotism had held seventeenth- and eighteenth-century European reading audiences in a state of awe and terror, it was the lot of the despots' wives that seemed to capture the nineteenth-century imagination. As Victorian notions of women's position in the domestic realm became more rigidly defined and more clearly articulated, so too did an antithesis to them: while the Victorians increasingly exalted women as mothers, homemakers, domestic "scientists," and partners to their husbands, they vilified the inmate of the harem who was, in their fantasies, cloistered, victimized, helpless — the mere object of lust, power, and limitless caprice. Just as the Victorian "angel of the household" was educated, skilled, and relatively autonomous at home, her alter ego was illiterate, unskilled, lazy, backwards, and helpless. Likewise, counter to the ideal Victorian husband who extended freedom to his wife and daughters, the Middle Eastern male was neither partner nor liberator. Rather, he was cruel and irrational, behaving despotically both in the private and political realms.

This fascination with the harem and its inmates fueled a taste for art and literature that journeyed into the Orient's inner spaces. At the same time that Europe's economic and territorial interests in Egypt advanced, travelers, painters, and photographers scrambled to the country in increasing numbers, bringing the harem and the private world of Egypt's upper classes home to audiences that were fascinated, repulsed, and titillated by what they read and saw. Early ethnographies such as Edward Lane's *Manners and Customs of the Modern Egyptians* (1836), for example, opened up the private world of Egypt's upper classes through detailed descriptions of the activities (real and imaginary) of harem women. One of the most widely read of Lane's chapters was that entitled "Domestic

Life (Women of the High and Middle Orders)," in which the author depicted women as heirs to a life of both pleasure and deprivation.[4] Activities such as pipe smoking, coffee drinking, reclining, gossiping, and the visiting of other harems constituted the focus of Lane's "investigations." Such ethnographies served to eclipse knowledge of the positions that upper-class women actually held in their homes and of the wide range of their activities and responsibilities. The result was a European fixation with Oriental indolence and cloistered, helpless, abused women.[5]

Of Hearth and the "Odd" Habits of Home

While in preceding centuries travelogues most often depicted Egypt as a region among the many in the Orient, the nineteenth century witnessed Egypt's appearance as a distinct "national" entity, full of particularly Egyptian institutions, behaviors, and proclivities. French historian Jean-Marie Carré, for example, has concluded that until the early nineteenth century, Egypt was represented in travel literature as a place that one simply passed through in order to get someplace else. Carré argues that while the publishing of Montesquieu's *Lettres persanes* in 1721 brought with it a whole host of other kinds of "letters" (from Istanbul, Moscow, or Lima), a *Lettres égyptiennes* never appeared.[6] Egypt was viewed by Europeans as occupying the borders between the "known" world and the world of monsters and extraordinary dangers.[7] Egypt was variously cast as the blessed territory in which the Holy Family sought refuge; as a repository of Hellenic heritage; as the house of Islam; as the capital of a dangerous empire.[8] Rarely did Egypt appear as a distinct entity.

In the early nineteenth century, however, a new obsession with Egypt materialized, and along with it came new devices for the study of Egypt — new categories through which the country could be analyzed. Some of the "lenses" through which Egypt had traditionally been viewed were maintained: Islam, for example, continued to be a category for assessing the ideologies and institutions of the modern Egyptians. Likewise, "despotism" continued to be the most common means of explaining the Egyptian body politic and the behavior of its rulers. At the same time, the traveler's attention was turned toward new arenas. While Egypt's body politic had not been forgotten, the domicile had become the focus for uncovering and understanding Egypt's secrets. The West's repertoire of stories about the "palace peculiarities" that first tainted and then undermined Ismaʻil's rule was informed by a very specific knowledge of his domestic habits, and of his "inner" nature, and the tellers of those stories were determined to label Isma'il and his behavior "Egyptian."⁹ The secrets found within the living spaces of Egypt's ruling elite were thus used to shape an Egyptian landscape on which the colonial experience was later played out.

Descriptions of Egyptians' living quarters were certainly included in travel literature that preceded the nineteenth century. However, early commentary is distinguished by the seeming disinterest in the subject of the home. Travelers often described Egyptian homes from the outside and from a distant vantage point, as if the task of depicting the domicile was to place it into some kind of grander vista or a larger cityscape. An eye for urban spatial arrangements and design was commonplace when living quarters were assessed, as illustrated in the description of Cairo written by the Englishman Abraham Parsons in the late eighteenth century:

In Cairo there are many broad streets and open, airy places, but this is the case only in the skirts [sic] of the town, as the greatest parts of the streets are narrow, the houses being from two, three and four stories, all of burnt brick which project so as to command a prospect to both ends of the street, which has this inconvenience, that they approach so close to those which are opposite as to make it disagreeable. The tops of the houses are flat, on which people enjoy the fresh air in the evening.¹⁰

Color, construction materials, and decorative style all caught the eye of travelers to Egypt in the seventeenth and eighteenth centuries, as did the general appearance of Cairo's homes. The Frenchman Jean Coppin, who visited Egypt in the late seventeenth century, never entered an Egyptian dwelling, but he enjoyed the facades of the different homes and was intrigued by the materials with which they were built. He had relatively little to say about houses in Cairo, but did remark that "generally the houses that make up a town aren't very nice to look at from the outside; their windows are closed and they have a rather melancholy countenance."¹¹ While Coppin's comments reflect a certain measure of distaste for his surroundings, they also display a kind of superficial disinterest, perhaps indicating that the domicile was relatively unimportant to his understanding of his surroundings.

When examining the exterior of the peasants' quarters, however, Europeans frequently gave lengthy descriptions of the size, shape, and manner of their construction. In a passage characteristic of the era in which it was written, Coppin's contemporary Antonius Gonzales said: "The *fellaheen*'s houses are for the most part built of sun-dried bricks and clay.

Their roofs are made of lath-work and boards, or of beams to which they attach palm fronds. On top of that, they put on two or three layers of clay, which under the hot sun becomes hard as stone and lasts a man's lifetime. All the houses in the villages are whitewashed."[12] Not a word about the home's interior appeared in Gonzales's descriptions.

By the nineteenth century, distant descriptions of Egyptian homes gave way to detailed accounts of the inner world of the domicile that were as minute in their description as they were thorough in their coverage. One author, calling herself "Riya Salima," perfectly summarized the nineteenth-century project of knowing the inner world of the Egyptian domicile when she said, "You will want to get inside the harem in order to know it intimately."[13] If the house was a mystery from the outside, it had only to be "entered" so that its contents could be revealed.[14]

Salima's text left no detail of the size, shape, or contents of the harem to the reader's imagination. Everything that she found and witnessed within the walls of the domicile was chronicled for the reader in exquisite detail:

Let us enter into one of these harems. . . . Here is the eunuch at the door. . . . Here we are in the entrance which is like ours but more open and with more light. There are many couches, a small, round inlaid table, a chandelier, a few small tables laden with ashtrays and cigarettes — these are the classic furnishings. This is where one receives guests during the summer, and where the family prefers to gather. As for the rest of the harem, the rooms don't seem to me to be as big or as luxurious.[15]

Here the position of Salima is much less that of an "observer" than an invited guest. Salima in fact wrote the book as if she was the owner of the harem, writing to a Western reader. "In providing you with a description of my house . . . I imagine the bizarre conclusions that you have drawn."[16] Her images are detailed and personal rather than disinterested and abstract.

The inside of the peasant hovel received as much attention as the harem. By midcentury, meticulous descriptions of every aspect of the peasants' quarters were also commonplace. The dirt, disease, and squalor that were attributed to the interior space of the hovel were as fascinating to the traveler as the contents of the houses themselves:

The internal arrangement of a *fellah* house is extremely simple . . . these rooms might be compared to two shabby bee-hives, about six feet at the widest part. The 'forn' mentioned in the story of Sheikh Abd-al-Haj is the most important piece of furniture. It is a kind of permanent bedstead, built of brick, and containing an arched stove or oven, which serves to give warmth in winter, especially at night, as well as for the purpose of cooking. The whole family, father, mother and children, sometimes spread their mats on this bed of ware, which, being fed with dung-fuel, bakes them gently until morning. . . . Chairs and tables are, of course, unknown and desired by the fellah, but some of them possess a sort of stand a few inches high, circular, and called a 'soofra,' resembling the article of furniture used in cities. . . . I admit that the poorest class of dwellings which I have described . . . cannot be visited without some danger of suffocation and some offense to delicate nostrils. I do not allow this to be a matter of reproach to the owners. Clean poverty and healthy misery are not to be met with every day, neither in Egypt nor elsewhere.[17]

The home, then, was not only besieged by the traveler but subjected to a very specific kind of investigation. Knowing Egypt's domestic spaces meant not only entering them but chronicling them in intimate detail. Egypt was seen not through the distant panoramas that characterized earlier literature but from an intrusive proximity. Knowledge and intimacy were combined in the quest to get inside Egypt's inner spaces and to expose their secrets.

Inside Ancient Egypt: Europe's Quest for the Pharaonic Past

Accompanying the nineteenth-century scramble to enter Egypt's domestic realm was a determination to uncover the secrets of its pharaonic heritage through the exploration of its ancient monuments. Mid-nineteenth-century Europe witnessed a fascination with Egypt's pharaonic heritage, an "Egyptomania" that sent an increased number of tourists to Egypt annually and swelled the ranks of societies dedicated to the study of Egypt's past. The result was a conflation of the past and the present and a tendency on the part of Europeans to attribute the pharaonic past to contemporary Egyptians and their institutions.[18] The territory between the Sudan and the Mediterranean thus quickly became filled with what Europeans claimed was a particularly Egyptian heritage. Modern Egyptians were cast as the descendants of a spectacular, admirable, and, most important, discernibly Egyptian people. Consequently, Egyptians were set apart from their contemporaries in North Africa, the Levant, and the Arabian peninsula in the Western imagination.

When Napoleon landed in Egypt in 1798, he had with him an entourage that included more than 150 scholars and technicians, including a number of cartographers and surveyors. He quickly put them to work uncovering Egypt's past.[19] The result of Napoleon's determination to find ancient Egypt was the establishment of Egypt as a "field of study"; and for the first time, Egyptian antiquities were subjected to serious and systematic investigations. Shortly after the invasion, Napoleon established l'Institut d'Égypte, designed to house his cadre of scholars and their projects. The result of their efforts was *Description de l'Égypte*, the production of which left no stone and no object unturned and unchronicled in a quest to "know" Egypt and to write its history.

The text set crucial precedents in the production of knowledge about Egypt. To begin with, it demonstrated that Egypt could best be known through thorough descriptions of all that was found there, from its languages, religions, monuments, and topography to its history and natural resources. Tribal relations, military conquests and defeats, and agricultural practices all found their way into the *Description*. A more thorough catalogue of things Egyptian has never been written by a European. The scholars who eventually wrote the *Description* did, in fact, spend a great deal of time chronicling the inside of Egypt's edifices. They entered and examined mosques and churches, fortresses, seats of government, private homes, and, to the delight of European audiences, pharaonic temples, tombs, and monuments.[20]

Egypt's pharaonic past became increasingly accessible in 1822, with Champollion's discovery of the Rosetta Stone, the cracking of its linguistic code, and the subsequent production of "knowledge" about hieroglyphics. "Guides" to the past such as the *Description* and access to the secrets of the hieroglyphs allowed for Egypt's literal invasion by Westerners in search of pharaonic history. A rush took place to "discover" the glories of Egypt's past. By the 1870s, the Thomas Cook Travel Company of London had produced a travel guide that included a complete dictionary of hieroglyphs and a "primer" for understanding the language; visitors to Egypt were encouraged to understand "ancient Egyptian" before learning simple phrases in modern Egyptian Arabic, and the Arabic-English dictionary was considerably less substantial than the "primer."[21]

Thus the early and mid-nineteenth century witnessed the growth of enthusiasm for a particular historical narrative about Egypt. This narrative tended to gloss over large periods of history and to leave others out. Absent from it were discussions of Roman and Hellenic invasions and settlements and, along with them, the establishment of Christianity as Egypt's once-dominant religion. Perhaps most important, it ignored the

Arab invasions that, beginning in the mid-seventh century, brought Arabic, Arab culture, and Islam to Egypt and the marginalization of pharaonic and Christian paradigms.[22] The resulting myopia about Egypt's past was well summed up by one late-Victorian traveler, for example, when he said that "to most of us, Egypt means three or four things only: A long, narrow strip of eternally, encircling water in the midst of a green avenue of country . . . all along its banks are . . . reeds in which dwells a kind of ubiquitous Moses . . . (and) a Lotus air where even mummies . . . are by no means out of place."[23] Egypt had ceased to be a central part of the Arab-Islamic world and had become the "land of the Pharaohs."

There were undoubtedly reasons besides the growing fascination with the pharaohs for the ascendance of this new territorial and cultural construction of "Egypt": the landing of Napoleon's troops and the subsequent struggle between England and France for dominance in Egypt; increased activity in India and the need to maintain safe passage to it *through* Egypt; as well as the establishment of Mohammad 'Ali's breakaway political dynasty in 1805. Nonetheless, by imbuing the territory known as Egypt and all its historically shifting borders with a predominantly pharaonic history — a history that none of the other territories in the Arab-Islamic Orient possessed — the Western descriptive genre and the travelogue of the nineteenth century did much to make the borders of Egypt rigid and distinct. The "plan" for touring Egypt inevitably placed the traveler inside the past:

Climb the Great Pyramid, spend a day with Abou on the summit, come down, penetrate into its recesses, stand in the king's chamber, listen to the silence there, feel it with your hands, — is it not tangible in this hot fastness of incorruptible death? — creep, like the surreptitious midget you feel yourself to be, up those long and steep inclines of polished stone, watching the gloomy darkness of the narrow walls, the far-off pin-point of light borne by the Bedouin who guides you. . . . Now you know the great Pyramid. You know that you can climb it, that you can enter it. You have seen it from all sides, under all aspects. *It is familiar to you.*[24]

Beginning with the pyramids of Giza, "knowing" Egypt entailed scaling and entering the monuments, ascending and descending such that the secrets of their construction might be revealed. Amelia Edwards betrayed the extent to which "knowing" ancient Egypt required penetration when she wrote about her first visit to Giza: "We started immediately after an early luncheon, followed by an excellent road all the way, and were back in time for dinner at half past six. But it must be understood that we did not go to *see* the pyramids. We meant only to look at them."[25] Travelogues and guidebooks taught travelers how to undertake the rigorous process of knowing the past, as evidenced by a passage from a handbook printed in 1885: "The ascent of the Pyramid is perfectly safe. The traveler selects two of the importunate Bedouin and proceeds to the Northeast corner of the Pyramids where the ascent usually begins. . . . The strong and active attendants assist the traveler to *mount* by pushing, pulling and supporting him."[26]

Travel literature also guided visitors through the pyramids' inner depths, providing vivid detail of what was found in them. Edward Lane's sister, Sophia Lane Poole, visited the pyramids in the 1840s and recorded both the activity of entering the pyramids and the "knowledge" that her visit to Egypt had afforded her. Her instructions for getting inside the pyramid were vivid, and her knowledge of its dimensions complete: "Before the traveler enters the pyramid he should divest himself of some of his clothes. . . . The passage by which we enter the Great Pyramid is only four feet high and three foot six inches in width."[27]

Lane Poole's descriptions of the inner realms of the pyramids, of their passages and their chambers, differed little from her descriptions of harems, illustrating the extent to which tours of Egypt in the mid-nineteenth century were shaped by peregrinations through the insides of both the ancient and the modern. While tours offered by fledgling companies like Thomas Cook defined Egypt through the sites and monuments, memoirs such as those written by Lane Poole attest to a second "tour" that outlined Egypt through realms that were hidden from the eye. Distinctions between ancient and modern were practically indiscernible when one looked from the inside out, as evidenced by descriptions of the Great Pyramid and Mohammad 'Ali's harem: "On emerging, we find ourselves at the foot of the Grand Passage. . . . This one ascending to the main chamber is, in comparison with those which lead to it, wide and lofty. It is lined above and below and on each side with blocks of limestone. The roof is formed of long blocs of stone leaning against each other."[28]

Lane Poole then entered and traversed the harem in precisely the same fashion: "We then ascended by an ample marble staircase to the *salon* on the first floor. This is a very splendid room, paved with marble as indeed are all the passages, and I imagine all the apartments on the ground floor. . . . The ceiling . . . is painted admirably in shades of dark and light blue. . . . The corners and cornices are richly decorated."[29] The portrait of modern Egypt that was the result of tours through Egypt, both those actually undertaken by tourists and those that took place in the armchair, were constructed out of Egypt's hidden spaces as well as its monuments, pulling the private world inexorably into the process through which Egypt was known.

European travelers were fond of using what they found inside of pharaonic monuments as keys to understanding modern Egyptians, for measuring the achievements of the past against those of the present. From the art that they discovered on temple walls, for example, travelers ascertained that modern Egyptians resembled the ancients: "Egyptians . . . have preserved the same delicate profile, the same elongated eyes, as mark the old goddesses carved in bas-relief on the Pharaonic walls."[30] In appearance, technique, and machinery, it was decided, the Egyptian *fellaheen* resembled their pharaonic ancestors, "the humble subjects of Amenophis and Seti," making them the robust descendants of the farmers who had once toiled on the banks of the flooded Nile and setting them apart from the ranks of the Orient's peasantry.[31] Finally, harem women were said to possess the visage of the Pharaonic princesses. It was often stated that "they would only have to do their hair in tiny braids in order to resemble Hofert Hari or Isenophé."[32]

By constructing the pharaonic past as the source and generator of Egyptian character, Western travelers inevitably constructed a yardstick by which the present could be measured. The obvious achievements of the ancient Egyptians served as reminders of modern Egyptians' potential, of the greatness that was in their grasp. At the same time, however, the pharaohs served as a sad reminder of that lost glory. Europeans found the modern Egyptians to be far less capable than their ancestors. Said Florence Nightingale after her trip to Egypt: "Without the [pharaonic] past, I conceive Egypt to be utterly uninhabitable."[33]

In Every Home an Odalisque: Everyday Habits of the Domestic Realm

Once Egypt's interior realms had been entered and their contents sorted through and catalogued, the activities of its modern inhabitants were subjected to the traveler's investigations. While both men and women and their daily activities were the object of the Western traveler's curiosity, Egyptian women and their habits attracted the most curiosity. Throughout the nineteenth century, the domestic realm was the arena in which foreigners "observed" women's daily habits and through which they could comment on women's position in Egyptian society.

Like depictions of the Egyptian house itself, descriptions of women and their daily activities changed markedly in the nineteenth century. In late-seventeenth-century literature, for example, it was women's appearance — their size, shape, and the style of their clothing — rather than their activities that made up the list of descriptions through which womanhood was presented: "The countrywomen are usually small and dark-skinned. Their beauty comes from their fiery eyes. The conversation that they make is very boring, and the way they dress is not pleasing. The women of the upper classes are better raised and nicer in every way."[34] Much like the discussion of homes with which this chapter began, this description of women is not wholly positive. The above "focus" on women, however, is distant and somewhat disinterested and does not take up either the "inner" or the "essential."

By the early nineteenth century, however, women embracing the tasks and burdens of domestic life began to take up the most considerable space in travel literature. Edward Lane devoted a great deal of his *Manners and Customs* to domestic life; the reader was caught up in lengthy discussions of food, furnishings, and the activities of the home's occupants. About the daily life of peasant women, he said: "The women of the lower orders seldom pass a life of inactivity. . . . Their chief occupations are the preparing of the husband's food, fetching water (which they carry in a large vessel on the head), spinning cotton, linen, or woolen yarn, and making the fuel called 'gellah,' which is composed of the dung of cattle."[35]

Often it was the most private domestic activities that were "reported" by the traveler: "As soon as it is light the poor woman gets up from her mat and shakes herself, or, if the weather is hot, she has been sleeping outside with her family. Having thus completed her toilet, she and her husband and children gather around a small earthen dish containing boiled beans and oil, pickles or chopped herbs, green onions or carrots."[36] Similarly, travelers entered the harem and recounted the daily agendas of its inhabitants for the reader: "The care of their children is the primary occupation of the ladies of Egypt . . . their leisure hours are mostly spent in working with the needle, particularly in embroidering. . . . The visit of one harem to another often occupies nearly a whole day. Eating, smoking, drinking coffee and sherbet, gossiping and displaying their finery are sufficient amusements to the company."[37] Accompanying this was a catalogue of the items used for preparing tea, eating meals, and smoking; men and women both were illustrated eating and smoking the pipe. Salima's tour of the harem was also accompanied by lengthy descriptions of the silver items used to make and serve refreshments, and with which tobacco could be consumed.

Habits such as smoking the water pipe were routine subjects in nineteenth-century travel literature. They represented the "exotic" and "debauched" activities that occurred in the Egyptians' private, domestic space. Because such "bizarre" habits took place indoors, the house became a source of intrigue and mystery. While habits like pipe smoking came to symbolize "inner mystery," female degradation, and Oriental fecklessness over the course of the nineteenth century, they did not represent debauchery in texts from earlier centuries.

Le Père Antonius Gonzales's seventeenth-century *Le Voyage en Égypte,* for example, contains an illustration that shows that the "odd" and the "depraved" habits that had come to be located in Egyptian homes were, at one time, depicted as having taken place outside, in open spaces.[38] Gonzales described pipe smoking as an act of innocents, of children, rather than the activity of the immoral, over-sexed inmates of the harem. At the same time, Gonzales depicted pipe smoking as a shared activity and not as the lot of the segregated realm of women. The smokers stood rather than reclined, such that laziness and fecklessness are not connoted. Finally, while the smokers appeared to be members of the urban, upper classes, they were not confined to the harem. Their activities did not take place in secret, or in closed homes, and there was no mystery about them.

As the nineteenth century progressed, the daily activities of both the harem and the hovel became not just the object of mystery and curiosity, but also a means through which commentary about Egyptian society could be issued. The most typical of that commentary was that women's habits were "peculiar," and that they illustrated the "degraded" position of women in Egypt. Prior to the nineteenth century, harem activities, while illustrating the luxuries of the Orient, did not necessarily connote "odd" or "degraded." In the late eighteenth century, for example, a certain Monsieur Savary noted that harem women lived a pampered existence, saying that slaves did most of the work while the "wives" relaxed: slaves served coffee, sherbet, cakes, and endless rounds of tea. As for their mistresses: "The women chat, they laugh, they frolic."[39] He also wrote that one of the women's favorite activities was the telling of stories. Women were said to sing little songs, to recite novels, and to perform dances for one another. In other words, the author reported that these women lived a life of leisure, but absent from his descriptions is any explanation that their activities were immoral, useless, or backwards.

Lane's descriptions of the harem resemble Savary's, but they contain a critical difference: attached to his narratives about women's activities is commentary, both direct and subtle, about the purpose of those activities, about their purported frivolity or lack of worth. To the above description about the women's telling of stories, for example, Lane added: "When their usual subjects of conversation are exhausted, sometimes one of the party entertains the rest with the recital of some . . . *facetious* tale."[40] According to Lane, women's conversations did not involve the use of intellect and were not designed to elevate or raise their moral state. Rather, stories were the lot of lies and make believe.

Others were more direct in denigrating the harem, calling its activities "perverse and idiotic" and its lifestyle "idle." Some compared what they saw in the harem directly to what they had read about Scheherazade in the *Thousand and One Nights*.[41] Upper-class women's behavior was most particularly criticized when it involved their relationships with men. If women were "idle" and idiotic in their telling of stories, they were lascivious when it came to their husbands. Again, Lane's text is instructive: "The wives of men of the higher and middle classes make a great study of pleasing and fascinating their husbands by unremitted attentions, and by various arts. Their coquetry is exhibited, even in their ordinary gait when they go abroad, by a *peculiar* twisting of the body."[42]

Just as the harem's activities were cast as taking place in hidden, remote spaces, domiciles themselves were often depicted as being "hidden" in dark, twisted alleys, on poorly lighted streets, on lanes so narrow that donkeys could barely pass through them, making the location of the domicile as mysterious as the activities that it contained. In many passages, the domicile's facade took on the same elements of treachery and secrecy that were the lot of its inner activities:

As we turn onto one of the narrow lanes that intersect the Mohammaden City [Cairo], we are struck not only by the vivid incongruities of the street scenes which travellers have so often described, but by the contrast between the noise and bustle of the crowded alley and the quiet silence of the tall houses that overhang it on each side. Here there is no sign of life; the doors are jealously closed, the windows shrouded by those beautiful screens of net-like woodwork which delight the artist and tempt the collector. If we enter one of these gates . . . we shall find the inner court almost as silent and deserted as the guarded windows that overlook the street. We shall see nothing of the domestic life of the inhabitants, for the women's apartments are carefully shut off from the court.[43]

Shrouded in mystery, the home contained Egypt's essence, as well as its secrets.

Outdoor Habits Veiled in the Harem's Intrigue

Over the course of the nineteenth century, the mysteries of the home began to be ascribed to women's activities within the public realm. In particular, veiling, segregation, and the relations between men and women in public became highly charged with negative meaning. The street became an extension of the harem, and the veil was made the public manifestation of segregation and seclusion.[44] The result was a blurring of Egypt's inner and outer realms and the creation of a seamless image of Egyptian behavior, wherein the public was but an extension of the private. In other words, the evils of the harem could be found everywhere.

Often, late-nineteenth-century travelogues compared veiled women outside of their homes to segregation, attributing both customs to the "closed world" of Oriental secrets. One traveler, for example, contrasted life in Egypt, which he thought to be generally open, to life for women:

Life goes on in the open streets to an extent which always surprises us. . . . People drink tea, smoke, pray, sleep, carry on all their trades in sight of the passers by. . . . *But, into the recesses of the harem and the faces of the women one may not look.* And this last mystery and reserve almost outweighs the openness of everything else. One feels as if he were in a masquerade; the part of the world which is really most important — womankind — appears to him only in shadow and flitting phantasm. What danger is he in from these wrapped and veiled figures which glide by, shooting him with a dark and perhaps wicked eye? . . . I seem to feel that this is a mask of duplicity and concealment.[45]

In earlier literature, the confinement of women to the domestic realm and the lack of interactions between men and women in public were devoid of any particular sociosexual meaning; upper-class decorum simply dictated the separation of the sexes. Another passage, for example, written in the late seventeenth century, claims nothing astonishing about the fact that men and women did not speak if they happened to encounter one another in the streets: "Married women and honorable unmarried women . . . never venture into places where men can be found. No one ever sees a man address a woman in the streets. . . . When women move about in the streets, they do so with modesty and in an edifying manner. When a man visits a private residence, women either cover their faces or retire [to their quarters] until he departs, even when their husbands are present."[46] While in nineteenth-century discussions of segregation and veiling such descriptions were usually followed by commentary about the evils of veiling and segregation as well as the barbarity of the men who perpetrated them, the above account was simply accompanied by further descriptions of the women who practiced such customs. Women, for example, were described as being "richly" dressed or covered in precious jewels. One author found women's character to be as pleasing as their clothing, which was, from head to toe, made of silver and gold.[47]

Coppin noted the absence of women in the streets and in Cairo's commercial districts, saying simply that "they are hidden in secret apartments of houses in such a way that people who visit those houses never see them."[48] The absence of women on the streets was noted in seventeenth-century literature, but was not the object of commentary. Likewise, descriptions of the veil before the nineteenth century seem to be included in travel literature as a kind of afterthought. Le Père Gonzales, for example, mentioned the veil only after a lengthy description of the various styles, colors, and materials that made up women's clothing of that period: "But when they *do* go out, you can't tell a thing about them, as they are entirely covered."[49] Coppin, like Gonzales, was as concerned with the turban, worn by men, as he was with the veil, and spent as much effort describing the ways in which men went about covering themselves. He claimed that both Egyptian men and women were so accustomed to covering their heads and faces that it was often difficult to tell them apart. Coppin paid great attention to the hierarchies of class and the corresponding color of turban that Cairenes wore and went to great lengths to inform the reader about how to tell the sexes and classes apart by the cut, style, and color of a person's headdress.[50]

Others attributed the use of the veil to honor and to the protection of women's "dignity" but did not connect the veil to any sort of cultural degradation. Said Abraham Parsons: "When the ladies walk out to visit each other, or go to their prayers at the mosque, or to the baths, which in general happens once a week, on Thursday, they are, on such occasions, attended by female servants only, who are as closely veiled as the ladies, it being a mark of infamy for a woman to appear abroad unveiled; all prostitutes, on the contrary, are obliged to appear with a naked face."[51] Here it was only "fallen women" who exposed their faces, and the veil was a sign of dignity and respect, rather than degradation. Love and passion were also cited as reasons for keeping women veiled, as was superstition. To the Frenchman Benoit Maillet, who wrote in the mid-eighteenth century, the veil was simply the means by which Egyptian women were protected from the "evil eye," and did not connote a social evil.[52]

By the nineteenth century, however, veiled women were being compared to the dead, to mummies, and to witches, illustrating the extent to which Europeans found themselves both fascinated and repulsed by women and the veil. Sir Frederick Treves explained: "In the crowd, too, are veiled women in black who would seem to be items detached from a funeral pageant, as well as bent old crones who, upon the addition of a conical hat . . . and a cat, would turn into witches."[53]

The veil was also a trope through which Victorian travelers discussed sex or the "sexual" nature of Egyptian society. Often it was noted that Egyptian women could be found — both inside the home and outside of it — naked but for their veils. Lane made reference to harem women who refused to be seen without a veil but who thought nothing of leaving their bodies unclothed. Peasant women, as well, appeared to know no shame when it came to "exposing" their bodies while keeping their visage covered: "There have been many instances of women who, upon being surprised naked, eagerly covered their faces. . . . The Egyptian peasants never give their daughters shirts till they are eight years of age. We often saw little girls running about quite naked . . . all wore veils."[54]

So common was the comparison made between home and the world outside of it, that veiled women often appeared simply to be extensions of the home itself and became part of the Egyptian cityscape — gray, mysterious, and frightening: "We find we are caught in a cul de sac and turn back. We come upon a creature entirely enveloped in a large brown or striped gray cloth, and as our glance lights upon it, it darts in at an open door. Another creature . . . that does not at once find a place of refuge squeezes itself close to a wall till we have passed by."[55] Here, veiled women are not only frightening, but possess the characteristics of animals. Brown and darting, they mimic the habits of Cairo's many rats, the removal of which, during the years of the occupation, was the obsession of many a British colonial official.

In Every Home a Family:
Motherhood and the Private Realm

As the balance of power between Europe and Egypt began to tilt in Europe's favor and as the merits of Egypt's body politic became cast in doubt, the question of what to do about reforming Egypt became more consistently articulated in the West. The result was a relentless "search" for the causes of Egypt's decay, a search that led to the harem and the hovel and to the implication of the private realm as the source of Egypt's ills (as well as its potential rejuvenation).

New to nineteenth-century travel literature was commentary about Egyptian men — rulers and ruled alike — as being the products of Egyptian home life. The habits and customs as well as the moral characteristics that were acquired by children in the harem and the hovel became more and more frequently attached to commentary about Egypt's public realm and its weaknesses. Victorian travelers to Egypt believed that both upper-class and peasant homes produced unsound citizens. One of the most deleterious results of the harem, as Victorians imagined it, was the result that the harem's alleged depravity, isolation, and sensuality had on motherhood. Since a woman's skills were, according to most travel literature, limited to sex, dancing, singing, smoking, and telling stories, it was thought unlikely that she would know how to be a good homemaker or a suitable role model for her children. She would bequeath no homemaking skills to her daughters, leaving the future of Egypt in jeopardy:

Egyptian society has its undoubted merits. . . . But in the essentials of civilization the Egyptians have everything to learn. In education they generally lack the rudiments, and in the higher department of morals they have hardly made a beginning. The fatal spot . . . is the position of women. . . . The early years of childhood, perhaps the most critical of a whole life, are tainted by the corrupt influences of the harem. . . . The reforming power of a lady is seldom possessed in the East. The restoring and purifying influence of wife on husband, of mother on child, of a hostess upon her guest is never felt. . . . In a word, *the finest springs of society are wanting.*[56]

Peasant women did not escape such critiques. Like their upper-class counterparts, Western travelers found peasant women lacking in domestic skills. Despite the fact that Westerners saw the hovel as a simple structure with little in it to demand a woman's attention, they believed that the widespread lack of education among the peasantry made it impossible for a young *fellaha* to run a family's domestic affairs. According to Mary Whately, "Of course it follows that the poor little things are not fit to guide the house. Even a peasant's household, where so little is to be done, cannot be left in the hands of a mere child."[57]

The peasants' putative laziness, stupidity, and love of filth were also listed as causes of the "low condition" of their living quarters. Charles Dudley Warner wrote: "Nothing but earthen floor and grime everywhere. . . . This is, on the whole, a model village . . . *probably the laziest in the world*. Men and women . . . were lounging about and in the houses, squatting in the dust, in absolute indolence, except that the women, all of them, were suckling their babies. . . . The men are more cleanly than the women, in every respect in better condition."[58] Laziness and stupidity also spilled over into the care of children, and peasant women were often called "Egypt's worst mothers." Another account stipulated: "From that time forward [birth], mighty little care is taken of the young *fellah* — at least to all outward appearances. He is weaned as late as possible, but when he can walk, is left to toddle about all day among the poultry and the goats, as naked as when he received the doubtful blessing of life. He is never or rarely washed, and swarms of flies constantly settle about his eyes. . . . Great misery occasionally induces a mother to sell or expose her child."[59]

From Every Home a Government: Tyranny and the Shape of the Egyptian Home

The odd habits of the Egyptian male — fecklessness, laziness, the tendency to recline and to waste endless hours in the consumption of tea and coffee, love of gossip and character assassination — were attributed to the habits of women in the home. If there was something "lacking" in a man's behavior or his character, it could be traced to the defects of his wife (or wives). But according to the nineteenth-century travelogue, the most deleterious effects of the harem and the hovel were not to be found on the streets or in coffeehouses. Rather, they manifested themselves at the level of government. As the century progressed, writers more frequently connected the condition of Egypt's homes with that of its body politic: mothers were not only responsible for producing spoiled children but for raising generations of men who were unfit to rule.

Europeans described the pashas who governed Egypt as being given to fits of anger and injustice. Pre-nineteenth-century writers such as Coppin and Gonzales, however, were more interested in the system of justice that allowed such abuses to go unchecked than they were with its causes. Neither referred to despotism as the *political* manifestation of a degenerate society, nor did they implicate women in Egypt's potential for misrule. In such an equation, despotism was the unfortunate byproduct of the system that produced it rather than the manifestation of its citizens' defects.

The relationship between the shape of the government and Egyptians' private lives began to be articulated in travel literature as early as the mid-eighteenth century. Accounts from that period, however, did not focus on women's participation in the shaping of rulers. Charles Perry, for example, who visited Egypt in 1743, attributed the alleged bad nature of the Ottoman government to the fact that Ottoman rulers were educated in the seraglio, from which they acquired their "negative" form of governing. Perry believed isolation, rather than "female influence," produced the seraglio's negative effects.[60]

The most striking antecedents to Victorian explanations of the relationship between the home and the political realm are found in a collection of letters written from Egypt in 1786 by Monsieur Savary to a cleric in Paris. Savary did not claim that women could ultimately influence the body politic; however, he did attribute the shaping of a society's morals to women and called on women to play a "role" in society that would extend beyond the domicile. "Women play a brilliant role in Europe. There they reign on the world's stage. Often the strength of nations is in their hands. What a difference there is in Egypt!! There, women are burdened by the shackles of slavery. Condemned to servitude, they have no influence on public affairs. Their empire consists only of the walls of their harem. It is there that their graces and their charms are weakened. Confined to the inner realm of the family, their activities don't even include domestic occupations."[61] While Savary claimed never to have entered a harem, he was inclined to believe that its activities left women in a state of "slavery," which confined their influence to a very limited realm.[62]

By the mid-nineteenth century, travelers routinely pointed to the home as the source of Egypt's misrule. According to many travelers, it was women who taught Oriental men to become tyrants. In the harem, men learned to be "chef, juge et pontiffe de la famille . . . il y commande."[63] Each family was said to form a small state in which the father was the "sovereign." In the family, according to Savary, each member learned his or her roles and duties. Chief among those duties was submission to the authority of others, especially that of the father. Savary evoked images of little kingships, saying: "The oldest man holds the scepter in his hands."[64] He who held the scepter was allegedly accorded all respect.

Victorian writers had the tendency to attribute the rise of "real" despotism in Egypt to events that occurred there in the nineteenth century. The reign of Mohammad 'Ali and the rise of his dynasty were consistently referred to as marking the beginnings of Egypt's real degeneracy: "As the grand sheikhs of Cairo enjoy more influence and power under this species of government than any other, they support the existing system with all their means; the soldier tyrannizes, the people suffer; the great do not feel any evils, and the machine goes on as it can."[65]

Nineteenth-century travelers claimed to "know" the nature of Mohammad 'Ali and his descendants as the result of their alleged access to the domestic realm. One of the conventions of Victorian travel literature that appeared more and more frequently as the century progressed was that of the "conversation" between travelers and Egyptians, in which the most revealing information about Egypt came from its most private spaces. It was such a trope that frequently allowed for the exposure of the "real" nature of Mohammad 'Ali's rule: travelers could claim to "know all about him" through alleged dialogues with members of his harem or his inner circle of ministers. The following, for example, was taken from a "conversation" between Nassau William Senior and one such minister — Artin Pasha — in which Mohammad 'Ali's proclivities toward the despotic were confessed:

He told me that he had read much about Machiavelli's "The Prince" and begged me to translate it for him. I set to work and gave him ten pages the first day, and the next day ten pages . . . but on the fourth day he stopped me. "I have read," he said, "all that you have given me of Machiavelli. I did not find much that was new . . . the next ten pages were no better, and the last were common-place. I see clearly that I have nothing to learn from Machiavelli. I know many more tricks than he knew."[66]

Mixed with discussions of the overbearing despotic nature of the Egyptian khedive were descriptions of the Egyptian lower classes as being wholly childlike and completely subject to the whims of their tyrant "father": "There is something, indeed there are many things, amusing in the first aspect of a barbarous population . . . but it soon becomes painful to live with beings with whom you cannot sympathize. The servility and degradation of the lower classes, the tyranny and insolence of the higher, and the rapacity and childishness of all, disgusted me more and more everyday. The government seemed, every day, to get worse and worse . . . because I saw more and more its workings."[67]

Egypt's "aristocracy" was similarly "known" to the traveler. Senior called upon a member of the khedive's inner circle (this time Tawfiq's) to account for the "truth" about Egypt's aristocracy and to illustrate the pressing need for reform of the ruling elite: "The Sheikhs and their families were the most ignorant, ragged and worthless aristocracy that ever had been. They would not work, they would not read; they passed their lives in smoking and contriving how to oppress the fellahs and deprive the government. . . . I shall return their sons in a year or two educated and civilized with more knowledge of men and things than they would have acquired in ten years squatting before the gates of their villages in the sun."[68]

Central to such narratives about Egyptian men was the role of Egyptian women in producing them. According to Senior's "conversations" with Egypt's elite, the degeneracy of both the rulers and the ruled resulted from their upbringing. Having no contact with the outside world, exposed only to the wiles of women, receiving only a Qur'anic education from his father — the Egyptian male knew nothing but the bad habits of the harem. His fate was simply to repeat the sins of his parents, marrying and divorcing, smoking and gossiping, until old age ended his career:

At fifteen he marries a girl of 11 or 12, but seldom, unless his family is very rich, keeps house; he and his wife live with his father or with her mother. By the time that he is 30, his wife has become old; he divorces her and marries another, and at 40 may have had nine or ten wives, but seldom more than one at a time.

Long before he is 50, the charms of the harem are over, and his life becomes every year blanker and blanker. . . . He does not read or write; he has little pleasure in society, for Orientals converse little and, indeed, have little to converse about.

There are no diversion parties, or balls, or theatres in our cities. There are no politics to incite interest except the intrigues of the Diwan. . . . He smokes for five hours; he enjoys himself; that is, reposes on a divan for three hours without smoking, sleeping or thinking; he squats cross-legged for two more in a coffee-house, hearing stories which he already knows by heart, told by a professional, and gets through to the remaining eight and one-half hours in bed, or on his bed, for he seldom undresses. How are you going to regenerate a people when such are the habits of its aristocracy?[69]

The answer to breaking the cycle of such presumed depravity and to instilling virtue in the ruling elite was the regeneration of Egypt's women. By the last two decades of the nineteenth century, travel literature increasingly called for women's education and training such that Egyptian men might be rejuvenated. The reform of Egypt's public realm was to start at home.

Every harem is a little despotism, in which the vices of despotism, its lawlessness, its cruelty, its intrigues, the pride and selfishness of its master, and the degradation of its subjects are reproduced on a smaller scale, but not with less intensity. Each wife is, of course, the envy of all the others. . . . The children . . . are trained up in the evil passions of family war, its stratagems, its falsehood, its spite and its revenge. . . . Early marriages give us mothers unfit to bring up their children. If polygamy degrades the wife, deprives the children, and turns the husband into a tyrant, does not that mean that institution alone accounts for Musulman inferiority?[70]

As nineteenth-century sojourners in Egypt began to raise their voices in defense of women's position in society, and as they called for women's reform and education as a panacea for the ills of public sphere in toto, travel literature traded in description for prescription. The aim of travel literature became not so much the chronicling of those things that Europeans thought they had found in Egypt, but, rather, the construction of a standard toward which Egypt might evolve. Egyptian women and the domestic realm were used as markers of Egypt's progress or, conversely, its retardation. The reform of women came to symbolize the reform of the body politic. Thus the exposure of the harem and the hovel was not simply a means of knowing Egypt; it became the critical first step in changing it. The intrigue with which earlier travelers viewed Egypt and its "peculiar' institutions was replaced with descriptions of superior European institutions, ideologies, and lifestyles, and the travelogue became an arena through which armchair reform was carried out.[71]

The Inner Realm on Display:
Egypt at the 1867 Universal Exposition at Paris

During the second half of the nineteenth century, at precisely the same time that European interest in Egypt had grown most intense, Egypt's interior spaces were frequently reproduced for the European public.[72] At the Universal Exposition of 1867 in Paris, for example, the nation known as Egypt was represented through the display of three buildings, representing different eras of the country's history. Visitors were instructed to go inside the displays in order to know Egypt, past and present. On display on the Champs de Mars — in order that "on se transporte en Égypte" — was a pharaonic temple; a Salamlik, or quarters of the (male) ruling elite, where official interactions took place; and an Okel, or caravansary.[73] The exposition's official literature called the temple and the Salamlik examples of "the two dead civilizations of the Pharaohs and the caliphs."[74] The Okel was presented as an example of Egypt under Isma'il Pasha, who oversaw an era of economic and industrial boom.[75] The guidebook that led visitors through the exhibits presented the contents of each building in extraordinary detail. No aspect of the buildings was left to the viewer's imagination. Visitors were informed that each detail had been scrupulously replicated, giving the display the utmost veracity. "The decoration — in general and in the minute details — the people and the things — all of it reproduces Egypt for us."[76] In the temple, guests were enjoined to examine the magnificent construction, the precision with which the ancients immortalized their gods, the spectacular art, the vivid colors of the paints, the magnificent hieroglyphs. Likewise, in the Salamlik, visitors appreciated the detail, but this time they saw artifacts of the inner world of Egypt's caliphs. Exquisite carpets, great quantities of gold and silver, weapons, furniture, silks, teas, spices — all were displayed in order to expose the mysteries of the quarters in which Egyptian rulers planned battles, wrote treaties, bargained over the spoils of war. In the inner world of the Salamlik, the past was recaptured.

The Okel was exposed in the greatest detail, as it was said to represent living Egypt. Step by step, floor by floor, brick by brick, the building's interior was revealed, and guests were lead through living quarters, commercial centers, military quarters, and stables for camels and donkeys. In addition, there was a reconstruction of an Egyptian library and a mosque school. The living quarters of the Okel commanded the most attention. One entered "by a wooden staircase, of several landings and a rather plain casing, which leads to the first floor and to the terrace where it ends, we are told, at a *lanternon* made entirely of *mashrabiyya*. Let's leave it in order to visit the big room. . . . The *mashrabiyyas* are worth seeing up close, and they are the most interesting part of our construction. They were taken from Hussein Bey's house in Cairo."[77] Visitors were asked to enjoy the vast quantity of objects that had been arranged in the Okel, many of which, it was claimed, were brought directly from Egypt, and to admire the great precision with which they had been laid out.

Perhaps the most outstanding feature of "Egypt" as it was "reproduced" at the exposition lay not so much in the fact that the nation's interior space was opened up for public enjoyment or for the general acquisition of knowledge about Egypt. Rather, it lay in the challenge with which visitors were presented as part of their tour. In the words of the official guide, they were asked to use their knowledge of Egypt's past in order to decide, to ordain, what the nation's *future* should be. "Today the exhibit offers to the admiring eyes of the whole world, in miniature and in one small site, all of Egypt, brilliant and splendid Egypt, revealing the grandeurs of its past, the rich promises of its present, and *leaving to public opinion the task of drawing conclusions about its future*."[78] A tour through Egypt's inner realms, past and present, ensured a vision of the future and gave Europeans the power to decide Egypt's fate.

Egyptian households, their interiors, and their customs were central to the construction of knowledge about Egypt in the nineteenth century. The Egyptian landscape that was created by tourist adventures and scholarly peregrinations was, to a great extent, shaped and structured by the harem and the hovel, spaces that were, ironically, largely hidden from the traveler's view. Women and their domestic activities were crucial to the West's understanding of Egypt and from whence its political and economic difficulties stemmed. Rather than asking why an obsession with Egypt's women accompanied the construction of "the Egypt question," we might begin to ask how "the Egypt question" could possibly have been constructed without them.

But Europe's obsession with Egypt's private realm and the subsequent attaching of the domestic realm to political and economic activities did more than simply conflate women and struggles that took place in the public realm. The relentless pursuit of "inner" Egypt and the uncovering of "secrets" that accompanied it resulted in the construction of two paradigms in which Egypt's progress or lack of it were to be measured. The first, which was the result of the equation made between modern motherhood and political success, pitted the habits and customs of Egyptians against those of the British in a race toward modernity. Proof that Egypt was not modern and, therefore, incapable of governing itself lay as much in the shape of relations between men and their wives as it did in the shape and function of its political institutions. Until its connubial relations were reformed, Egypt could not inch closer to modernity.

At the same time, the nineteenth-century construction of the pharaonic past and the juxtaposition of the great achievements of the ancient Egyptians with the chaos and disorder of the present also served to highlight modern Egypt's backward state. In such a construction, Egyptians had not only failed to "make it" to modernity, as it was defined by the Europeans, but it had "slipped" from their previous days of glory. Having thus suspended Egypt in time, between a golden past and a modernity that they could not yet grasp, the British called for an open-ended period of reform.[79]

The use of the essential, inner realm to define Egypt also created a kind of "subjectivity" from which the Egyptian was expected to speak. The role and position of women, the habits and activities of the home, formed the discourse of modern Egyptian-ness. Women were central to dialogue between Egyptians and Europeans about modernity and its trappings, not only because the early years of the occupation left discussions about the political realm outside of their grasp, but because the very definitions of "what to do about Egypt" necessitated that women be evoked in every "modern" utterance.

Finally, the above discussion of Egypt as it was shaped by tourism and travelogues challenges the most common notions about the relationship between knowledge about "the other" and the creation of colonial policy: "We came, we saw, we were horrified, we intervened."[80] While Britain's policy in Egypt was to a large extent shaped by the officials who interacted with the Egyptian ruling elite, it is easy to argue that Isma'il's antics had been "known" to the British government long before he was forced to abdicate. "The Egypt question" was thus not the product of the "horror" experienced by European banks and governments when Isma'il's accounts were perused and the "truth" discovered. Cromer and his associates may have been horrified by what they "saw" in the most private spaces of the palace and the harem, but they did not discover or uncover it. Such horrors had long since been unmasked through popular literature. Thus, the basic narrative about Egypt's invasion and occupation must be rewritten to include what it was that the British knew about Egypt prior to the occupation, what it was that horrified them, and how the policies of intervention and occupation were therefore configured.

CHAPTER 3

Domesticating Egypt

The Gendered Politics of the British Occupation

Among the many foreigners present in Egypt at the time of the British occupation was English nobleman Wilfrid Scawen Blunt (1840–1922). Blunt was a curious figure among the expatriate community. On the one hand, he was a tourist searching for an escape from England's climate and hoping to add to his stock of Arabian horses.[1] On the other hand, his interest in learning the Arabic language brought him into increased contact with Egyptians outside of tourist circles. Among them were al-Azharites Jamal ad-Din al-Afghani (1838–97) and Mohammad 'Abduh (1849–1905). Through his interactions with these men, Blunt's interests in Egypt and Arabic were transformed into an unofficial involvement in Egyptian politics. Blunt supported al-Afghani and 'Abduh's brand of Islamic modernism and nationalism and did his utmost to arrange audiences for them with other sympathetic Westerners in Europe and Egypt.[2] In both Cairo and London he petitioned for British withdrawal from Ireland and Egypt. Blunt's concern about European encroachment into Islam mirrored his long-standing support of the Irish national movement, and he earnestly attempted to convince Her Majesty's Government that an extended occupation of Egypt would not serve the crown's interests.[3]

Blunt was the first British witness to the occupation to publish his memoirs about his experiences in Egypt.[4] Whether this particular accomplishment was the result of his haste to circulate his views about the occupation or a by-product of his relative life of leisure is unclear. The title of his memoirs, however, *Secret History of the English Occupation of Egypt,* does suggest that Blunt had an agenda, as does the following quote from the original manuscript, published in 1895. Blunt wrote: "It is not always in official documents that the truest facts of history are to be read, and certainly in the case of Egypt, where intrigue of all kinds has been so rife, the sincere student needs help to understand the published parliamentary papers."[5]

Blunt's hunch that official documents about the occupation did not expose a full account of British motives in 1882, or of the British understanding of the country and the people they invaded, is easily confirmed through close readings of dispatches to and from the Foreign Office and the memoirs of the officials who oversaw the British protectorate. While Egypt's heavy debt to European bondholders and the British desire to safeguard their trade routes — aspects of the occupation that are clearly recorded in parliamentary papers — were certainly crucial factors behind the occupation, other official documents and private memoirs reveal that discussions of Egypt and "the Egypt question" included debates about Egypt and the Egyptians that transcended concerns with land and money. Those discussions included images that bore a great resemblance to travel literature and art. They cast the homes and families of elite Egyptians as central to understanding Egyptian politics.

Blunt's call to read between the lines of official records reveals that there were motives behind the occupation that, while not necessarily "secret," were as essential to the occupation as were the Suez Canal and Egypt's increasingly tenuous ability to pacify its stockholders. The critique of the additional agendas behind the occupation and the images associated with them is important for a number of reasons, not the least of which is the further illustration of the relationship between European image and Egyptian reality that was discussed in chapters 1 and 2. At the same time, however, traditional accounts of the financial and territorial motives behind the occupation fail to answer many lingering questions about why the occupation took place and how the subsequent protectorate was structured: Why did the British choose to take on another "colony" despite the anti-imperialist climate in Great Britain? Why did they choose an open-ended tenure in Egypt? Why were the colonial elite so determined to reform a country in which they claimed to have found evidence of economic solvency and self-governing institutions? Blunt was correct in suggesting that answers to such questions lie in literature not normally included in official records.

Official documents and memoirs were as laden with images of corrupt Egyptians and family practices as was the travel literature that was written before and during the occupation. While the British did not overtly state that they were occupying Egypt because of the sexual practices of the khedives and of the ruling classes, they do imply that they had to stay in Egypt because — and despite compelling evidence to the contrary — something was wrong with Egyptians that made them incapable of governing themselves. Those deficiencies were often linked to the moral condition of male Egyptians, a condition that was also linked to their familial and sexual practices. Just as the family and its politics were central to the literary construction of an Egyptian landscape, familial politics appeared as a central ingredient in the construction of the "veiled" protectorate.

Invasion and Occupation

The British occupation of Egypt and the official commencement of Anglo-Egyptian rule began early in the summer of 1882. The British allegedly reacted to the wave of antiforeign sentiment that characterized Egypt's political climate in the early 1880s and that appeared to threaten British foreign trade. In response to an outbreak of rioting targeted at Europeans in the harbor city of Alexandria earlier that summer, the British fleet landed troops off Egypt's northern coast in order to quell the riots and restore order.

Between June and September 1882, a number of battles took place, in Alexandria and elsewhere, between the British, who had both territorial and economic interests in maintaining order in Egypt, and Egyptians who wished to put an end to foreign influence in their political and economic affairs. The Egyptians who participated in the rebellion rallied under the slogan "Egypt for the Egyptians" and in support of Ahmed 'Urabi, who proposed the creation of a constitutional regime. 'Urabi and his supporters — native Egyptian army officers and landed, commercial, and administrative elites — were the product of reform programs begun by Mohammad 'Ali and continued and expanded by Isma'il. The Egyptian army officers wanted parity with their Turkish and Circassian counterparts within the military ranks. Many elected members of the Chamber of Deputies, opened by Isma'il in 1866, wanted their role within the government to be less consultative and more executive. Arabophone-Egyptian landowning elites and professional graduates from the state's schools — the *effendiyya* — hoped to ascend to greater heights within the central administration, thereby taking a greater hand in the running of the state. Between 1858 and 1882 Arabophone Egyptians had a near monopoly on high positions within both the military and the civilian administrations but still felt excluded from certain posts.[6] The goal of the "Egypt for the Egyptians" movement that united all of them was the curtailment of the khedive's powers and the limiting of European encroachment into Egyptian affairs, both of which were seen by the Egyptians as blocking their access to power. While the 'Urabists were successful in taking control of Cairo in July of 1882, forcing the Khedive to take refuge in Alexandria, the British invasion that began in mid-July limited the 'Urabists' control to Cairo by early August. By September 19, 1882, the British forces were successful in defeating 'Urabi and his followers, and the British colonial experience in Egypt began. While the invasion of Egypt was, on the surface, designed only to put down the rebellion, protect European nationals, restore public order, and bolster the power of Tawfiq, the British did not leave Egypt until 1952.[7]

The 1882 invasion came six years after the country had witnessed a financial crisis. Egypt was in debt, and, in accordance with a joint agreement that had been drawn up between Isma'il and certain European financial houses and their governments, a Public Debt Commission had been established in 1876. The purpose of the commission was to oversee the repayment of the loans contracted by Egypt's rulers, past and present, and to maintain khedival authority and public order intact.

Isma'il had managed to increase Egypt's foreign debt from 3.3 million to 98.5 million Egyptian pounds, money he used to implement a series of urban and agrarian reforms. European observers claimed that, despite his talents for modernization, Isma'il was fond of extravagant spending and that he had an insatiable appetite for all things European. According to Viscount Alfred Milner (1854–1925), private secretary to the banker G. J. Goschen (1831–1907), whose investigations into Egypt's finances in the 1860s led to the establishment of the commission, Isma'il was "luxurious, voluptuous, ambitious, fond of display . . . he was, at the same time, full of the most magnificent schemes for the material improvement of the country."[8] In his haste to transform Cairo into a second Paris (Isma'il considered Egypt to be a European, rather than an African, nation), the khedive spent vast sums. By 1876, he had spent much and repaid little, causing his creditors to doubt his ability to repay at all.

In the early 1870s Isma'il attempted to remedy this precarious financial situation by restructuring loans and increasing the production of certain cash crops, particularly cotton. In 1871, he promulgated the Muqabala Law, through which landowners got a perpetual reduction on their taxes in exchange for paying six years' worth of taxes up front. Because landowners were slow to show enthusiasm, the law was made compulsory in 1874. Additionally, Isma'il sold off parts of his estates as well as those of his family members. In 1875, the Khedive sold Egypt's shares in the Suez Canal Company to Great Britain, handing over a prodigious stake in, as well as control over, Egypt's maritime economy. The results of Isma'il's attempts, however, were apparently so meager in the face of such enormous debt that, in 1876, in a move designed to delay repayment indefinitely, Isma'il declared bankruptcy, sending his European creditors into a panic.

The formation of a Public Debt Commission was the result of that panic. Isma'il agreed to the commission's formation in an attempt to regain financial solvency; in actuality, however, its creation was Egypt's first step toward the loss of political independence. The consequent increase of European intervention in Egypt's financial affairs led, less than a decade later, to the 'Urabi rebellion and gave meaning to the slogan "Egypt for the Egyptians." The commission consisted of four representatives from European creditor nations as well as two controllers, one French and one British, and was designed as a system of dual control for France and Great Britain, both of which had accumulated economic and territorial interests in Egypt. As the system was configured, the khedive and his ministerial entourage would continue to rule Egypt, but they would do so under the supervision and tutelage of a group of foreign administrators who would oversee the Egyptian economy. These outsiders would also manage Egyptian affairs d'état, such that the capital loaned to the royal family made its way back to Europe. The architects of this scheme argued that keeping a khedive on the throne with all of his authority intact would ensure public order and facilitate the tasks facing the commission. Solvency could thus be achieved without a revolution.

By the time of the occupation, the number of Europeans residing in Egypt had reached ninety thousand, up from sixty-eight thousand in 1870 and from the six thousand expatriates who resided there in 1840.[9] The modernization projects of the khedives attracted Europeans to Egypt, where they were often granted concessions for development projects such as that given to Ferdinand de Lesseps for the construction of the Suez Canal. Others profited from the state's use of their technical skills. In the 1860s and 1870s in particular, Europeans were employed in the Suez Canal project, the expansion of Egypt's railway system, and in many of Isma'il's urban modernization projects. The cotton boom in the 1860s and Egypt's increased trade with Europe led to the growth of Egypt's foreign commercial community, which tended to be located in ports such as

Alexandria and Port Said as well as the capital. The size of this community grew along with Isma'il's mounting debt. Finally, the size of the British community tripled as the result of the occupation. The long-standing Ottoman tradition of granting capitulations to expatriates in their territories placed Europeans above Egyptian law. Life in Egypt thus held considerable allure: Europeans found in Egypt a heady atmosphere of reform and economic growth in which they could live cheaply, invest freely, and enjoy the many supposed adventures of the Orient.

Life in Egypt also allowed Europeans increasing power. As the khedives borrowed European money and expertise, they found their own power circumscribed by "concessionaries, contractors and bankers [who] exploited their position to create a vast field of opportunities for their own profit."[10] Additionally, foreign consular offices used the power vested in them by the capitulations to obtain useful contacts within the administration and to protect European merchants from complaints bought against them by Egyptians.

The reaction of elite Egyptians to the growing size and power of the European community was mixed. Elite Egyptians, too, were profiting from increased trade with Europe and from the modernization of their country. Outward signs of success for Egypt's upper classes included access to Western education, imported European goods, and holidays in Europe. But just as certain Cairene neighborhoods became exclusively European and new sporting and cultural clubs extended membership privileges to Europeans alone, the presence of the commission and the creation of a mixed cabinet was a signal to the Egyptian elite that their aspirations were threatened by their ruler and by the West alike.

The creation of a cabinet staffed by European ministers angered Egyptian notables and higher-ranking members of the army and the central administration who had come to expect a role in running Egypt's affairs. The cabinet formed under Prime Minister Nubar (1825–99) in 1878 in response to the founding of the Debt Commission was in fact the first executive cabinet in Egyptian history.[11] But neither the khedive nor the Egyptians who served on it were happy with its formation because of the role that Europeans played in it. Indeed, Nubar's mixed ministry reflected a turning point in Egyptian history: Until that time Egypt had been governed directly by Isma'il, who was aided by notables and state-trained administrators who headed and staffed administrative departments. The presence of Europeans on the cabinet not only diminished Isma'il's authority but increased the importance of Isma'il's prime minister by making him a liaison between the khedive and the European cabinet members.

In addition to increasing the level of Egyptians' resentment toward Europeans, the establishment of the Public Debt Commission led to the rise of secret, political societies in Egypt. The formation and proliferation of the societies were encouraged by Isma'il because their members seemed to be as angered by European intervention in politics as they were with the khedive's role in exposing Egypt to such a level of Western interference. Certain prominent members of the Chamber of Deputies met in members' homes to form the National Society, which by March 1879 demanded the formation of a national government that would exclude Europeans. Members of the National Society drew up a National Project of Reform (La'iha wataniyya), which recommended, among other things, that Egyptians themselves could solve Egypt's financial crisis, that dual control should be limited to financial affairs, and that the chamber must be granted greater control over politics. The demands of the National Society were similar to those of the 'Urabists within the military.[12]

The platforms of the 'Urabists and the National Society reflected frustration with Isma'il's heavy-handed rule and with European influence in Egypt. But they also indicate a determination on the part of Arabophone Egyptians that they should not be blocked from the highest echelons of the civilian and military administrations. In April 1879, Isma'il formed a new cabinet with Sherif Pasha, leader of the National Society, at its head. The khedive stated that he wished to comply with the interests of the nation, and a draft of a constitution was submitted to the Chamber of Deputies for discussion. Some members of the military remained unsatisfied with Isma'il's gestures. The appointment of an increasing number of Britons to military positions and serious arrears in back pay to Egyptian officers made their satisfaction unlikely. But Isma'il had succeeded in putting together what looked like an alliance between himself, his prime minister, and the Chamber of Deputies.

Great Britain and France were uneasy with the alliance and with the Egyptians' apparent determination to withstand further European interference in their affairs. When on April 22, 1879, Isma'il decreed a financial arrangement that was contrary to what European nations wanted or expected, Germany took the lead in courting Ottoman sultan Abdulhamid II (r. 1876–1908) to encourage Isma'il to abdicate his throne. Abdulhamid was struggling to salvage a disintegrating empire and was only too happy to get rid of an ambitious member of the dynasty that had tried to cut itself off from Ottoman rule entirely since the turn of the nineteenth century. On June 26, 1879, the sultan ordered the deposition of Isma'il and the ascension of his son Tawfiq to Egypt's throne. Isma'il left Egypt to live in exile in Naples and, later, Istanbul, where he died in 1895. Tawfiq ruled Egypt until 1892.

Tawfiq appeased European political and financial figures, who found him more compliant and more suitable a ruler than his father had been. To Egyptian nationalists, however, he was a weak and easily manipulated puppet. By 1880, Tawfiq had set up a procedure for the repayment of Egypt's loans such that 60 percent of the state's expenditures went to Europe at the expense of further investment at home. Nationalists thus saw Tawfiq's ascension as marking the end of a period of relative autonomy and prosperity and the death knell of Egyptian self-rule.

For the British, keeping Tawfiq on the throne was crucial for a number of reasons. They equated a strong, stable khedival presence with the successful safeguarding of their economic and territorial interests; in actions and in character, Tawfiq appeared to be less likely than his father to resist the designs and demands of a foreign administration. At the same time, the British saw in the new khedive certain tendencies towards constitutional, liberal rule and deemed him more likely than his father to succeed at "modern" politics. Because of such proclivities, the British believed that real economic and political reform, without which Egypt could never stand as a modern, independent nation, could begin under Tawfiq's rule.

By the early 1880s, the security of Egypt was of tremendous importance to certain European nations. Since the landing of Napoleon's troops in Egypt in 1798, the country had been of both real and presumed importance to both Great Britain and France. For Great Britain, Egypt provided the surest and quickest access to India. For France, containing Britain's territorial ambitions was of paramount significance. The construction of the Suez Canal not only tied up a considerable amount of French and British capital but increased both parties' territorial ambitions in North Africa.

Upon taking power in 1879, Tawfiq set about building a stable government by inviting Sherif to form a new ministry. Sherif would only agree if Tawfiq would promulgate a constitution. Thus, in September 1879, the khedive chose Riad Pasha, known to be against constitutional reform, to serve as his prime minister and to form a new ministry. While Riad oversaw the implementation of certain policies that were pleasing to some Egyptians, such as tax reform measures and the abolition of corvée labor, he was forced to agree to the formation of an international commission that led to greater European control over Egypt's finances. Such agreements, in addition to Riad and the khedive's absolutist approach to governing, led to further resistance from army officers, landowners, and government officials.

On November 4, 1880, certain members of the Chamber of Deputies joined forces with anti-khedive army officers to issue a manifesto demanding further autonomy for Egypt. It also called for greater control over the khedive — in other words, a constitution. Between November 1880 and the outbreak of the 'Urabi-led rebellions of June 1882, Tawfiq was thus locked in a power struggle with the military and the Chamber of Deputies. By the time of the uprisings, those who positioned themselves against Tawfiq had learned that they could, in fact, force the khedive's hand on certain issues. They succeeded, for example, in getting "their men" placed in important governmental positions. At the same time, those same forces witnessed the khedive's ability to crack down on them when necessary through decrees limiting such things as the length of military service and the arrest of dissenters. This standoff appeared on the verge of resolving itself in late December 1881, when the tone of Tawfiq's address to open the Chamber of Deputies reflected a mood of collaboration.[13] But when a joint note from Great Britain and France promising support for the khedive arrived in early January 1882, the situation changed. The 'Urabists were convinced that the European powers planned to step up their intervention into Egyptian affairs. Lacking any other source of support, members of the Chamber of Deputies moved in the direction of an alliance with the 'Urabists. Both groups were now united in favor of a constitution and against furthered European involvement in their affairs.

Tawfiq was forced to dismiss his prime minister and appoint the 'Urabist candidate Mahmud Sami al-Barudi (1839–1904) in February 1882. 'Urabi then immediately set about bringing the Chamber of Deputies under his own control. He also made the changes within the military that he thought had been needed for years, helping Arabophone Egyptians achieve better status and pay. 'Urabi forced al-Barudi to dismiss European officials from the government, presaging the removal of all European influence from Egypt. To many Egyptians of all classes, 'Urabi looked like the hero who might finally rid Egypt of Christian, European influence.

When in early June of 1882 an atmosphere of triumph against the West turned into antiforeign demonstrations in Alexandria, 'Urabi's forces were either unwilling or unable to contain the violence. This brought the attention of French and British troops off the Alexandria coast. 'Urabi's forces prepared a military confrontation against them, speculating that the

Sultan would come to his assistance. Great Britain demanded of the Sultan that 'Urabi be dismissed; the Sultan wavered but refused to send troops to Egypt. By July, the khedive had taken refuge in Alexandria, and the 'Urabists continued to build up their political and military power. When the 'Urabists refused to give in to British ultimatums to cease building defenses along the Mediterranean coastline, the British prepared to attack. When England made it clear that an attack was forthcoming, the French withdrew their forces. The battles that led to the British occupation began on July 11, 1882, culminating in the September occupation.

British policy began to be shaped officially in the fall of 1882 with the arrival in Egypt of Lord Dufferin (1866–1918), British Ambassador to the Sublime Porte at Istanbul and Her Majesty's Envoy Extraordinaire. His task was to investigate Egypt and submit a report about its political condition to London. In this account, Dufferin spelled out the potential difficulties that the British might encounter in their attempts to quell the anarchy and chaos of the 'Urabi rebellion. His suggestions served as a basic outline for British rule; Dufferin persuaded the British government that withdrawal needed to be preceded by a reform of the Egyptian administration. Such reform would ensure the stability of the Egyptian polity as well as its economy and limit the duration of an occupation. Dufferin wrote: "Europe and the Egyptian people, whom we have undertaken to rescue from anarchy, have alike a right to require that our intervention should be beneficent and its results enduring; that it should obviate all danger of future perturbations, and that it should leave established on sure foundations the principles of justice, liberty and public happiness."[14]

Lord Cromer was dispatched to Egypt in late summer 1883 to oversee the establishment of a British administration in Egypt that would strengthen Egyptian governing institutions and assure that Dufferin's goals were attained. As consul general, Cromer laid the foundations for an administrative structure in Egypt that lasted through the first decade of the twentieth century. Cromer implemented a system of administration that was designed to oversee and "tutor" the different ministries of the Egyptian government. Dufferin recommended that the Egyptians have village and provincial councils as well as a general assembly and a legislative council, members of which would be elected by the provinces and the villages. Eight ministers would be responsible to the khedive. While in theory foreign administrators were supposed to yield to the power of the khedive, his ministers, and the assemblies, in fact the British exercised enormous power and influence over them. Foreign Secretary Lord Granville (1818–91), in what later came to be known as the Granville Doctrine, recommended that the Egyptian ministers be advised that they would cease to hold their offices were they not to follow the advice of their British overlords.[15]

Granville's advice led to a pattern of rule that Milner later described as a "veiled protectorate," the length and goals of which were as uncertain as they were indefinite. The Dufferin Report and the Granville Doctrine both suggested that Egypt possessed centralized authority, a liberal economy, and forms of representative government, the hallmarks of European nation-states.[16] British Agent Edward Malet openly referred to Egypt's political system as constitutional.[17] At the same time, however, both documents belied British confidence in the Egyptian ability to participate in the institutions that would eventually be handed over to them.[18]

The tenets of the protectorate thus depicted Egypt as being both politically sound and unstable, modern and less than modern (Milner wrote that no country on earth could vie with Egypt in such idiosyncrasies).[19] Concomitantly, the vague goals of the protectorate and its open-ended duration placed the British in the position of being at the same time committed to reforming and governing Egypt and hurrying to take their exit. "The question," Milner wrote, "is often asked why, if we do not intend to keep the country, we should be at such pains to improve it?"[20] The ambiguities of the protectorate were multiple.

1882: An Uncertain Occupation

Why did the British expose themselves to a potentially lengthy involvement in Egypt despite the less-than-enthusiastic atmosphere for reform at home? Scholars typically attribute Egypt's official entrance into the British colonial orbit to decreased British confidence in the willingness of Egypt's leaders to participate in a European-dominated foreign trade or foreign rule. Territorial reasons can also be cited: As early as the 1870s, some Britons argued for an invasion of Egypt out of fear that Britain would lose its coveted routes to India. Intense debates occurred in parliament and in the press over whether or not the British could trust that these routes were actually safe in the hands of Isma'il.[21] Once the occupation had taken place, it was also commonly argued that the interests of bondholders in Egypt had, in fact, led to the invasion. A new kind of imperialism was taking place as the result of overseas investment.[22] Surplus capital, some argued, and its investment outside of Europe had led to the right kind and degree of jingoism necessary for the launching of a burdensome invasion.[23] Finally, certain Britons believed that England had a duty to occupy Egypt because of Great Britain's special aptitude for "governing or directing more backward nations."[24]

Since 1961, with the publication of Ronald Robinson and John Gallagher's *Africa and the Victorians,* the British government's willingness to occupy Egypt has been most frequently attributed to "freakish events" such as the 'Urabi rebellion that threatened Great Britain's overseas trade. According to the Robinson and Gallagher thesis, the invasion of Egypt was proof that the Palmerstonian policies of informal empire had failed. British policy in the Near East from 1840 to 1880 was based on an imperialism of free trade, or informal empire, designed to create a local class of merchants and traders who, as a result of increased prosperity, would adopt the politics of liberalism. These locals would become grateful to the British for advancing free trade and thus welcome further tutelage from them. A sympathetic local population would ensure political stability and the easy maintenance of British supremacy. According to Robinson and Gallagher, the 'Urabi rebellion and its aftermath served as significant proof to the British government that indirect European influence was in fact doing more harm than good. Chaos at the periphery of the empire — such as the 'Urabi rebellion — drew the British into an occupation they did not want or need. The policies of Palmerston's informal empire were hence transformed into the reluctant imperialism of an invasion.

Critics are skeptical of Robinson and Gallagher's analysis. Juan Cole's analysis of the events leading up to the 'Urabi rebellion, for example, suggested that Robinson and Gallagher were wrong, empirically and conceptually, in finding anarchy and impending collapse in the Middle East.[25] Cole claimed that Robinson and Gallagher's views of social change in nineteenth-century Egypt — particularly their depiction of a putative clash between conservative, "Moslem" tendencies and a new, liberal stratum as well as their notion of fragility of Ottoman institutions — distorted the reality of the 'Urabi rebellion and its supporters. He claimed that the Robinson and Gallagher thesis also distorts the causes of the occupation and British policy and intentions in Egypt.[26]

Likewise, in his reassessment of Robinson and Gallagher's *Africa and the Victorians,* A. G. Hopkins suggested that the Conservative government that ruled Britain from 1874 to 1880 was not as hesitant about the occupation as Robinson and Gallagher suggested. Hopkins particularly cited Benjamin Disraeli's (1804–81) purchase of Isma'il's shares of the Suez Canal bonds in 1875 as giving the British government a direct investment in Egypt and, along with it, a greater interest in seeing Isma'il keep his word. Hopkins suggested that Disraeli's acquisition of the canal shares blurred distinctions between neutrality and commitment.

When the Liberals took power in 1880, William Gladstone's policy of free trade imperialism was the minority opinion to full-scale occupation of Egypt. Hopkins pointed to Sir Charles Dilke (1843–1911), under-secretary of the Foreign Office, as emblematic of a general "casting about for ways of substituting British supremacy for Dual Control."[27] When the French took Tunisia in 1881, many considered Egypt to be a concession for Great Britain. On the eve of the 'Urabi rebellion, in other words, the metropole was already poised to solve the Egypt problem with an occupation.

Differences in interpretation notwithstanding, the impetus for the invasion was a perceived crisis as well as an unwillingness on the part of the British to upset any balance of power relative to other European nations. Despite the variety of arguments for and against an invasion, a resounding chorus called for action in the face of the potential loss of access to Egypt and therefore to other parts of the British Empire. Indeed, journalist Edward Dicey's (1832–1911) impassioned assertion that the British route to India could not be guaranteed by an unjust and incompetent khedive did not differ much from Dilke's conviction that Isma'il and the 'Urabi movement posed sufficient threats to convince parliament, as well as popular opinion, that an occupation was not only justifiable but an outright duty.[28] Calls for the occupation were made in a language that cast Egypt and its political and economic institutions as threatening and unstable.

Justifying an Extended Stay in Egypt

Once the occupation of Egypt had become a fait accompli, however, little accord existed over what to do with it. The Gladstone government was reluctant to keep Egypt; British officials in the field hesitated to predict how long it would take to secure the country. What resulted was a kind of "policy of ambiguous policy," through which a decision to either stay in Egypt or leave it could be legitimated. Such a plan was not deliberate but was, rather, Cromer's response to his perceived predicament. He wrote: "I came to Egypt with a hearty desire to aid to the best of my ability the successful execution of Mr. Gladstone's Egyptian policy. I thought I understood that policy and, if I understood it rightly, I felt assured that it met with my general concurrence. I soon found, however, that I was pursuing a phantom which constantly eluded my grasp."[29]

Gladstone's determination to leave Egypt and Cromer's reluctance to confirm the possibility of a quick withdrawal resulted in numerous investigations by British officials into Egyptian institutions and ideologies. To be sure, Egypt had been studied before: The G. J. Goschen and Stephen Cave missions of the 1860s and 1870s had been designed to investigate Egypt and its government and to articulate a strategy for recovery. Goschen and Cave's inquiries were responsible for the creation of the Public Debt Commission that was set up to monitor the Egyptian government until it began successfully to pay back its loans. But while the reports issued by Goschen and Cave appear to have been based on actual investigations into Isma'il's financial affairs and on inquiries into records of his transactions with European banks, the investigations preceding and accompanying the occupation of 1882 reveal a mixture of inquiry and fantasy.[30] As officials like Dufferin and Granville began their investigations, they challenged the notion that Gladstone's policy constituted a quick invasion followed by a quicker withdrawal. In a dispatch to Gladstone written shortly after the occupation, Granville noted: "Indeed, from the first moment when we began to look around in the country which we had rescued from anarchy, it was clearly seen to be wanting in all the conditions of independent life."[31] Neither Dufferin nor Granville was ever clear about the source of their discoveries. Blunt criticized Dufferin's investigations into Egyptian institutions, accusing him of simply throwing open the doors of his "embassy to anyone who could give information."[32] Dufferin claimed that his conclusions about Egypt were based on information "thoroughly threshed out by those with whom it has been my duty to put myself into communication."[33]

Gladstone wanted Dufferin to gather information about the potential reform of Egypt's military and its political institutions, since the idea of a rapid reform program supported Gladstone's desire to leave Egypt quickly.[34] Granville and Dufferin were thus charged with assessing both Egypt's political realm and its military, a task that proved overwhelming given the paucity of information about Egypt that the Gladstone government possessed prior to the occupation.[35] Dufferin responded to Gladstone's requests after only ten days in Egypt, stating that the establishment of liberal governing institutions in Egypt would be "more or less a leap in the dark."[36]

The reasons behind Dufferin's conclusion are markedly unclear. Dufferin's predecessor Cave had once concluded that Isma'il's resources (if properly managed) were sufficient to meet Egypt's liabilities.[37] Malet, Egypt's consul general from 1879 to 1883, later informed the Foreign

Office that Egyptian rule was, in fact, constitutional. Dufferin himself indicated that Egypt possessed what he called a Chamber of Notables that had "exhibited both wisdom and courage" (although it was also his belief that the chamber was easily swayed by the will of the khedives).[38] In the Egyptian military, Dufferin saw evidence of order and loyalty.[39] In other words, Dufferin's report to the Foreign Office contains evidence of Egypt's potential for self-government. Dufferin in fact enjoined Her Majesty's Government to administer the "Valley of the Nile" through "the creation, within certain prudent limits, of representative institutions, of municipal and communal government . . . though aided . . . by sympathetic advice and assistance."[40] In the same paragraphs within which he alluded to Egypt's potential, however, he concluded, "A certain quality which can best be expressed by the term 'childishness' seems to characterize the Egyptian people; and that they can proceed at once to exercise full-blown constitutional functions, which occasionally come to a deadlock in highly organised communities, is not to be expected."[41] Egyptians thus appear both capable of governing themselves and childlike.

The rhetoric of Dufferin's correspondence with the Foreign Office — correspondence that would certainly be labeled "official" — often reads like travel literature. In writing his reports, Dufferin seemed to rely on hearsay and stories about Egyptian heritage rather than actual encounters with Egyptian elites and the institutions within which they functioned. In the fashion of nineteenth-century Orientalist discourse, Dufferin apparently had no qualms mixing real investigations into Egyptian institutions with hearsay and fantasy: Straightforward assessments of Egyptian institutions were juxtaposed with unsubstantiated descriptions of allegedly barbaric governing practices. On one occasion he reported objectively to Granville: "A Chamber of Deputies has actively existed . . . with this in view I think we should try to introduce the Representative Principle into the government of Egypt."[42] On another, Dufferin exclaimed, "My Lord, the most painful characteristic which *strikes a traveller* on visiting Egypt is the universal use of the 'Courbash,' or lash, administered with great severity on the most trivial occasions at the Caprice of petty officials."[43] Dufferin's representations thus render Egyptian ministers both capable and wanting.[44]

Cromer was equally forthright about attributing his knowledge of Egypt and the Egyptians to the travel accounts of his compatriots. What he understood about Isma'il and his character, for example, he had gleaned from Nassau William Senior's *Conversations and Journals in Egypt and Malta* (1882). In his memoirs, later to be published as *Modern Egypt*, Cromer wrote:

It should be remembered that Ismail was utterly uneducated. When Mr. Senior was returning to Europe in 1855, he found that an English coachman who had been in Ismail's service, was his fellow-passenger. Of course, Mr. Senior at once interviewed him. The man's account of Ismail's private life is worth quoting. *I do not doubt its accuracy.*

> "Ismail," he [Senior] said, "and his brother Mustafa, when they were in Paris, used to buy whatever they saw; they were like children, nothing was fine enough for them; they bought carriages and horses like those of Queen Victoria or the Emperor, and let them spoil for want of shelter and cleaning. . . . The people he liked best to talk to were his servants, the lads who brought him his pipes and stood before him with their arms crossed. He sometimes sat on his sofa, and smoked, and talked to them for hours, all about women and such things. . . . I have known him sometimes to try to read a French novel, but he would be two hours getting through a page. Once or twice I saw him attempt to write. His letters were half an inch high, like those of a child's copybook. I don't think that he ever finished a sentence." (Conversations, vol. 2, p. 228.)[45]

In dispatches that often read more like nineteenth-century travel literature than "official" comment on finances and territories, assessment of the Egyptians' capacity for self-government was couched in descriptions of institutions that, on the surface, seem to have had little to do with the ability of the Egyptian military and body politic to function. Dufferin's and Cromer's tendency to conflate travel literature with solid fact was emblematic of what Edward Said has called the "citationary nature of Orientalism": the confidence Europeans felt about making claims about the Orient when those claims could be anchored in literature of any sort.[46]

The most striking examples of the blurring of fact and fantasy to produce a vision of Egypt on the eve of the occupation were reports about the character of the khedives. In the early years of the British tenure in Egypt, for example, Cromer's secretary, Henry Boyle, penned a "Memorandum on the Background of the Khedival Family."[47] The memorandum was intended to serve as a guidebook for British administrators in Egypt but was never printed or circulated. Boyle claimed that he wrote the book in order to show the mentality of the Egyptian royal family, such that administrators might understand the country over which they were governing.[48] The text describes the character of many members of the royal family: Ibrahim was reported to have died from too much sex and champagne; all of Mohammad 'Ali's descendents — including Tawfiq — were listed as capricious and cruel; Tawfiq's cousin, Princess Nazli, was supposedly brilliant but besotted with champagne; and Tawfiq's aunt Jamila, Boyle had concluded, was a lesbian who kept a chaotic, disorderly household.[49]

Boyle's memorandum reveals a tendency on the part of the British to conflate the character and habits of the khedives with Egypt and its institutions in toto: "For all practical purposes, the Khedive and Egypt are identical."[50] Cromer and Dicey both compared Cromer with Louis XIV of France: "He, in his own person, was the state."[51] This link between character and politics was often used by the British to describe or even predict Egyptian politics. As Cromer wrote to the Foreign Office in 1882: "I have no reason to suppose that, should any disturbance occur . . . the Egyptian Government would be disposed to use excessive or unnecessary severity in its suppression. *The personal character of the Khedive is, indeed, of itself almost a sufficient guarantee that no such tendency exists.*"[52] Dicey echoed Cromer's predictions about Tawfiq's potential response to domestic disturbances, saying that "by character, by disposition . . . Tewfik Pasha is very unlikely to imitate the example of his father."[53] To understand the character of the khedive, apparently, was to understand Egypt.

Despite the fact that Isma'il was out of power when the occupation took place, the characteristics of his rule and of his behavior seemed to be conflated with the inability of the Egyptian government to govern. Speaking of Tawfiq, his ministers, and the Egyptian army officers who had mutinied shortly after Tawfiq's ascension in 1879, for example, Malet concluded: "The traditions of the days of Ismail Pasha stalked like spectres across their paths."[54] Isma'il and his character continued to symbolize political crisis and mismanagement.

Isma'il occupied a curious place in the minds of the Europeans who thought that they knew and understood him. To some Europeans, he had been a praiseworthy ruler. He had, in fact, created a modern military, laid one thousand miles of railroad track, dug fifty thousand miles of irrigation canals, and established hundreds of primary and secondary schools throughout Egypt. The Cairene upper classes spent their leisure time in well-landscaped parks and gardens, in museums and galleries, at the zoo, or visiting one of the world's finest opera houses. Such accomplishments led many Europeans to consider Egypt a marvelous instance of progress.

Others were not so convinced. In one of his many articles on Egypt in the journal *The Nineteenth Century*, for example, Dicey, claimed that such programs were in fact undermined by his perverted ambition. While Isma'il had been successful in transforming Egypt, Dicey stated his "mode of carrying out his objects" was "wholly unjustifiable" because of the "sensual self-indulgence" that undergirded his private life.[55] Europeans inside official banking and governing circles loved to tell stories about Isma'il and his peculiar behavior, stories that became commonplace European knowledge about Egypt. Wrote Cromer: "Ismail was too well known in Europe to play the part of the constitutional monarch."[56] One story, recorded by Boyle for his memorandum, illustrates what Europeans felt they *knew* about Isma'il and his rule: "Ismail was visiting Vienna . . . there he saw an enormous mirror which he wanted for his Abdine palace. He sent Bravay [a Frenchman and friend of Isma'il] to inquire the price, which was 20,000 francs. But in Bravay's account the mirror was priced at 20,000 Napoleons [worth much more than the franc at that time], and no questions were asked."[57]

Tales of financial frivolity were coupled with stories about Isma'il's penchant for savage, capricious rule. The most commonly told were those about his attempts, often successful, to kill off ministers with whom he disagreed. One of the most notorious tales was that of the khedive's desire to kill his minister, Nubar, with whom he had become suddenly angry. Isma'il wanted to throw Nubar off the ship on which both men were traveling to Egypt from Istanbul. Nubar was only able to save his life by appealing to the vanities of the khedive: He tricked Isma'il into telling stories about himself until the ship landed in Alexandria, too late for Nubar's execution to take place.[58]

Lord Milner believed that the causes of the khedive's bankruptcy were as much moral as financial. "The tremendous financial smash which marked the closing years of the reign of Ismail Pasha," he wrote, "was the result of a disregard, not only of every economic, but every *moral* principle."[59] Milner later condemned Isma'il's decadence: "Over and above the millions wasted in entertainments, in largess, *in sensuality,* in the erection of numerous palaces — structurally as rotten as they are aesthetically abominable — he threw away yet other millions upon a vast scheme of agricultural development."[60] He concluded that it was not merely the wild ups and downs of Egypt's finances under Isma'il's reign that indicated a need for European intervention but also the effects that Isma'il's behavior had on the morality of Egypt's citizens.[61] Despite the exterior success of Isma'il's reforms, his sensuality appears to have thus rendered him less capable than his Victorian contemporaries.[62] Such descriptions of Isma'il's character placed him in the position of being at once modern and backward, capable and incompetent. Dufferin and Granville did not condemn Isma'il's reform programs simply for the accumulation of debt but for Isma'il's putative lack of morality in carrying them out.

Stories circulated not only about Ismaʿil's immorality but about the dis-reputable origins of Tawfiq. A common tale was that Tawfiq "owed his exalted station to an accident. Ismaʿil on one occasion visited a lavoratory in the Palace and found there one of the minor slaves of the Harem — known as Kandilji — whose duty it was to look after the lighting of the Harem apartments. The girl attracted His Highness's notice and in due course Tewfik saw the light of day. As he was Ismail's eldest son, his mother became Birinji Kadin [the first lady] and Tewfik was heir to the throne."[63]

The sexual politics of Ismaʿil's mother, Khosayr Hanem, also figured prominently in the British project of characterizing and knowing Egypt. It was said that she was given to driving through Cairo in search of good looking men to take home to her palace. She allegedly had all of her young lovers executed after they spent the night in her boudoir.[64] Whether these rumors were true or not, their circulation cemented the relationship between the private life of Egyptian elites and their political aptitude. As Victorian templates for connubial as well as parental behav-ior were assigned to the Egyptian body politic, the domestic habits of the khedives and their wives were not merely the object of British fascination or scorn. Rather, they became elevated to the standard by which the British measured and understood Egyptians and their politics. Dicey in fact concluded that Ismaʿil's achievements were considerable for a "prince born and bred in the harem."[65]

Despite the stories that circulated about his origins, the British looked upon Tawfiq with greater favor than they had Ismaʿil, referring to him as Ismaʿil's "better son."[66] If the British were judging the Egyptian khedives by their willingness to share power with their fellow Egyptians, then such positive reports of Tawfiq's reign are surprising, for Tawfiq suspended his father's Chamber of Deputies immediately upon taking the throne. The despotism that had been so abhorrent in the father was clearly tolerated in the son.

Other criteria clearly influenced British opinion about Tawfiq's gov-erning qualities. Dufferin stated in early 1883 that Tawfiq — his suspension of the Chamber of Deputies notwithstanding — was more like European rulers than his father had been. He wrote, "The Prince now sitting on the Khedival throne represents, at all events, the principle of autonomous government, of hereditary succession, and commercial independence."[67] Malet found Tawfiq to be powerless but inoffensive and highly grateful to the British to whom "he knew that he owed his life and his throne."[68] While Milner found Tawfiq to be less civilized than his father had been (he spoke no European languages perfectly, for example), he nonetheless found that "at heart Tewfik was really much more like a constitutional ruler of the Western type than an Oriental despot, while Ismail was an Oriental despot with a Parisian veneer."[69]

While many reports about Tawfiq were actually unflattering, he was consistently "recommended" by the British for the job of ruling Egypt. In 1882, Cromer wrote:

If Egypt is in the future no longer to be ruled by a Khedive but by an independent Sovereign, the next question which will arise will be the choice of that Sovereign. I conceive that the present Khedive must certainly be chosen.[70] . . . If an Oriental is to be chosen, I do not think that a better choice could be made than that of the present Khedive. . . . He is not a man of any considerable power or ability, but I believe him to be not only one of the most honest, but also one of the most humane and conscientious Orientals whom I have ever come across.[71]

The khedive's moral life and domestic habits were frequently juxtaposed with commentary about his fitness for rule. Dicey described Tawfiq as "a man of 27, spare of figure, with a plain but not unkindly face, gifted with good intentions, but with narrow views; a devout believer in Islam; . . . a good husband; a man of moral domestic life; a frugal administrator — such was the Prince who, by the irony of fate, became the successor of Isma'il the Magnificent."[72] Blunt concurred with Dicey that Tawfiq was an apt ruler, adding to his description of Tawfiq's "virtues" that the khedive's domestic life was well-conducted as compared with most of his predecessors and not unadorned with respectable virtures.[73] The fact that Tawfiq was monogamous made its way into most official accounts of the occupation. Regardless of the fact that Tawfiq's tight-fisted hold on power was unpopular with Egyptians, his domestic life appears to have made him the man for the job of governing Egypt.

Despite the British enthusiasm for Tawfiq, however, and their ill-conceived convictions that he did not evince "any of those ruthless and despotic instincts which signalized the Egyptian Satraps of former days," Dufferin ultimately informed Gladstone that Egyptians were incapable of reforming themselves: "It is true that Egypt is neither capable of re-vindicating [national independence] nor fitted to enjoy (constitutional government), in the full acceptation of either term, but she may count on the former being secured to her by the magnanimity of Europe, while she may trust to time for the development of the latter."[74] Regardless of Tawfiq's allegedly Western qualities, Dufferin claimed that Egyptian institutions were too steeped in despotism for the "seeds of liberty" to take root without instruction from the British.

As in colonial India, where subjects were required to be "English in tastes, in opinions, in morals, in intellect" but never fully English, Tawfiq embodied the ambiguities of British colonial policy in Egypt.[75] As a man who the British found capable of constitutional rule and, at the same time, malleable and pliant, Tawfiq was symbolic of what Homi Bhabha has called the essential ambivalence of colonial rule. As a "mimic man," Tawfiq could never be fully modern, but his apparent ability to be reformed made him a suitable cog in the colonial machinery.[76]

Egyptian ministers were subject to the same kind of analysis by colonial officials. In the late 1870s, Cromer linked the personalities of the pashas to their ability to rule, stating that "more depended on the character of and personal influence of the individuals who were chosen than on the special functions which might be assigned to them by a Khedival Decree."[77] Milner insisted that it was the unfitness of the pasha class to govern that necessitated the veiled protectorate. His experiences with them led him to believe that the pashas' interest in government rested on little more than personal caprice: "Left to themselves they do not have the strength of character to resist the gradual return of former evils."[78] He reviled Gladstone's hopes for a quick evacuation of Egypt, stating that to do so would return the country to the days of "corrupt and effete Pashadom."[79]

After assuming the position of consul general, Cromer claimed that the domestic behavior of the Egyptian ministers with whom he was supposed to work alarmed him the most. In 1891 he wrote: "There can be no doubt that a real advance has been made in the material progress of this country during the past few years. Whether any moral progress is possible in a country where polygamy and the absence of family life blights the whole social system is another question."[80]

In most British accounts of Egypt from this period, the roots of "effete Pashadom" were left vague. Dufferin once alluded to Granville that nepotism led to ministerial inefficiency overall.[81] According to Cromer, the harem had produced the "idiosyncrasies of Pashadom."[82] For Cromer, Tawfiq's monogamous relationship with his wife was evidence that ridding Egypt of seclusion and polygamy would produce better government. Was it any accident that it was a man with no harem who decided to cooperate with the British and thereby usher in a period of political and economic reform?

Thus, no matter what one cites as the cause of England's intervention into Egyptian politics, the British conclusion that the character and the morals of the Egyptian elite shaped the Egyptian political realm and affected its ability to function added a further dimension to "the Egypt question." The veiled protectorate — the basis of which was an occupation that would stay in place until the practices of both the political and private realms were reformed — was rooted in attitudes about Egypt and its ruling elite that often had little to do with immediate financial and territorial crises. When Gladstone finally conceded that an occupation would have to accompany invasion, he said: "We have now reached a point at which to some extent the choice lies between *moral* instruction and evacuation . . . and the question is . . . whether we are to try to prepare Egypt for a self-governing future. I believe we have already made our choice."[83]

Regenerating Egypt: The Family Politics of the Occupation

Based on investigations into all aspects of Egyptian life, Cromer concluded that when rule by Egyptian khedives ceased to be despotic, liberty would follow.[84] But, in reality, the formulation of a policy through which Egypt would be set on the right track was not so easy. Two opinions circulated about whether or not Egypt would, once abandoned by the British, return to reactionary forms of government. The first, proffered by Lord Dufferin, was that the Egyptians could, in fact, be "tutored" under the "aegis of [British] friendship." His opinion was that: "the magic wand of education and the subtle force of example would combine to produce a 'civic sense' — that spirit of liberty without license, or reasonable independence, which is the Anglo-Saxon ideal. And when in the space of a few years a voter's heart should beat beneath every *galabieh* [traditional Egyptian garb], and a voter's sturdy intelligence fill every Egyptian head, then we could withdraw our Army and our Advisors . . . and all would be gloriously well."[85]

The second opinion came from Lord Cromer, who was not so optimistic. In his view, reform and evacuation were irreconcilable. Only Gladstone's hatred of facts, Cromer claimed, led the prime minister to support the idea of an evacuation.[86] Cromer claimed that reform of any kind was a long and uncertain business. He also doubted that Egyptians could actually be reformed, stating that the Anglo-Saxon ideal of which Dufferin spoke lay well outside the Egyptians' grasp.

Cromer depicted Egyptians as being akin to small children, needing constant care and supervision. He told Granville that Tawfiq understood the duties of a constitutional ruler about as well as Cromer's six-year-old son.[87] Cromer was fond of comparing Egyptians to children in early stages of development who are capable of little initiative and model their behavior after that of their parents. Explain once "to the Egyptian what he is to do and he will assimilate the idea rapidly. He is a good imitator and will make a faithful, even sometimes a too servile copy of the work of his European master. . . . On the other hand, inasmuch as the Egyptian has but little power of initiation, and often does not thoroughly grasp the reasons why his teachers have impelled him in certain directions, a relapse will ensue if English supervision be withdrawn."[88] The implication was that Egyptians could be reformed if the British were present to guide their actions, but that the country would slip back into decay were European supervision withdrawn.[89] Such sentiment was but an echo of Stephen Cave's earlier assessment of Egypt. In 1876 he wrote: "Egypt may be said to be in a transition state . . . she suffers from the defects of the system out of which she is passing as well as from those of the system into which she is attempting to enter."[90]

Cromer's rhetoric about reform did not always translate into official policy. Indeed, he was often accused of overlooking the Egyptians' moral and intellectual advancement in favor of a purely material development of Egypt's resources. The source of the ambiguous official policy, however, was Cromer's conviction that the morals of modern Egyptians prevented their final reform and, hence, their emancipation. In casting the moral realm as the utmost stumbling block to modernization and liberation and in claiming that the domestic realm produced effete Egyptians, Cromer linked family politics to the process of modernizing and liberating Egypt.

This formulation is made particularly clear in Cromer's memoirs, *Modern Egypt*. In his summation of Egyptian society, Cromer pointed to polygamous relationships both as Egypt's defining characteristic and as the source of its political and economic condition. Consistent with his 1891 memorandum to Nubar Pasha in which he linked political and economic progress with monogamy, Cromer argued in *Modern Egypt* that the whole fabric of European society rested on family life. "Monogamy fosters family life," he wrote, "polygamy destroys it."[91] Family life in Europe, he argued, served to foster in European men the kinds of traits and talents that could be transferred to the political realm and make it successful. Without a sound domestic order, little chance existed that such traits could be inculcated in Egyptian men. Neither the monogamous habits of many Egyptian officials nor the repeated attempts of Isma'il and

Tawfiq's high-ranking administrators to promulgate a constitution seemed to convince Cromer that elite Egyptians behaved much like Europeans of similar class.

Reform would take place by training Egyptians to be like their European masters in habit and taste in order to replace the deleterious effects of polygamy and seclusion with the basic tenets of European society. "If ever the Egyptians learn to govern themselves," Cromer claimed, "if, in other words, the full execution of the policy of 'Egypt for the Egyptians' becomes feasible, the Egyptian question will, it may be hoped and presumed, finally cease to be a cause of trouble to Europe, and the British nation will be relieved of an onerous responsibility."[92]

The first step toward training Egyptians to govern themselves was weeding out the practices of the harem.[93] Underscoring all of Egyptian civilization, Cromer wrote, was the degradation of women that resulted from the existence of the harem. In perhaps the most often-quoted passage from *Modern Egypt,* Cromer linked the Egyptians' inability to reach European standards of modernity and self-sufficiency with the condition of its women:

Looking then solely to the possibility of reforming those countries which have adopted the faith of Islam, it may be asked whether any one can conceive the existence of true European civilization on the assumption that the position which women occupy in Europe is abstracted from the general plan. As well can a man blind from his birth be made to conceive the existence of color? Change the position of women, and one of the main pillars, not only of European civilization but at all events of the moral code based on the Christian religion, if not Christianity itself falls to the ground. The position of women in Egypt, and in Mohammedan countries generally, is, therefore, a fatal obstacle to the attainment of that elevation of thought and character which should accompany the introduction of European civilization, if that civilization is to produce its full measure of beneficial effect.[94]

The two worst manifestations of this degradation, found at all levels of Egyptian society, were, according to Cromer, veiling and seclusion. Seclusion had "baneful" effects on society, the most important of which was that it limited women's intellectual development and, hence, that of men. "Moreover," he wrote: "inasmuch as women, in their capacities as wives and mothers, exercise a great influence over the characters of their husbands and sons, it is obvious that the seclusion of women must produce a deteriorating effect *on the male population,* in whose presumed interests the custom was established and is still maintained."[95] According to Cromer, the next step in making "better" pashas — after the eradication of the harem — was the restructuring of the Egyptian educational system.[96] The old-fashioned Egyptian pasha, Cromer claimed, was undisciplined, afraid of change, immoderate, prejudiced, self-deceived, and nepotistic; he needed to be replaced with men of better character. Despite his sometimes skeptical stance toward the project of educating Egyptians, Cromer often cited the system of public education as being an arena in which old traits might be replaced with Victorian habits and sensibilities. But hope for the creation of better character in Egyptians was in vain without the reform of the family and the education of women. "The position of women in Egypt," Cromer argued, "is a fatal obstacle to the attainment of that elevation of thought and character which should accompany the introduction of European civilization, if that civilization is to produce its full measure of beneficial effect."[97]

Despite his position that Egyptians were ultimately not reformable, Cromer did concede that education and exposure to Europeans had begun to change Egyptians in both habits and tastes. "Enlightened Egyptians," according to Cromer, were catching on to monogamy, and, therefore, exhibiting more appealing political tendencies. Cromer cited two Egyptian ministers, Sherif and Riad, as "monogamous notabilities" morally sound and capable of solid political judgment.[98] Cromer seemed to forget that Sherif and Riad were on opposite sides of the debate about constitutionalism, and that monogamy had not rid Riad of his tendencies toward absolutism. The domestic practices of reformed Egyptians, and their manifestation in the political arena, apparently held the key to Egypt's success. Domestic practices served as proof, however insubstantial, that an open-ended period of reform was necessary as well as beneficial.

Conclusion

As the private realm of Egypt's khedives and its elite class was made synonymous with Egyptian institutions, elite domestic behavior became conflated with the success of the body politic. Despite the very concrete territorial and economic concerns that led the British to occupy Egypt, their formulation of the veiled protectorate appears to have been shaped by anecdote, impression, travel literature, and the British conclusion that Egyptians were not fit for self-rule. The British overlooked the fact that Ismaʿil fell victim to policies that allowed for the continued emergence of landed, commercial, and administrative elites with a greater stake in

Egyptian power. While the Chamber of Deputies was hardly a parliament, and while Isma'il cannot be termed a constitutional ruler, the British overlooked Isma'il's increasingly slippery grip on absolutism.

Nonetheless, British officials confidently attached behavior in and outside houses to an indefinite program of reform that they claimed would create a generation of capable Egyptians and then liberate them. "England," wrote Dicey in 1880, "will allow Egypt to enter a new stage of its history."[99] Like a child possessing much potential but no autonomy, Egypt needed to be led, taught, supervised — *parented* — such that it could, at some indeterminate point, be emancipated.[100] According to Cromer, "It was originally contemplated that the occupation should be of short duration, and should come to an end when the Khedive's authority was again fully established. It was found, however . . . that the work of reform . . . was not to be set on foot in such a short while, as had been hoped by some authorities, but would require Egypt to be *nursed* and *tended to a slow maturity.*"[101]

The paternal nature of the veiled protectorate is easily seen in the structures of the protectorate itself. Cromer did nothing to strengthen the constitutional forms of the khedivate; rather, he worked as what M. W. Daly has referred to as an "estate manager," increasing the number of British advisors to oversee the work of the Egyptians. The Egyptian administration was left in place and put under the parentage of British supervisors.[102] Egyptians were not dismissed from their governing positions and replaced by Europeans, nor were Egyptian governing institutions closed down — in fact, new positions were created, albeit with very limited functions. "Native rule" was thus maintained, but it was subjected to the overbearing presence of British supervision. Foreign Secretary Lord Salisbury called it "advice," but Cromer made it clear that "they [the Egyptian elite] must, on important matters, do what they were told."[103] While "reform" of the Egyptian elite remained central to the ideology of occupation, Cromer had no policy or "plan" for it.[104] Egyptians would be both free to work and enslaved by their overseers until the reform of its political institutions took place.

The politics of the veiled protectorate were thus likened to the politics of sound motherhood — of raising Egypt to a new level of development.[105] Reform of Egyptian home life would produce a new parentage, replacing Isma'il's immoral lineage with a new one. In this equation, women or images of them and their place in the Egyptian domicile were not directly responsible for the political or economic crisis that caused the occupation. Women were, however, implicated in the construction of the

Egypt problem and its solution. While such women were merely specters, indistinct visions of harem inmates, they were consistently evoked in the construction of the Egypt the British thought they were occupying and reforming. In the gendered politics of the veiled protectorate, women were not necessarily seen, but the image of their seclusion in the harem and their relationship to Egyptian rulers was a constant presence.

Imperialism thus did not merely result in the feminization of the Orient, as Edward Said has argued, but rather in its concomitant infantilization.[106] Both the British and, later, Egyptian nationalists used images of Egyptian women to symbolize, respectively, the backwardness and strengths of the Egyptian body politic. Each group could claim to protect, nurture, and herald feminine Egypt as an indication of its success at reforming her.[107] In the British equation of colonial discourse, Egyptian men had to be transformed themselves before they could claim the authority to reform Egypt. In order to take their positions as fathers of a new Egyptian order, Egyptian men had to endure a "childhood" before "growing up."

Thus, while territorial and economic concerns explain the invasion of Egypt, British occupation and the relationship that developed between the two parties arose out of the understanding the British had of Egypt and the Egyptians. The contract that was established between the British and the Egyptians between 1882 and the 1919 Revolution was based on an understanding that the British would leave after Egyptians matured and demonstrated a new assortment of virtues, morals, and behaviors. The genesis of such new cultural and social codes was to be their homes. For Egyptians to demonstrate that they were ready to take Egypt's political and economic affairs back into their own hands, they would have to show that the affairs of their domiciles were in order. For the politics of the occupation to be overruled — for Egypt to claim that it was a nation ready for self-rule — a set of modern, Egyptian domestic behaviors would have to be shaped, learned, and, finally, put on display.

CHAPTER 4

The Home, the Classroom, and the Cultivation of Egyptian Nationalism

From the latter decades of the nineteenth century onward, British administrators and Egyptian nationalists who worked within the colonial administration subjected elite Egyptian schoolchildren to a reform of their personal behavior that was designed to fit the needs of the Egyptian state — both as it transformed itself and as it struggled to liberate itself from the British. After 1882, as British government officials called for the creation of more productive, more modern Egyptians to serve the state, the classroom became the laboratory in which Egyptian youth learned and practiced new habits, behaviors, and relationships. Given Egypt's history of reform prior to the British occupation, Egyptians and British both played roles in transforming domestic practices. The most fundamental lesson that turn-of-the-century Egyptian children learned, however, was that their cultural traditions were responsible for Egypt's backwardness and its subsequent occupation. Teachers of all subjects taught Egyptian children that only when they learned and practiced a new set of traditions in their private and public lives would they be capable of ushering Egypt into a modern, independent age.

Beginning under Isma'il, the classroom became an arena in which the state could begin to exert its influence over greater numbers of Egyptian citizens, subjecting them to curricula that reflected the goals and ideals of the government. While Isma'il's nascent public educational system did not succeed in transforming the domestic practices of elite Egyptians, it did lay the groundwork for extending state control over a greater number of classrooms and for standardizing curricula that would later extend into the students' home life.

Isma'il's reign also witnessed the rise of foreign, missionary education in Egypt. Foreign education, for girls and boys alike, exposed young Egyptians to a discourse about the state of their homes and the condition of the body politic in which backward households were blamed for the fall of nations. The quest to gain access to Egyptians' souls resulted in an assault upon their domiciles — an intrusion that was not unlike the European travelers' quest to gain access to Egypt's inner spaces. This time, however, discourse about the home and the family was accompanied by concrete recipes for transforming backwardness into modernity. The landscape constructed and fostered under Isma'il's predecessors, and later written about by Rifa'a al-Tahtawi, was increasingly labeled "modern Egyptian." By the turn of the twentieth century, *effendi* schoolchildren learned that the behavior that took place in their increasingly modernized homes was proper, Egyptian, and nationalist.

Under British rule, the Egyptian household became central to the education of young Egyptians within the public educational system. For both the British and the Egyptian nationalists who worked within the colonial government, transforming the habits of young Egyptians was central to making them more modern, more productive, and more likely to be loyal to a central state. At the same time, however, lessons about the household and its practices served as an arena in which Egyptians circumvented censorship and British control of public education. Modernity, loyalty, and the roots of revolutionary platforms were all couched in lessons on domestic practices.

The classroom was thus the arena in which the generation of *effendi* Egyptians who participated in the demonstrations of 1919 cultivated notions about their roles in creating an independent, Egyptian body politic.[1] In the classroom the habits and customs of modernity were shaped, the sins of the domicile purged, and the mores of the new nation articulated.[2] In the 1919 Revolution, graduates of the nascent Egyptian educational system from the 1880s onward demonstrated a host of modern habits, relationships, and behaviors emblematic of the nation's readiness to govern itself.

The Egyptian Classroom and the Expansion of State Hegemony

Central to the modernizing programs of Mohammad 'Ali and his grandson Isma'il was the creation of a nascent, "national" educational system that progressively brought the goals of the state to bear on the thoughts, habits, and behavior of Egyptian schoolchildren — especially those of the upper classes.[3] The result was the production of a class of Egyptians trained to be effective state functionaries as well as a cadre of Egyptians whose behavior had begun to be molded by the state. While the behavior was hardly uniform or "national" under Isma'il's reign, the state became increasingly responsible for shaping the minds and morals of young Egyptians.

Mohammad 'Ali first began the process of bringing education under the control of the state in the 1820s in order to create both a European-style military and a body of civil servants who would be loyal to him and his new governing apparatus. Isma'il later continued his grandfather's educational reforms, with the goal of bringing an increased number of Egyptians under the control of a state-sponsored curriculum. In both measures he was largely successful. Isma'il oversaw the creation of courses designed to shape the habits, customs, and behavior of the young Egyptians who passed through the educational system, extending the hand of the state into the most private realms of its students' daily lives.

Historians mark Isma'il's educational reforms as having fallen into two periods. From 1863 to 1871, Isma'il continued the work of Mohammad 'Ali, funding schools that provided the state with a European-style military. Then, from 1871 to 1879, he pursued the creation of a nascent public educational system. In 1863 he reestablished the Egyptian Ministry of Education, which had been closed during the reign of his predecessor, 'Abbas. In 1868, thanks to the energies of his deputy minister of education, 'Ali Mubarak (1823–93), Isma'il also re-opened the School of Administration and Languages, which played a central role in the production of state-sponsored school curricula and school administrators. Once the Ministry of Education and the School of Administration and Languages were in place, Isma'il and 'Ali Mubarak opened a number of government-sponsored primary and preparatory schools, a polytechnic school of engineering, a school of medicine, industrial schools, a school of surveying and accountancy, and a school of Egyptology.[4]

One of Isma'il's most effective measures for bringing Egyptian education under his control was putting a significant percentage of the *kuttabs,* or mosque schools, under direct government supervision and then subjecting them to state-controlled curricula. The extension of the state's hand into religious education took place in 1867 when 'Ali Mubarak formed a committee to reform the *kuttabs* and to augment their curricula. According to Mubarak's autobiography, he wanted the schools to combine a mixture of traditional Qur'anic education with courses that would meet the state's quest for loyal, competent functionaries.[5] The outcome of the work done by Mubarak's committee was the law of the tenth of Ragab — November 7, 1867 — that placed all *kuttabs* with sufficient *waqf* income under the control of the government.[6] Those *kuttabs* would now be administered by the government while their expenditures were met by *waqf* moneys.

As the result of this new law, three kinds of schools were under state control by the late 1860s and early 1870s: village-level elementary and primary schools, primary schools in the urban centers and provincial capitals, and preparatory schools. Graduates of the primary schools were eligible for entrance in the preparatory schools, a diploma from which lead to jobs in the government bureaucracy. The graduates of the elementary schools were not targeted for the preparatory schools. In order to extend state education to the rural populace however, Isma'il and his ministers decreed that each of Egypt's regions *(mudiriyya)* with a population of ten thousand or more was entitled to a "first-degree" school, the goals and curricula of which corresponded with the governmental primary schools. Students in the first-degree schools learned the Qur'an, reading, writing, penmanship in Arabic, basic arithmetic and fractions, geography, and hygiene. The state opened second-degree schools in districts with five thousand to ten thousand inhabitants; because students were not expected to continue with their education after graduating from the second-degree schools, their curricula was augmented with Arabic grammar and syntax, geography, and national and natural history.[7]

The importance of the state's role in opening new schools, bringing the *kuttabs* under its auspices, and increasingly taking charge of school curricula lies in the efforts of the state to create a uniform education to serve its needs. Students at all levels were increasingly subjected to regular exams "above all for the good of the students and, consequently, for the benefit of the state," and textbooks were increasingly prescribed by the Ministry of Education. All teachers were required to have a certificate, granted by local notables or a by a delegate from the Ministry of Education.[8] The seeds of uniformity were thus planted.

Isma'il also endeavored to create a uniform public educational system by restructuring the teachers' college, Dar al-'Ulum, which was originally opened during Mohammad 'Ali's reign. The goal of the college was to modernize and routinize the education of al-Azhar graduates who were teaching in the primary schools and the *kuttabs*. The Dar al-'Ulum project was only marginally successful under both rulers, and the project of building and running a modern teachers' college was only accomplished under Tawfiq's reign. The importance of Isma'il's renewed interest in the project, however, lies in his attempts to bring a corps of teachers fully under state management.[9]

An increase in the state's interest in and attention to girls' education also marks the reign of Isma'il. The khedive first began planning the construction of a girls' school in 1867 under the guidance of his foreign advisors. As conceptualized in 1867, the school was to accommodate five hundred girls between the ages of nine and eleven and to consist of a five-year program of study. According to Octave Sachot, who was sent to Egypt by the French Ministry of Education to report on the condition of public education there, the curriculum was set to include "reading, writing, religion, moral instruction, Turkish (for rich girls), the four laws of arithmetic, . . . child raising, home economics and the culinary arts, and needlework."[10] The staff was designed to include five teachers of *tarbiyya* (child raising), two professors of home economics, a specialist in cooking, and ten instructors of sewing and needlework.[11] Sachot alerted Egyptian officials that he found their system of women's education lacking, as there was, at that time, only a school for midwives.[12] Sachot warned that the neglect of girls' education would place government projects at risk.

A girls' school was opened in 1873, thanks to the patronage of Isma'il's third wife, Cheshmet Hanim. Egypt's first official girls' school, al-Siyufiah was dedicated to the training of Muslim girls, although Coptic girls' schools and foreign missionary schools for girls had opened earlier and had included a small number of Muslims. Upper-class families at that time, both Muslim and non-Muslim, also had begun the habit of hiring foreign governesses and tutors to teach their children. Al-Siyufiah's students were recruited from families of large landowners and government officials as well as the white slaves owned by such families. The 298 students who were enrolled there in 1875 learned Turkish, Arabic, religion (including the Qur'an and morals), needlework, and laundry. The deposition of Isma'il in 1879 forced his wife to withdraw her support of the school, and the project was taken over by the Waqf administration. Al-Siyufiah was then combined with a similar school for girls founded by the Waqf administration and re-named al-Saniah.

A number of reasons prompted the growing interest in girls' education, both on the part of the state and the families who chose to have their daughters educated.[13] According to a report written by Egyptian state official Yacoub Artin Pasha, the original goal of girls' education was the production of better domestic servants to run the household economies of the upper classes and to take a hand in the raising of their children. When white slavery was abolished in 1877 and a new rank of servants had to be created, al-Siyufiah trained the young women who would seek employment in upper-class homes. This, according to Artin, was one of the reasons why poor families sent their children to the first girls' schools. The girls were fed and clothed for free by the school's administration. At the same time, they learned the tastes and habits of the Egyptian upper classes, which were constantly changing as the result of the influx of ideas, tastes, and fashions from Europe and elsewhere.[14]

According to Artin, the 1870s witnessed the growth of the practice of educating girls among the educated elite. Upper-class men, many of whom married educated women, sent their daughters to school to signal that they were of a privileged class and that they were part of the "modern" world. Many such men had contact with fellow Egyptians whose daughters had been to missionary schools or had private, foreign tutors. An al-Saniah education was a means of acquiring the fashion and etiquette of the upper classes without the expense of private tutoring or the fear of having one's daughters directly exposed to foreigners.

Isma'il's increased interest in educating Egyptian girls also stemmed from the constant critiques waged by Europeans against Egyptians and the position of women in Egyptian society. The khedive and his ministers were well aware of European critiques of the moral state of Egyptians, of the allegedly poor condition of their home life, and of the role of un-educated women in ruining the morals of those men who might run the nation. On February 9, 1875, Riad Pasha, then deputy minister of Public Education and of the Waqf administration, sent a communiqué to one of Isma'il's secretaries. Attached to it was an article from the previous day's edition of the French journal *Le Courrier de Port Said,* which criticized the state of girls' education, the family, and the Egyptian nation. Riad suggested that Isma'il read the article, which implied that any political reform program had to entertain "la politique genereuse" of educating girls as well as boys. The article claimed that through women's education, the home life and the moral life of all Egyptians could be salvaged; in extending its hand into the home life of the nation, the state would assure its own moral and political future.[15]

Finally, the project of educating women was one of the ways in which Isma'il endeavored to imitate Europe and to make himself, at least in appearance, into a European-style ruler. In August 1869, Isma'il urged Nubar Pasha to acquire the semblance of a school for girls before the arrival of Empress Eugénie from France for the opening of the Suez Canal; he thought that she should see not only the splendors of Egypt's technological development but also the extent to which the state took care of its citizens.[16]

Thus, by the time of Egypt's financial crisis in the mid-1870s and the first stirrings of "the Egypt problem," one could find the roots of a "system" of education run by the state, with the particular interests of the state in mind. By the time of the occupation, the number of students in the government primary schools and in the *kuttabs* under state control was 4,445 — up from 1,399 in 1878.[17] The "national" program of study under Isma'il's reign, while still in a fledgling state, was designed to produce Egyptians who were loyal to, and who could work efficiently for, the government. The state had placed itself in charge of choosing the curricula that it deemed necessary to the project of modernizing Egypt. The students' minds and bodies were becoming increasingly the product of the government.[18]

Model Homes for a Heathen Nation: Missionary Education, the Household, and the Making of Modern Egyptians

In addition to state-sponsored education, foreign missionaries addressed the manners and morals of young children and the quotidian nature of their home life. Approximately 130 foreign schools opened during Isma'il's reign, sponsored by English and American missionaries, Greeks, Germans, Italians, and others. Some foreign schools were opened to educate the children of expatriate businessmen. Others formed part of European and local Christian benevolent projects. For foreign missionaries, in particular the American Protestants, reshaping manners and morals was the first step in the process of conversion: to attend to the inner realm of the soul, the inner realm of the domicile had to be cleaned up. The American Protestant educational endeavor mirrored and often reinforced the process through which the home and the family were being targeted by the state. Until the late nineteenth century, when state-sponsored primary and secondary education began to spread and become "popular" with the middle and lower classes, the American Protestants had the lion's share of Egyptian students, and theirs were the most consistently full classrooms in Egypt.[19]

For the Protestants who ventured to Egypt and for those who read about missionary activities at home, Egyptian households and their activities were central to the process through which foreigners came to imagine who the Egyptians were and how they behaved. The missionaries who traveled to save Egyptians' souls had, thanks to art, fiction, and the travelogue, preconceived notions of what they would find in Egypt. One of the places that missionaries most readily searched for sources of heathenism among the Egyptians was the domicile. American Protestants at home and abroad believed that the Egyptian home was the source of Egyptians' lethargy, indolence, and perversion.

The educational branch of the American Presbyterian missionary enterprise in Egypt began during the winter of 1853, when a Dr. Paulding, who had been a medical missionary in Damascus, went to Cairo to sojourn in a warmer, dryer climate. What he saw in Cairo convinced him of the need for missionary work in Egypt. Accordingly, he wrote to the Board of Missions urging the importance of Egypt as a new "educational field." In November 1854, Paulding was joined by the Reverend Thomas McCague and his wife, both of whom had sailed from Philadelphia on September 30 in order to begin the task of educating Egyptians. They were joined by a Dr. Barnett of the Damascus mission, and an "Egyptian team" was born.[20]

The small group purchased a house "favorable for residence, religious services and a boys' school" in Azbakiyya, which was then the largest Coptic quarter in Cairo. Barnett began preaching, and Rev. McCague taught English in the boys' school while he learned to speak Arabic. McCague's wife had difficulty finding literate Egyptian women to help her teach young girls; thus, she attempted to bring a few Egyptian girls into her home to train them to be homemakers as well as teachers. Due to the fears of most Egyptian families that working and learning in a foreigner's home in such a capacity would ruin their daughters' opportunities for marriage, the McCagues soon realized that a girls' school would have to be opened outside of their domicile. They found rooms suitable for instruction, and the couple opened their doors to female students in 1855. Their curriculum was simple: An Egyptian woman taught sewing and served as governess while Mrs. McCague taught English, spelling, and reading. Other accounts state that the couple had employed a young Egyptian man named Abdullah to teach Arabic. According to their private correspondence Mrs. McCague was driven to push for girls' education by her fascination and repulsion with Egyptian home life. The home, she thought, was not only the source of heathenism but thwarted the progress of conversion. In a letter to a cousin dated April 5, 1855, Mrs.

McCague made much ado of Egyptian houses, their construction, and their inner activities:

But to return to the description of the houses with which I commenced. . . . There is no regularity in their construction. The principal aim is to make them as private as possible. . . . The females occupy the lower story, which is called the 'hareem.' . . .

The dwellings of the lowly orders are very mean. . . . The entrance to these hovels often resembles the entrance to a cave and there are small apertures in the wall for the admission of light and air. . . .

The women of the higher classes generally spend their time in visiting, gossiping, eating, smoking, taking care of the children and embroidering handkerchiefs with gold and colored silk. . . . But the women of the lower orders are condemned to greater drudgery than the men. Their chief occupations are the preparing of their husbands' food . . . when they go out with their husbands, he rides while she walks behind and carries the bundle if there be one.[21]

Mrs. McCague's repulsion with the inner world of Egyptians led her to formulate a basic mandate for girls' education in Egypt: Reform of the inner world of their domiciles had to come before any other religious or educational task could begin.

This distaste for Egyptian home life led to a swarm of missionary activities in and around Egyptian houses. Of particular interest to the early missionary educators was work that got them inside the Egyptians' homes. They called this task *zenana* work. A pamphlet on missionary activity explained that *zenana* was the Indian term for harem, and that the term had been adopted by the Presbyterians to mean "home work" in general. The point of *zenana* work was to take the message of the scriptures to women whose isolation in their homes kept them from attending the mission schools. Because most missionaries found the condition of women's homes to be appalling, however, the missionary project took on a new twist: If *zenana* work could not succeed in converting Egyptian women to Christianity, it could, at least, train them in the basics of housekeeping and home economics. New domestic habits would serve to "elevate women's spirits," even if they were not ultimately made into Christians.

Facing the challenge of entering Egyptian homes either for the purpose of religious conversion or conversion to the "science" of modern home economics was the task of the educational mission in Egypt. While the regeneration of Egypt was the task of male and female missionaries alike, women had the special task of penetrating the Egyptians' domestic realm so that its women and children could be saved. An article in the

Women's Missionary Magazine dated October 1887 and entitled "Home Training and Its Present-Day Difficulties" targeted the domestic arena as being the "hope" for Egypt's renaissance. Because of their "special" ability to have access to the private realm, this work was targeted for women and called "women's work." Women's work was the cornerstone of the project that would rejuvenate the Egyptian spirit as well as the Egyptian domicile. One missionary recounted: "With God's help the needle, in the finger of the missionary's wife, was the simple instrument that opened the gates of steel to admit Christian teaching and influence."[22]

Women's work also included the classroom. The missionaries could not always succeed in getting inside Egyptian homes; they could, however, open classrooms in which future generations of Egyptians could be reached and trained. While boys and girls alike were educated in the mission schools, the women's societies talked at length about girls' education, and the *Women's Missionary Magazine* was often full of columns and articles on how best to educate young Egyptian girls, make them into proper wives and mothers, and thereby assure Egypt's first step toward "salvation."

There does not appear to have been any standard curriculum in the Egyptian mission schools until about 1910, but different sources allude to the courses that served as standard fare in many schools. An 1888 annual report of the mission in Egypt referred to a kind of basic curriculum. Students took geography, math, grammar, catechism, English, French, algebra, geometry, trigonometry, physiology, and philosophy. All subjects seem to have been studied by boys and girls alike, except for the last four, which were for boys alone. In addition to the above coursework, girls had supplementary courses in household subjects.[23]

An article from the *Women's Missionary Magazine* entitled "The Khayatt School" summed up the nineteenth-century missionary educational "project" for girls. The school, located in Luxor and named after the local family that paid the expenses of the teachers, taught primary and secondary school in a converted house to about two hundred girls. The girls got a strong education in what was referred to as "the common branches," what Westerners would undoubtedly call reading, writing, and arithmetic. At the same time, they learned how to make their own clothes and take care of household duties. Also part of the curriculum was a strong dose of discipline: "M. Sitt [is] standing on a low rostrum behind a little table telling . . . the story of Joseph . . . to a long row of girls who have never learned to 'toe the chalk line.'" The girls learned manners and cleanliness: — "A rush is made to bring chairs for us, while one of the little readers offers her book that we may see what is being read. . . . The teachers are all clean and neat in their dress, and one rarely sees among pupils what we would call here a dirty face."[24] This emphasis on order allowed girls to display that they were educated. Graduates of the school were said to leave in a much "improved" condition, visible in their manners and their appearance: "It is interesting to see the improvement in the girls as one goes from lower to higher classes . . . every year seems to show increased cleanliness and tidiness of person as well as intelligence of face."[25]

By the early 1880s, Protestant missionary schools reported substantial enrollment of both boys and girls. By the turn of the twentieth century, at which point enrollment in the schools hit its peak, there were 176 American Protestant schools enrolling 11,014 students. This number represented a substantial increase from 1875, when twelve schools enrolled 633 students.[26] The opening of more government-run primary and secondary schools, as well as the government's increased interest in girls' education, detracted from the number of parents interested in missionary education, and enrollments began to decline around 1900. By the 1880s, the missionaries also began to report that they had a goodly number of Muslims enrolled in their schools, although the vast majority of their students were Christians, most of whom were Copts.[27] In 1883, the annual report claimed that 650 Muslim students were enrolled in the schools. The boys' boarding and day schools in Haret as-sak'ain in Cairo claimed 493 students, 137 of whom were Muslim. The girls' school of the same neighborhood boasted 294 students, a small percentage of whom were Muslim. Among the schools' pupils, the report claimed, were Ahmed 'Urabi's four daughters.[28]

At the end of the nineteenth century, as the Americans' mission to convert to Christianity slowed down, it was replaced by a mission to civilize. The home was thus transformed from being the site of potential conversion to that on which "national" refashioning could take place. By 1900, as the result of more than half a century's work in the region, Protestant missionaries ceased to consider Egyptians to be simply a part of the heathen hordes and saw them, rather, as "Egyptians," possessing of very specific needs and characteristics. "Egyptian homes," "Egyptian villages," and the "Egyptian nation" appeared, full force, in missionary literature, wherein Egypt and the Egyptians took on very particular problems that could be solved through the educational mission. The reshaping of the home as a kind of "first step" toward Egyptian national regeneration — rather than Christian conversion — became a common topic. While reli-

gious education was certainly not written out of the missionaries' curricula, the point of the missionary educational project became the rejuvenation of Egyptians as a *nation*.[29]

Carrie Buchanan, one of the prominent figures in the Egyptian field in
the early twentieth century, saw missionary work as constituting a
"national affair." For her, the string of missionary schools throughout
Egypt gave the "nation" a sense of boundaries and brought Egyptians
together in a kind of "national" spirit:

> If one could be lifted up above the land of Egypt on 'the wings of the morning,'
> and could take a view of the whole country — of the beautiful Nile valley — from
> the sea right on to the Sudan, you would see a fine network of schools. At the
> great centers, Alexandria, Tanta, Zagazig, Cairo, Fayoum, Assiut, Luxor and
> Khartoum, the lines are drawn in and tied and strengthened. All kinds of classes
> are gathered into this great net. . . . Some of the best citizens of the land have been
> taught the true principles of right service to their country.[30]

The parallel nature of the state's modernizing project and the missionary civilizing project is brilliantly illustrated in *Farida's Dream,* a pamphlet published by the missionaries around the turn of the century. It consisted of a "story" recorded by Miss Rena Hogg, who was a central figure
on the Egyptian missionary scene during the first two decades of the
twentieth century and took up the struggles of a young Egyptian girl
from a village to accept the message of the Gospel and to "learn" the ways
of the modern world. It is not clear whether Farida is a Muslim or a
Christian. In her "dream," as it was allegedly recounted to Miss Hogg,
Farida became aware of what she had to do in the process of transforming herself and her village:

> The village had been suddenly roused from its drowsy, leisurely life by a cry in its
> lanes, 'The Pasha is coming! Make everything clean!' And immediately it was as
> if the place were under the ban of the plague and a medical inspection imminent.
> Such a sweeping of courts began, such a burning of rubbish and daubing of
> whitewash upon mud walls! Every inhabitant was astir and at work in a fever of
> expectation. . . .
> She needed no Joseph to interpret her dream. One look into that face had
> made everything clear. To be ready for the Pasha her home must be cleansed from
> wrong.[31]

Ultimately, however, the task of cleaning up in preparation for the pasha's
arrival became more than just Farida's task: The entire village had to
"clean" up before contact between it and the pasha could really take place.

Farida's story can be read two ways. Its obvious message is a Christian one and highlights the putative missionary goal of converting the Egyptians to the religion of Christ the Pasha. The other message is, however, a secular one, and in it the pasha is clearly a khedive or a state functionary. His entrance into the village and into the hearts of its inhabitants, like that of his religious counterpart, wakes the nation from its "leisurely life" and brings activity and productivity. In either reading, however, the acceptance of a new order, religious or secular, brings the "nation" to life — "conversion" to the science of home economics was the implicit basis of becoming "modern."

One of the central platforms for "waking" the village and bringing it to life was the restructuring of the family. Missionaries believed that home life and its crucial contribution to modernity had not existed in Egypt prior to the missionaries' arrival. As the twentieth century progressed, missionary literature came to be the mouthpiece for familial reform and the missionaries claimed that they had been responsible for introducing "the home" and the activities associated with it into Egypt.[32] The missionaries were determined to shape Egyptians in the model of the Victorian monogamous couple, assigning very specific roles and behaviors to each family member and claiming that national progress would come only when proper domestic habits and inclinations were taken up. The classroom would provide the model on which future generations of Egyptians could shape their family life. Minnehaha Finney, a career missionary and author of much of the curriculum that was used in the schools from about 1915 onward, taught that missionary homes and families as well as the families of Egyptian Christian converts should provide the model after which Egyptians could pattern their new national habits and customs. Finney referred to a married Egyptian couple, both graduates of the mission schools, and the home that they kept as an important example to the others in the village:

I am thinking of one teacher's home which pleased me greatly; a few bright pictures made the mud walls attractive, the dirt floors well swept with a bright colored mat here and there did not look like dirt floors; the little baby slept in a "carton" box, well padded, and when the mother set the sleeping baby in her little bed out in the sun for her sun-bath it was the talk of the village. That young mother had scores of opportunities to demonstrate to those village women the way to make a real home out of their simple surroundings.[33]

The girls' boarding school at Luxor had a "model house," which was a typical village house arranged "so as to be kept clean easily. The classes in

Domestic Science have their Home Making lessons in the Model House."[34]

At the helm of the new, modern family would sit a fine homemaker, who would, of course, be skilled in the domestic sciences. The *Women's Missionary Magazine* reported, for example, that as the result of education, daily meals in Egyptian homes had become true *family* meals with both sexes and their offspring dining together. Hogg visited the homes of many of her school's graduates and was happy to see that they were applying what they had learned in school to their home life: "Baking, washing, ironing, cleaning — all had their fixed days and hours. . . . *One needs to be familiar with the easy-going methodlessness of the East to realize the greatness of the advance involved in this grasp of the importance of system.*"[35]

The American missionaries were fond of claiming that through their educational mission, and in particular the familiar reform that they emphasized, Egyptians had entered into a new era of national consciousness and pride in their national history. Buchanan saw the graduates of her schools — boys and girls alike — and the Egyptian parents who allowed them to be taught there as part of the "New Orient" that Egypt was becoming. That pride, she said, was expressed in the fondness that Egyptian children felt for telling stories about Egyptian history, in presenting pageants about different eras of Egypt's past, and in bringing their parents to school to attend such productions, the ultimate goal of which was a celebration of "the new nation."

Buchanan told the story of Mrs. Hind Ammun, a graduate of the Girls' Boarding School in Cairo, who, after her husband's premature death, found herself wanting to do something to "help the nation." Thus she set about writing a history of Egypt, hoping that it could be used as a text in either the mission schools or those of the government. She submitted the text to the minister of education, an Egyptian, who accepted the manuscript for publication and offered her a royalty on the first edition. But he said he could never have such a history published with a woman's name on it; he suggested that she change her name to Hassam Mahmoud. The minister said, "This splendid lady drew herself up in all the dignity of her new womanhood and replied, 'But I am a woman . . . and I have written a true history of Egypt and I wish . . . [those] facts to appear on the title page.'"[36] The minister consented, apparently realizing that education — even in Christian missionary schools — and the creation of an Egypt "worthy of a true history" were part of the same project. At the time of Mrs. Ammun's death, she was under contract with the government to write another history book for use in the government's primary schools.[37]

Thus the education that was at first designed to spread the Gospel to secluded women and then "clean up" the domestic realm now took credit for the production of Egyptians' sense of their "worthy history." The rejuvenation of the home was not only being credited with helping the national good but also with creating a sense of "national." To foreign missionaries and their students, nationalism was the result of familial and domestic reform.

Staking Territory, Shaping Identity: The Private Realm in the Politics of Occupation, Nationalist Riposte, and the Construction of National Narratives

After the British occupation of Egypt, the national educational system became the site of very contested debates between the British, who dominated the educational system, and Egyptian nationalists, many of whom worked within the state bureaucracy and held positions in the Ministry of Education or on one of its many central and provincial educational boards. For nationalists, education was a means of continuing the process of cultivating loyalty, efficiency, and productivity in Egyptian civil servants. As the Egyptians' struggle against the British intensified, however, the educational system also became a means through which notions of "the nation," its history, its future, and its characteristics were cultivated.

The British had very specific ideas about educating Egyptians and creating a literate Egyptian class, which clashed with those of the Egyptians. The British blueprint for the Egyptian educational system had everything to do with their determination to maintain the country's "agricultural spirit" and promote its agricultural productivity. The kind of education that might have led to real intellectual or industrial growth would have diverted energies and resources away from agriculture, threatening the supply of cotton to the mills back home. In 1905, Cromer stated that any education that detracted from the Egyptians' fitness for agricultural labor would be "a national evil."[38] But to run Egypt's affairs without making Egypt a formal colony, the British needed an educated class. Here, they drew on their experience in India, best summed up by Thomas Macaulay, who, in July 1833, told the House of Commons that effective trade and government between the British and the Indians depended on the creation of an educated class. India would, he surmised, become little more than a costly dependency if "the diffusion of European civilization" in India were to be halted.[39]

Fears of rebellion, however, added a tension to the prospect of educating Egyptians, and therein lay the conflict between the British administration's "blueprints" for resolving "the Egypt question" and their actual implementation. In theory, the length of British tenure in Egypt depended on the creation of a new class of Egyptians who could govern themselves well and wisely. However, if the British were to assure themselves final say in the occupation's terminus, the project of educating Egyptians would have to be contrived very carefully. Cromer, in fact, thought that Macaulay's advice had been somewhat misguided, given the extent to which the spread of Western-style higher education in India had created a class of discontented ideologues. In 1906 he wrote: "Here, I am trying to take to heart the lesson of India. . . . All I want of the next generation of Egyptians is for them to read and write. Also I want to create as many carpenters, bricklayers, plasterers, etc. as I possibly can. More than this I cannot do."[40] Thus the ambiguities of the British colonial project in Egypt once again asserted themselves. Egyptians had to be made productive along the lines dictated by the British, but they could not be made overly productive. Some Egyptians would learn English in order to work for the colonial state; others would learn only Arabic, shutting themselves out of government work and limiting their prospects to agriculture.[41]

The result of such tensions — between the interests of colonizers and nationalists, the precarious balance between economic productivity and limited military expenditures — was a functional but circumscribed system of elementary, primary, and secondary education. Keeping with their general policy for administering Egypt, Cromer kept the Ministry of Education intact, and, within it, maintained the practice of centralizing the ministry and of allowing the minister of education — an Egyptian — to have almost total authority over it.[42] While the educational budget during the Cromer years was extremely low — about 1 percent, lower than it had been during the years of Isma'il's gravest financial crisis — and while Europeans tended to dominate governing and advisory boards within the ministry, Egyptian ministers appear to have had a relatively large say in dictating the inspection of schools, the creation and regulation of curriculum, and the appointment of teachers.

The British first caught the real ire of the nationalists in 1891 when the Ministry of Education was subsumed into the Department of Public Works (Nizarat al-ashghal), reducing the role of the minister of education to that of a subminister within a larger department. During the 1890s, a battle also waged between the British and the nationalists over the language of instruction: The British preferred that instruction at the primary and secondary levels take place in English. (Until 1904, when the French agreed to relinquish their interests in Egypt, a battle also waged between the two European nations over which of their languages would be the language of instruction.) The nationalists preferred Arabic and eventually "won" in their struggle for its hegemony in the classroom; even before Cromer's departure from Egypt in 1907, most of the instruction in Egyptian elementary and primary classrooms was in Arabic, while many secondary courses were taught in a European language.[43] Sir Eldon Gorst (r. 1907–11) who succeeded Cromer, was predisposed to the Arabization of the Egyptian educational system and to making the system more rational by instructing Egyptians in their native tongue.[44]

Struggles also took place between the British and the Egyptians over what Egyptians were capable of learning. Because the overwhelming majority of students in the public schools were Muslim, Cromer opined that they were not capable of absorbing what he called a "classical" education, since modern political thought and philosophy were anchored in Christian traditions. Furthermore, Cromer understood that political theory and modern history were swords that could be taken up against the occupation. Consequently, his policy toward the teaching of subjects that might inculcate democracy in young Egyptians was premised upon the sentiment that they were both useless (Egyptians would not catch on) and dangerous (they *should* not catch on). Part of the educational "politics" of the occupation was the limiting of such courses or their elimination from the curriculum altogether. Were the ideals and practicalities of democratic self-rule to be inculcated in young Egyptians, it would have to be done in another arena.[45]

One of the most effective measures taken by the British against the Egyptians was the limiting and circumscription of curriculum, a strategy that effectively isolated Egyptians from the process of narrating their history — past and present — or from shaping the institutions that would define their future. Cromer determined that courses on ancient and modern Egyptian history, for example, were unnecessary for the "lower orders" (elementary-school students), whose education was to consist merely of reading, writing, arithmetic, and basic courses in manners; likewise, he saw history as superfluous to the Egyptians who were being pushed through the educational system in order to serve the state. Thus, even in the most superior state schools, there was a real dearth of such courses. When history courses did appear on school schedules, they occupied a very limited number of hours each week. The lack of history in the public school curriculum and the dangers of its absence from the classroom were lamented by members of the Egyptian National Party at a party congress held in Brussels in 1910. In his speech to the congress, "l'Angleterre et l'instruction en Égypte," delegate Rifaʿat Wafik claimed that the limiting and elimination of history from the curriculum was one of the most powerful instruments of British rule in Egypt.[46]

In 1906, Egyptians were able to assert themselves more directly into curriculum debates. That year, a regular Ministry of Education was once again created, and Saʿad Zaghlul was appointed minister of education, a post he held until 1910. But it was actually with the re-creation of the ministry that the British were able to gain the most control over education, which they accomplished through the establishment of the position of *mustashur* (counselor, or adviser), who could, and did, supersede decisions made by the Egyptian minister on any matter. From 1906 until 1919, that position was held by Douglas Dunlop, who held Egyptians in contempt and who did little to promote either the spread or the improvement of public education or to include Egyptians in its management. While after January 1910 a new Provincial Council Law allowed Provincial Councils to finance and "promote education of all types," the Ministry of Education, under the tight reigns of the British, continued to shape the policies and the programs of the Egyptian educational system.[47]

Thus, while the original structure of Ismaʿil's Ministry of Education remained relatively intact under the British occupation, in truth it was ultimately guided by the demands and the desires of the British for the system. The British plan for Egyptian education included a very low budget — 1 percent of the total budget until 1922, when it was raised to 3 percent — as well as the mandate that the goal of education was, in the case of the lower orders, religion, reading, writing, and "civility," but nothing more. In the case of the middle and upper classes, education was limited to the training necessary to serve the government. In order to limit the number of primary- and secondary-school graduates to what the economy and the administration could absorb, Cromer began to charge tuition for the public schools. He also initiated the practice of examining graduates: Admission into the bureaucracy was based on proof that exams had been successfully passed. The examinations were made extraordinarily difficult, such that few students succeeded in passing them.

Despite low budgets and stalemates between the two parties over the politics of educating Egyptians — the goal of education and its price; the ceilings on the levels of education that Egyptians could aspire to; the rudimentary nature of the elementary-school curricula as it was conceived by

Cromer — the educational system continued to expand, centralize, and add further numbers of Egyptians to its grasp. Cromer reported, for example, that despite the raising of fees, there was an increase in boys enrolled in the primary schools from 5,785 in 1902 to 6,070 in 1903. By 1904, the number of students in schools under government inspection had risen to 140,000 — up from 92,000 in 1903.[48] In 1905, the number of students enrolled in government-funded *kuttabs* had risen to 7,410, a number that rose again to 11,014 by 1907, the year that Cromer left Egypt.[49] By 1911, four years after Gorst and Dunlop began granting a limited number of scholarships to secondary-school students, there were 202,095 students enrolled in 3,644 government-inspected schools as well as 3,535 enrolled in the government's thirteen higher primary schools.[50] Both the British and the Egyptians continued to take part in shaping Egyptians to make them more productive, civilized, and modern. The Egyptian government's quest to modernize Egyptians and the determination of Europeans to make Egyptians useful and civilized often overlapped. Despite differences in their goals, both groups sought to shape Egyptians in their thoughts, habits, and customs.

Egyptian nationalists co-opted British discourse and responded to it within the ambiguities inherent in the British mandate for Egyptian education — between extending education to Egyptians and limiting its scope and focus, between cultivating an educated class and limiting its horizons. Indeed, it was often in the molding of Egyptian schoolchildren's manners and habits that Egyptian nationalists were able to resist the British desires to limit the Egyptians' education and at the same time succeed in creating productive, modern Egyptians. Textbooks of all sorts carried recipes for personal conduct, which often couched powerful lessons in history and politics. Just as often, they connected personal behavior to the project of overturning colonial rule. Sometimes such lessons appeared in texts on manners and morals — in other words, in texts that were, in fact, designed to teach students to behave properly and to be more "modern." Just as often, however, lessons about behavior and its role in liberating Egypt appeared in textbooks on subjects such as reading, math, and geography. In both cases, the message was the same: The personal behavior of the Egyptians was the motor behind history past and present, behind the success of the economy and the fate of the political realm. Learning to count and to read, like learning to brush one's teeth, would lead the nation to triumph.

The public school curriculum in the years following the occupation reveals an increased concern with the private life and the behavior of

Egyptian schoolchildren. In 1885, for example, the public, primary-school curriculum included a course called *durus al-ashya'*, or "object lessons," which included such topics as clothes, keeping one's clothes clean, the use of soap, the house and all its rooms, and how to best build a house.[51] It also included *adab* and *tarbiyya*, which consisted of lessons in basic manners, hygiene, health, clothing, and behavior in and outside the home. Notes to instructors of *durus al-ashya'*, included in the curriculum guides from 1885 and 1887, defined *adab* and *tarbiyya* as being akin to "parental advice or example" given to the student by the instructor.[52] The students emulated the instructor and learned the manners and behaviors that would befit them outside of the classroom.

In 1896 *adab* and *tarbiyya* were separated from *durus al-ashya'*, which, by 1901, was clearly defined as serving to improve the child's intelligence and augment his interest in the "things around him" both in the Europeanized and privately run primary schools and in the elementary schools.[53] In the new curriculum there was a separate class on manners and behavior, called either *tahdhib* (self-edification) or *al-diyanna wal-tahdhib* (religion and self-edification). By 1901, this class sought to produce "the best of human behavior for interactions, at home and outside the home." It addressed the "care of the body, proper clothing, manners for eating, correct times for eating," and the cultivation of private behavior that would assure the preservation of "the order of the public sphere *[al-hi'a al-'umummiyya]*." [54]

By 1907, a course called *al-tarbiyya al-qawmiyya* (national *tarbiyya*) had come into existence when Sa'ad Zaghlul, then minister of education, re-enacted a khedival order of 1867 that called for the separation of Muslims and Christians for classes on religion. Students separated for *diyanna* (religious instruction) were now brought back together for *tarbiyya* and *tahdhib*, making those subjects a national rather than a sectarian affair.[55] The course was taught in the primary and secondary schools as well as the elementary schools, which by 1916 were teaching 10,421 girls and 27,337 boys. By the 1920s, the name of the course was changed to *al-tarbiyya al-wataniyya wa al-akhlaq* (national upbringing and morals).[56]

The "private politics" of habits and manners were the building blocks of programs that taught nationalism and productivity. Cleanliness and personal hygiene, as well as habits and mannerisms proper to the modern era, were central to textbooks on subjects ranging from reading to *adab*. Arabic-language readers, for example, couched cultural critiques in lessons on the Arabic alphabet and grammar and included concrete instructions for self-improvement. A reader published in 1916, for example, contained a chapter called "What Do You Need to Conserve the Health of Your Body?" It included short passages on such topics as cleanliness, proper bathing, and proper clothing. This chapter was immediately followed by another, entitled "Advice on Manners," which addressed eating and drinking in a clean and orderly fashion. Permeating the text were sentences such as "Keep your body upright in walking and sitting; be balanced in your eating and drinking habits"; "Keep your things neat and organized"; and "Always keep your face, hands and clothes clean."[57]

The domicile figured centrally in such textbooks. A reader first printed in 1905, entitled *Reading and Pronunciation,* presented the Arabic alphabet and then listed several hundred simple words, including "wood, bricks, carpenters, engineers, and plumbers." It then repeated those words in the context of basic lessons, asking questions: "What do homes need? . . . How do we build proper houses?" The answer was that "proper homes" — the kinds of homes that produced sound, modern, Egyptians — required "order, cleanliness, and ventilation." Huts, tents, and dark or crowded quarters were listed as dwellings that belonged to "another world," a premodern world, and thus had to be done away with so that a new era could be ushered in.[58]

Cleanliness and personal habits were also addressed in textbooks used to teach *al-tarbiyya al-qawmiyya.* Such texts taught students that their private habits were important to the preservation of their health but also had a bearing on the good of the nation. A book written for the teaching of such a course around 1910 taught students that their love of the nation as small children consisted of doing everything that parents and teachers told them to do when it came to learning manners, "such that you can, later on, be capable of serving your nation. The behavior of ignorant people is vile and is by no means the kind of behavior that will serve the country."[59]

"Private" and "personal" also extended from manners and cleanliness to include the cultivation of "private" characteristics and sensibilities. Virtues such as courage, valor, honesty, and integrity were to be cultivated in the student's private life and applied to the national struggle. Textbooks on morals published in the decades leading up to the revolution outlined the extremely personal nature of habits and customs, as well as virtues and sentiments, that would lead to the creation of a strong and independent nation. All of the characteristics that would later define independent Egypt were first to be cultivated within Egyptians in their personal activities. Textbooks gave very clear instructions for how personal behavior suitable to the nationalist agenda was to be shaped and applied, connecting the good of the self and that of the nation at every turn.

One textbook on morals and virtues, printed in 1913, consisted of a series of dialogues between imaginary students and their teachers. Of particular interest to this study is the first chapter of a text entitled *Kuttaib fi al-tarbiyya al-awaliyya wa al-akhlaq* (Short texts on basic *tarbiyya* and morals) in which the relationship between the construction of self and nation was laid out:

> *Teacher:* I told you how you can become a virtuous man. Remind me of how that is.
>
> *Student:* First of all, I develop strength of self. By that I mean that I should strive to develop my mental faculties — my intelligence, my feelings, and my will. Second . . . I work against all defects of character, guarding myself against anything that might threaten my character. Finally, I devote myself to a love of virtue.
>
> *T:* Where is happiness found?
>
> *S:* I find happiness in the performance of my duties, in the love of work, in the love of my family, in the love of the nation . . . I find happiness in knowledge, in manners, in industry.[60]

The cultivation of manners and virtues, while ultimately the goal of the educational system, was a task that, according to textbooks on many subjects, was to begin at home. The above lesson continued by teaching the student that love of the nation began with the love of his family, and that his family was part of a bigger collective, known as the nation. Manners and morals shaped both families and made them prosper; behavior for the success of one could not be obtained without tending to the other. While the immediate lesson in most of these texts had to do with the shaping of behavior appropriate to the immediate family, children learned that the condition of their family had its bearing upon the nation in toto: "The Nation consists of a group of families. And if the families that make up the nation are enlightened, refined, rich, strong, then so too will the nation be all of those things. And if those families are possessing of fallen morals, if they are poor, if they are uneducated, then the nation, like those families, will be corrupt, poor and backwards."[61]

The modern family was most commonly defined as consisting of a husband and wife and their children. Polygamy was very clearly discouraged, as was the habit — often referred to by Europeans as emblematic of a bygone age — of sharing the domicile with members of the extended family. Thus the family was redefined to fit the models of Victorian domesticity. Arabic readers often contained lessons with titles such as "A Man and His Wife," "A Mother and Her Son," and "A Father and His

Daughter," which laid out very precise definitions for household rela-tionships. Typical of these textbooks were prescriptive phrases such as "A father hopes for love between him and his wife . . . and he sees to the ease of the mother and her children. The father must be generous and stead-fast in the *tarbiyya* and education of his family."[62]

Thus the process of liberating Egypt was made into a very personal struggle for Egyptian schoolchildren. Despite the overwhelming pres-ence of the British in the administration of Egypt's public education system, Egyptian children were taught that they were involved in a per-sonal struggle to save their nation. They learned that their every action, from cleaning and dressing to interacting with their relatives, had a higher meaning. Shaped in the domestic realm, and then transported into the world outside the home, their habits and morals would serve as the foundation upon which modern, independent Egypt would be built.

Mothers of the Future, Visions of the Past: Modern Motherhood and the Making of a New Order

The task of liberating the nation had enormous implications for Egyptian motherhood: once the child learned that his behavior was crucial to the national "project," he learned that a reformed, educated, rational mother would teach him the kinds of morals, virtues, and behavior suitable to an Egyptian in all his affairs. Thus the task of producing mothers who could carry out the national mission became more urgent. Women's education became a project not only of creating educated, literate women but of producing mothers who could lead the home and national family into a new era.

On the eve of the revolution, girls' education had made significant strides since the early days of al-Saniah. In 1899, Cromer reported that girls' education was making "slow but satisfactory progress." More than one thousand girls attended government-sponsored *kuttabs,* and more than two hundred girls attended government-sponsored primary schools in Cairo.[63] By 1912, more than twenty-five thousand girls attended schools under state guidance and inspection.[64] In 1917, al-Saniah enrolled ninety-one women in courses designed to produce primary- and secondary-school teachers.[65]

Two basic premises seem to have underscored the turn-of-the-century mandate on public education as it pertained to girls. The first was that

young women needed a strong moral training. Untrained, poorly educated women were held responsible both by Europeans and Egyptians for
the decay that was found in Egyptian homes and that allegedly manifested
itself in the political and economic behavior of Egyptian men. To remedy
this, girls had to be subjected to a strong moral training so that they could
produce better men.[66] The second premise was that a "modern" home life
was to accompany moral training in the production of a salient motherhood and along with it, a sound modern citizenry. Such a modern home
life was to be cultivated through the science of home economics and modern child rearing and in the industry of sewing, cooking, and cleaning.
While in the 1870s, courses on washing, ironing, and sewing had been created in order to offer "une vie professionielle" to the lower classes
through the production of servants for the upper classes, by the turn of
the century middle- and upper-class women were being taught similar
skills in order to make their homes modern and, therefore, moral. The
project of educating women was not restricted or bound by concerns
about making better women but, rather, had the greater objective of shaping the nation's future.

The question of the cultivation of modern motherhood as a remedy for
what ailed Egypt culturally and politically was placed on the educational
agenda both by Egyptians and the British. Yacoub Artin, for example,
who summarized the achievements of the Egyptian educational system
and offered prescriptions for its improvement in the late 1880s, discussed
the importance of women's education to the national project. Quoting al-
Tahtawi's *al-Murshid al-amin lil-banat wal-binin,* Yacoub stated that the
modernizing project depended upon the creation of a class of women
who could, in *governing* their homes well, produce a generation of men
who would better serve the state. In modern nations, he said, the benefits
of educating women far outweighed the inconvenience of it, for sound
mothers created sound nationalists.[67]

Like many Egyptians, Cromer believed that elevating the moral and
political status of Egyptians would come only through the improvement
of Egyptian women. In an annual report on the condition of Egypt and
the Sudan, Cromer said, "I need not dwell on this subject at any length.
It forms only one part of the very difficult and vitally important social
question connected with the position of women in Egypt and generally
in the East. Possibly, [the situation] will be modified by the spread of education."[68] His policy notwithstanding, Cromer was hesitant to provide the
education through which the lot of Egyptian women was to be improved.
In 1904 he said:

How far the movement now rapidly progressing in favor of female education will eventually modify the ideas, the character and the position of the next generation of Egyptian women remains to be seen. Should any changes in their position take place, it is greatly to be hoped that they will be gradual. . . . Nevertheless, it is equally true that until a gradual change is effected in the position of women in this country the Egyptians, however much they may assimilate the *outward forms,* can never hope to imbibe the true spirit of European civilization in its best aspects.[69]

Despite Cromer's determination that the development of women's education move slowly, the number of educational endeavors designed for girls, and the number of girls enrolled in the public schools, continued to increase. In 1904, for example, the Ministry of Education found both the funds and the enthusiasm necessary for the creation of the Bulaq Normal School for the training of young women to be teachers in the *kuttabs.* There were a number of reasons for the creation of a corps of female teachers to work in those schools. The first was the problem of getting Muslim parents to agree to have their young girls taught by men. The second was the difficulty in finding teachers to instruct the young girls in what was thought of as the "female" branch of elementary education, designed to produce modern mothers and homemakers. Female teachers for girls in the *kuttabs* were to combine the roles of moral training and guidance with a thorough knowledge of the Qur'an, and at the same time they were to be masters of the domestic sciences. Their task was to teach sewing, ironing, washing, cooking, housecleaning, as well as the basics of child rearing.[70]

By 1908, the annual report shows that there were some sixty women enrolled in the school, taking courses such as "the usual book subjects, plain needlework, simple cookery, laundry work and cottage gardening." The same report also states that graduates from the Bulaq Normal School were in great demand, both in Cairo's *kuttabs* and those in the provinces, where the girls' schools were either understaffed or the demand for girls' education had led to the opening of new schools.[71] By 1909, there were more than nineteen thousand girls enrolled in the nation's *kuttabs,* leading Gorst to conclude that "the movement in favour of female education is not restricted to the upper classes."[72]

According to Cromer, the demand for girls' schools grew steadily throughout the first decade of the twentieth century. By 1905 he reported that "the reluctance of parents to send their daughters to schools has been largely abolished. Demands for . . . other [public] schools and . . . private schools . . . have greatly increased."[73] The year he left Egypt, Cromer stated that the "government schools for girls are full to overflowing, and private enterprise is seeking to establish girls' schools in different parts of the country."[74] This he attributed to a change in taste among Egyptian men, to a growing demand that wives be educated "partners" and sophisticated homemakers: "The steady output of boys from the secondary schools and higher colleges has indirectly stimulated the movement for female education, for the younger generation are beginning to demand that their wives should possess some qualities other than those which can be secured in the seclusion of the harem."[75]

Parents began to show an interest not only in securing an education for their daughters but in dictating the *kind* of education that their daughters received. Some thought that female education was too geared toward teaching and asked for a more general education, including an emphasis on the domestic sciences. Some, according to Cromer, regularly visited al-Saniah and, when they found the curriculum lacking, announced that they would find a foreign school or a private tutor.[76] Cromer also noted that most of the girls enrolled in al-Saniah and the primary schools had parents who were paying for their tuition. This convinced him that the number of middle- and upper-class families interested in educating their daughters had increased; previously, the school admitted girls from the lower orders and paid for their tuition.

By 1916, the curriculum for the girls' higher elementary schools, the largest and most well-funded of the *kuttabs,* included Arabic (reading and writing), religion, geography, and a little history. It included a course on general accounting as well as one on "accounting for the home" *(al-hisab al-manzili).* The girls spent two hours a week studying health and hygiene. Finally, they spent twelve hours a week on courses in home economics *(al-tadbir al-manzili),* needlework, washing, ironing, and cooking.[77] Girls in the lower elementary schools also studied needlework and hygiene, albeit for a lesser number of hours. Their curriculum included a subject called "occupations," assumedly cooking and washing.[78]

Girls enrolled in the government's primary schools had a separate course called "moral instruction" in addition to the above-mentioned coursework classes in English. Like their counterparts in the elementary schools, they spent a substantial number of hours learning the domestic sciences, including a class called "housewifery."[79] The curriculum for al-Saniah that same year differed little except in the inclusion of English, physical education, and science. Students also took accounting, home economics, embroidery, cooking, washing, and ironing.[80]

Finally, when the Egyptian University was opened in 1908, it included a series of evening lectures for women. According to the university's "plan of operation" for the 1911–12 academic year, this "women's section" was dedicated to "creating familial happiness among individuals." The curriculum for teaching women included courses on *tarbiyya* and morals, given in French. In addition, they were to have lectures in Arabic on the history of Egypt, both ancient and modern. Finally, courses on home economics included hygiene, choosing the home and its foundation, marital life and happiness of the family, and household manners and morals (*al-adaab al-manziliyya wal-akhlaq*).[81] The home economics course was taught in Arabic in order to make it accessible to the widest audience.

The domicile played a central role in curriculum designed especially for girls, just as it did in the above-mentioned texts for boys. Because building the nation was described as a family affair, the home in which the family resided was the focus of great attention. The home played a number of roles: its location, shape and size, as well as all of its activities constituted a central trope in the textbooks that described how the modern family was supposed to function and how the Egyptian family was to be remade. The home was used to teach the manners and morals befitting the modern home. Instructors used the home as a symbol in stories about history, the nation, and modernity. For women, ordering the home and its activities became intrinsic to defining and illustrating a nationalist agenda.

The quite popular and well-circulated text, *al-Tadbir al-manzili al-hadith* (Modern home economics), which teachers used to teach domestic sciences both in private and in state-sponsored primary and elementary schools, made much ado of the home, both as a physical structure and as the foundation on which the modern nation would be built. An entire chapter of the tenth edition of the book, printed in 1916, was called the "Place of Residence," and included such topics as "How to Chose a Home," "Where the Domicile Should be Located," and "Health and the Home." In the chapter, girls learned that: "the most important thing in the life of a human being is choosing the site of the place of residence. Health, comfort and familial happiness all depend upon this choice. . . . The slaving, toiling, and frustrations that mankind must put up with outside of the home are made easier when one has the right domicile."[82] Girls then learned that the house needed to be near a market, as people could not do without the buying and selling of household goods. The proper home was not to be far from the husband's place of work, as a good part of the day would otherwise be lost to his going to and fro. For health reasons, the house was not to be too close to cemeteries, hospitals, gas works, or standing water. Water pipes should not be situated inside walls, nor should they be too great in number. They were not to be made of poor-quality lead or clay. Windows were to be big and numerous enough to let in the requisite amounts of light and air.[83]

Some texts gave girls explicit instructions on how to clean, organize, and order the interior of their homes. They should organize the house according to seasons and divide it properly for hygienic reasons: the eating and reception space was to be on the ground floor; the first floor was to contain bedrooms and dressing rooms only; higher floors were to be reserved for servants and washrooms.[84] One textbook taught young women what the rooms in their houses should contain. About the *salat al-istiqbal* (reception room): its wood floors needed to be cleaned once or twice weekly. The best curtains were made of heavy material. A medium-sized table in the center of the room, accompanied by three or four small chairs, formed an ideal smoking area. Screens on the windows should prevent the entrance of dirt and insects. Women should hang family pictures in the reception room and should display maps of Egypt, statues of famous figures, and paintings representing Egyptian history.[85] This kind of house would set modern Egyptians apart from the traditional orders.

Once the structure of the modern home was established, clear instructions for life inside it were given. Future mothers were supplied with very precise definitions of their roles: They were the helpmates to their husbands, the support for their spouses. The modern mother was "responsible for taking care of household affairs; she oversees the *tarbiyya* and refinement of her children, and she instills good morals in them when they are small. If she herself is refined, and if she is aware of her responsibilities, then she will be the source of the family's happiness, as well as that of the nation. She will be the foundation for their good *tarbiyya* and their success in life. The mother is the child's first school."[86]

The girls' curriculum in the prerevolutionary decade adhered to the principle that the child's first school was the home. The following "Hymn to Home Economics" *(Nashidat al-tadbir al-manzili)* is emblematic of the role of the home in the creation of a cadre of future nationalists. The hymn was used in *al-tadbir al-manzili*, which was, after 1907, a central part of public and private education from state-run primary and elementary schools to the foreign schools and day schools provided by beneficent organizations. The hymn gives a remarkably good summary of this new "science of the home":

Oh Girls of the New Generation, rise in renaissance, the dawn has come.
Remember God — pray, worship Him, and put on your work clothes.
Organize the things that you must do today.
Wash and make sure that everything gets clean; iron and fold your clothes
    with great care.
Prepare nutritious food for your family.
Sift, crush and clean wheat.
The science of home economics, girls, holds the key to womanhood.
In it lies the secret to good economizing and to a happy life.
Girls, shape the morals of a child, plant virtues and a desire for self-
    refinement in him. Teach him how to rely upon himself.
Teach him all this, and he will know how to love the Nation.[87]

The home, then, was situated as the bedrock of modernity, upon which the nationalist project would be built. The "science of the home," as it was taught in *al-tadbir al-manzili,* assured not only that the home would function as a clean, modern "classroom" but that mothers would be competent teachers. *Al-tadbir al-manzili* was designed to highlight women's place within the nation, to delineate their position as mothers, to describe the mother's concomitant duties and activities, and to teach girls the rights and responsibilities that came along with motherhood. Classroom lessons would be applied to girls' domestic life, ensuring that the new order of Egyptians would be clean, organized, and morally sound. The success of independent Egypt depended on reformed home life.

While children of both sexes were to be the product of reformed home life, this recipe for modernity and political modernization cemented a role for women inside the domicile. The domicile was to be the laboratory in which both boys and girls learned to love the nation; the modern home without the presence of a woman behind its walls, however, could not succeed.

Conclusion

Outside the classroom, young Egyptians were also subject to lessons about their family in the press. Young subscribers to magazines called *al-Talba* (The students), *al-Madrasa* (The school), *al-Talmiz* (The student), *Anis al-talmiz* (The students' companion), and *Dalil al-tulab* (The students' guide) were exposed to general news and current events as well as columns on such topics as education, science, history, short stories, games, and "literary sayings." The magazines served as a general guide to the expectations facing educated, middle-class Egyptians.[88]

Children's journals often alluded to the activities through which children "practiced" the home economics of nationalism both in the private and the public realms. Sometimes those activities were as simple as structured play in model homes, wherein teachers supervised children in the practice of cleaning and cooking and acting out the roles of good fathers and good mothers.[89] Some magazines, like *al-Tarbiyya* and *al-Talba*, carried a "girls' column," or *"bab al-banat,"* which described activities like bathing dolls and "tea parties" for both boys and girls as part of "practicing" home life.[90] In addition to lessons learned at school, games and activities were designed to complete the child's lessons in behavior appropriate to the new order.

Other activities asked children to apply the principles of *tadbir al-manzil* to arenas and projects that, on the surface, appear to have nothing to do with the domicile. *Al-Tarbiyya* and *al-Talba*, for example, routinely recounted events in which students were required to demonstrate the principles of order, routine, and cleanliness that they learned at home and in the classroom in a distinctly public arena. In early March 1905, for example, *al-Tarbiyya* announced that the Ministry of Education had held its annual celebration of fitness *(hafla sanawiyya fil-riyada al-badaniyya)* in al-Gazira Square on February 16. According to the journal, the students demonstrated the goals of the Ministry of Education by performing various kinds of organized marches up and down the square and by playing certain kinds of sports and games. In attendance were teachers, members of the government, both foreign and Egyptian, and the khedive himself. When the students passed before their audience, they chanted "Long live the Khedive; long live Egypt." Those in attendance were said to have been most impressed with the order and discipline of the children, as well as the fitness of their bodies. It was reported that the marches "embodied the goals of public education, the life of the nation, and the progress of Egyptian youth."[91] Various schools and students won prizes for foot races, jumping, hurdling, and tug of war. Prizes were also given, however, for discipline and order; those schools that performed the best organized marches were given special merit. By applying the tenets of *tadbir* and home economics to their physical bodies, students thus not only impressed their leaders and won distinction but extended the project of reforming domestic space into a distinctly public realm.

Because journals were subject to less scrutiny from the colonial government than were school curricula, the messages delivered to children in them were often outright revolutionary.[92] In late November 1908, for example, the journal *al-Talba* published the contents of a speech given by its editor 'Abd al-Hamid Hamdi at the opening of a new theater in Cairo, Dar al-tamthil al-'arabi (the Arab theater).[93] Nationalism, as it is portrayed in Hamdi's address and in other editions of *al-Talba,* was presented as a concept that was taught, or performed, for an audience that would learn and practice it. Hamdi presented the nation as a theater in which various acts of morality, courage, and valor were acted out and in which behavior was shaped. Learning one's lessons well in the theater qua school of morals, he said, was crucial to the national drama's dénouement: only when all the actors had learned to play their proper roles could the drama's final act — liberation — take place.

Hamdi linked the national theater to the children's homes, telling the students in his audience that in their homes they were to learn and play roles that would ultimately reform their families and make them stronger. At the same time, in the theater of the reformed family, children would actually be practicing the drama that would ultimately liberate their nation.[94] He said:

The nation is to the continent what the family is to the home. Now let us assume that we have a family living in the house in the middle of the woods, and that the father of this family is a tyrant, prohibiting the family members to move about freely, telling them that they have only to eat and drink and do what he deems their responsibilities, and that anything other than those things will incur his anger and his punishment. Let us also assume that the family members do not know any better, and that they do not have the kind of information that would inform them that they have more rights than just eating and drinking and staying confined to the house, or that they must completely obey the tyrant who lords over them. Is it reasonable for us to think that, given the circumstances, the family is going to want to, or be able to, participate with the father in the affairs of the home? Is it even going to occur to the family that such participation is their right?

This is an example of a nation governed by an autocrat, a tyrant, in the middle of the jungle of ignorance. It neither knows its rights, nor is it capable of attaining them. It would never occur to them to ask for independence.[95]

In this drama, that of the dethroning of the autocrat, the tyrant father only disappears when children act their domestic roles properly. For the nation to have within it an informed, politically active body politic, the good father has to replace the tyrant father as the head of a reformed family. Hamdi continued:

Let us return to the family: If it was granted to them that they be guided to the knowledge of what their rights and responsibilities were toward the father, then it would not take the family long to demand a more reciprocal relationship, nor would it take long for the family members to take an active role in the administration of the home's affairs. And if the family were made to know its neighbors, and made to know their relationship to those neighbors, then both their domestic affairs and their external affairs would improve. This is the same thing that happens to the nation when knowledge spreads within it: all those within it start to recognize what their responsibilities to the leader are, and what his responsibilities to them are. The nation begins to recognize its rights, and then demand them; slowly, the family begins to participate in the running of the nation's affairs.[96]

In equating the nation and its reform with that of the family, Hamdi delivered a powerful message to Egypt's children: The unseating of the old khedival order, responsible for the political, fiscal, and cultural decay that had brought about Egypt's occupation, was a familial affair in which they were to play a central part.[97] On their shoulders fell the burden of learning the roles that would bring about the downfall of the tyrant father and the ascension of his replacement.

The 1919 Revolution saw symbols such as *bayt al-umma* (house of the nation), which was the nickname for Sa'ad Zaghlul's home, and *umm al-masriyyeen* (mother of the Egyptians) the nickname of Zaghlul's wife, Safia. Such titles were not merely endearing terms for beloved leaders. Rather, symbols such as "house" and "mother" embodied the national struggle as they were defined in the classroom.

Schoolchildren were not isolated from or unfamiliar with the ideal behavior of those who would ultimately lead the nation to independence. The modern, morally sound, organized behavior of the leaders of the new order embodied by the Zaghluls in 1919 was replicated for schoolchildren daily, both in the classroom and in the domestic realm that they were helping to transform. Children learned that the roles played by leaders in the private realm brought the nation success in the political realm. As they acted out those roles along with their leaders, children participated directly in the birth of their nation.

CHAPTER 5

Table Talk

The Home Economics of Nationhood

From the 1870s onward discussions of the home and the family and their relationship to politics were not limited to state-produced literature. In an active, popular, and privately funded press, a generation of educated Egyptians, both Ottoman-Egyptian and Arabophone, articulated sentiments about themselves and politics that echoed state-sponsored projects. *Effendi* debates over what it meant to be Egyptian were full of references to domestic and marital habits. Likewise, their critiques of Egyptian politics reflected the idea that Egypt's advancement toward constitutional government could be measured by the behavior of its elite classes. After the British occupation of 1882 and the subsequent imprisonment or exile of many prominent publishers and journalists, the native press went dormant for a decade. But in the years following Tawfiq's death in 1892 and the ascension of his son 'Abbas Hilmy II (r. 1892–1914) to the throne, political journalism reemerged and flourished.

Unlike Tawfiq, 'Abbas was openly against the occupation and encouraged *effendi* journalists to use the press to voice their opposition to the British. From the early 1890s, the tendency to couch discussions of nationalism and politics in domestic terms became more common as elite Egyptians used the press to counter British claims about the state of their homes, families, and, hence, their body politic. Until 1907, when the British allowed Egyptians to form political parties, the press alone provided the *effendiyya* with an arena for expressing nationalist sentiment and for shaping political platforms. The pages of privately printed books and periodicals from the early 1890s onward thus voiced the aspirations of an increasingly articulate and frustrated generation of Egyptians in discussions that often appeared to be more about housekeeping than political reform. By the eve of World War I, at which point 144 locally produced journals played a substantial role in shaping public opinion, Egyptians of all classes had become exposed to the family politics of challenging British rule.[1]

Cultivation, Domestication, and Critique: The 1870s and the Spread of Gendered Nationalism

From the last years of Isma'il's reign onward, the press was increasingly the arena in which students and graduates of the state's civil schools articulated their desires and demands.[2] From the mid-1870s onward Egypt could claim a private press that concerned itself with politics, making it accessible to ordinary Egyptians. Isma'il himself was enamored of the periodical press and saw it as symbolic of Europe's cultural and political progress. His willingness to allow private Egyptians to fund and print their own newspapers, coupled with substantial increases over the course of the 1860s and 1870s in the number of literate Egyptians, led to an astonishing boom in the late 1870s in the number of privately printed books, Egyptian newspapers, and Egyptians who could read them. Between the early 1860s and the early 1880s, the press went from a readership of zero to tens of thousands.[3] Despite scant circulation statistics for the 1870s and 1880s, many have estimated that some periodicals circulated thousands of copies. Acknowledging individual copies that circulated among family members, "readership" estimates climb even higher.[4] The nascent press was often censored or shut down and its editors were frequently exiled from the last days of Isma'il's rule through the early 1890s. Nonetheless, a new relationship evolved between the embattled Egyptian government and a class of Egyptians struggling to define themselves as well as their relationship to local and international politics.

Isma'il's enthusiasm for the press (he started his own propaganda organ in 1866, *Wadi al-Nil* [The Valley of the Nile]), favorable market forces, and an increasingly enthusiastic reading audience led to the emergence of a whole host of privately funded periodicals from the late 1860s onward, including *al-Ahram* (The pyramids) — later to be one of Egypt's most widely read newspapers — which began circulation in August of 1876. Christian editors such as Salim al-Naqqash (*al-'Asr al-Jadid* [The new era], founded in 1880; and *al-Mahrusa* (1880) [The divinely pro-

tected]) and Mikha'il 'abd al-Sayyid (*al-Watan* [The nation], 1877) took
advantage of the press boom to join Muslims 'Abdullah Nadim (*al-Tankit
wal-Tabkit* [Mockery and reproach], 1881) and Hasan al-Shamsi (*al-Mufid*
[The informer], 1881) — among others — in discussing local and international events, the khedives, the rising influence of Europeans in Egypt,
Westernization, Islamic reform, independence, the economy, taxes, and
education. *Al-Ahram* was the only newspaper in the 1870s that concen-
trated on reporting hard news; the rest of the periodicals were filled with
essays and editorials, many of which waged fiery critiques against a government that appeared to ignore the demands of the *effendiyya* to take a
greater role in matters of state. The lion's share of these periodicals were
published in Arabic.[5] While editors differed in political orientation —
some encouraged continued Ottoman sovereignty while others demanded Egypt for the Egyptians — they appear united in their demands
for increased political participation for Arabophone Egyptians in politics.
Because of its popularity in the period leading up to the 'Urabi revolt,
Tawfiq passed a press law to limit journalists' activities in 1881. The law
allowed the government to suppress publications if they appeared to vio-
late public order or propriety.[6]

During this period the family began to appear as a trope in the periodical press. It served to criticize khedival politics, European intervention
in local affairs, and resistance to the rise of constitutional government in
Egypt. The familial trope became a means of lampooning the ruling elite
and for describing Egypt's position in the "modern" world. The most
outstanding examples of political critiques couched in domestic, familial
images are found in Yaqoub Sannu°'s (1839–1912) satirical journal, *Abu
Nazzara Zarqa'* (The man with the blue spectacles). *Abu Nazzara,* as it
was known, made its first appearance in Egypt in 1877. In 1878, Isma'il
exiled its editor to Paris, but loyal readers smuggled the journal into
Egypt. Research suggests that it was widely read and read out loud to illiterate Egyptians.[7] One foreign sojourner in Egypt wrote of Sannu°'s
papers that "there was hardly a donkey boy of Cairo, or of any of the
provincial towns, who had not heard them read, if he could not read them
himself; and in the villages I can testify to their influence."[8] The journal
waged relentless invective against Isma'il, his government, and foreign
occupation. *Abu Nazzara* was written in colloquial Egyptian-Arabic in
order to heighten the distinction between the Ottoman Turkish spoken
by many members of the ruling elite and to make the paper accessible to
the *fellaheen.* Indeed, even those periodicals in the 1870s and 1880s that did
not print in colloquial Arabic used a simple prose style that reflected an

interest in as wide a readership as possible.[9] The journal frequently criticized Isma'il's treatment of the peasants and the urban working classes and contrasted the life of the peasantry with Isma'il's extravagant lifestyle. *Abu Nazzara* consistently lamented the paucity of arenas in which Arabophone Egyptians could participate in politics.

Sannu' was a product of Egyptian state education. The son of an Italian emigrant to Egypt, he was an Egyptian Jew raised in Alexandria. His father served as tutor to one of Mohammad 'Ali's nephews, and Sannu' himself served as a tutor in the khedival household after returning from an educational mission to Europe. Sannu' taught at Cairo's Polytechnic Institute in the 1860s and turned his attention to writing theatrical satire in the early 1870s. He incurred the wrath of Isma'il for his pointed comments about the khedive's household, polygamy, the increased influence of Europeans in Egypt, and his bold support of Isma'il's uncle, 'Abd al-Halim, as contender for the throne. He was thus exiled to France in 1878.[10] Sannu' depicted Isma'il's delight at his banishment in a caricature published in the September 15, 1878, edition of *Abu Nazzara*. Underneath the dancing khedive, the caption read: "Say this about Abu Nazzara: He's traveling tomorrow, oh my brothers! In our Egypt he was a blossom. May he prosper and return to us. Say this about the *'sheikh al-hara'*: Tomorrow he'll be absorbed [in other things], oh my brothers! Abu Nazzara came to a bad end. You haven't heard the last of him."[11]

Abu Nazzara posed arguments in favor of the establishment of some form of constitutional rule in Egypt and paeans to the readiness and ability of Egyptians for such rule. It did so through caricatures of Isma'il and his family — sad (and sometimes vulgar) reminders of why truly representative politics had not yet found a home in Egypt. Such critiques of khedival politics are illustrated by Sannu's many caricatures of Isma'il, whom he frequently referred to as "Pharaon" (the pharaoh) and whom he commonly depicted as fat, clumsy, and idiotic. Sannu's caricatures hint at a sordid domestic life, bad parentage, and errant children attempting to run Egypt and its political and economic affairs.

The frivolities of Isma'il's private life were often used to critique the khedive and his policies. On one occasion, Sannu' depicted the khedive surrounded by Parisian show girls. Sannu's choice of Parisian women can be read either as a jab at Isma'il's fondness for all things French, or as a reference to Sannu's place of exile. The khedive's attire in this particular caricature made him out to be something akin to a mystic: He was barefoot and donned a robe rather than trousers and a waistcoat. Later, after Isma'il had himself been exiled, Sannu' chose to cast him as a European

FIGURE I. "Punish him with a belt." *Abu Nazzara Zarqa'*, June 24, 1879.

"peasant," dancing amid a group of women. The Arabic caption read: "The banished one acts the part of a 'Napolitani,' and lessens his anxieties through dancing."[12] In both cases, the company of women and indulgence in senseless gaiety appear to mark the tenor of Isma'il's politics. A kind of idiocy is indeed central to both caricatures. A set of wings attached to the khedive's back in the September 15, 1878, caricature suggests a kind of other-worldliness. Indeed, various depictions of the khedive from the late 1870s have him wearing wings and threatening — or promising — to use them to fly away. Magic and mysticism, rather than prudence, appear to guide his actions.

Isma'il, as an errant, incapable child, was the subject of a front-page cartoon from *Abu Nazzara* from the summer of 1879 (see Figure 1).[13] Tawfiq sits on the khedival throne, surrounded by a large crowd of applauding Europeans. A German who resembles Bismarck holds Isma'il on his knee. The fallen khedive's trousers have been pulled down, exposing his buttocks. His feet are held by an Egyptian *fellah* while the German vigorously spanks him. The Arabic caption reads: "Punish him with a belt.

FIGURE 2. "The milk of knowledge." *Abu Nazzara Zarqa'*, August 19, 1879.

Give him one on his arse. He's a disobedient boy. He doesn't listen to what our leader says." The *fellah* suggests that he be punished with a belt, an allusion to the frequent use of the courbash to which the peasants were subjected under Isma'il's reign. (The French caption calls the punishment well deserved but insufficient.) Isma'il is captured as idiotic, childlike, and wholly helpless in front of his replacement, Tawfiq, and the Europeans who orchestrated Tawfiq's rule.

The journal also critiqued the childhoods of Egypt's rulers. Another image from *Abu Nazzara* shows politics to be the lot of motherhood — in this case, unsound motherhood (see Figure 2). The cartoon depicts the transfer of power from the hands of Isma'il to Tawfiq. The new khedive is depicted as an infant at the breast of Prime Minister Sherif, who was known to support nationalism and constitutional rule. Sherif was originally appointed by Isma'il in 1879, shortly before Isma'il deposition, and he resigned shortly after Tawfiq took power because of the new khedive's unwillingness to champion parliamentary politics. The foreign nations that encouraged the Ottomans to depose Isma'il stand in the background. In French the caption reads: "The Premier of Egypt offers his Master the milk of knowledge; their friends celebrate his crowning and offer him pretty presents."[14] In Arabic, the caption states: "Sherif the wet nurse offers his 'bizz' [teat] to the 'little Pharaoh.' The great nations have brought him toys which they use to satisfy him upon the arrival of the *firman*[15] [announcing Tawfiq's ascension to the throne]. The sons of Egypt witness [such acts] and are agonized by them."

A number of readings of this caricature are certainly possible. Sherif's career as Egypt's Prime Minister (1879, 1881–82, and 1882–84) was tied to the country's nationalist movement. Sannu°'s decision to clothe Sherif as a "woman" might be an indication of his ire at the nationalists' inability to establish constitutionalism in Egypt, the failure of Isma'il and his ministers to stop the transfer of power to a weak khedive, and their failure to stave off European interference in Egypt's affairs. But Sannu°'s decision to clothe Sherif in female attire and depict him breast-feeding Tawfiq suggests another agenda. One has to wonder if perhaps the lampoon is also aimed at Tawfiq: Did Sannu' mean to suggest that Tawfiq was cooperative with the British and leery of legislative reforms because of the very lineage that produced him? Does Sherif represent the aspirations of the nationalist movement, or does he symbolize Tawfiq's heritage as the bastard son of a deposed ruler and as a puppet khedive? While Sherif's presence in the caricature suggests the potential power of the prime minister to infuse Tawfiq with the virtues of nationalism, the presence of the West indicates that Sherif failed. In such a light, the triumph of foreign interference in Egyptian politics seems to be represented as the product of lineage, and breast milk as the transmitter of unsound rule. The European powers with their rattles and other children's toys are reminiscent of nannies, again evoking domestic images and linking them with the occupation.

In the spring of 1882, years after Isma'il's deposition, the family politics of the royal household were once again subjected to lampoon. At this time, Khedive Tawfiq struggled to control both the actions of his cabinet and his relations with the European powers. In yet another image from *Abu Nazzara*, Isma'il sneaks up on a robust female servant, licentiously gazing at her backside, and, finally, giving in to the "devil," who appears to lead him on. A eunuch witnesses events (see Figure 3).[16] The caricature is called the "Question du Cabinet" and is reminiscent of the commonly circulated stories of Tawfiq's birth in which Isma'il overtook a comely slave girl in a harem "cabinet d'aissances" and, hence, secured a male heir

Question de Cabinet

FIGURE 3. "The cabinet question." *Abu Nazzara Zarqa'*, May 12, 1882.

for himself. Once again, the khedive's political follies appear to be conflated with unsound patrilineal and domestic practices.

Thus, prior to the occupation, the private life and domestic habits of the khedives had already become targets for critiquing the body politic. Even in the early stages of articulating nationalism and alternatives to khedival rule, Egyptians could not detach the political realm from domestic behavior. Domestic politics were positioned to create behavior worthy of a modern nation-state.

The Press, Political Culture, and the Making of a Nationalist Lexicon

The exile of many dissident editors, the Press Laws of 1881, and the events of 1882 all served to limit and silence the press throughout most of the 1880s. One historian refers to the press in the period from 1882 to 1892 as having experienced an "intellectual paralysis" as the result of the shock of the occupation.[17] When 'Abbas Hilmy II took the throne, however, a new era of freedom and activity was inaugurated, and the number of non-governmental, privately funded newspapers increased tremendously. 'Abbas encouraged a press that vociferously denounced the occupation and encouraged a renewed and reformed khedival rule. The release and return of imprisoned journalists coupled with 'Abbas's tolerance led to an articulate anti-occupation press of many varieties. Cromer's determination not to curtail freedom of the press in Egypt played a significant role in the continued development of the free press until the outbreak of World War I. As the result of his tolerance, however, the occupation — as well as the occupiers — became the target of the *effendiyyas*'s intellectual focus.

Throughout the 1890s and into the first decade of the twentieth century, the politics of the occupation, the paucity of administrative opportunities for Egyptians, and the lack of organized political parties caused "the Egypt question" to continue to be the outstanding issue of the day. The task of defining "Egypt," its aspirations, its history, its citizenry, and the "nationalist" riposte to the occupation, shaped journalism throughout that decade. In other words, while the objects of the nationalist struggle were clear, the terms of the struggle were as yet undefined. While no consensus materialized about the nature of the struggle against the British, the habits of hearth and home were a common thread in the fabric of emerging political movements.

Immigrant Syrian Christians played a central role in the Egyptian press after 1882. Indeed, 15 percent of papers published between 1873 and 1907 were founded by expatriate Syrians. Syrian-Egyptian papers did not tend to report news; rather, they were aimed at cultivating reading habits among the Egyptian *effendiyya* and to spreading the ideals of the French enlightenment.[18] The hugely successful *al-Muqtataf* (Selections) was first published in Egypt in 1896 by Yaqoub Sarruf (1852–1927) and Faris Nimr (1856–1951) in order to encourage the exchange of ideas among Egyptian intellectuals (both native-born and émigré). The paper was reported to have a circulation of three thousand by 1892 — an outstanding number of readers for that time.[19] Likewise, Jurji Zeidan's (1861–1914) *al-Hilal* (The crescent) opened in 1892 and was "concerned with the human condition." It specialized in articles on Arab history and culture as well as the Arabic language.[20] Like *al-Muqtataf, al-Hilal* was immediately successful and enjoyed a circulation of ten thousand by 1897.[21]

Syrian-born Muslim Rashid Rida (1865–1935) joined his fellow Syrians in contributing to the intellectual blossoming of the 1890s. His periodical *al-Manar* (The lighthouse), published between 1898 and 1935,

addressed the issue of the "Islamic community's cultural and political orientation," advancing the position that "Islam, properly interpreted in light
of modern developments, was the only response to the challenges of the
day."[22]

Native-born Egyptians also joined the rush to publish in the 1890s.
With the backing of 'Abbas, 'Ali Yusuf (1863–1913) published *al-Mu'ayyad*
(The strengthened), which remained in circulation for twenty-three years
following its first edition of 1889. The paper supported an "Islamic, anti-
British cause" and published articles by Mustafa Kamil, Mohammad
Farid, Ahmad Lutfi al-Sayyid, and Sa'ad Zaghlul — all of whom became
central figures in the Egyptian nationalist movement.[23] Yusuf later used
the paper to promote the goals of his party, al-Hizb al-Islah al-Dusturi
(Constitutional Reform Party) after its founding in 1907. Mustafa Kamil
(1874–1908) published his own journal, *al-Liwa'* (The standard) in
1900 — a journal that would later serve as the mouthpiece for his political party, al-Hizb al-Watani (Nationalist Party). Like 'Ali Yusuf, Kamil
promoted an anti-British stance but in terms that were Egyptian secular-
ist, rather than Islamic. The People's Party (Hizb al-Umma), led by
Ahmad Lutfi al-Sayyid (1872–1963), published *al-Jarida* (The paper) in
1907, again articulating a form of Egyptian, secular nationalism.

While the political platforms — like the intellectual orientations — of
each of these papers differed, they seemed to be united by their attention
to defining what it meant to be an educated Egyptian around 1900. The
political essay took pride of place in the press of the day; the two hundred
thousand readers who bought weekly and monthly newspapers in 1900
read essays and editorials on such topics as politics, economics, history,
and Western and Islamic civilization. Inherent to essay writing in the
1890s and early 1900s was a struggle to define the Egyptian condition and
to "place" Egypt relative to other nations and to the West that had
occupied it.

Throughout the 1890s, Egyptian-ness was most frequently evoked and
articulated through debates and discussions that, at least on the surface,
had little to do with the high politics of the British, the khedives, and constitutions. While certainly engaged in the struggle to define Egypt's role
in the battle against imperialism, the press in the 1890s also helped define
modern Egypt. The press discussed issues such as financial self-sufficiency,
advanced knowledge of science and history, and table manners.
Discussions about domestic politics defined "Egypt," "Egyptian," and
"Egypt-ness" as they pertained to resistance and national transformation.
Such discussions transcended ethnic or religious categories — Muslim-

Copt, pro- and anti-Ottoman, Syrian-Christian émigré — that are usually attributed to turn-of-the-century Egyptians.[24] Discussions and debates about households and their activities made "Egyptian modern" into a kind of new religion, a foundation for nationalism, and a means of shaping a common, national (bourgeois) culture.

Periodicals from the 1880s were already publishing articles on the home, its contents, and its inhabitants. Mona Russell, for example, cites an 1881 article from *al-Muqtataf*, "The Decoration of the Home," as well as later articles on decorating the table and arranging the salon and home furniture.[25] Likewise, throughout the 1880s *al-Ahram* published reports of the "royal couple" Tawfiq and Amina at events connected to the state: a military parade in Alexandria in 1883;[26] the opening of a new railway station and the inauguration of public utilities projects in the Delta;[27] and the grand openings of new theaters and other houses of culture in Cairo.[28] Despite the presence of the British in Egypt — or perhaps because of it — Tawfiq and his wife appeared to have been linked to the continued progress of the Egyptian state. In both cases the home and domestic habits were vaguely tied to modernization.

From the 1890s onward, however, that connection became more explicit. Newspaper columns dedicated to topics pertaining to the home often set the terms for defining Egyptian "national" and Egyptian "modern." Political journals were full of articles on women and "questions" about their position in Egyptian society. Oftentimes, periodicals dedicated to "politics" and "science" also included columns called *tadbir al-manzil* ("household organization" or "home economics") in which subjects superficially pertaining to women actually couched greater discussions and debates. Definitions of Egypt, narrations of Egyptian history, and articulations of nascent bourgeois nationalist culture all coalesced in columns on home economics.

Jurji Zeidan's monthly journal, *al-Hilal*, for example, carried a semiregular column called "Hadith al-ma'ida," or "Table Talk."[29] According to the editors, the column was included in the journal to give "healthy advice on food and drink and other household needs." By early September 1900, it also came to include advice on the family and its health: "We call it table talk in order to indicate that it includes the kinds of things that should be talked about, in terms of food, and, at the same time, humorous and useful topics of discussion."[30] The table was thus positioned to address health; at the same time, food, eating, and table manners shaped discussions that were considered useful to Egyptian families.

'Abdullah Nadim (1845–96), who was exiled for his role in the 'Urabi rebellion and only brought back to Egypt in 1892, also included the discussion of household topics in his monthly journal *al-Ustadh* (The professor), which was published between August 1892 and June 1893. *Al-Ustadh* was best known for carrying satirical attacks on Lord Cromer and his policies, so much so that Cromer demanded Nadim's expulsion from Egypt. The journal did not have a regular *tadbir al-manzil* column, but "household" topics and debates involving the domestic realm were as frequent to it as articles on politics. A sampling of articles from 1892 reflects the editors' preoccupation with political agendas of the day: "The Path by Which Public Opinion Can be Established"; "Our Progress: Yesterday and Today"; "Uplifting the Nation;" "The Constitution"; "Progress and Politics"; and "Copts, Muslims and Unification."

Articles on politics also dipped into the domestic realm, and household issues were often used as a means of discussing nationalism, politics, and national "progress." Articles such as "National Life," from August 30, 1892, and "Why They Progressed and We Did Not, Even Though We Were All Created Equally," from November of the same year, both attached "progress" and "nationalism" to the ability of governments to centralize and enforce education. The journal argued that government reorganization in Egypt had strengthened the family not only because it had improved Egypt's material landscape but also because it had provided the education for establishing new templates for behavior.[31]

Discussions of manners and morals, inside the home and out, were often a means through which Egyptian-ness was negotiated. A long article called "Morals and Habits," printed in *al-Ustadh* over the summer of 1892, used women's clothing as a means of articulating class and regional differences within Egypt and to distinguish Egyptian women from others (Arabs and Turks, for example). Precise, detailed discussions of women's clothing served not only to provide a "national" panorama of habits but rather to highlight the editors' "knowledge" of women and their personal habits, both in and outside the home.

The household was most thoroughly revealed, interrogated, and politicized in *al-Ustadh* through fictional "conversations" between women of different classes, on the "problems" they faced at home: how they arranged their households, took care of household affairs, raised their children, and interacted with their neighbors. A "conversation" from 1892 between two fictional characters, "Hanifa" and "Latifa," revealed the different kinds of problems women had with their sons. The women discussed what to do about their sons' drinking, for example, and their laziness. They plotted how to go about getting their sons engaged to "good" women, future wives who would not only continue to supervise the behavior of these men but oversee a solid domestic realm and produce sound children.[32] Likewise, "Hafsa" and her daughter, "Salma," talked about organizing the pantry, both for optimal savings and the preservation of the health of each of the household's members. The home, Hafsa claimed, was like a little kingdom, wherein order in the pantry (the cabinet), would assure order, health, and productivity at every level.[33]

Two final female characters, "Zakiyya" and "Nefissa," argued about which type of education would make them productive at every level of their lives. Nefissa's school taught piano, ballroom dancing, and foreign languages along with reading, writing, and sewing. Zakiyya's school taught her reading, writing, math, morals, *tarbiyya,* and household organization. She convinced her friend that the most important part of education was the lessons to women about organizing their homes, since the home was where "Egyptian" customs were formed and shaped. Ballroom dancing, she argued, was a fun and fancy art, and there was nothing inherently wrong with learning it. But, like the learning of foreign languages, it would lead Zakiyya's friend to marry a foreign husband, live in a foreign household, and practice foreign customs at home. She would therefore produce children who did not have "Egyptian" habits and morals and who would be unlike their Egyptian peers.[34]

Marital practices and the habits of couples inside and outside of the home were common topics of discussion in the early nationalist press. Newspapers and magazines discussed proper ages for marriage, the pros and cons or arranged marriages, and choosing the "right" spouse. Rashid Rida's *al-Manar* often ran articles about the home, questions pertaining to families, and "Egyptian behavior." In one such article, Rida claimed that if reformers really wanted to create a sense of Egyptian identity, they had to start by reforming Egyptian home life. He argued that the biggest problem affecting domestic life was the marital practices of a new generation of Egyptian men, who were refusing to marry women who were not well educated. The education of women who would influence their husbands and children at home was, according to Rida, the first step in the struggle to create a national Egyptian lifestyle. Rida explained, "However you want your men to be, make women that way, for their hand is the one which carries the greatest influence."[35]

Perhaps the most outstanding example of the convergence of science, politics, and "the domestic sciences" from the 1890s was the monthly journal *al-Muqtataf,* published by Faris Nimr and Yaqoub Sarruf.[36] *Al-*

Muqtataf ran articles on history, economics, science, and politics. In addition, it ran a regular column on *tadbir al-manzil*. According to the "banner" that accompanied the column each month, the editors included *tadbir al-manzil* as a regular feature in order to "explicate and illustrate topics of general importance to members of the household *[ahl al-bayt]* and knowledge about the *tarbiyya* of children, the planning of meals, clothing, living quarters, decoration, and things to that effect. This knowledge will benefit each member of the family."[37]

The January 1, 1895, edition of *al-Muqtataf,* for example, ran a cover story on "the future of civilization," which appraised the political systems of Western Europe and the United States and sized up the institutions, individuals, and relationships that characterized modern politics in those societies. The article was a translation of an essay by the American writer Henry George and was serialized over several editions. On May 1, "The Future of Civilization" was followed by a *tadbir al-manzil* column that discussed the subject of "cleanliness." The anonymous author of "The Secrets of Cleanliness" asked why it was that Egyptian clothes and bodies got so dirty and what could be done about it. He began by discussing Egypt's "cleaner" past, saying:

If a high priest from the pharaonic era, one who witnessed the days when the ancient Egyptians like Ramses the Great ruled the earth, when naked and barefoot women washed and drank water from the Nile and its canals, water that in those days was not polluted, saw what the Nile has become, he would cry. After witnessing how the ancients worshipped the Nile, not even letting their animals go in it, he would be horrified to see the corpses of animals that regularly float down it, as well as the sewers of the cities and villages that regularly empty into it. He would prefer to go back to living in the land of the dead.[38]

The author did not claim to know why Egypt and the Egyptians had become so dirty, especially, he said, given the injunctions against dirtiness found in both Islam and Christianity. He did claim, however, that modernity was characterized by cleanliness and that it required cleanliness; therefore, teaching Egyptians the "secrets of cleanliness" would not only bring them into the age of modernity but would also allow them to imitate their great ancestors. Egypt, he claimed, was characterized by special dirt problems; all countries faced dirt, but Egypt's geography produced difficult conditions that modern Egyptians had to understand and overcome. His approach to Egypt's problem was quite scientific:

What is true about Egypt is that clothes get dirty easily because of the dust in the wind that sticks to them, as well as the dirt that the body excretes. . . . You can't get that kind of dirt out by brushing it off, or by shaking it out, or by washing with water alone, because the human body excretes twenty-three ounces of sweat every twenty-four hours. When it dries, it doesn't go away; rather, more than an ounce of it sticks to our skin. We don't feel it, but we produce it from our ordinary everyday activities. It gets into our skin, and from our skin it gets into our clothes. . . . It won't come out unless you mix an alkaline solution with the water in which you wash the clothes.[39]

The author then went on to describe the proper mixtures of soap and solution and the correct temperature of hot water.

Tadbir al-manzil thus played a number of roles in the male-authored nationalist press. It prescribed the direct application of science to the home, ensuring that knowledge and scientific activity were not overlooked in the domicile. The author's insistence upon "Egyptian dirt" created a common culture or common Egyptian-ness, presenting a problem with which all Egyptians were bound to struggle. Finally, the scientific battle against dirt within the modern Egyptian household allowed Egyptians not only to become modern but to reconcile themselves with their ancient history. The modern application of science made the home the vehicle through which modernity was claimed and past greatness articulated.

The creation of Egyptian-ness through the home was also a prominent feature of the women's press in the 1890s.[40] *Al-Fatah* (The young woman) was edited by Hind Nawwal (c. 1860–1920) and was the first Egyptian women's magazine. The journal made its first appearance on November 30, 1892, and was announced as a "Scientific, Historical, Literary, Satirical Newspaper." *Al-Fatah* regularly carried a *tadbir al-manzil* column and featured articles on such topics as health, economics, and *tarbiyya*. Like the male-authored press, it contained articles that consistently blurred the boundaries between public and private, domestic and political. In its fourth issue, for example, from March 1892, the journal ran an article in its *tadbir al-manzil* column called "The Politics of the Home," in which the relationship between the home and the public realm was clearly delineated. The author claimed that *tadbir al-manzil* was one of the most important issues of the age because it was a science through which moderation or balance was known and practiced between husbands and wives, mothers and children, housewives and servants. Such balance was crucial to relations both inside the home and in the public sphere: "The house that is well-mannered and well-furnished enables its [male] owner to learn and take charge of the rights and responsibilities he has to the members of his household, *and those outside of his household*. It enables the master of the house to supervise his servants and to supervise the politics of his servants with his children."[41] Those politics included teaching children obedience, manners, science, and the knowledge of their rights and responsibilities. The science of home economics, then, was responsible for shaping social relations, those of equality and disparity; relations outside the home would thus depend on lessons learned at home, and the domicile was rendered indispensable to politics. A subsequent issue of *al-Fatah* claimed that lack of attention to the politics of the home, as they were shaped by *tadbir al-manzil*, led nations to ruin. Nations that neglected *tadbir al-manzil* also "neglect human rights, ruin the morals of their citizens, weaken their minds, and lessen their chance of earning a living."[42] Far from being separate from politics, or being the lot of women alone, home economics is depicted here as shaping morals and productivity, and as ruining nations or helping them to advance.

Alexandra Avierino's (1872–1926) *Anis al-Jalis* (The intimate companion) did not have a regular column on *tadbir al-manzil* but did frequently include articles on such topics as *al-hayah al-manziliyya* (domestic life); *sh'un al-manzil* (domestic affairs); *al-hayah al-zoujiyya* (married life); *mamlaka fil bayt* (the house as a kingdom); and *tarbiyyat al-atfal* (the *tarbiyya* of children). Accompanying such articles were discussions of kingship, science, geography, civilization and the progress of nations, and work and productivity.

Avierino also published *Le Lotus*, for Egyptian francophones at home and abroad, and called it a "Revue Mensuelle, Littéraire, Scientifique, Artistique." Designed for women, the magazine promised to "maintain local color, discuss habits and customs of the Egyptians, and provide a place where the healthiest manifestations of intelligence can be found."[43] *Le Lotus* did not have a *tadbir al-manzil* column but often carried articles on the household and other issues pertaining to private life. One such article was called "The *Fellah* and His Private Life," in which household practices were used as a means of describing "Egyptians." Drawn mostly from Edward Lane, the text offered little more than European descriptions of the *fellah*'s home. The author insisted that private life offered the best vehicle for understanding "this great majority of Egyptians" and that reforming the *fellah*'s private life would make the difference between civilized Egypt and an uncivilized one.[44] The same issue also contained an article called "La Sultane Adroite," which was a fictional account of a sultan and his favorite wife; the wife's superior skills in home economics helped her husband run his kingdom and make sound political decisions.

Homes as "schools" of virtue were also the topic of fiction that often circulated in the turn-of-the-century press. Most journals had "literature" columns in which poetry and short stories were printed in serialized form. Romantic love, friendship, political progress — all took place against the background of a reformed, scientifically sound home. In such fiction, conflict — of whatever nature — was always resolved when homes were "cleaned up," women were educated, and sound mothers taught their sons the "secrets" of nationalism.

In March 1909, a monthly periodical called *Jama'iyyat al-Hayah* (The 'Hayah' Organization), which billed itself as a "magazine concerned with religion, self-refinement, literature, science, sociology, and history," published in its "Story of the Month" section a piece entitled "Nationalism and Love."[45] Written by an Egyptian, Mohammad Effendi Ahmad 'Abdalfatah, the story concerned a certain Indian national, "Krishna," who, while studying at Oxford University in England, meets and falls in love with an Englishwoman, "Brit." Krishna realizes that his love for Brit contradicts the work that he has done in creating an Indian Nationalist Party (called the Red Palm) at Oxford, designed to teach his fellow nationals how to make and use dynamite and how to use it against their colonial oppressors. Despite his fellow party members' admonishments against his growing love for Brit (he could not, they said, love a Briton because of his commitment to his nation), his feelings for her persist.

The tale is a long and somewhat tortured one, full of intrigue, espionage, and counterespionage and full of tragedy for both lovers. When young Krishna returns to India from England, having finished his education and, with it, his career in explosives engineering, he is met at the train station by his mother. She hands him a shirt that has been soaked in blood, the shirt of his dead father who, in Krishna's absence, had been martyred for the Indian nationalist cause. Krishna kisses the shirt and promises his mother that he will avenge his father's death, a promise that he intended to keep until memories of his beloved fill his mind.

His mother is quick to notice that his eyes shone with bittersweet memories, and she is pleased and delighted until Krishna confesses the nationality of his betrothed. In anger and disbelief, she refuses to embrace him, to recognize him, or to let him enter her home until he has renounced Brit and sworn vengeance for his father's blood. At this point he realizes the path that he must choose: "His mother's words influenced him greatly. He was suddenly overwhelmed by images of his father's grave. And it was his mother — his mother who had loved him and raised him and taught him the love of the nation — his mother who handed him the blood-soaked shirt and asked him to avenge his father's death. He took the shirt from her, placed it in his suitcase, and promised not to return to her until he had avenged his father."[46]

As the result of his mother's admonitions, Krishna redoubles his efforts with the members of the Red Palm Party, and they start a newspaper called *The Voice of Truth*. As the result of the journal, certain Indian nationalists destroy a number of British businesses. When a British judge sentences the journal's editor to death, Krishna decides to get revenge. He travels to Calcutta and enters the man's house late at night. Once there, he discovers the judge to be Brit's father. Forced to choose between nationalism and love, Krishna chooses nationalism and kills the judge. Krishna returns to his mother, recognizes her as his first "school" of nationalism, and, once again, is welcomed into her home.

The lesson in this story, and in many like it that were in circulation at the turn of the century, is that it is *mothers* who teach their sons to love the nation and, more important, not to betray it. Krishna's "career" as a nationalist began and ended in the same way, in a proper home with proper domestic relationships, overseen by a strong mother.

By the turn of the century, then, the home became a predominant vehicle for defining a nationalist lifestyle, for critiquing lifestyles that did not "support" the process of modernizing or liberating Egypt, and for talking about politics. While women are central to these discussions — as better housewives, partners, mothers, and educated women — men, too, shared enormous implications. While women were the target of reform through education, men were expected to be the indirect beneficiaries of home economics — to take what they had "learned" at home into the public realm. *Tadbir al-manzil* was not just women's work: In order for the nation to be strengthened, men had to be versed in it — transformed by it — as well.

Marketing Modernity:
The Commodities of a Nationalist Lifestyle

The project of recasting oneself as a middle-class nationalist was not just a matter of intellectual debate. The press was also full of advertisements for commodities that promised modernity. Often, such commodities were marketed to "improve" the consumer's health; just as often, however, they were pitched as "nationalist" products that configured the body, as well as the home, into the new constellation of modernity, self-sufficiency, and political capability. Those who purchased and used such items improved themselves and contributed to the struggle against imperialism at the same time.[47]

The most common products on the turn-of-the-century market were medicinal. *Effendi* Egyptians showed a remarkable preoccupation with the condition of their body and with the purchase of potions and remedies designed to promote better health. During the 1890s, *al-Hilal* was full of ads for remedies of all kinds, both imported and locally produced. Pills, oils, and creams of various sorts all promised better health and greater longevity. The Huile de Foie de Morue, for example, advertised in *al-Hilal* throughout the 1890s, claimed to work against pallor, anemia, and tuberculosis in adults as well as children. It promised to shorten the period of convalescence following an illness and to provide greater strength.[48] Such advertisements for health products continued into the twentieth century. Editions of *al-Ahram* from early 1905, for example, were full of ads for things like toothpaste, backache remedies, general pain killers, cough syrups, and potions for the cure of anemia.[49] Other products, like Gardenia Flor (a new cologne, shaving lotion, and soap imported from Paris), were promoted, if not for health, then for the general improvement of the body, physical appearance, and hygiene.[50]

Products also promoted what was often called a new lifestyle. For smokers, for example, many tobacco products promised "a nationalist lifestyle." On March 9, 1905, an ad for a tobacco factory promoted a certain brand of tobacco "for those who wish for a nationalist lifestyle." Other tobacconists referred to their stores as "nationalist."[51] Other ventures offered European clothing for men and women. Clothing was generally advertised as promoting better appearance and better comfort. In 1910, *al-Ahram* advertised Unshrinkable Underwear, which was designed to last longer than other underwear and to provide better comfort. It was sold in fine stores all over Egypt and available for adults and children.[52] Books were often promoted as "nationalist" or as promoting "nationalism." *Al-Hilal* often ran ads for texts on history and geography; Egypt's place in the modern world as well as its formidable role in the past apparently had a healthy market.[53] Zeidan wrote a number of histories of Egypt, which *al-Hilal* promoted. Products for the household also took up considerable space in such advertisements. Turkish baths, porcelain bathtubs, and electric baths hit the market in early 1905. That same year, The Store of Success (Mahal al-najah) advertised the "best products" for the home — tablecloths, tableware, and bedspreads.[54] Stoves, ovens, and such household items as chafing dishes frequently appeared in the advertisements, as did innovations in home furnishings.[55]

Advertisements for men's products intermingled with appeals to women. For example, magazines and newspapers promoted the increased availability of products for the workplace, including gas-run engines, electrical appliances, and heavy machinery for factories. Banks also routinely advertised in the turn-of-the-century press. Accompanying such advertisements were ads for products promoting women's health. Such advertisements did not occupy separate sections for women but, rather, appeared among ads for banks, businesses, and machinery. One ad promoting a cure for a menstrual remedy appeared sandwiched between ads for gas engines and men's clothing. While the women's press ran ads for products designed specifically for women's consumption, ads in periodicals like *al-Ahram* and others like it promoted and enhanced male nationalists' knowledge about the "problems" plaguing women's bodies while offering solutions and remedies. Most products promised to make "better," stronger, more productive women. Doan's advertised a special product for women, "a remedy for women's illnesses alone." The ad warned that sick women could not do housework or attend to children; the pills kept such lack of productivity from occurring.[56]

The ads revealed a heightened sense of knowledge about women's bodies and what ailed them. The Doan's ad, for example, boldly stated: "Women get sick more often than men do . . . that's why we've produced a remedy to cure them alone." Likewise, an ad for Hemagen Tailleur Menstrual Remedy noted that "certain illness . . . need special remedies." Puberty for young women and its attendant ailments was also addressed in advertisements. Bink Pills (Hubbub bink) helped girls through puberty: "One of the most difficult and crucial periods . . . for young girls . . . During puberty, girls often feel weak, sometimes they become anemic."[57]

Remedies and information about women's bodies occupied the same status among "modern nationalist" products such as literature, clothing, and tobacco. "Scientific" knowledge of women and their bodies was, like proper behavior, attire, and home furnishings, included among the templates of Egyptian-ness. Journals frequently ran articles on such topics as "women and science," "women and natural history," "the effects of tight clothing on a woman's organs," and "climate and women's health." Women served as a vehicle through which scientific knowledge was heralded and through which nationalists forged a proprietary relationship over "their" women.[58]

Finally, healthy children and their *tarbiyya* figured into the turn-of-the-century commodities market. The press frequently advertised books on how to raise healthy, disciplined children.[59] Ads also promoted "proper" clothing and food especially designed for children. *Al-Ahram* and *al-Hilal* frequently ran an advertisement for Phosphatine Falière's Children's Food that consisted of a group of healthy children, all dressed in European clothing, diving into an enormous serving dish; it contained no copy, but the children in it were robust, happy, and energetic.[60] Such images of children often accompanied "nationalist" men in other advertisements. An ad for Doan's Pills from the turn of the century, for example, pictured a man with a bad backache at home in a modern dining room with his wife and daughter. His daughter looked very much like she might have eaten Phosphatine food for children. Advertisements also featured books on child rearing, such as *Adab al-Fata'* (Children's manners) and *Kitab Tarbiyyat al-Atfal* (A book on the *tarbiyya* of children).[61]

The display of economic solvency and scientific knowledge that heralded nationalist platforms in turn-of-the-century Egypt thus included "the woman question." Acknowledging and promoting the needs of women served to prove that nationalist men were "modern." Bathtubs, home furnishings, and modern child raising all played a role in constructing bourgeois Egyptian nationalism. Eating Phosphatine, like washing with alkaline solution, connoted not only knowledge of modernity and its trappings but a concern for Egypt's condition and its progress.

The Best Face for the Nation is a Woman's: Modernity, Nationalism, and "the New Woman" Debate

The structures of early nationalist discussions about "politics," modernity, and reform reveal the relationship between (male) nationalists and "the woman question." The texts that opened the nationalist debate over the position of women in Egyptian society are two works by Qasim Amin (1865–1908): *Tahrir al-mar'a* (The liberation of women), published in 1899, and *al-Mar'a al-jadida* (The new woman), published in 1901 in response to the reaction of Cairo's learned elite to his first text. In them, Amin advocates for advancing women's position in society and explains his position on the use of the *hijab* (translated as "veil" by translator Samiha Sidhom Peterson) as well as his stand on such things as divorce and polygamy. Amin called for advancing the education for girls, reforming divorce laws, and rethinking the use of the *hijab* and its place in

Islamic history; thus, both feminist and nationalist scholars have claimed him as Egypt's first "feminist" and as the father of the Egyptian feminist movement.[62] Likewise, his texts have been credited with "starting" the debate over what to do about Egypt's "woman question." Scholars disagree over the authorship of Amin's two texts (some, for example, claim that they were actually penned by Mohammad 'Abduh, who was Amin's intellectual mentor) and over his definition of "reform."[63] Historians concur, however, that his texts inaugurated a general nationalist preoccupation with the condition of Egyptian women as well as a determination to better it.

Amin's texts also produced an intense reaction among Egyptian intellectuals of all persuasions and resulted not only in the rise of great debates in the press but in the publication of texts that served as countertreatises to Amin's positions.[64] Amin was attacked — and praised — for the kinds of reforms he advocated for women, especially educational reforms. His commentary about the "veiling" of women also led to great debate. But whether one was for Amin or against him, discussions of his work had something in common: In all of them, women and their activities — domestic or otherwise — symbolized Egypt's political condition.

Amin's intellectual projects provide insight into the question of whether Egyptians of Ottoman origins viewed themselves as Egyptian in turn-of-the-century Egypt. Amin's father, Mohammad Bey Amin, was a landowning Ottoman Turk, who married an Arabophone Egyptian from Upper Egypt. Mohammad Bey had been the governor of the province of Kurdistan until its uprising against the Ottomans, at which point he ended up overseeing the Bahariyya province in Egypt at the beginning of Isma'il's reign. He became a high-ranking member of Isma'il's army. His father's heritage and position within Isma'il's administration would certainly have placed Qasim Amin within the camp of Ottoman Egyptians with high expectations of a good position within the administration — expectations that would most likely have been met — and a dismissive attitude toward Arabophone Egyptians. Yet Amin's work can be read as a primer on how to be Egyptian and on how to liberate the Egyptian nation from foreign occupation.

Amin was very much the product of Egyptian state-building projects. He was educated in state-run primary and preparatory schools in Alexandria and Cairo. He attended the School of Law and Administration. A student mission took him to France in 1881, where he obtained a French law degree from the University of Montepellier in 1885. He went on to get a degree in Islamic law. When he returned to Cairo, Amin was appointed judge in the mixed courts and then to the government courts in 1887. In 1889 he was appointed as the principal judge for the region of Beni Suef, where he stayed for two years before being transferred to Tanta. There he had contact with men who had participated in the 'Urabi movement, among them 'Abdullah Nadim. Amin wrote in French and Arabic, not Turkish. So, while his origins were Ottoman Turkish, his education placed him in the growing ranks of *effendi* intellectuals whose outlook and interests appeared to be inclusively Egyptian.

A rereading of Amin's texts in the context of the great flurry of discussions about domestic politics and their relationship to the nation-state prior to the appearance of Amin's work suggests alternate ways of looking at the rise of "the new woman" debate. Amin's agenda in both *The Liberation of Women* and *The New Woman* had much less to do with liberating women than it did with exposing the home and its domestic relations as a means of illustrating that Egypt was "modern" and politically capable, and, therefore, of securing a place for itself among modern, independent nations. The woman question, as it appears in Amin's texts and others like them, was a means of claiming a national history for Egypt, of highlighting the strength of its various institutions, and of charting a course for its future. By lifting the *hijab* off of Egyptian society and, therefore, exposing the condition of its private realm, modern Egypt — in all its various manifestations — was put on display. Scholars typically translate Amin's use of the word *hijab* to mean "veil." Because Amin argued that the first step in transforming Egypt was abolishing the *hijab*, it has usually been argued that taking a stand against the "veil" was central to promoting a reformed position for women.[65] Such an argument conforms, more or less, to nineteenth-century European discourse about the veil as representing debauchery, social and political decay, and the Egyptians' general disregard for women.[66]

Thus in interpreting *hijab*, scholars have failed to make the connection between the structures of modern nationalism and the nationalists' general obsession with cleaning up the domestic realm (an obsession that included "the woman question").[67] Amin frequently used the term *hijab* to mean a kind of garment, especially when he discussed the different kinds of "veils" used in Egypt, distinguishing between such things as the *birqa'a*, which was a veil that covered the face, and the *habara*, a long, cape-like cloak. He also used *hijab* to mean the segregation and seclusion of women from society, the treatment of women as property, the subjection of women to an uneducated state, and a determination to keep them ignorant of their legal rights.[68] In other words, he appropriated the term *hijab* to transform the state of women and society.

Throughout *The New Woman,* Amin refers to social and political reform as being tantamount to "lifting the *hijab*" from Egyptian society. Such an act did not merely expose women's faces or grant an extension of women's rights. Rather, the purpose of lifting Egypt's *hijab* was to expose the home and its practices and to use what was found there as a means of addressing the condition of Egypt's political realm, history, structures, and future. Amin was not discounting the literal burden of wearing a garment. But, by expanding his readers' understanding of *hijab* and its "lifting" to mean a general uncovering of Egypt and all its institutions — especially its families — he transformed early nationalist debates, particularly as they pertained to gender and domestic reform.

Indeed, Amin placed the heart of Egypt's historical development — political and otherwise — in the family and familial structures. His view of history, as it developed toward modernity, was that changes in family structures and domestic relationships were instrumental, in fact crucial, to progress.[69] Before publishing his two texts on "women," Amin used 'Ali Yusuf's journal *al-Mu'ayyud* as a forum in which to discuss the process of reforming and modernizing Egypt.[70] Between 1895 and 1898, the articles were published as a series called "*Asbab wa nata'ij*" (Reasons and results) and constituted an inquiry into Egypt's social, political, and economic condition. The articles addressed topics such as independence, productivity, class differences in Egypt, the social and financial consequences of Waqf properties, and *tarbiyya* and its role in "producing" Egyptians.

In his introduction to the series, Amin pointed to history as an indicator both of the past and of its "truths" as well as of the future and its promise. What drove history, he claimed, was not random fortune; he believed in causality and therefore dedicated his inquiries to uncovering what was driving Egypt forward. His answer was the reform of the habits and customs — and, therefore, the very nature — of its inhabitants. He said:

The condition of a nation both in happiness and in misfortune, in progress or decay, does not happen by accident; rather, that condition is the result of a crisis which does not resolve itself except through the transformation of the inner condition of that nation.

If a nation is energetic, well-mannered and civilized it will be successful in the world. And if it is lazy and ignorant and ill-mannered, it will fall into misery.

When a society knows where it has come from it will know where it is going and how to get there. Change comes from no other source, not from the will of the one person or a hundred people, not from the issuing of one law or hundreds of them. It only comes from history.[71]

Amin's task, in the remainder of *Asbab wa nata'ij*, as in *The Liberation of Women* and *The New Woman*, was to show Egyptians where they had come from and how they could "progress." History, according to Amin, had a motor: Because the family could change a nation's habits and customs for the better or worse, it moved history and caused nations to advance. Amin claimed that history had passed through a series of stages, all of which were reflected in (and which, in turn, affected) the shape and structure of the family. In what Amin calls history's first stage — its nomadic stage — families did not exist and, therefore, men and women both lived free. Women did not marry, and paternity was established based on whomever a child happened to resemble. In such a state, he claimed, women were independent, gained their own living, and were the equals of men. He believed that the Germanic tribes and the Arabs had passed through such a stage. He also claimed Siam and Dahomey, in Africa, were still in such a condition, as were Tahiti, Melanesia, and parts of India and Africa.

Societies advanced and entered into "stage two" of history when they became sedentary. At that point, the "order of the household" was founded and women lost their independence. Heads of families owned their wives, acquired them like they would slaves or livestock, and thought nothing about their freedom. Men married more than one wife in order to maintain them as property rather than partners. In such a system, women inherited neither money nor property and could not divorce or gain custody of their children. Men placed their wives in the domicile and forced them to remain there.

"Stage three," according to Amin, resembled its predecessor in many ways but contained important differences. Government had come to take on the characteristics of the family: Tyrannical rulers held their citizens captive just like the tyrannical husband-father held his wife and children captive. Men in stage-three societies were not free from the tyranny of their rulers. Therefore, as a means of empowering themselves, they tyrannized their wives. Accordingly, women in such societies had very few rights — they could, for example, inherit money and property — but were wholly subservient to the whims, desires, and wills of their husbands, fathers, and masters. Amin elaborated: "This kind of autocratic government was the first to appear in the world. It weakened, then disappeared, after having lasted for generations in Western Europe. It was replaced by a constitutional order, based on the principal that a ruler does not have the right to people or to their properties, except to the degree that the law obligates him."[72]

"Stage four" occurred when societies were governed by constitutions. According to Amin, the transition from stage three to stage four occurred when "men progressed in their thinking to the extent that they realized that handing their will over to the disposal of a sovereign was an affront to their dignity and a transgression of their rights." The structure of families also started to reflect this. According to Amin's schemata, stage four was reached when the family and, along with it, the government were reformed and wholly resembled one another. When the tyrant father-husband was dethroned and replaced, both inside and outside the home, with a just and enlightened ruler, the social order would then advance to its final stage. One could not be reformed without the other: "If someone should ask which of the two has influenced the other, we can say that the two conditions are reciprocal: the form of the government influences that of the home, and the customs of the home influence the political order."[73]

In Europe and America, Amin stated, men and women were as free in their private lives as they were vis-à-vis their rulers. Amin thought this was especially true in America, where he believed government had ceased to interfere in the lives of its citizens: "Men are completely free in their private lives; the authority of the government and its interference in the affairs of the individual are almost nonexistent."[74] He cited England, France, and Russia as examples of nations in which tyranny had either ceased to exist or was in its "death throes"; consequently both the political and the domestic realms enjoyed relative levels of freedom: "We see that the Westerner's home is based on strong pillars, just as we see the Western nations to be in perpetual development."[75]

In Amin's "tour" of countries in *The New Woman* (the text is, indeed, reminiscent of the travel literature discussed above), he acknowledged that a society could dethrone its tyrants — and reform its men — by first reforming its women.[76] Peter the Great knew this and hence abolished segregation; Catherine the Great completed his work by insisting that women be educated.[77] English women knew the sciences, worked in industry, and took great part in charitable and municipal organizations. As the result of women's education and exposure in countries like Russia and England, he claimed, great changes had come about in family life. And as the form of the family continued to evolve, so too did that of the government.

Egypt, according to Amin, was still at stage three. He claimed that nothing had ever approximated constitutional "order" among the Arabs: "The Arabs' form of government consisted of an unbound [bound to no governmental contract] sultan or caliph who ruled through administrators who, like him, were unbound. Thus the ruler and those like him ran their administrations in the manner that they saw fit. . . . There was nothing in the system that forced them to revert back to rule according to the Shari'a."[78]

Such unchecked power, he claimed, could also be found in the Arabs' domestic realm. Amin said, "Women are slaves to men, and men are slaves to rulers. Egyptian men are oppressors in the home and oppressed outside of it."[79] In their households women were not free, and outside their homes men were equally oppressed, even though, according to the law, men and women had innumerable rights.

Amin could not explain why tyranny was not quick to disappear in Egypt despite the Egyptians' great efforts at reform and their strong desire for it. He did argue that it would disappear, however, if the home was remade. Starting with women, Egypt could be "pushed" into its final stage of history: Amin's "new woman," and the effects that she would have on the domestic realm, would put an end to Egypt's political slavery. Through "the new woman," men would acquire the moral and intellectual virtues and capabilities that would lead them to put an end to tyranny in the public realm.

Amin advocated the abolishment of polygamy and the creation of marriage as a partnership, in which both men and women would learn and practice their rights and responsibilities to one another. Women who could divorce and choose their partners freely, he claimed, would be a critical first step in abolishing the old order, in which women were merely chattel, and ushering in a new era in which men learned from their wives just as their wives learned from them. Education, coupled with the right to divorce, would give women a sense of independence (they would, ideally, no longer be dependent on men) and would make women attractive partners to men:

What is more beneficial for men than having, by their side, a companion who accompanies them day and night, in residence and in travel . . . a companion with brains and a good upbringing . . . a woman who manages his income and promotes his work and reminds him of his duties and points out his rights? . . . She is a friend who adorns his house and gives pleasure to his heart and fills his time and dissolves his troubles. . . . I say without hesitation that unless we develop such tender feelings in ourselves such that men form bonds with women in the above-mentioned ways . . . then all we have done so far and all that we will do in the future for developing the state of our nation will be in vain.[80]

This partnership would be aided further by the new woman's ability to order and organize her home. Her knowledge of domestic affairs would not only make the home a clean, healthy, productive space but also a place where men would want to spend more time.[81]

Finally, the new woman would be the source of further generations of new men. Women's education would prepare them to be the source of modern *tarbiyya* in their homes, producing generations of Egyptians who would be sound in body as well as mind. Amin said, "Let me state a simple truth: that all the faults we see in children — lying, fear, laziness, and stupidity — result from the fact that mothers are ignorant of the laws of *tarbiyya*." Educated women were to replace laziness and stupidity with the sciences, with history, with the basics of home economics. Their homes would either be laboratories of modernity or "replicas" of the sins of the past. Amin continued, "The axis of education revolves around the mother. The child, male or female, from the moment of birth up to the age of puberty, knows no other model than his mother, associates only with her, and reacts only to his feelings according to the patterns she has presented to him. His mind is a blank page, and his mother writes on it as she wills."[82]

Amin was also concerned with what he called "moral *tarbiyya*." The healthy bodies and minds of Egyptian children were clearly important, he argued, but had little impact on society when children were morally unsound. He attributed the morals of his generation to the fact that most of their mothers had little education or moral instruction. He said, "The woman . . . passes her morals along to her children who, in turn, pass them on to those they come in contact with. Thus, morals become those of the community after they are the morals of the family and after they are the morals of the mother. . . . A good mother is more beneficial to the species than a good man, and a corrupt woman is more damaging than a corrupt man."[83]

Amin illustrated the importance of reformed households to the nation through the examples of nationalist men who were the products of them. He began with the example of a "questionable" nationalist, Ibrahim al-Hilbawi, who, as a lawyer, represented the British against the accused Egyptians in the trials following the massacre at Denshawi. In 1906, in the Delta village of Denshawi, a group of British officers on a shooting trip accidentally shot and killed the wife of a local Egyptian official. In the flight that ensued, several Egyptians and two British officers were shot and some of them killed. Four of the Egyptians accused were hanged and four others were sentenced to life imprisonment. The British handed down harsh sentences as a means of discouraging future incidents. The Denshawi episode, however, became a nationalist rallying cry, leading Egyptians of all ranks to question British rule in their country. Amin quotes letters from al-Hilbawi that appeared in *al-Mu'ayyad,* wherein al-Hilbawi wrote about seeing Crete from a ship that took him back to Egypt from Europe. He wrote:

This is the first time that my eyes have seen this island since it was separated from the Ottoman Empire. . . . While passing it by, I tried to remember regretfully the events that preceded this decree, and those that took place during and after it. There was murder and shedding of the blood of the island's Muslims. . . . I tried to remember this as a true Muslim who feels the pains of his fellow Muslims. I found in myself neither space in my heart nor blood that could be affected; nor will you find in me any space for sorrow or mercy.[84]

Al-Hilbawi was possessed by similar feelings when he reached Egypt. On the train from Alexandria to Cairo, he passed by the battlefields on which Egyptians clashed with the British in 1882, leading directly to the occupation: "This was the first time in my life that I had passed by Tel el-Kabir and al-Kassasin and al-Mahsama and Nafisha. All these points had been taken as defense lines against the British army in the year 1882, and it should have been that in passing by these places for the first time, that the pains of sadness and the memory of the loss of the glory of the country and its independence would have been aroused in me. In spite of that, I felt no pain or distress."[85] Amin attributed al-Hilbawi's inability to feel anything for his country (as well, assumedly, as his ability to deceive his countrymen by prosecuting them) to the fact that he hadn't learned patriotism as a child. ("The real reason for this loss of feeling . . . is the neglect of *tarbiyya* in childhood.")[86] In other words, he blamed it on al-Hilbawi's home life and on his mother.

Amin juxtaposed al-Hilbawi's experience with one that he witnessed in France, where he believed that proper homes produced exemplary nationalism, saying:

When I traveled in France I saw a boy of ten who was beside me while I was watching a group of French soldiers returning from the battle of Tonkin. When the French flag passed him, he stood up with respect and raised his hat and saluted the flag and watched it with his eyes until it was gone. To that young child, the homeland was embodied in the flag that passed in front of him. It aroused in him the feelings of love that his *tarbiyya* had instilled in him, to the extent that I felt that he was a completely grown man.[87]

The reform of the domestic realm created a kind of *moralpolitik*, in which Egypt's triumphant entrance into its fourth and final stage of history would be witnessed only by a new order that would begin in the domicile and that would be overseen by women. *The New Woman* thus appears not to be the impassioned discourse of an enlightened feminist but, rather, an example of a gendered, nationalist discourse in which the virtues and victories of the public realm — the victories and the sentiments of men — were wholly dependent upon the politics of the families from which those men came. Amin did not call for women's participation in the public realm. He claimed that few Egyptian men were ready for political responsibilities. Amin's "new woman" and the order of her home were wholly responsible for the creation of a new man. That new man, in turn, was subject to a whole litany of new behaviors: Monogamy, partnerships with women, "scientific" domestic practices, and, finally, a new relationship with a just ruler were all evoked in Amin's prescriptions for liberated, "uncovered" women. "The new woman" and the social and political changes that were part of her creation were the building blocks of a new political order that further generations of men would enjoy. The actual shape and structure of that political order remained, at the turn of the century, remarkably vague. What was clear, however, is that it would rest on the foundation of a new domestic régime.

Debates about women were subsumed into Egypt's first articulations of party politics. Cromer left Egypt in 1907 after the outcry against him, both in Egypt and Great Britain, that resulted from the Denshawi massacre of 1906. Cromer was replaced as consul general by Gorst, who attempted to appease the Egyptians by allowing them to organize themselves into political parties. Gorst's successor, Lord Kitchener (r. 1911–13), also attempted to address some of the political and economic grievances held by the *effendiyya* against the British administration by allowing more Egyptians access to higher-ranking administrative positions within the government. By 1910, the bureaucracy had become flooded by educated Egyptians, products of both private and public education.

The formation of political parties lifted indigenous politics out of the realm of the press. The parties consisted of middle-class intellectuals, reformers, and activists with different visions of how their nation's future would manifest itself. Three major parties prevailed in Egypt on the eve of World War I: Sheikh 'Ali Yusuf's Constitutional Reform Party, which advocated independence for Egypt within an Islamic framework; the People's Party, headed by Ahmad Lutfi al-Sayyid, which espoused a kind of secular, liberal constitutionalism; and the National Party, headed by

Mustafa Kamil until his death in 1907 and then by Mohammad Farid (1868–1919), which demanded immediate evacuation by the British. Kamil and his contemporaries believed that while Egypt had bonds with the Ottoman Empire, it also formed a distinct territorial entity that had to be respected and defended by Egyptians.[88]

Household reform appears to have been part of each party's agenda. Lutfi al-Sayyid demanded the education of women and the reorganization of the family as the first steps toward the destruction of tyranny in Egypt and constitutional government.[89] His platform for the eventual establishment of a constitutional regime in Egypt was the creation of a system of public education in Egypt that would "rid the nation of its childlike ways" and teach Egyptians sound familial relationships.[90] Egypt's political situation, like its economic one, would not, he claimed, be remedied without the total transformation of the Egyptians' most personal relationships, the reform of which would be his party's charge.

The minutes taken from a National Party congress, held in Brussels in 1910, also indicate that the household had become central to shaping party platforms. Debates over the construction of hospitals and schools and the education of women took up as much floor time at the congress as did the discussion of "politics." Debates about Egypt's readiness for self-government, over the shape and function of its legislature, for example, were sandwiched between lengthier and more heated debates over infant mortality, cleanliness, motherhood, and education.

One party member, Hamed al-Alaily, in a speech entitled "The Future of Egypt: The Moral and Intellectual Aspects of Egyptian Nationalism," claimed that it was only through the resuscitation of Egypt's households and the salvation of its children that the politics of parliaments and legislation would come about. He said: "It is not the cotton-bales or the loans of fund-holders that are at stake, but . . . men and women . . . and children. . . . When this aspect of the political movement is realized by our compatriots and our sympathizers . . . a mighty wave of pity and indignation will roll over their awakened souls."[91]

The result of such politics would not only be the attraction of more Egyptians to nationalism but the total transformation of the Egyptian landscape. "The Egypt question" would be answered from the bosom of Egypt's domiciles:

If we exert ourselves from this moment . . . our children will inherit from us a land flowing with milk and honey, blessed with independence and all the virtues that follow in its train as the flowers come with spring. . . . Well-filled granaries, overflowing marts; smiling cottages and lovely palaces of art, magnificent libraries and noble places of worship; brave men true and intelligent, and sweet women — worthy helpmates for men — homes lit up with the light of love and virtue and resounding with the prattle of joyous children. All this and even more than this, all that Greece ever dreamed of or Rome ever planned, all that England has achieved.[92]

The role of the party was thus to maintain a double vigilance. While on the one hand preparing for an active political future, the party had also to concern itself with nurturing the nation's children and securing its future home life. By the mid-1920s, all of the party "platforms" included cleaning up the domicile, protecting maternity, safeguarding the future of Egypt's children: Article 5 of the National Party's bylaws was dedicated to the continued spread of education and the protection of maternity and childhood. The Liberal Constitutional Party, founded by 'Adly Yeghen in 1921 as the result of his difficulties with the Wafd and Sa'ad Zaghlul, pledged to improve the hygienic conditions of the entire country, both inside and outside the home.[93]

Conclusion

In May 1915, a new journal appeared on Cairo's literary horizon, edited by 'Abd al-Hamid Hamdi, who, earlier in the century, had also started a weekly magazine for children called *al-Talba* (The students). The new journal was hailed as a "weekly social, literary critical newspaper," and it contained, like many of the other journals discussed above and found in Cairo and Alexandria in the two decades leading up to the 1919 Revolution, the mixture of "political," literary, and "domestic" discussions and debates that were the requisite fare of journalism at that time. Called *al-Sufur*, which is best translated as "uncovering," or, "unveiling," the paper immediately gave the appearance of being a women's journal. Like many of the papers discussed above, however, *al-Sufur* was not targeted at women but, rather, referred to the political agendas of the day as being synonymous with "the woman question," or more specifically, with debates over the *hijab*. Hamdi explained in the journal's opening issue:

We are publishing *al-Sufur* because Egypt's young intellectuals saw the need for it. The meaning of "*al-Sufur*" includes more than what usually comes to mind when one hears that word, especially in the ways that pens have been wildly discussing it in connection with "the woman question." Women are not the only ones in Egypt to be in *hijab*. Rather, our position, our virtues, our morals, our ability, our knowledge, our security — all of these things, in Egypt, are in *hijab*. . . . We are an *umma* in *hijab*, in the true meaning of the word. In this journal we will uncover those things that are covered. We named the paper *al-Sufur* in order to highlight where we can get to in terms of progress and reform.[94]

Hamdi listed the kinds of behavior that he thought represented *hijab* in Egyptians and their social and political institutions: He pointed to the rich who flaunted their money and did nothing for the poor; to men who claimed to be wise but did not heed their own counsel; and to governments that harshly punished even the smallest of crimes without recognizing their tyranny to be the greatest crime. Finally, Hamdi condemned men who promised their wives fidelity, "leaving them home safe behind their curtains, while [they went] out of the house and committed adultery." In other words, the behavior of men in and outside of their homes were all, in the words of the author, "the worst examples of *hijab*."[95]

"The woman question," then, as it appeared in the turn-of-the-century press, was not wholly about women. Rather, it served as the means through which the political realm was often addressed, critiqued, or exalted.[96] Discussions about the *hijab*, in Qasim Amin's work and elsewhere, couched agendas that ranged from the unseating of political tyranny to economic solvency to reformed marital contracts. "The woman question" asked men to accept a new order of things, a new code of behavior, while claiming to demand a new set of values and behaviors from women.

As it was presented in the above journals, "the woman question" created an increasingly analogous relationship between the body familial and the body politic. Table talk, home economics, and "uncovered Egyptians" formed the basis of new ways of talking about politics, modernity, and science. The habits and customs of modern Egyptians, in their domiciles, formed the pillars of a new, gendered body politic in which the images of sound homes, reformed marriages, and good mothers embodied and gave meaning to "Egypt" for bourgeois, nationalist "Egyptians." Early articulations of constitutionalism, reform of the khedival order, and the inclusion of greater numbers of Egyptians in the

quotidian affairs of governing Egypt reflected a continued preoccupation with *"l'ordre feminin"* and the shaping of political discourse through
domestic affairs. In the decade leading up to the revolution, "the woman
question" was thus not just an abstract means of discussing nationalism,
or of couching political commentary and critique in social terms; rather,
it was also central to the process in which political aspirations and platforms became concrete.

CHAPTER 6

Reform on Display

The Family Politics of the 1919 Revolution

In the spring of 1919, after enduring the humiliation of Egypt's transformation from an informally occupied territory to a formal protectorate state, the imposition of martial law, the dismissal of local forms of self-government, and the difficult years of World War I, the Egyptians delivered an answer to "the Egypt question." In a series of sometimes bloody demonstrations, strikes, and boycotts, which lasted, intermittently, through early 1922, Egyptians of all classes endeavored to show Great Britain, as well as the postwar diplomatic community, that their period of colonial tutelage needed to come to an end.[1] Having withstood almost forty years of manipulation of their political, social, and economic institutions, Egyptians informed their colonial masters that they were ready for self-rule.

The demonstrations of 1919 and 1920 appeared to unite disparate elements of the Egyptian population. While a number of factors brought different Egyptians to the demonstrations — the grievances of some were clearly economic; other complaints were overtly political — a common desire to see the British leave Egypt ignited the revolution and seemed to unite Egyptians in a conflict that was both local and international in nature. One of the most commonly told stories about the revolutionary demonstrations is that the struggle against the British transcended class and sectarian differences, providing Egyptians, at least for the revolutionary moment, with a "new religion."[2] Within the constructs of nationalism, Egyptians — rich and poor, Muslim and Christian, peasants, workers and landed elites, men and women — took to the streets, arm in arm, not only to make the quotidian tasks of governing Egypt impossible for the British but also to demonstrate that a new order of things — a new stage of existence — had come to pass.

The rhetoric and iconography of the *effendiyya* during the 1919 Revolution alluded to Egypt's rebirth, its passage from one stage of existence to another. Among the most volatile factors of the World War I era were insinuations made by the British that the end of the war would lead directly to negotiations over Egypt's future independence; such expectations were further heightened by Woodrow Wilson's postwar declaration of his principles of self-determination. Both sets of promises evoked the vague language and goals of the occupation as it began in 1882, in which Egypt was depicted as a child being raised to maturity by its colonial master. The formation of political parties after 1907 and the brief tenure of Egypt's Legislative Assembly (1913–14), through which Egyptians demonstrated to the British that they were "grown up" and capable of self-governing, led to expectations that emancipation was at hand. Said one revolutionary, Morcos Fahmy, in a letter addressed to Egypt's high commissioner General Allenby: "The movement [the revolution] is but the beginnings of emancipation . . . an emancipation that will allow this so-called minor to take, without trepidation, a few necessary steps in order to fortify its muscles and begin its march to adulthood."[3] According to Fahmy, Egypt's yearnings for maturity were part of an evolutionary process through which all nations advanced.[4] Fahmy beseeched the British to allow the Egyptians to continue with the "evolutionary cycle" that they had begun, "without intervention and without coercion . . . despite their faults and their weaknesses."[5]

The rhetoric and the iconography of the revolution frequently engaged and contested the language and images of the occupation. Indeed, revolutionary circulars intercepted by British intelligence reveal that the long list of promises made by the British, including the false promise of liberation after World War I, served to fuel revolutionary fervor.[6] The revolutionary demonstrations, press coverage, poetry, short stories, and political caricatures all evoked images of emancipation and raising the nation-child to maturity. The iconography of the revolution depicted reformed *effendi* nationalists giving birth to the new independent nation and nurturing it. Gaining Egypt's independence was a family affair in which the nation's promise was "delivered."

Images of the reformed family and its domestic habits were crucial to the revolutionary movement in two particular ways. The first was the display of Egypt as a nation. At the end of World War I, the British rejected the notion that the Egyptian people formed a nation and that the Wafd, the delegation of elite Egyptians who demanded direct negotiations with the British at Versailles, represented the interests of the Egyptians in toto. The British claimed that Egyptians did not know the difference between "nationalist" and "extremist" or "revolutionary."[7] It thus became incumbent upon the *effendiyya* — the Wafd's targeted source of support — to present an image of national unity, both to the British and to the Egyptians whose loyalty the Wafd needed to gain.[8] *Effendi* revolutionaries used familial, domestic imagery — including images of mothering and nurturing — to display to the British that Egypt was indeed a nation and that the Egyptians formed a national "family" despite the varying agendas that they brought to the demonstrations.

Similarly, the *effendiyya* frequently depicted the Wafd leadership and its supporters as the natural heads of this national Egyptian family. The emergence during the revolution of the familial imagery that the *effendiyya* had learned in the classroom and articulated in the turn-of-the-century press cemented the Wafd's relationship to the revolution and to the Egyptians. While the Wafd leadership saw itself as representing and promoting the ideals of liberal government — as fighting for an Egypt for all Egyptians — it had not, in fact, been elected by the Egyptians to represent them in Europe. Familial imagery demonstrated that despite its ad hoc nature and its upper-class origins, the Wafd had created — given birth to — the Egyptian people that it was determined to represent. The role of mother — sometimes embodied by a female, sometimes played by a male — gave the nationalist movement the appearance of cohesion, structure, and strength.

At the same time, the use of *effendi* family politics in direct confrontations with the British proved that secular, middle-class reform had the power to free the nation. By presenting the revolution as the logical outcome of middle-class reform, and by connecting that reform with the Wafd and its agendas, the *effendiyya* claimed that their habits and values were distinctly Egyptian — and politically useful. Monogamy, domestic reform, the education of women, and the application of scientific motherhood to the home were considered nationalist strategies that constituted the proven recipe for independence and self-rule.

The *effendiyya*'s drive to represent the nation and to create a parental link between the Wafd and the Egyptians represent understudied aspects of the 1919 Revolution: the creation of a nationalist, revolutionary culture *after* the revolution had begun and while the revolution's leadership was overseas.[9] Most historians agree that the 1919 Revolution was a spontaneous uprising, ignited by the circumstances of World War I and by the refusal of the British to negotiate directly with the Egyptians in the post-war conferences.[10] While the desire of the Egyptians to represent them-selves at Versailles certainly echoed the sentiments expressed by political parties a decade earlier, those political parties had been rendered dormant by the war and thus had not been able to coach a revolutionary movement into existence. Party leadership was therefore not available to shape and lead a revolutionary movement until the Wafd presented itself to the British as a delegation of negotiators and until the masses rallied behind their efforts.[11] The leadership of the Wafd was itself surprised at the out-pouring of support it received from the masses when it first encountered difficulties with the British.[12] Did the revolution thus invent the Wafd, or did the Wafd shape and sponsor the revolution?[13]

The revolution did indeed force the British to recognize the Wafd as Egypt's representatives. But did the revolution create a Wafd that repre-sented the interests of "all Egyptians"? The Wafd was not a party of social revolutionaries or champions of the lower classes, and it was not in fact interested in a starting a revolution.[14] As a group of elite landowners and financiers, the Wafd leadership was mostly interested in gaining the support of the middle and upper classes for its campaign to represent Egypt.[15] But once its role was established and the Wafd leadership was ensconced in Europe to negotiate a postwar agreement, a discourse link-ing the Wafd to the Egyptians was created by Wafd supporters back home. For the *effendiyya* — students and professionals alike — the image of the family and the rituals of reformed domesticity represented the Wafd's ability to rule Egyptians. The display of the reformed, bourgeois family during the revolution brought the logic and imagery of the occupation full circle and the ideals of the middle classes to the fore.

World War I, the Protectorate, and the Outbreak of the Revolution

The informal and indefinite nature of the British occupation of Egypt changed when the Ottomans, still Egypt's de jure sovereigns, sided with the Germans and thereby declared war on the British. The British thus made Egypt into a formal protectorate state on December 18, 1914. On the following day, the British deposed 'Abbas Hilmy II and replaced him with a puppet ruler, his uncle Husein Kamil (r. 1914–17). The protectorate detached Egypt from the Ottoman Empire and gave the British virtual legislative and executive powers there; Husein Kamil's title was changed to sultan in order to acknowledge Egypt's separation from the Ottoman Empire. The British put Egypt under a state of martial law in which freedoms of assembly and the press were curtailed and then abolished. The Egyptian government, headed by Prime Minister Husein Rushdi Pasha and the sultan, became mere facilitators of the British war efforts. Because of the war with the Ottomans in the Sinai and the Hijaz, and difficulties with the rebelling Sanusi Bedouin in Cyrenaica on Egypt's western border, Egypt quickly came to house large numbers of British troops.

The war saw untold hardships for the Egyptians.[16] By 1916 the British invasion of Palestine had begun taxing Egyptian civilian resources. The forced recruitment of labor for the Allied armies in the Middle East and elsewhere and the requisition of animals, buildings, and food placed a tremendous burden on the Egyptian peasantry. Between 1916 and 1919, one and a half million *fellaheen* were conscripted by the British, totaling one-third of Egyptian men between the ages of seventeen and thrity-five.[17]

The local economy was damaged by the British war effort. In September 1914, the British passed a decree that limited cotton production and forced the production of foodstuffs and cereals in its stead. Cotton production in the Delta was thus limited to one-third of each landowner's holdings; consequently, during the war years, the export value of cotton decreased 50 percent.[18] This both angered peasants and subjected them to enormous financial hardships. Such changes also alienated the large land-owning class, including men like Sa'ad Zaghlul and 'Ali Sha'rawi, who later played central roles in the movement to end the protectorate. While such men indeed benefited from the structure of the Egyptian economy during the war years, they resented the implementation of policies that were not of their own design.[19]

Finally, the urban masses were significantly affected by the war. While the working classes initially benefited from the growth of a local industry that produced substitutes for imported goods, they were harshly affected by changes in local living conditions. Peasant migration to the cities, in part the result of changes in agricultural production, put pressures on the urban infrastructure, and the loss of building materials to the war effort resulted in a severe housing shortage. Rents consequently went up, leaving urban dwellers the victims of price inflation. It is estimated that monthly expenses for the poorest of Cairo's inhabitants tripled between 1914 and 1919; at the same time, wages decreased.[20] High prices of food and other goods and the loss of Egyptian capital to British troops led to massive inflation.[21]

By the end of the war, most Egyptians felt that they were facing intolerable conditions. Their khedive had been deposed and replaced by the British; they had been forced to declare war on Istanbul; their own political institutions were closed down in favor of unilateral British rule; and their land and goods had been confiscated or converted. High prices made it impossible for many to eat and find shelter. Crime rates increased in the urban areas, as did prostitution, disease, suicide, starvation, and drug use. Nationalism thus ceased to be merely an ideological platform for the elite and became a rallying cry for all those afflicted by the war and the protectorate.

Perhaps the most duplicitous aspect of the establishment of the British Protectorate in Egypt was the promise to end colonial rule. Sir Milne Cheetham, the acting consul general in Egypt in 1914, stated that England in fact wished to "accelerate progress towards self-government for Egypt."[22] Such promises were as vague and open-ended as the veiled protectorate itself and created the expectation that the end of the war would lead to Egyptian independence.

The years before the outbreak of World War I had, in fact, seen an increased participation of the *effendiyya* and the landed classes in governmental affairs. Egypt's Legislative Assembly, from which the revolution's leaders actually emerged, portended a more active role for Egyptians in politics but was shut down by the war. The assembly, like the political parties earlier in the century, was part of the British administration's program of appeasement: It was an extension of Egypt's original Legislative Council, formed in 1883 as the result of the Dufferin Commission's recommendations for "training" Egyptians in the arts of self-government. Formed at Kitchner's urging, the assembly was designed to be a means of checking the power of ʿAbbas Hilmy. It turned out, however, to be a nationalist forum. The assembly met for the first time in January 1913 and was suspended when the protectorate was announced in December of the following year. The suspension of the assembly, according to historian Afaf Marsot, was enough to convince men like Saʿad Zaghlul, long-time supporters of the British, that Egyptian designs on self-government were not forthcoming.[23]

The emerging leader of the liberal nationalist movement was Saʿad Zaghlul, who was elected vice president of the Legislative Assembly just prior to the war's outbreak. By the time the Legislative Assembly was suspended, Zaghlul stood in opposition to the British government and to the puppets it maintained in the Egyptian government. Like Zaghlul, most of the men who later emerged as the leadership of the Wafd were

Western educated and solidly rooted in the middle and upper classes —
landowners, industrialists, merchants, *effendiyya*. Zaghlul, Mohammad
Mahmoud, Hamad Basil, 'Ali Sha'rawi, and 'Abdullatif al-Makabati were
all large landowners; Isma'il Sidqui was an industrialist; Ahmad Lutfi
al-Sayyid and 'Abd al-'Aziz Fahmy represented the *effendiyya;* and
Mohammad 'Ali and 'Umar Tussun were members of the royal family.
The Wafd leadership and many of its supporters accepted the ideals of
constitutional liberalism as de rigueur. They were therefore prepared to
cooperate as long as the British made good on their promises to leave
Egypt once the Egyptians could demonstrate political maturity. One
Wafd supporter later recounted in his memoirs: "We in Egypt always
regarded the British Occupation as temporary and on that understanding,
based on reiterated pledges, we were prepared to cooperate without relin-
quishing our claim to be finally an independent people. . . . We were
eager to advance on those lines."[24] The British referred to the author of
these words, Amine Youssef, as an "extreme, *though reasonable,* nationalist. He acknowledges what Great Britain has done for Egypt, but he
appeals to her to grant complete independence to that country now on
the ground that 'The moment has come when she can claim her sovereignty, justified by her moral and material conditions.'"[25]

Egyptian nationalists like Youssef attempted to force the British to
make good on their promises about the negotiation of independence
shortly after the signing of the armistice. On November 13, 1918, Sa'ad
Zaghlul, 'Ali Sha'rawi, and 'Abd al-'Aziz Fahmy visited the British resi-
dency in Cairo to meet with Egypt's high commissioner, Sir Reginald
Wingate. Encouraged by the end of the war and Woodrow Wilson's
espousal of the principals of self-determination (Wilson was considered
a "messiah figure" in Egypt in the postwar period), Zaghlul and his associates presented Wingate with a program of complete autonomy for
Egypt.[26] They also requested permission for travel to London to discuss
Egypt's future directly with the British government.

The British were not prepared to respond affirmatively to either of
Zaghlul's requests. By the time the war ended, the British were still
uncertain about what they wished to do with Egypt; it was clear, however, that emancipation was not included in their options. In September
1917, an Egyptian Administration Committee, consisting of Lords
Balfour, Curzon, and Milner, was established to determine the status of
postwar Egypt. A memo submitted by Lord Milner made their position
clear: "Unless we lose the war, Egypt will in [the] future be as much a
part of the British Empire as India or Nigeria, whether we proceed to

annexation or, as I personally think better, we content ourselves with a form of the Protectorate."[27] Balfour found Zaghlul's plans for Egypt extravagant and claimed that Egypt was not ready for self-government of any nature. While he declared himself willing to negotiate later with Egypt's prime minister Husein Rushdi, who had supported Britain's goals for Egypt throughout the war, he wholeheartedly denounced Zaghlul's intentions.

Also on November 13, Zaghlul set out to establish a delegation of Egyptians who would speak for the nation and its interests. Historian Maurius Deeb characterizes this delegation as a synthesis of the National and Peoples' Parties of the years leading up to World War I. From the National Party the Wafd took its organizational infrastructure, several prominent members, an urban base of support, and a firm conviction to oust the British from Egypt; from the People's Party they gathered rural support and a commitment to liberal ideology. As such, they made allies of the urban *effendiyya;* the rural, medium-landowning element; the landed elite; and large landowners and industrialists.[28]

Members of the Wafd were united by their experience in the defunct Legislative Assembly as well as by a desire to seek independence from Great Britain though legal means and to represent the will and the wishes of the Egyptian people directly.[29] To gain popularity, Zaghlul undertook a public speaking campaign and traveled throughout Egypt. In order to strengthen his position in the eyes of the British, he initiated the *tawkilat* campaign — the collection of signed depositions from all of Egypt's representative organizations stating that the Wafd was their sole, authorized representative in all political negotiations with the European powers. The *effendiyya* were instrumental in getting the *tawkilat* signed in the provinces, acting as representatives of the Wafd. The *tawkilat* had the effect of igniting nationalist sentiment and was "unwittingly a silent rehearsal for the 1919 popular uprising."[30]

When members of the Wafd learned that a Syrian delegation was being allowed to attend the Peace Conference at Versailles, they became more radical in their demands and tactics. Organized meetings at Zaghlul's home and public denunciations of British rule took place with greater frequency. When Prime Minister Husein Rushdi and his associate 'Adly Yeghen resigned in outrage over the treatment of the Wafd, the British were left with no sympathizers in Egypt. Consequently, the British government began to view the Wafd as dangerous. On March 6, 1919, Zaghlul and other members of the Wafd were warned that their activities could be punished under the sanctions of martial law. Two days later,

Zaghlul and fellow Wafd members Hamad Basil and Isma'il Sidqui were arrested and exiled to Malta.

The result of their exile was the beginning of a series of demonstrations in Cairo that lasted throughout March and engaged Egyptians of all classes and occupations in active rebellion against the protectorate. On March 9, students from the faculty of law and from al-Azhar led demonstrations in Cairo's streets. They were quickly joined by students from other faculties and later by secondary-school students. On March 10, the students joined ranks and marched toward central Cairo, joined by tram workers declaring themselves on strike.[31] Soldiers fired on the demonstrators, resulting in the revolution's first fatalities.

The demonstrations soon spread throughout Egypt. On March 12, the British fired on three thousand demonstrators in Tanta, killing eleven and wounding fifty-two. Another thirteen were killed at the mosque of al-Sayyida Zeinab in Cairo on March 14. By March 15, many communications facilities had been destroyed; in Qalyub, railway tracks were pulled up and trains were attacked. British military personnel were attacked and killed. By March 16, three thousand Egyptians were dead, one hundred villages were destroyed, sixty-three railway stations were burned, and railroad tracks were damaged in two hundred places.[32]

Women joined the demonstrations on March 16, carrying banners that read "Long Live Freedom and Independence" and "Down with the Protectorate." On that same day, eighty thousand revolutionaries gathered at al-Azhar to hear speeches given by the Wafd Party. By March 19, certain provinces were in open revolt: in the Delta and Upper Egypt, the *fellaheen* destroyed crops and burned railway stations. By the end of March, the country was in open revolt, and joined the Wafd in demanding independence.[33]

In late March, General Allenby arrived in Egypt with authority to take whatever measures necessary to restore order. He quickly discovered that only military intervention would quell the disturbances. Sensing the difficulties facing the British in Egypt, the impracticality of such an intervention, and the importance of allowing the Wafd to attend the Peace Conference, Allenby released Zaghlul on April 9, 1919. By April 11, Zaghlul and other members of the Wafd were en route to Paris, where they remained in negotiations with the British for the duration of the revolution.[34]

Once Zaghlul was in Paris, a Central Committee was created to continue the Wafd's mission in his absence.[35] The most important tasks facing the Central Committee were maintaining communication with

Zaghlul, raising funds for the Wafd, and mounting a campaign to create national support.[36] To both ends, the Central Committee set about increasing Wafd membership, both in Cairo and the provinces.[37] Their first targets were the village notables, inasmuch as the notables could provide funds for the Wafd's coffers and lend support to the Wafd's agenda at the local level (as Wafd members, it was also hoped that the notables would sit on branch committees).[38] Citing correspondence between the Central Committee's first secretary, 'Abd al-Rahman Fahmy, and Zaghlul in Paris, Deeb states that notables with educated sons in Cairo were most readily brought into the Wafd fold.[39] According to Deeb, the *effendiyya*, as sons of the village notables, were at home in the country as well as the city, and therefore capable of presenting the Wafd agendas in language appealing to their fathers.[40] The *effendiyya* thus served as the ideological link between the Wafd and the provinces. The British accused the *effendiyya* of subjecting innocent Egyptians to their machinations and of bringing the masses into a movement that was not designed to represent their interests.[41]

The Central Committee was quick to note that enthusiasm for joining the Wafd at the village level increased after students returned to their villages following the school strikes in late March 1919.[42] Students took the "spirit of the revolution" back to the provinces to local families. Students were active in demonstrations, in creating and distributing leaflets and brochures, and in mounting press campaigns.[43] British intelligence reported that "a large measure of the work of agitation is entrusted to the students."[44] The British were not so much nervous about the presence of the Wafd in Paris as they were by the success of the *effendiyya* in consolidating a movement in the Wafd's absence.[45] While the Wafd leadership was absent, the revolutionary movement grew and spread.

Indeed, if the establishment and exile of the Wafd started the revolution, then the *effendiyya* — both professionals and students — were central in transforming the symbols of disparate uprisings into a nationalist movement with the Wafd at its head. Historian Mohammad Anis claims that the revolution must, in fact, be understood as two revolutions. The first occurred in March 1919 and caused the disturbances that ultimately got the attention of the British. The second, he claims, began in April and created the movement that the Wafd would continue to lead. It was during this second revolution that the *effendiyya* — as the "Wafd's missionaries" — displayed the often domestic symbols through which the "crowds" of demonstrators were transformed into a "people" united behind the Wafd.[46]

When a continuation of the protectorate was accepted at the Peace

Conference in May 1919, the demonstrations and strikes in Egypt resumed. The Wafd's Central Committee, formed on the eve of Zaghlul's departure, continued to organize local committees that made it difficult for local government — British or Egyptian — to do its work without consulting and including the Wafd. Further strikes in support of the Wafd and against martial law broke out, as did another series of strikes by civil servants and workers.

Allenby appeased the Egyptians by telling them that a British commission, led by Lord Milner, would be sent to Egypt to listen to Egyptian ideas about autonomous government, albeit one that would remain under British protection. News about the incipient arrival of such a commission led to a greater degree of agitation, a situation that the Wafd leadership seized upon in order to organize further public disturbances and disorder. Once the Milner mission arrived in Cairo on December 7, 1919, Egyptian students immediately set about organizing and executing its boycott.[47] On December 10, the Central Committee of the Wafd issued a press communiqué stating that the Egyptian nation had decided to boycott Milner for three major reasons, perhaps the most important of which was that Milner and his peers wished to negotiate while assuming the Protectorate a fait accompli. During the mission's stay, the initial portion of which was spent in sequestration inside the Semiramis Hotel, its members received more than a thousand telegrams from the Egyptian populace. Most spoke in favor of an end to the protectorate; all the telegrams listed Sa'ad Zaghlul as Egypt's representative. While Milner was able to meet with Husein Kamil's successor, Sultan Fuad (r. 1917–36), and certain Egyptian ministers, he spoke with very few of the men who had any influence over the majority of Egyptians.[48] Despite Milner's December 29 announcement that his presence in Egypt was dedicated to "listening" to Egyptian requests, the boycott continued. Those with whom Milner did speak stood firm in their requests for Egyptian independence.

Milner left Egypt in March 1920. In June, 'Adly Yeghen was sent to London as an intermediary to begin talks between the Wafd and Milner that continued through November of that year. As those negotiations progressed, splits formed between Zaghlul, who would not settle on an agreement until an Egyptian national assembly could vote on it, and Wafd members ('Adly Yeghen included) who were willing to conclude the negotiations without the direct support of the Egyptian masses. Milner's report on conditions in Egypt and their causes, published on February 26, 1921, suggested that the protectorate was neither tenable for Great Britain nor satisfactory to the Egyptians. Allenby asked Sultan Fuad to inform the Egyptians that the British government was willing to formalize Milner's proposal, which Zaghlul asked the Egyptian nation to accept, despite his reservations. 'Adly Yeghen was asked to form a ministry to represent the Egyptian people, and Allenby promised to back it. Upon his assumption of the premiership, 'Adly promised to invite Zaghlul and the Wafd to continue negotiations with the British until they reached an agreement that represented the people's will.

Privately, however, 'Adly attempted to prevent Zaghlul from returning to Egypt, fearing that Zaghlul's popularity would undermine his newly established premiership. His fears were confirmed when, on April 4, 1921, Zaghlul returned to a hero's welcome — a clear indication of the people's preference for Zaghlul. To campaign against 'Adly, Zaghlul relied once again on the *effendiyya* (students in particular), asking them to take the message to the provinces that the 'Adly cabinet did not represent Egypt's will. Zaghlul succeeded in inviting British Labour Members of Parliament to Egypt, so that he could show them that the 'Adly ministry was not legitimate. The result of the visit, according to Deeb, was the issuing of a manifesto by the MPs that an election for a National Assembly should be held and that the assembly should elect the Egyptian cabinet.[49] While the assembly was never formed, 'Adly resigned on December 11, 1921.

For his role in bringing the 'Adly cabinet down, Zaghlul was again deported, this time to the Seychelles on February 20, 1922. Zaghlul's popularity surged, both among the masses and among those who had previously left the Wafd. The absence of the Wafd leadership from Egypt made the British more willing than ever to come to a settlement with the Egyptians, and one week after their exile — on February 28, 1922 — the British announced their willingness to recognize Egypt as an independent state. In exchange, Britain made several demands: it would retain sovereignty over its communications in Egypt; its troops would be held in Egypt in order to defend Egypt against aggressions from foreign powers; Britain would be allowed to protect minorities and foreigners within Egypt's borders; and it would be given sovereignty over the Sudan. On March 1, 1922, Egypt's newest prime minister, Tharwat Pasha, formed the cabinet that drafted Egypt's first constitution. On March 15, Egypt claimed its independence. The new constitution was unsatisfactory to the Wafd, King Fuad (the constitution changed his title from sultan to king), and the British, yet it formed the basis of an arrangement between Britain and Egypt that lasted until 1936.[50] Zaghlul emerged as the father of a revolution that took place largely in his absence, and as the leader of an independent Egypt, despite his reservations about the shape and structure of the new Egyptian polity.[51]

Building the Nation:
The Political Realm in Feminine Garb

The *effendiyya* who shaped and circulated the revolution's icons and propaganda pushed a dual agenda. They were dismissive of any nationalism that was not bourgeois, thereby claiming that it was their brand of behavior that suited the struggle against the British. At the same time, however, their discourse about the "nation" and the "national struggle" reveals a belief that Egyptians of all classes and creeds made up an Egyptian family — a family that, once "fathered" by the Wafd, would succeed in gaining independence.

Thus, a study of the press and propaganda during the revolution is a study in contradictions. Eyewitness accounts of the demonstrations attest to the fragmented nature of the Egyptian "nation." The "crowds" who participated in the demonstrations were depicted not only as having been divided along class lines but as differing in their demands on the British as well. Not even the Egyptian press called all revolutionaries "nationalist." Those who participated in a fashion deemed "orderly" by the press were called nationalists; those who did not were left out of the nationalist fold. "Non-nationalists" were in turn called mobs, rabble (*ra'a*), and riffraff (*gauga'*). Egyptian depictions did not much differ from the British accounts of certain demonstrators, which read: "A drawing by Hogarth of a scene made up of Dante's inferno and the French Revolution, add to that . . . oriental fanaticism — and you have something like this mob. Many of the crowd no longer produced any sound from their throats, others were foaming at the mouth, and I myself saw three fall over in fits on the ground."[52]

At the same time, however, the press often portrayed demonstrators — of all classes — as representing an Egyptian "nation," despite the differences in their behavior and their agendas. The *effendiyya* presented images of disparate masses transformed into a united, Egyptian populace — an Egyptian people (*umma*). What appeared to make a national movement out of crowds was the figure of "Egypt," represented and protected by the Wafd, behind which all Egyptians could rally.

To cement the relationship between the Wafd and the masses, the Central Committee made good use of the Egyptian press. The rise of nationalist sentiment in Egypt after 1918 and the rapid development of technology led to an increasingly "politically zealous" press and to a

greater interest in the press on the part of the Egyptian masses.[53] When
the Central Committee was put to work creating a support base for the
Wafd, they therefore had both an established vehicle for their "propaganda" and an eager audience. While neither the Wafd nor its later
detractors had official journals until 1922, support for the revolution and
for the Wafd's platforms was given by a goodly number of journals,
including *al-Ahram* (which continued to be Egypt's most widely read
daily newspaper) as early as 1918.[54] By 1919, *al-Ahali* (The people), *al-
Mahrusa, al-Nizam* (The order), and *al-Afkar* (Thoughts) were counted
by the British as "violently nationalist."[55] Often it was the "nonpolitical
press" — journals such as *al-Lata'if al-Musawwara* (Illustrated niceties),
founded by Iskander Makarius in 1915; and *al-Kashkul* (The scrapbook),
founded by Sulayman Fawzi in 1921 — that contained highly political messages about the revolution, the Wafd, and the Egyptian nation.[56] Both
journals represented, lauded, and lampooned national leadership through
the use of political caricatures, a medium that would later become a staple of the Egyptian press. While periodicals such as *al-Lata'if al-
Musawwara* and *al-Kashkul* did not have a very large circulation, they
were influential precisely because their illustrations and caricatures could
be understood by the illiterate.[57] The themes of both journals were
indeed representative of the more widely circulated newspapers.

Articles from the Egyptian press reporting the organized marches that
took place on March 17, 1919, for example, depict the apparent
dichotomy between "nationalist" and "non-nationalist" behavior.
Undertaken with the permission of the British authorities, those marches
swept through Cairo with a cast of thousands. The demonstrations were
successful in shutting down government work and businesses for the
duration, but no property was damaged and no conflict with the British
authorities occurred. According to *al-Ahram,* the demonstrators proceeded through Cairo, led by the police chief. Following the police came
the first rank of demonstrators — a group of students — carrying the
Egyptian flag. Students were followed by ranks of workers, also carrying a flag that read *"al-'umal"* (workers). The march lasted for six hours.[58]
Press reports did not linger on lengthy descriptions of the members of
the demonstrations' ranks. Rather, they turned the readers' attention to
those who had apparently been a disruptive or uncivilized element in
previous demonstrations, strikes, and attacks on the British. They
scolded disruptive forces for working against the revolution and its purposes. Straightforward narrative accounts of the demonstrations gave
way to commentary about them.

By contrast, the "perfection" of the orderly demonstrators of March 17 illustrated the powers of nationalism and sound nationalist behavior to resuscitate the nation. Apparently speaking to the British, an anonymous writer in *al-Ahram* wrote: "We aim our words at those who would not or did not see, and to those who have heard bad things spoken about them. . . . The demonstrations proceeded with an order that filled our hearts with joy," expressing what the periodical *al-Mahrusa* had also called the "best manifestations of living, developed nations."[59] Workers, warehouse and store owners, and merchants were listed as having participated in the most civilized, orderly fashion, marching, watching, and cheering from the sidelines.

Al-Mahrusa also dedicated its opening columns to praising the "civilized" nature of the *effendiyya*-led marches of March 18, saying that such demonstrations were crucial to countering what the British said and thought about Egypt.[60] The March 21 edition of *al-Mahrusa* compared the students' role in the demonstrations with that of the riffraff, saying that the students followed the "right model" *(al-manhaj al-salimy)* because their demonstrations were undertaken with wisdom, order, and presence of mind.[61]

Apparent in these two descriptions of anti-British demonstrations is the notion that there was a proper, Egyptian nationalism that needed to be revealed before the Egyptians were ready to govern themselves. The *effendiyya* seemed to believe that bourgeois nationalism had resuscitative powers, that it had created a "living, developed" nation, and that it would — if left unhindered — continue to bring the masses into the fold. Whether or not the Wafd leadership actually believed that "nation" transcended differences in class and political agendas is secondary to the fact that what they displayed in the press — both for the British and their fellow Egyptians to see — were images of the Egyptian nation in which all classes claimed membership. The unruly orders could clearly be brought into the fold with the right sort of leadership.

Revolutionary images of Egypt and its "proper leadership" reflect the debates and discussions about the Egyptian nation that had been in circulation since Mohammad 'Ali's era: Egypt was a "family" of people, it was modern, it had been reformed. Strains that were common to the turn-of-the-century press and the classroom — in which it was argued that Egyptians could demonstrate their modernity and their commitment to liberating the nation through their personal behavior — surfaced during the revolution and were connected to the Wafd's struggle against the British. While the revolution was the unplanned reaction of many classes to the conditions of the war years and to the unfulfilled promises of the

FIGURE 4. "Come dance with me, my dear Egypt." *Al-Lata'if al-Musawwara,*
December 8, 1919.

British, the imagery of the *effendiyya* and the Wafd reflected the projects
of personal and domestic reform that had been so central to shaping
nationalism for more than a century.

Indeed, one of the most common images from the Egyptian press during the revolutionary period was that of Egypt as a being — an entity —
distinct from other nations, possessing its own history, customs, and traditions. As in translations from Mohammad 'Ali's era, in debates about
"the new woman" from the turn of the century, and in children's textbooks, the entity known as Egypt was placed relative to other nations so
that its progress could be measured. Not surprisingly, Egypt was depicted
in the gendered, feminine images that had been so central to the
effendiyya's nationalist consciousness since the late nineteenth century.
One caricature, for example, published in *al-Lata'if al-Musawwara* the day
after Milner's arrival in Egypt in December 1919, illustrates Egypt as
different from Syria and Albania and from the colonial powers that
sought control over them (see Figure 4). Egypt is represented as an elegant, ancient Egyptian, a kind of pharoaonic princess. Allusions to the

pharaonic past include Egypt's attire, the lotus that adorns the column behind her, the palm trees, as well as the furniture in the background.[62] Syria, clothed presumably in some sort of traditional costume, is a dancing girl. She sways freely and happily in the embrace of her French suitor, Henri Gouraud, later to become mandate Syria's high commissioner.[63] At the same time, Fiume (Albania), clothed in what appears to be Tyrolean attire, has clearly succumbed to Italian General D'Annunzio, who led the siege of Fiume, with whom she seems pleased to dance. Egypt refuses the overtures made by her suitor, an unnamed British officer. When he invites her to dance, she refuses his embrace, and gives him the cold shoulder and a piece of her mind. (He says: "Come dance with me, my dear Egypt." She replies: "On the life of your father, have some mercy!") What is suggested here is that it was a distinctly Egyptian entity rather than an Arab or European one that would ward off imperialism and give Egypt its independence. For the educated classes, the connection between reform and Egypt's ability to thwart the British might well have been clear. But even the uneducated, for whom the relationship between the revolution and state-sponsored reform was neither important nor obvious, could take pride in Egypt's clearly victorious stance.

The fact that Egypt is depicted as a woman suggests that it was the virtues of Egyptian womanhood that could either lead a nation to "give in" to imperialism or ward it off — provide it with morals and courage, or corrupt it.[64] While Egypt's posture is defensive, and evokes both power and modesty, the other two nations rather immodestly open themselves to be taken by France and Italy. This particular Egyptian "woman" is thus placed in the position of defending Egypt in the public sphere through the values and virtues that, according to the press and to public-school pedagogy, were hers to cultivate in the private realm. While Egypt as a "woman" was central to revolutionary iconography, it is hard to imagine that this clearly public, political role — albeit for an imaginary woman — did not evoke the same discomfort and debate that had been intrinsic to "the woman question" in the early twentieth century, at least for some Egyptians.

This awkward relationship between the power of womanhood — albeit imaginary — to confront the British and the crucial role that women were to play in the domestic realm is evoked in another caricature, which also connected the crucial role of domesticity with the revolutionary struggle. The seemingly innocuous images of domestic activities that were so central to the turn-of-the-century press and classroom were also used during the revolution to depict the Egyptian nation. The image, also from

FIGURE 5. "What will you have, my lady?" *Al-Lata'if al-Musawwara*, August 20, 1920.

al-Lata'if al-Musawwara, resurrects discussions of "table talk." Printed in August 1920, at which time Sa'ad Zaghlul and his fellow Wafdists were in London negotiating with Milner for an end to the protectorate, the cartoon is a clear indication of the extent to which domestic practices and national liberation were part of a similar agenda. The waiter represents England; the diner is Egypt. He asks her: "What will you have, my lady?" She responds: "A platter of independence and, along with it, a dish of freedom." International diplomacy, here, is forged in a modern dining room (see Figure 5).[65]

At this dining room table cum drawing table of international politics — clearly public space — a refined, well-mannered woman does Egypt's bidding. Egypt, as a modern, literate woman, knows the protocol involved in dining in the league of modern nation-states. This is not the image of a clumsy, backward, colonized entity seeking entrance into the league of refined, modern nation-states: this woman — while obviously not European — asks for what she wants with all the ease of a Western counterpart. While her attire suggests the maintenance of a certain degree of "non-Western-ness," it also reveals that Egypt is modern and has a taste for the latest fashions. Her arms are bare, her shoes are "Euro-chic." This woman is sitting upright and dining at a table, an emblem that directly contrasts with images produced in the West in the nineteenth and early twentieth centuries, in which women were portrayed as endlessly lounging and reclining. In such depictions, women engaged in far less "functional" activities than this caricature suggests — gossiping, smoking, sexual intrigue — and were passive, voiceless, and without will. In this very public image — again, a contrast to Orientalist images of seclusion — the Egyptian nation qua woman is neither passive nor voiceless.

This image of Egypt suggests that modern, reformed womanhood ultimately made England subservient to Egypt. Again, while the illiterate masses would not have made the connection between this caricature and "table talk," they could certainly see England's deference. This waiter not only serves Egypt but bows to her. It is she who is in control, she who commands. Evoking the lessons of nineteenth-century, state-produced travel literature, this caricature suggests that modern Egypt had not only reached Great Britain's "level" in the hierarchy of modern nation-states but had surpassed it. Would Milner recognize this and similarly bow to the Egyptians? Domestic imagery also appeared in revolutionary propaganda designed to counter British claims that the revolution had no goal and that revolutionaries had little mission other than the destruction of the British and their property. *Effendi* nationalists readily contested such depictions of their nationalist movement and countered the British insistence that their revolution consisted of little more than rabble-rousing.[66]

Again, "table talk" connected reform to the revolution. An intelligence report from June 1919, for example, given to the members of the Milner mission, also evokes the various forms of "table talk" that were so common during the decades leading up to the revolution. This memo, part of a police folder on the activities of the "Waez Printing Office and the Printing at Shareh (sic) el-Khelwati," stated:

Essamul Dine was found in possession of a copy of el-Defaa al-Watani [National Defense] and a paper in which it was written in his own handwriting under the heading 'Banquets':

General Sir Edmund Allenby offered a big banquet . . . in Savoy Hotel. . . . We have been able to know the "menu" of the banquet. It is as follows: 'Independence of Egypt per force à la Mayonaise; the Union of the Nation; Freedom of meetings and that of the press; Egyptian (cervelle) with bluff, and Money per force.' The drinks are our blood, our sweating.[67]

As in early-twentieth-century newspaper columns wherein "hadith al-ma'ida" couched discussions that had less to do with eating and drinking than with the politics of creating a new national family, 'Essam ad-Din's paper attacks British politics in the terms that were most common to shaping Egyptian nationalism in the decades leading up to the revolution. What appears to be a description of British cannibalism also reflects the lexicon of *effendi* nationalism. While the banquet was clearly public, the struggle was waged at the table.

The Wafd leadership was given a legitimate role in creating a nation-state through its interactions with "Egypt" the distinct nation, "Egypt" who embodied national reform programs. A caricature printed in April, 1922, when the first Egyptian constitution was being penned, depicted members of the Wafd Party sitting at the feet of a splendid female nation. Across her extended arms were the words *"al-umma al-misriyya"* (the Egyptian nation), and her sash read *"istiqlal"* (independence). Wafd members held scissors, measuring tape, sewing pins — all that the (male) nationalists needed to clothe Liberated Egypt in "her" new attire (her dress, sandals, and headdress alluded to Greco-Roman ideals). She commanded them: "This dress is missing something! I want a different design." According to the caption, their response to her was simply, "Be tolerant of us . . . be broad minded . . . wait until we're finished, and then you can be the judge!!!"[68]

The caricature clearly depicted the Wafd Party as the ultimate author of the nation-state; it created its institutions, the limits and functions of those institutions, and granted suffrage or denied it. Indeed, it offered a counter to Milner's claim that the nationalist movement was a "Frankenstein" that Sa'ad Zaghlul had created.[69] However, the nation's voice — a woman's voice — appears to be essential enough to the national project that she, ultimately, had the last word in the nation's design. If the feminine nature of the nation was left unsatisfied, its male authors would surely be put back to work.

Similarly, *al-Kashkul* chronicled the process of writing a constitution through images of men clothing lady Egypt.[70] In *al-Kashkul's* rendition, Egypt's prime minister, Husein Rushdi Pasha, puts the final touches on Egypt's overcoat. The magazine's editors chose pharaonic rather than Greco-Roman imagery to depict Egypt: the cobra in her headdress and her anklet and arm bands evoke the same pharaonic imagery used in the depiction of the dancing "Egypt" (see Figure 4). Her high-heeled and elegant shoes seemed to suggest that this pharaoh was modern, the result of the reform programs that placed Egypt on an equal footing with the European nations. In both images, Egypt dwarfs the men who clothed her. Men

FIGURE 6. "The awakening Egyptian youth." *Al-Lata'if al-Musawwara,*
October 11, 1920.

bow to lady Egypt and look small in comparison to the nation. Thus the
images deliver a double message: on the one hand, men created the nation-
state. On the other, (female) Egypt is slightly out of their grasp. Was the
emergence of modern Egypt thus the result of reform, or was it the
inevitable manifestation of eternal Egypt's history, strength, and potential?

An image of Egypt's independence as the result of male efforts yet at
the same time out of their grasp was clearly not uncommon to the revolutionary press. The relationship between the female form of the nation
and the *effendi* struggle to build a body politic is also well illustrated in
another caricature from *al-Lata'if al-Musawwara* (see Figure 6). Here, the
potentials of the body politic are clothed in Western garb: Egypt, or a
vision of what Egypt might have become, is depicted as a kind of ethe-
real beauty queen, just out of reach of the fettered, "Awakening Egyptian
Youth" *(al-shabab al-misry al-nahid)*. She is "Freedom and Total Independence" *(al-hurriyya wal-istiqlal al-tam)*. The young *effendi* beckons to
her: "Come to me, come to me oh my beloved" *(illayya illayya ya habibti)*.

The caption reads: "This caricature needs no clarification for it shows the restrictions placed on the Egyptian youth who cannot progress to fulfill their aspirations unless their fetters are cut. Who can cut them except a strong government?"[71]

Upon closer examination of the caricature, one discovers that the *effendi* youth is fettered by "foreign habits." As if he has asked the three foreigners next to him (depicted as a cocaine dealer, a vendor of "drinks," and a pigeon breeder) to free him from his fetters, they respond that "tomorrow" *(bukra fil-mish mish)* they will let him go.[72] It is then that he turns to his beloved Egypt for succor and salvation; she is not fully embodied, but she does not reject his advances. The "nation" in this cartoon, like the images that preceded it, is feminine. But the ultimate form of the nation-state appears to be interchangeable. Here freedom and independence, without which there could be no nation, are represented as European (modern European, in fact; this woman's clothing is quite stylish). This mixture of clothing styles attests to the fact that the form that the nation-state would take at the time was still quite fluid. While always essentially female, the nation had many aspects.

The interchangeable nature of the Egyptian nation in these caricatures attests to the fact that the process of middle-class self-fashioning that was so central to the turn-of-the-century press and the classroom was still in process when the revolution took place. Just as *effendi* revolutionaries filled the press with discussions (and illustrations) of the shape of the nation, they also discussed the "personal" nature of becoming free. Monogamy, the freedom to choose one's spouse, household fashions and clothing styles, the proper education of children — all were as essential to the display of *effendi* nationalism in 1919 as were allegiance to the nation and the Wafd. Just prior to the outbreak of the revolution, for example, *al-Sufur* carried an article called "If I Were Free." What appeared to be a discussion of independence from the British was in fact a discussion of marital life:

If I was free and had a wife whose arm I could take and with whom I could stroll we would discuss events . . . heedless of those who surround us. . . . I wouldn't try to convince her of my opinions, nor lead her in any direction. . . . If I was free and God blessed me with sons and daughters . . . they would be educated such that the curtain between them and me would be lifted. If I was free . . . If I was free . . . oh, freedom.[73]

Freedom here was not just the struggle against an occupying power but rather the continued attachment of middle-class habits to the independence movement. Companionate marriage, lifting the curtain between

men and women, and the importance of family evoked the relationship
between political success and domestic habits that had marked Egypt's
long march toward independence.

The *effendiyya's* preference for modern, reformed women, like love of
the nation, was a frequent image in the press during the revolutionary era.
In July 1922, *al-Kashkul* carried a depiction of a dapper, sophisticated
young man gazing at a beautiful woman and saying, "You are the giver
of life, and there is no life without you, oh Egypt."[74] His Egypt sported
a knee-length skirt and high heels; her face was uncovered. The besotted
effendi — books at his feet, papers in his pocket — betrays the trappings of
a modern education and an affinity for Western clothing. His attention to
his appearance, like his quest for knowledge, has led him to his beloved.
Education and personal behavior produced clear nationalist allegiances
and aspirations. Is this not the woman he would chose once he was free?

After the revolution began, the press continued to run articles promoting habits and customs that characterized independence. Articles such
as "The Choice of a House," "*Tarbiyya* and the Future of the Nation," and
"Politics and Morals" formed the staples of the revolutionary press as they
had in the decades leading up to it.[75] Just as in the press at the turn of the
twentieth century, the right kind of morals, dress, behavior, and houses
would lead the nation to independence.

"The Woman Question" burned as hotly in the revolutionary press as
it had at the turn of the century. Articles and debates on the *hijab,*
women's education, motherhood, the proper and "natural" roles of
women in society, and comparisons between women in the East and West
accompanied articles on independence and constitutionalism. Women's
appearance and behavior appeared to be as crucial to the revolutionary
moment as they had been to the process of shaping middle-class nationalism in prior decades. The activities and behavior of "real" women was
thus as important as the morals and virtues of the "imaginary" women
who were used to represent the national struggle. In "Yesterday and
Tomorrow," *al-Lata'if al-Musawwara's* cartoonist Ihab Effendi depicted an
Egyptian woman ("Yesterday") and her granddaughter ("Tomorrow").
The caption indicated that "Tomorrow" was an example of what would
happen to Egyptian women if they persisted in imitating the West:
"This picture shows the difference between what Egyptian women wore
years ago and what the women of tomorrow, their granddaughters, will
look like if they continue to accelerate the pace at which they adopt the
dress and adornments of the West."[76] For the readers' inspection, the journal presented the shortening of the *"niqab"* up to the knees, asking how
far these women should go. While it is not enormously clear — either

from the caption or the caricature — whether or not the cartoonist or the editorial staff found "Yesterday" superior or inferior to "Tomorrow," the image of women here does illustrate the changes in habits and customs that accompanied Egypt's struggle for self-rule.

But what of the women of "today"? During the revolution, images of idealized, "fashioned" womanhood — women depicted as the nation, as the nation's history and its ideals, as the ideals of Westernized, male nationalists — clashed with the goals and aspirations of real women. Educated wives of the Wafd members and their *effendi* supporters appeared in the press and on the streets during the uprisings and the Anglo-Egyptian negotiations. They joined forces with the Wafd both in support of the national movement and in an attempt to bring the goals of reform (education, in particular) to fruition for women by attaining a role for them in the liberated body politic. When the revolution began, women harnessed their experiences as administrators in the arenas of education and beneficent activities to lead demonstrations against the British and to create the Wafdist Women's Central Committee in January 1920. Like its male counterpart, the Women's Central Committee served as an auxiliary to the Wafd. The Wafdist women organized demonstrations and boycotts of British goods, collected money and jewelry to help finance the nationalist struggle, and dealt directly with British authorities when male Wafdist leaders were exiled or imprisoned.[77] Because of the admiration shown for these women in the press (regardless of their views on women's education or the *hijab*, male nationalists did not argue against the contribution women were making to the revolution), and the gratitude of the Wafd for the women's efforts, it was not unreasonable to expect that women (at the very least the Wafd women) would be granted some sort of role in the political realm once independence had been gained. Unclear at the time of the revolution was whether *effendi* revolutionaries were responding to the contributions of "real" women or to the ideals of womanhood that were so central to representing the nation.

Mothers of the New Order: Nurturing the Infant Nation

At the time of the revolution, the image of the independent, Egyptian nation was clearly born of an ideal mother. Motherhood was key to cementing the relationship between the Wafd and the masses during the revolution, and motherhood challenged the aspirations of real women to participate in politics. The *effendiyya* presented images of mothers and motherhood that would ultimately save the nation from the British as well as guide the actions and decisions of Egyptian leaders. While the role of male nationalists in fashioning, authoring, and structuring the nation cannot be denied, iconography from the revolution suggests that male actions were irrelevant if not born of the right Egyptian "mother" and steeped in the virtues of (sound) motherhood. The Wafd was given greatest credence when it participated in "nurturing the nation," making motherhood essential to the revolution. When the revolution died down, however, women would be required to continue to nurture the nation from their homes.

In some newspapers and journals from the revolutionary era, the relationship among the home, domesticity, and motherhood was not much different than it had been in the turn-of-the-century press and the classroom. In other words, middle-class readers were reminded that if they loved their (real) mothers, and if those mothers were reformed and savvy, Egypt's independence would follow. In others, independent Egypt was embodied as a mother, and loving her was attached to a very concrete display of Egyptian institutions: a constitution, a national bank, Wafd leadership.

Motherhood, for example, guaranteed Egypt's financial solvency. In yet another image from *al-Lata'if al-Musawwara*, "Mother Egypt" is seated on the back of the Sphinx (often used in the revolutionary press to symbolize the nascent Egyptian nation). She breast-feeds the infant "Bank Misr," which was founded in 1920 by a group of Egyptian large-landowners and industrialists as a means of funding an independent, Egyptian economic policy. It was intended to be a purely "Egyptian" bank. Bank Misr is surrounded by the Bank of Rome, the Bank of Athens, the Anglo Bank, the Ahly Bank, the Belgian Bank, and the Credit Lyonais (see Figure 7). The cartoon's caption reads:

This picture represents Bank Misr and the Egyptian nation and the foreign banks in Egypt. Bank Misr is represented as a newborn baby, being breast-fed the milk of his mother. And who is his mother? None other than the Egyptian Nation, the beloved, splendid Egyptian Nation sitting on its oldest and most famous manifestation — the Sphinx. While mother Egypt attends to breast-feeding her newborn — about whom she is overjoyed — the child's older brothers sidle up to take a look. Their eyes are full of jealousy and rage, but they cheer each other on by saying: 'Will the baby live? Will the baby live?' We say: 'Yes the baby will live if he continues to nurse from the breast of his mother!'

The author's message is clear: Egypt's financial solvency would come about when its citizens, children, and institutions were thoroughly

FIGURE 7. "The baby will live if he continues to nurse from the breast of his mother." *Al-Lata'if al-Musawwara*, August 2, 1920.

nursed by the blessings of motherhood. Modern motherhood (a glance at Mother Egypt's shoes suggests that she was "modern") would instill in Egyptians morals and virtues, the absence of which, according to some, had led Isma'il Pasha into the grips of colonialism. The sins of the ancien régime were purged through breast milk. Similarly, on August 27, 1919, the journal depicted mother Egypt leading her sons into a wide-open New Bank Misr. In the background, the sun rises from behind the pyramids, here symbolic of "Egypt's Rebirth" (*nahdat Misr*).[78]

An important feature of both caricatures is that the relationship between Mother Egypt and Bank Misr does much to forge a connection between Egypt's financial elite (most of whom profited from the British occupation, particularly during the war years, and many of whom favored a continuation of the protectorate) and the nationalist movement. In the second caricature particularly, the Egyptian masses are included in an elite undertaking through the figure of mother Egypt. In both caricatures, men appropriate birth to cement their relationship to the nation.

The role of modern motherhood in bringing Egypt to independence was also the subject of numerous advertisements of products that promised perfect motherhood in both its political and domestic manifestations. An advertisement for Lactagol baby formula appeared in the summer of

FIGURE 8. "Healthy sons for the nation." *Al-Lata'if al-Musawwara,* August 27, 1919.

1919 (see Figure 8). Its subject appears to be straight out of one of the demonstrations: women marching and carrying placards. Rather than reading "Freedom and Total Independence," as did many of the placards carried by women in the demonstrations, the advertisement says: "Nationalist Mothers: Your most sacred duty is to raise healthy sons for the Nation. So feed them 'Lactagol.'"

Revolutionary iconography alludes to the fact that there were very particular recipes for motherhood that had to be strictly applied in order for independence to take place. An image from early 1920, when the Milner

FIGURE 9. "Milner and Egypt." *Al-Lata'if al-Musawwara,* January 2, 1920.

mission was still in Egypt, suggests that when those recipes were not followed, the nation would be subject to disaster (see Figure 9). Here, Lord
Milner is Egypt's "nanny." According to the cartoon's caption, he "with-
holds from Egypt the milk that it needs to survive; instead, Milner gives
Egypt a rattle — a toy — to distract it and keep it quiet. Egypt, of course,
responds by screaming louder." Written on the bottle is "complete independence," and the rattle reads "personal freedom," a reference to the concessions the British were willing to grant the Egyptians without, in fact,
granting them independence. Reminiscent of the caricatures of Isma'il
taken from *Abu Nazzara Zarqa',* Milner and his mission in Egypt are not
only lampooned as a woman but as an inauthentic mother.[79] While his
sins were "political," their genesis was his home.

During the revolutionary period, mother Egypt gave Egyptians a
common heritage and provided them with a new lineage — regardless of
their class background. The Wafd Central Committee used motherhood
to encourage nationalist sentiment among the masses. This circular was

sponsored by the committee and distributed by the students of one of Cairo's preparatory schools. It read:

To all the notables of the country, its *omdas* [*sic;* village chiefs], its wealthy men, its representatives and men of distinction, its *ulemas* [*sic*] and people of respect, its advocates and doctors, its engineers and craftsmen, its merchants and farmers, its students and employees, its ex-ministers and farmers, its elders and youths and to all its people the following earnest call and important admonition are directed: Verily your mother Egypt, who nourished you with her good production, suckled you with the flowing water of her Nile, let you enjoy her breeze, opened for you her wide breast . . . calls you with a voice chosen with tears and a breast full of burning sighs and communicates spiritually with the nobility of your souls.[80]

The new lineage of Egyptians produced by Mother Egypt was frequently contrasted with the old generation of Egyptian rulers in circulars that made the rounds during the revolution. The sexual politics of the khedives that were so frequently discussed in the nineteenth century also formed a common motif in revolutionary discourse and were used to distinguish between the family politics of the old regime and those of a new, independent Egypt.

How beautiful is the child of an adultress, who slept with a he mule or a wild donkey. He was born five months after the marriage, while the mule is generally born after 8 months. We are going to deliver ourselves from the rule of a wicked king in the future. Kings do their work skillfully, but Fuad is being "used" (like a woman) in his grand palace. . . . Hell, where is thy torture for the husband, the wife and the child of a harlot. And 'Down with Milner.'[81]

Similar circulars insisted that the sultan abdicate "his filthy throne, which is painted with shame," and allow 'Abbas Hilmy II, deposed at the beginning of World War I, to re-take his throne. "'Abbas, you are welcome — the heart of the country is longing for you."[82]

Likewise, during the demonstrations, revolutionaries in Cairo and Alexandria chanted the poetry of the popular poet Bayram al-Tunisi (1893–1961), which frequently equated the sexual habits of the monarchy with corruption. Some of his favorite topics were the marital and sexual habits of the royals and their result on the Egyptian body politic.[83] Al-Tunisi's satirical poems got him arrested, and he lived outside of Egypt for twenty years after the revolution. The following poem paints a picture of palace corruption and the resulting birth of a bastard child — Egypt's future king. Al-Tunisi wrote (and Egyptians chanted):

The corruption in the Bustan Palace has rocked the ages[84]
As has the corruption of the royals
The sentry has charged off to fetch a client
While the nanny has gone out to buy a loaf of bread
See what the unborn child inherits
And what unknown strain gets let into the family of Mohammad 'Ali
Sultan Fuad, your son's rear end has just seen the light of day
He came out glistening under the sign of Cancer
God blessed you with the birth of a boy.
What a pity that the month (of his birth) was not quite right.[85]

Al-Tunisi apparently wrote poetry about the royal family in order to counter images of Fuad and Nazli that were published in the pro-British newspaper *al-Muqatam* during 1919 in order to illustrate the virtues of the line of royals that the British had placed on the Egyptian throne during World War I. While *al-Muqatam* presented Fuad as embodying wisdom, political ability, and morality, critics like al-Tunisi argued that his marriage was a sham, that his son was a bastard, that Fuad himself bankrupted the royal family through his gambling debts — so much so that he was forced to beg for food at the homes of his friends.[86] Clearly such a man was not fit to lead an independent nation.

Who would be fit to rule in Fuad's place? Images of adultery and its resulting damage to the political realm were countered by illustrations of a new Egyptian lineage — born of Mother Egypt — that would ensure independence for the Egyptians. If Fuad were indeed morally and financially bankrupt, the new generation of Egyptians would not be.

Domesticity, the Good Father, and the End of Colonial Rule

In addition to portraying Egypt as a nation, the *effendiyya* nationalists created images of the Wafd as the natural head of a united Egyptian nation. Here the rhetoric about the new fathers and the new families that was so central to the school lessons and the national press in the decades leading up to the revolution manifests itself in concrete images. Wafd supporters depicted the Wafd leadership as the reformed fathers who were capable of leading Egypt into an independent era. Sa'ad Zaghlul and his wife Safia became the father and mother of Egypt; their home was Egypt's home. The Wafd leadership participated in and encouraged activities that were maternal in nature — the family politics of the reformed middle classes were put on display. Images of the Wafd leadership appeared in the press as giving birth to the Egyptian nation and nurturing it to maturity. The ability of the Wafd to lead the nation was frequently evoked through its relationship to Mother Egypt and to activities associated with maternalism and domesticity. Mother Egypt and her delegates provided Egyptians with a common heritage, a common lineage, and a common connection to the struggle of ousting the British.

Motherhood and its role in giving birth to the nation-state was not simply captured in political caricatures or, as chapter 4 suggests, aimed at young women in the classroom. Rather, "motherhood," or an active role in nurturing the nation, took a central role in promoting the role of the *effendiyya* in the revolution. The popular press from the time of the strikes, demonstrations, and boycotts suggested that there were very specific scripts for playing the role of a good nationalist or displaying one's affections for and intentions toward the nation. Acting the role of the "good mother" was, for elite men as well as women, central to the drama of national liberation. For the Wafd leadership, playing clearly domestic roles was a way of revealing sound and sincere nationalism and, therefore, claiming political leadership.

In 1919 and 1920, it was not uncommon for journals and magazines to illustrate "good" or "sound" nationalism by telling stories about the lives and activities of men who were labeled as "exemplary nationalists." The *effendiyya* were frequently depicted in the context of their public and private lives in order to highlight the kinds of activities, sentiments, and virtues that had come to form the culture of modern nationalism. Among the stories told about those exemplary nationalists were anecdotes about their upbringing, domestic habits, and familial affairs. One journal described Mohammad Tawfiq Nasim (1875–1938), twice head of the Egyptian ministry and an early Wafd member, as being a man of enormous political capability and fit to lead the nation to full and proper independence.[87] How, and on what basis, was this concluded? Nasim's power, it was claimed, was based on the fact that he "had never once been tempted to drink alcohol." Furthermore, he had a sound relationship with his wife and "enjoyed the pleasures" of his domestic life. For those reasons, young nationalists were enjoined to aspire to his example and to emulate him in every way.[88]

'Adly Yeghen was similarly feted in *al-Lata'if al-Musawwara*. At the time the article was printed, 'Adly was liaison between Sa'ad Zaghlul in London and the Milner mission in Egypt.[89] The author, Fuad abu al-Sa'ud, wrote that 'Adly's virtues as a nationalist, as well as his popularity among Egyptians, stemmed from his upbringing and his home life. Egyptians' "confidence" in him at the time of the negotiations between the British and Sa'ad Zaghlul was rooted not only in his education, experience, and political abilities but in his domestic affairs, past and present.[90]

In such stories, which were written as short biographies, male bourgeois nationalists were enjoined to behave outside the home in the same way that women had been asked to behave inside the home since the turn of the century. Sound nationalists were consistently depicted as "rearing" the nation's children and as embodying the virtues that were required of the "good mothers" who stayed at home. 'Ali Bey Fahmy Kamil, for example, was a wealthy Egyptian who had, in early 1919, donated an annual fund of three thousand Egyptian pounds, earmarked for the education of poor Egyptian children. Ali Bey's virtuous nationalist spirit was attributed to his upbringing, to a righteous domestic life, and to a *tarbiyya* provided by his mother that early on established in him proper nationalist morals and principles. Recognizing the role that such a home life had played in his childhood, 'Ali Bey was said to have been determined to make a similar life possible for future Egyptians.[91]

Included in this list of nationalists who nurtured the nation was Dr. 'Abd al-'Aziz Nazmi, founder of various philanthropic organizations, including an orphanage for children called the Freedom Orphanage (Malga' al-hurriyya). The editors of *al-Lata'if al-Musawwara* and other journals such as *al-Ahram* characterized all of the doctor's charitable activities as "truly nationalist," including the establishment of a society for the protection of children, a society for the feeding of the poor, a school for nurses, and societies against the spread of prostitution and the continuation of white slavery. At the same time, he was credited by the press as actively creating a nationalist Egyptian youth through his activities in charitable organizations.[92] The domicile in which Nazmi nurtured the aspirant nation extended to include Egypt's poor. The founding and funding of the Freedom Orphanage took pride of place in the press during the spring and summer of 1919. The project was often pitched as a means of reclaiming Egypt's "lost" youth from the Europeans who were busy building schools, hospitals, and orphanages to take care of Egypt's disadvantaged. Philanthropy was not new to Egypt. But the establishment of the Freedom Orphanage seemed to capture the imagination and the enthusiasm of the Cairene public during the first months of the uprisings.

The Freedom Orphanage project actually began in early 1918, the brainchild of a group of university students determined to help Cairo's poor and homeless. According to *al-Sufur*, the students attempted to raise one thousand Egyptian pounds to build a shelter and to coordinate their efforts with the Waqf Ministry. When their attempts failed, Nazmi took on the project as a private endeavor. Continuing to work with the students, he determined that the orphanage should be given the name "Freedom," and that the local population would fund it. In April and May of 1919, the press was full of announcements of public meetings of the orphanage's governing board and advertisements for local theatrical performances, the proceeds of which were donated to the orphanage.[93]

Al-Ahram waged a large campaign for money to build the orphanage. Beginning on April 9, 1919, with a "call to action" from Nazmi, the paper listed, almost daily, the names of Egyptians who were contributing to the campaign and the amount of money that they had pledged. Said Nazmi:

It is impossible for any human being to describe the joy of being potentially close to freedom, a freedom that each person, each people, has the right to. . . .

In celebration of this joy, and the victory that we've achieved through our demonstrations, I suggest to each member of my great nation, and especially the youth, to participate by giving one piaster to the Freedom Orphanage, to raise the level of *tarbiyya* of homeless and orphaned children. . . .

Today, I myself am participating by contributing 1,000 piasters. . . . I would request that you send your contributions to the editors of *al-Ahram*, who will put the money in the bank. Let this be but the first of many nationalist, beneficent projects.[94]

Al-Ahram listed donors by name, place of residence, occupation, and amount contributed. By April 12, hundreds of donors had donated a total sum of 3, 915 piasters — contributions ranged from one piaster to one thousand. By April 14, the list included many hundreds of professionals, bureaucrats, merchants, students, and housewives. Throughout the summer of 1919, merchants advertised "sales," the profits of which would go straight to the orphanage.[95]

By midsummer 1919, the orphanage had opened its doors to children who had apparently been picked up by the police.[96] On July 5, 1919, *al-Ahram* reported that the orphanage housed sixty-nine boys and twenty-two girls, and that the Waqf Ministry had earmarked three thousand pounds annually to be given to the project. On that day, members of most of Cairo's major newspapers toured the orphanage, and it was generally reported that it was "giving birth to" productive men and women. According to *al-Ahram*, the children performed marches and various

FIGURE 10. "The Egyptian nation." *Al-Lata'if al-Musawwara*, June 9, 1919.

kinds of exercises for the visiting journalists and demonstrated some of the activities that they learned in school, such as sewing and ironing and washing.[97] Portraits of the children and the orphanage that were printed in *al-Lata'if al-Musawwara* showed the children as clean and well dressed, orderly and obedient. Those images were contrasted with pictures of children who had not benefited from the nationalists' care — those children were filthy, ragged, and miserable.[98]

In the summer of 1919, *al-Lata'if al-Musawarra* printed a cartoon depicting the project of raising money for the orphanage and its role in shaping the nation. In it, Egyptians are depicted as a family of men and women, rich and poor, Muslim and Christian (*al-umma al-misriyya min jami' al-tawa'if*), gathered around a figure that, we are told, represents humanity and the Freedom Orphanage itself. Here, *effendi* nationalists join women, the *fellaheen*, and a priest (see Figure 10). The woman says: "The women of Egypt thank *al-Lata'if al-Musawwara*." The *effendi* at her side says: "The literati and the students bow down in praise. Bravo! Bravo!" The *fellah* says: "The masses as well thank *al-Lata'if al-Musawwara*." The woman's placard reads, "The Egyptian Nation (*al-umma al-misriyya*)." These are the Egyptians who have participated in the collection of funds for the orphanage. At their feet are a group of clean, healthy, well-dressed children — "children of the rich" — presumably the product of modern households and a proper upbringing. Next to them, however, is a group of naked, scrawny, faceless children, all of whom plead for the nation's assistance. Unlike those children who stand with the men and women of the nation, these children have no faces and are indistinguishable from one another.

In the center of the cartoon we find another female image, the orphanage itself, to which the nation looks for guidance. She is a mother figure (she holds a small baby), but here she wears a slightly different garb than that of the mothers pictured above; she is clothed in the garb of a Greco-Roman warrior, of the kind often used in French revolutionary iconography to represent the ideals of constitutional government.[99] She wears a sash that refers to her as "humanity" *(insaniyya)*. It is to her that the men and women of Egypt look; it is from her that the faceless poor seek assistance. At her feet, a clean, well-dressed child hands her a sack of money to support the orphanage. She thanks him in the name of the faceless, voiceless poor. In his interaction with her, in his participation in the fundraising, he acquires face, voice, and citizenship.

The young child also represents *al-Lata'if al-Musawwara* itself, which had dedicated the proceeds of a special issue to the campaign to raise money for the orphanage. The sack of money represents that contribution. He says: "My lady. It wasn't enough to talk and write like my older and bigger brothers have done. I collected this for you and hope you will use it to help the poor who ask help of you." *Al-Lata'if al-Musawwara* is juxtaposed with a group of old pashas who represent other periodicals. They are inactive, dejected; they look at Mother Egypt but do not interact with her. They attempt to defend their status and their actions:

al-Ahram: I announced the campaign, I drummed up support, I made a lot of noise and advertised the names of those who participated. Doesn't that count?

al-Afkar: Oh, no my friend! Writing is one thing. Digging in our pockets is another.

al-Basir: This little boy must have been born in early 1919.

al-Watan: This little boy is brave. We must praise him if we're good editors . . . or, should we hit him?

al-Ahali: Not a bad idea.

al-Minbar: Didn't I do enough in criticizing the selling of [remainder of caption unclear].

The old order, as it is depicted here, neither cooperates fully with Mother Egypt nor participates in the creation of her citizenry. Clearly, "New Egypt" is given voice and citizenship through its role in nurturing children, in playing a maternal role in the national household.

Similarly, the Egyptians who showed up to protest the presence of the Milner mission in Cairo were depicted as a kind of family by the editors of *al-Lata'if al-Musawwara*. The Egyptians of both sexes and all classes who paraded in front of Lord Milner included babies as well as the elderly. Milner, depicted in his quarters at the Semiramis Hotel, looked out over the Egyptians who addressed him, asking them: "What? Where? When?" They respond, "Complete independence." The caption read: "It was made clear to the Milner Mission: all the children of Egypt — men, women, poor, middle class, rich, babies, old folks on the brink of death, the answer is the same. Their word, their request, their hope, their vision is total independence."[100]

The maternal nature of nationalism, as it was embodied in philanthropic activities, was immortalized by the poet Hafith Ibrahim, called "the Poet of the Nile," whose poems were carried in most magazines and newspapers during the revolutionary period. His poem to Nazmi's orphanage, also entitled "Malga' al-hurriyya," equated nationalism with raising the nation's children. Like the founder of the orphanage, Ibrahim called upon his fellow male nationalists to ensure the nation's success by caring for its youth.

You men who are earnest about nationalism — The time has come to ensure the future of those who will inherit the nation.

Build orphanages, factories, irrigation canals, agricultural syndicates.

Who knows — perhaps those whom you help will turn out to be a full moon to light the way; they might turn out to be another Sa'ad [Zaghlul]; they might turn out to be another [Mohammad] 'Abduh; they might become another poet like Shauqi or they might turn out to be a brave knight. . . . How many souls of great men rest within the bodies of orphaned children?[101]

The children of nationalist projects were thus given a new lineage. They were not the offspring of the old order of pashas and khedives whose actions had led to the occupation. Rather, they were the "offspring of Mustafa, sons of Farid, and cubs of the Lion SAAD [sic]!"[102] They were the children of men who gave themselves over entirely to the nationalist project of reforming the national household.

The nurturing, maternalist activities of the elite classes during the revolution, as they are illustrated in the attempts to build the Freedom Orphanage and in Hafith Ibrahim's poem created a paternalistic relationship between the new ruling classes and the Egyptians over whom they governed. While gendered, feminine activities were central to the creation of sound nationalists, it was men who claimed to give birth to them and men who would ultimately govern them. The paternal nature of "right" nationalism to the disruptive activities of mob rule reflects the ideals of early-twentieth-century lessons for young schoolchildren about the importance of order and discipline to reforming both their real and national households.[103] Shaped by the maternal virtues of the reformed household and led by the men who practiced it, nationalism would make citizens out of riffraff.

Freedom Begins in the House of the Nation (Bayt al-Umma)

In the revolutionary press, as well as in subsequent recollections of the events of 1919, Sa'ad Zaghlul is depicted as the model of bourgeois, nationalist sentiments and behaviors as well as the head of the Wafd and its spokesperson. His home served as a starting point for many of the revolution's demonstrations; it was a prominent icon, as "*bayt al-umma,*" throughout the revolution. The British kept a sharp eye on the Zaghlul residence, reporting not only its role as departure point for the demonstrations but as a venue for numerous political meetings disguised as "tea parties."[104]

In fiction published in the years of the revolution, Zaghlul was characterized both as a father politician, giving birth to freedom and independence, and as a good parent, encouraging order, good will, strong virtues, and sound relationships in both his literal and his national homes. In stories that were carried in the press, political struggle always involved some sort of conflict within the family.[105] Usually it was nationalism or nationalist projects overseen by Zaghlul or dedicated to him that brought the family back to order. Once the family was remade, political success always followed. The domestic behavior of Sa'ad Zaghlul and the *effendiyya* thus became synonymous with political triumph.

Between January 9 and February 20, 1922, *al-Lata'if al-Musawarra* published in serial form a story called "Zaghlul Misr," or "Egypt's Zaghlul," which illustrates the relationship between concern for the family and the national struggle. "Zaghlul Misr" depicts the aspirations of young nationalists as well as model characters for producing a strong nation. It is full of "bad citizens" and "good ones," and ends only when good citizens are made out of bad ones, and proper families are made out of both.

"Zaghlul Misr" tells the story of Farid, a committed, *effendi* nationalist who calls Sa'ad Zaghlul and the revolution his "earthly religion." While participating in one of 1919's many demonstrations, he is tossed a red ribbon that features the slogan "Long Live Egypt's Youth" and the initials "A. T." Farid has no way of knowing who the ribbon belonged to; nonetheless, he places it in his jacket, above his heart. Shortly afterward, he is approached by several students who tell him about a secret "nationalist" meeting being held that night; they give him its time and location and encourage him to attend. Confused, both about the red ribbon and the secret meeting, Farid goes to sit in a café. There, he gives a young boy money and asks him to go and purchase a pack of cigarettes; when the boy returns, a large, fat man is on his tail, attempting to beat him with a stick. We discover that the boy, Mohammad, is an orphan who begs for the fat man, 'Am Hamad, in order to earn his keep. ('Am Hamad is the story's first example of a "bad citizen" — he abuses children, exposing them to indolence and vice.) Mohammad does not know who his parents are, nor where he comes from; the only thing he remembers about his childhood is that a woman — another bad citizen — came and took him from his home and gave him to Umm 'Ali, 'Am Hamad's wife.

Umm 'Ali is described as "huge, vulgar, unkempt . . . a shameless adulteress, capable of destroying a huge army simply by sticking out her tongue." Farid enjoins his companions to help him to rid the nation of such examples of womanhood; they respond that total independence (al-istiqlal al-tam) depends on it. The group of young, middle-class nationalists vowed to make the upbringing of Mohammad their responsibility.

The antithesis of such imagery — or the "good nationalist woman" — appears in the next scenes, set during another demonstration. Farid passes by a car full of women, one of whom chants nationalist slogans and, at the same time, warns her fellow demonstrators about traitors in their midst who seek to destroy the revolution. Farid stands for a long while and watches the woman, saying to himself: "This woman is not my mother, but my pride for her is great. How great it would be for me to be the son of a woman like her. Thank God that I am a member of the same nation that she is." Farid and his companions agree that the woman represents nationalism, motherhood, and independence. Because of his encounter with her, Farid feels compelled to attend the secret meeting.

Fearful of what might happen to him at the meeting, Farid climbs up on a roof adjacent to the meeting place in order to see who will attend. As he stands on the roof, steeped in self doubt, he reaches into his pocket and pulls out the red ribbon, reminding himself of the courage of others, especially the woman from the demonstration. It is at that moment that he is approached by an unknown woman, wearing a red ribbon like his, who tells him that she is the *murabiyya,* or nanny, of 'A'isha, the woman who originally threw him the ribbon. She has been sent, she confesses, to warn him about traitors attending the meeting; to urge him to attend it so that he could warn anyone else wearing a ribbon like his to flee.

The action then moves to Sa'ad Zaghlul addressing a delegation of women. Farid is at the meeting to hear Zaghlul's speech. At the meeting, 'A'isha confronts Zaghlul by saying, "Remember, if there had not been a mother or a wife to carry life's burdens with you, you would not have turned out to be a capable leader." Zaghlul responds by saying that he knows very well that a woman, his mother, was his first *"watan."* Farid and Zaghlul meet, and Farid finds himself invited to travel with his hero to Upper Egypt in order to help him bring Egyptians into the ranks of the Wafd.

In the meantime, Farid has been "set up" by traitors who attended that secret meeting. The young boy Mohammad discovers the setup and tries to warn Farid, but it is too late; Farid has left for Assiut with his would-be assassin 'Am Hamad in pursuit. As 'Am Hamad is about to kill Farid, 'A'isha's *murabiyya* shows up and intervenes, saving his life at the very last moment. 'Am Hamad, wounded in the skirmish, is nursed back to health by Farid and the nanny and thus becomes a nationalist. The nanny helps Farid back to Cairo and the two marry. Mohammad finds his real parents, who convert to nationalism. All live happily ever after, as does the nation.

This story is noteworthy not only for the clear connection it makes between the political realm and the domestic one (good nationalists were virtuous and cared for children; bad citizens abused them; good nationalists married virtuous women; bad citizens married "adulterous shrews"), but also for showing the role that middle-class domesticity plays in the saving of the nation. The *murabiyya* — a woman trained in the sciences of the home — warned Farid away from the meeting and eventually saved his life. And 'A'isha, without overstepping cultural boundaries or conventions, reminded Sa'ad Zaghlul of the importance of his home. Middle-class nationalist males — raised by the likes of the *murabiyya* and 'A'isha — guide the nation's children and make them into nationalists. Nationalism, in Zaghlul's Egypt, was able to restore the family, as is evidenced by young Muhammad's reunion with his family. The happiness of Muhammad's literal family was reflected in that of his national one.

It's a Girl!

Gender and the Birth of Modern Egyptian Nationalism

Each year, the Egyptian press commemorates the anniversary of the demonstrations that mark the 1919 Revolution. Given the remarkable nature of their appearance in the demonstrations, it is usually women who are chosen as the symbols of the revolution and whose participation in the Egyptian nationalist movement attracts the most commentary. Usually the story goes something like this: Egyptian upper-class women, for centuries the victims of the harem, woke up to the evils of the patriarchal system that had enslaved them. At the same time, they became aware of the possibilities of the reform of the domestic realm and supported "maternalist" activities as a means of empowering themselves. Concomitantly, they supported nationalism as a means of ensuring Egypt's future as well as their own. In 1919, they took to the streets, en masse, in support of Egyptian independence, nationalism, and liberation from the old order of things. When the revolutionary struggle died down, these women organized Egypt's first feminist union, hoping for an extension of their revolutionary activities through participation in elections and parliamentary activities. Having discovered a political voice, having participated alongside men in the struggle for independence, women thought themselves the rightful heirs to all the political rights that an independent Egyptian polity would grant to men.

In July 1995, *al-Ahram Weekly*, in commemoration of the U.N. International Conference on Women, published an article called "Half a Nation: A Century of Feminism." In it, the struggles made by women to participate in the Egyptian public life were recounted and placed in the context of women's first entrance into the public arena in 1919. The article stated:

In the 1919 Revolution, women took to the streets for the first time in demonstrations, demanding national sovereignty. With national independence — albeit incomplete independence in 1922 — the first organized women's movement began. Huda Sha'rawi led women in forming the first explicitly feminist organization — *al-Itihad al-Nisa'i al-Misri* (the Egyptian Feminist Union) in 1923. The Union headed a movement within which women articulated a feminist and nationalist agenda.

The earliest manifestations of "feminist consciousness" surfaced as a new culture of modernity was being shaped in nineteenth-century Egypt. Women gave expression to this new gender awareness at the moment the old urban *harem* culture, predicated on female domestic seclusion and other forms of control over women, was being eroded in the midst of pervasive modernizing transformations. Upper- and middle-class women observed how men in their families were freer to innovate while they were more restricted. Speaking with other women, thinking about their common experience, they discovered different ways they, as women, were controlled. As they imagined their new lives, women began to withhold complicity in their own subordination.[1]

The suggestion here is that the overturning of an old order, central to which was the harem, would bring women out of seclusion and into the political arena. And the implication is also that men championed changes as much as women did, including disbanding the harem, welcoming women into the revolutionary demonstrations, and encouraging women's full participation in public culture, including the political realm. Egypt's modernization and political emancipation, in other words, were expected to produce concrete changes for women, central to which was an active role in the new body politic.

But there is also an epilogue to this telling of the revolution and the role of women in it: The union of women (or feminism; usually the women who participated in the demonstrations are referred to as feminists) and nationalism failed.[2] In this narrative, the forces that brought nationalists and feminists together on Cairo's streets in 1919 were to be short-lived; male nationalists failed to grant women suffrage, or any part in the running of Egypt's nascent, body politic, when they penned Egypt's constitution in 1922. Thus continued *al-Ahram:* "The month after the creation of the Union a new constitution was promulgated declaring all Egyptians equal, with equal civil and political rights and responsibilities. Three weeks later this equality was violated by an electoral law that restricted the exercise of political rights to *male* Egyptians."[3] The

nationalist movement that preceded and sponsored the revolution represented the agendas of men alone and was not, ultimately, designed for
women. While crucial to the revolutionary moment, women were not
ultimately to be a part of the political agenda.

Such a conclusion has unfortunate implications for nationalists of both
sexes. It holds that while women were capable of championing and
sponsoring causes that have been referred to in recent scholarship as
"maternalist," they were not ultimately capable of translating philanthropic activities into political roles for themselves. In Egypt, women first
claimed "political" space for themselves by attaching calls for women's
education and modern health care to their support for nationalism — a
union that they supported in the female-authored and sponsored press
that took rise at the turn of the century.[4] In the decades preceding the revolution, women used their increased access to education in order to take
an active role in the domains they had previously written about: they
became educators and doctors, worked on the boards of hospitals and
orphanages, and created "secular philanthropic societies" such as the
Mabarrat Mohammad 'Ali, which was a dispensary for women and children.[5] When the revolution began, women harnessed their experiences in
such arenas to lead demonstrations against the British, and to create the
Wafdist Women's Central Committee. Thus organized, the Wafdist
women organized demonstrations and boycotts of British goods, collected money and jewelry to help finance the nationalist struggle, and
dealt directly with British authorities when male Wafdist leaders were
imprisoned.[6] The Egyptian Feminist Union (EFU), formed after the revolution ended, attempted to translate such roles into the postrevolutionary era as suffrage and direct political participation. Because the
EFU was not successful in attaining an active political role for women, it
has been concluded that while "maternalism" was successful in elevating
the position of women in Egyptian society and in organizing women col-
lectively, it failed as a concrete platform.

Likewise, the male nationalists who championed the efforts of women
in "maternalist" activities prior to and during the revolution are seen as
having used concern with the plight of Egypt's women and concern for
the nation's household in order to promote nationalism. Once independence had been gained, male Egyptian nationalists apparently turned
their backs on the women who practiced nationalism and hoped to
extend their revolutionary activities into active political participation.[7]
Men are said to have taken on "the woman question" (central to which
were discussions about the role of women as mothers, women's educa-

tion, the *hijab*, or "veil," and appropriate divorce and inheritance laws for women) in order to modernize Egypt and to ensure the creation of a nation-state that could ward off continued colonial domination.[8] Feminist and nationalist historians read Qasim Amin's *The Liberation of Women* and *The New Woman* and believed that "liberation" meant suffrage and political agency and that "new" meant a radical departure from the past.[9] By writing women out of the constitution, male nationalists appear to have turned their backs on the women's movement that men themselves participated in creating and sponsoring, leaving historians to question both the impetus for the intense debates that "the woman question" engendered and the motives behind its disbandment.

Postrevolutionary history and the writing of the first Egyptian constitution thus present historians (both of women's movements and of nationalism) with a number of unanswered questions. Perhaps the most tenacious of which asks why women were apparently excluded from the political realm after they had been welcomed into the struggle from its conception.[10] Egypt's first steps toward independence featured women organizing demonstrations, marching, standing for long hours in the hot sun, and subjecting themselves to arrest and gunfire from the British. These stories seem to offer proof that Egypt was ready for liberation. One has to wonder how such stories continue to be generated in the relative absence of women's participation in the political arena that marks postrevolutionary history.[11]

Such questions about the role of women in revolutions or their postrevolutionary fates are not confined to Egypt. To be sure, women or images of women have been central to a number of revolutionary movements and have been evoked to represent the glories of the liberated body politic, the modern nation, and the emancipated home. The American and French Revolutions, the Chinese Revolution of 1911, and the Bolshevik Revolution of 1917 are all examples of revolutionary moments wherein women and their emancipation became central to men's political rhetoric about the overthrow of an old order and the ushering in of a new era.[12] Women in these revolutions became synonymous with progress and modernity, and their participation alongside men in the political arena served as proof that the new order promised democracy, equality, and liberation for both sexes. Many historians argue that, like their Egyptian counterpart, each of these revolutions illustrate failed promises. Postrevolutionary societies could be as oppressive in their political, educational, and economic policies toward women as the regimes that preceded them.

These examples seem to demonstrate a universal phenomenon wherein women in revolutionary contexts play a role that is highly political only to have the political realm denied them after the revolutionary struggle dies down. It has certainly been hypothesized that women and notions about them are less crucial to the construction of new regimes than to the overthrow of old political orders. The Egyptian case appears to be no exception.

The lack of an active female presence in the political realm after the Egyptian 1919 Revolution represented the logical result of gendered debates about the Egyptian nation, national reform, and nationalism in the nineteenth and early twentieth centuries. Domesticity and the feminine and maternal activities it connotes were central to shaping the nation-state from the nineteenth century onward. For the independent Egyptian nation to continue to be undergirded by the domicile, women would have to stay at home. Did Egyptian men thus engender a body politic to exclude women, or did they inherit a set of modern, European constitutional ideals that were gendered in such a way as to depend upon a modern, reformed female presence within the home?[13]

In the 1919 Revolution, a half-century of debate, discussion, and reform was made manifest in the symbols through which bourgeois Egyptians argued that their nation was ready for independence. Those symbols brought the activities of the reformed, domestic realm into the spotlight of the political arena. Indeed, the above chapters have illustrated how crucial the domicile and its inhabitants — both real and imaginary — were to discussions and debates about the Egyptian body politic. The Egyptian domicile was central to the ways in which Egypt, as a territorial, political, and cultural entity, was conceptualized, first by European tourists and, later, by government officials. The penetration of Egyptian homes throughout the nineteenth century and the production of knowledge that accompanied it made Egypt a gendered, feminine territory to be taken and dominated by Europe.

The Egyptian state sponsored a travel-writing project, however unwittingly, through which modernity was described in terms that linked household arrangements to political structures. The debut of this project corresponded with changes in the marital and domestic arrangements of Egypt's elites — changes that were in fact precipitated by transformations in Egypt's body politic. The choice of a house, the proper arrangement of its contents, and the relationships that took place inside its walls distinguished a new class of state servants who, as the century progressed, saw themselves and the landscape on which they lived as modern Egyptian.

For the Europeans who came, with ever-increasing frequency, to "know" the Egyptians over the course of the nineteenth century, elite Egyptian households represented backwardness rather than modernity. The most infamous of Egypt's households was Isma'il's. The alleged peculiarities that took place there were offered as proof that Europe's interests in Egypt, territorial and otherwise, had to be safeguarded by an occupation. Once the occupation had thus been legitimated, the private politics of the khedives and their ministers were used to gauge Egypt's movement toward modernity, economic solvency, and political capability — its very ability to be reformed.

In the years surrounding the British occupation, the domicile served as a trope through which Egyptians discussed the state's successes and failures. Proper marital relations, breast-feeding, and *tarbiyya* became symbolic of political prowess. Table manners and the science of home economics were not isolated to the women's press, as it took off in the late nineteenth century but, rather, came to shape a whole political culture. Issues and arguments that, on the surface, appeared to be about "women" (and the debate over the *hijab* is but one example) in fact couched strident critiques of Egypt's past, its body politic and the occupation, as well as prescriptions for how to lead Egypt to a better future.

The iconography of the revolution reveals that central to the demonstrations of 1919 was an attempt on the part of bourgeois Egyptian nationalists to expose the private realm of their households and to display the reform that had taken place within them. The transformation that had taken place in Egypt over the nineteenth century in general, and since 1882 in particular, was displayed from the inside out. In the words of one nationalist: "We want the whole world to know that security reigns in our beloved country . . . we want it to know even our most intimate secrets."[14]

Revolutionary iconography also illustrates the gendered nature of the Egyptian body politic in 1919. A multitude of meanings was attached to "woman," "feminine," and "female." The nascent Egyptian nation-state depended on the existence of certain female prototypes, the characteristics of which informed the political, as well as the private, domain. The bourgeois "mothers" of both sexes who demonstrated in the 1919 Revolution signified that Egyptians had reformed the political, economic, and private realms of their nation. Nurturing that nation, both at home and in the public realm, was a powerful political act. Charity and concern for the poor indicated not only an engagement in politics but the adoption of all the behaviors required by the modern, Western political realm.

But the iconography of the revolution also reveals a cementing of the relationship between modern *effendi* habits and Egyptian nationalism. By using press accounts of the demonstrations to distinguish between orderly marches led by middle-class nationalists and disorderly bands of "rabble" and "riffraff," the *effendiyya* secured their class behavior as the proper nationalist behavior. The lower classes that were not willing to be brought into the fold by following the *effendi* recipe for sound nationalism were dismissed from the ranks of those who had fought for the nation. The "rabble" may thus have contributed to making Egypt ungovernable for the British, but they did not help give birth to the nation.

At the same time, dressing the "nation" in the symbols of middle-class domesticity served to infuse the semi-independent body politic that was won in 1922 with elite values. Dining in restaurants, wearing European fashions, decorating with Western furnishings, nannies, baby formulas — all seemed to suggest that bourgeois, "Egyptian modern" had secured the victory of modern Egyptian independence.

Finally, linking Sa'ad Zaghlul and his fellow Wafd delegates to those symbols transformed members of a class of Egyptians that had profited from the British occupation into the leaders of a national movement against the occupation. The caricatures and slogans that were so central to the revolution suggested links between the Wafd and the masses that apparently even surprised the Wafd. Thus Sa'ad Zaghlul and his contemporaries appeared to have given birth both to the nation and to be champions of the culture that created it.

One can only guess why the British failed to recognize the political significance of charity. Perhaps the omission indicates that by 1919, templates for judging the political potential for non-European peoples had changed. In April 1919, Consul General Wingate asked the British Foreign Office to counter Egyptian nationalist "propaganda" with its own forms of propaganda in the European press. However, they failed to include domestic practices along with Bolshevism, anarchy, and potential pan-Islamism as images of nationalism.[15] And yet in Egypt, as in other parts of the world that were colonized or occupied by the British in the middle and late nineteenth centuries, domestic practices served as powerful templates for measuring the success or failure of a people — indeed, the very ability of a people to call themselves a nation. Such images also reappeared when colonized peoples began to demand independence. An alternate reading of the British failure to reckon with the family politics of the 1919 Revolution is that they recognized that the Egyptians had fulfilled the contract that was set in place in 1882 and were ready to govern themselves.

Notes

Introduction

1. Public Records Office (hereafter, PRO), Foreign Office (hereafter, FO), Great Britain, 141/522/9085, Apr. 10, 1919. This particular file contains reports for the Foreign Office regarding European and American coverage of the 1919 demonstrations.

2. PRO/FO 141/751/8941, Dispatch no. 216, Cheetham to Curzon, May 11, 1919. My emphasis.

3. Seth Koven and Sonya Michel have defined maternalism as the championing of domestic activities (child rearing and day care, for example) by women as a means of securing political agency for themselves. See their edited volume, *Mothers of a New World: Maternalist Politics and the Origins of Welfare States* (New York and London: Routledge Press, 1993).

4. The seminal work on Egypt in the British colonial imagination is Timothy Mitchell's *Colonising Egypt* (Cambridge: Cambridge University Press, 1988). While he and I look at different British measures of the Egyptians' alleged inability to govern themselves, I am indebted to his paradigms.

5. See Lata Mani, *Contentious Traditions: The Debate on Sati in Colonial India* (Berkeley: University of California Press, 1998); Partha Chatterjee, *The Nation and Its Fragments: Colonial and Postcolonial Histories* (Princeton: Princeton University Press, 1993); and Tanika Sazkar, "The Hindu Wife and the Hindu Nation," *Studies in History* 8: 2 (1992): 213–35.

6. Mrinalini Sinha, *Colonial Masculinity: The "Manly Englishman" and the "Effeminate Bengali" in the Late Nineteenth Century* (Manchester and New York: Manchester University Press, 1995).

7. See Ronald Hyam, *Empire and Sexuality: The British Experience* (Manchester and New York: Manchester University Press, 1990).

8. Sir Edward Grigg Papers, pt. 7, Grigg to Lord Passfield (Sidney Webb),

Sept. 11, 1929, Bodelian Library, Oxford, cited in Susan Pederson, "National Bodies, Unspeakable Acts: The Sexual Politics of Colonial Policy-Making," *The Journal of Modern History* 63 (1991): 653.

9. *Parliamentary Debates* (Commons), 5th ser., vol. 233 (Dec. 11, 1929), cols. 600–603, cited in Pederson, "National Bodies, Unspeakable Acts," 658.

10. On the use of domestic and familial practices to dominate non-Western peoples by other colonial powers, see, for example, Julia Clancy-Smith and Frances Gouda, eds., *Domesticating Empire: Race, Gender, and Family Life in French and Dutch Colonialism* (Charlottesville: University Press of Virginia, 1998); and Lynne Haney and Lisa Pollard, eds., *Families of a New World: Gender, Politics, and Nation-Building in Global Perspective* (New York and London: Routledge Press, 2003).

11. See Sazkar, "The Hindu Wife"; Partha Chatterjee, "Colonialism, Nationalism, and Colonized Women: The Contest in India," *American Ethnologist* 16: 4 (1989): 622–33; and idem, "A Religion of Urban Domesticity: Sri Ramakrishna and the Calcutta Middle Class," in *Subaltern Studies 7: Writings on South Asian History and Society*, ed. Partha Chatterjee and Gyanendra Pandey, 40–68 (Delhi: Oxford University Press, 1992).

12. Pederson, "National Bodies, Unspeakable Acts," 663.

13. PRO 533/392/11, cited in Pederson, "National Bodies, Unspeakable Acts," 660.

14. The Egyptian Revolution is usually defined as having taken place between 1919 and 1922.

15. On Victorian family ideals, see Leonore Davidoff and Catherine Hall, *Family Fortunes: Men and Women of the English Middle Class, 1780–1850* (Chicago: University of Chicago Press, 1987).

16. The impositions of European ideas on non-Western cultures is well discussed in Edward Said, *Culture and Imperialism* (New York: Knopf, 1993); and Mary Louise Pratt, *Imperial Eyes: Travel Writing and Transculturation* (New York and London: Routledge Press, 1992).

17. Leila Ahmed, *Women and Gender in Islam: Historical Roots of a Modern Debate* (New Haven: Yale University Press, 1992).

18. This argument is made in Beth Baron, "Mothers, Morality and Nationalism in pre-1919 Egypt," in *The Origins of Arab Nationalism,* ed. Rashid Khalidi, 271–88 (New York: Columbia University Press, 1991); and Rebecca Joubin, "Creating the Modern Professional Housewife: Scientifically Based Advice Extended to Middle- and Upper-Class Egyptian Women, 1920s–1930s," *Arab Studies Journal* 4: 2 (1996): 19–45.

19. This tendency is described most keenly by historian Beth Baron, who writes: "Preoccupation with tracing the origins of feminism, however broadly defined, has led to an approach which treats the idea like a baton, passing from one thinker to the next." See Baron, *The Women's Awakening in Egypt: Culture, Society and the Press* (New Haven: Yale University Press, 1994), 4.

20. Ahmed acknowledges European attitudes toward women in Islamic societies and the changes in women's education in Egypt. She does not thor-

oughly elucidate, however, the process through which such idioms were introduced into a general political and intellectual climate or how they were learned or interpreted.

21. On the role of gendered female roles and imagery in shaping masculine culture, see Michael Roper and John Tosh, *Manful Assertions: Masculinities in Britain since 1800* (New York and London: Routledge Press, 1991).

22. Margot Badran, *Feminists, Islam, and Nation: Gender and the Making of Modern Egypt* (Princeton: Princeton University Press, 1995), 4.

23. Baron, *The Women's Awakening in Egypt*, 8.

24. Ibid., 61. Similarly, Baron argues that while the male press had politics as its central preoccupation, women wrote mainly about topics pertaining to the home.

25. The use of domestic experiences as an analytical category has allowed scholars in other fields to transcend rigidly defined categories of male and female, masculine and feminine, private and public, and to illustrate the extent to which political transformation implicated and shaped the lives of both women and men. Historians of the Ottoman Empire and modern Turkey, for example, have begun to use household politics as an analytical category for uncovering gendered ideologies and institutions, relations among middle- and upper-class urban families, and the relationship between families and the state. See Leslie Pierce, *The Imperial Harem: Women and Sovereignty in the Ottoman Empire* (Oxford: Oxford University Press, 1993). On the transitional period between the end of the Ottoman Empire and the rise of modern Turkey, see Alan Duben and Cem Behar, *Istanbul Households: Marriage, Family and Fertility, 1880–1940* (Cambridge: Cambridge University Press, 1991). See also Duben, "Turkish Families and Households in Historical Perspective," *Journal of Family History* 10 (1995): 75–97; and idem, "Household Formation in late Ottoman Istanbul," in *International Journal of Middle Eastern Studies* 22 (1990): 419–35. The authors show that national ideals required certain preoccupations with heterosexuality, reproduction, and parent-child relations that affected the behavior and sensibilities of men and women alike, both inside their homes and in the public sphere.

26. This is the argument put forth by Carole Pateman in "The Fraternal Social Contract," in *Civil Society and the State: New European Perspectives*, ed. John Keane (London: Verso Press, 1988); and idem, *The Sexual Contract* (Stanford: Stanford University Press, 1988).

27. See Afaf Lutfi al-Sayyid Marsot, *Women and Men in Late Eighteenth-Century Egypt* (Austin: University of Texas Press, 1995); and Jane Hathaway, *The Politics of Households in Ottoman Egypt: The Rise of the Qazdaglis* (Cambridge: Cambridge University Press, 1997).

28. André Raymond, "Essai de géographie des quartiers de résidence aristocratique au Caire au XVIIIième siècle," *Journal of the Economic and Social History of the Orient* 6 (1963): 58–103. See also Nelly Hanna, *Habiter au Caire aux XVIIième et XVIIIième siècles* (Cairo: Institut Français d'Archéologie Orientale du Caire, 1991). See also Janet Abu-Lughod, *Cairo: 1001 Years of the City Victorious* (Princeton: Princeton University Press, 1971); and F. Robert Hunter, *Egypt*

under the Khedives, 1805–1879: From Household Government to Modern Bureaucracy (Pittsburgh, Pa.: University of Pittsburgh Press, 1984).

29. See Afaf Lutfi al-Sayyid Marsot, *Egypt in the Reign of Mohammad 'Ali* (Cambridge: Cambridge University Press, 1984).

30. Mona L. Russell, "Creating the New Woman: Consumerism, Education, and National Identity in Egypt, 1863–1922" (Ph.D. diss., Georgetown University, 1997). See also Hunter, *Egypt under the Khedives.*

31. See Hanafi al-Mahalawi, *Harim muluk misr, min Mohammad 'Ali ila Faruq* (Cairo: Dar al-Amin, 1993).

32. Mary Louise Pratt calls this process transculturation. Her study, *Imperial Eyes,* examines transculturation in light of European travel literature, its role in creating colonial discourse, and indigenous responses to the guises of travel literature. The best example of a study of the effects of the colonial experience on British culture in England is Sinha, *Colonial Masculinity.*

33. I am indebted to Deniz Kandiyoti for expanding my understanding of modernity and what it meant to be both Ottoman and Turkish "modern." I found her personal conversations enormously helpful, not to mention her printed work, especially "Gendering the Modern: On Missing Dimensions in the Study of Turkish Modernity," in *Rethinking Modernity and Nationalist Identity in Turkey,* ed. Sibel Bozdogan and Resat Kasaba, 113–32 (Seattle: University of Washington Press, 1997). She is not, of course, responsible for my interpretations of her work.

On women as symbols of modernity in the nineteenth- and twentieth-century Middle East, see Lila Abu-Lughod, ed., *Remaking Women: Feminism and Modernity in the Middle East* (Princeton: Princeton University Press, 1998), especially Abu-Lughod's introduction and Kandiyoti's afterword.

34. This argument is made by Edward Said in *Orientalism* (New York: Vintage Press, 1979), and later taken up by Timothy Mitchell in *Colonising Egypt.*

35. On women as symbols of the new Egyptian nation, see also Beth Baron, "Nationalist Iconography: Egypt as a Woman," in *Rethinking Nationalism in the Arab Middle East,* ed. James Jankowski and Israel Gershoni (New York: Columbia University Press, 1997), 105–26; and Lisa Pollard, "The Family Politics of Colonizing and Liberating Egypt, 1882–1919," *Social Politics* 7: 1 (2000): 47–79.

36. Deniz Kandiyoti, "Identity and Its Discontents: Women and the Nation," in *Colonial Discourse and Post-Colonial Theory,* ed. Patrick Williams and Linda Chrisman (New York: Columbia University Press, 1994), 429–43.

Chapter 1: My House and Yours

1. See Bernard Lewis, *The Muslim Discovery of Europe* (New York: W. W. Norton, 1982).

2. Here my thinking has been greatly influenced by Benedict Anderson, *Imagined Communities,* extended ed. (London: Verso, 1991); and Anne Godlewska and Neil Smith, *Geography and Empire* (Oxford: Blackwell Publish-

ers, 1994). The most persuasive account of the project of "mapping" and knowing the world, as a tool of European dominance and national resistance, is found, however, in Thongchai Winichakul's *Siam Mapped: A History of the Geo-Body of a Nation* (Honolulu: University of Hawaii Press, 1994). Winichakul argues that the Siamese nascent "state's" control over both political power and technology in the mid-nineteenth century led to the construction of Siamese "territoriality." Territoriality included the state's attempt to classify an area, to communicate that classification to its citizens through the construction and strict enforcement of boundaries. Intimate knowledge of the inner, domestic realms, he notes, appear on late-nineteenth-century Siamese maps, just as locally produced maps also placed Siam in an international context. Locality, or territoriality, had both an international and a very personal dimension.

3. I do not wish to argue that the home and its inhabitants had not been discussed and debated over the course of Islamic history. Quite to the contrary, relationships between men and women, as well as domestic affairs, were often the subject of debate, just as they were often used as a trope for commentary about issues that often had little to do with marriage and domestic activities. What I do mean to suggest, however, is that early-nineteenth-century reforms in Egypt brought about markedly new ways of talking about the home and the family and attached the domestic realm to political and economic constructs that had been heretofore discussed differently in the Islamic world. For provocative discussions about women and the domestic realm as tropes for other kinds of agendas, see Denise A. Spellberg, *Politics, Gender, and the Islamic Past: The Legacy of 'A'isha bint Abi Bakr* (New York: Columbia University Press, 1994); Fatima Mernissi, *The Veil and the Male Elite: A Feminist Interpretation of Women's Rights in Islam,* trans. Mary Jo Lakeland (Reading, Mass.: Addison Wesley, 1991); Fatna A. Sabbah, *Woman in the Muslim Unconscious,* trans. Mary Jo Lakeland (New York: Pergamon Press, 1984). See also the early chapters in Leila Ahmed, *Women and Gender in Islam.*

4. Jamal al-Din al-Shayyal, *Tarikh al tarjama wal-haraka al-thiqafiyya* (Cairo: Dar al-Fikr al-'Araby, 1951), pt. 3.

5. On the role of the state and its servants in the creation of a body of literature called "modern history" in nineteenth-century Egypt, see Jack A. Crabbs Jr., *The Writing of History in Nineteenth-Century Egypt: A Study in National Transformation* (Cairo: American University of Cairo Press, 1984).

6. Afaf Lutfi al-Sayyid Marsot, *Egypt in the Reign of Mohammad 'Ali* (Cambridge: Cambridge University Press, 1984).

7. Juan R. I. Cole, *Colonialism and Revolution in the Middle East: Social and Cultural Origins of Egypt's 'Urabi Movement* (Princeton: Princeton University Press, 1993), 28.

8. Khaled Fahmy, "The Era of Mohammad 'Ali Pasha, 1805–1948," in *The Cambridge History of Egypt,* vol. 2, *Modern Egypt from 1517 to the End of the Twentieth Century,* ed. M. W. Daly (Cambridge: Cambridge University Press, 1998), 142.

9. Ibid., 145.

10. Hunter, *Egypt under the Khedives,* 22.

11. Ehud Toledano, "Social and Economic Change in the 'Long Nineteenth Century,'" in *The Cambridge History of Egypt,* vol. 2, *Modern Egypt from 1517 to the End of the Twentieth Century,* M. W. Daly, ed. (Cambridge: Cambridge University Press, 1998), 256.

12. Hunter, *Egypt under the Khedives,* 103.

13. This is Hunter's argument in *Egypt under the Khedives.*

14. Ehud Toledano makes a compelling counterargument in his *State and Society in Mid-Nineteenth-Century Egypt* (Cambridge: Cambridge University Press, 1990). He claims that the distinction between the two groups remained rigid throughout the later decades of the nineteenth century. See, esp., pp. 68–93.

15. F. Robert Hunter, "Egypt Under the Successors of Mohammad 'Ali," in *The Cambridge History of Egypt,* vol. 2, M. W. Daly, ed., 183.

16. Ibid., 192.

17. Cole, *Colonialism and Revolution,* 101.

18. Hunter, *Egypt under the Khedives,* 52.

19. Cole, *Colonialism and Revolution,* 101.

20. Toledano, "Social and Economic Change in 'the Long Nineteenth Century,'" 260.

21. Hunter, *Egypt under the Khedives.*

22. Al-Shayyal, *Tarikh al tarjama,* 200.

23. Ahmad 'Izzat 'Abd al-Karim, *Tarikh al-ta'lim fi 'asr Mohammad 'Ali* (Cairo: Maktabat al-Nahda al-Misriyya, 1938), 329.

24. Al-Shayyal, *Tarikh al-tarjama,* 46.

25. Ibid., 73. The need for translations and translators was first made real in 1827 when Egypt's first modern medical school was opened and neither professors nor students were proficient in a common language.

26. Louis 'Awad, *Tarikh al-fikr al-misry al-hadith, min al-hamla al-faransiyya ila 'asr Isma'il* (Cairo: Maktabat Madbouli, 1987.)

27. Al-Shayyal, *Tarikh al-tarjama,* 147.

28. 'Abd al-Karim, *Tarikh al-ta'lim,* 333.

29. The school functioned until 1849, when Mohammad 'Ali's successor, 'Abbas I, had it closed; it did not open again until Isma'il's reign.

30. al-Shayyal, *Tarikh al-tarjama,* 45.

31. Beginning in the 1830s, dozens of texts on medicine and how to take care of the body were translated. The first was an Arabic version of Bayle's *Anatomie du corps humain* (Anatomy of the human body) (1833), followed in that same year by the publication of an Arabic version of *Les Règles de l'hygiène et de la médecine appliquée au corps humain* (The rules of hygiene and medicine, applied to the human body). The relationship between the body and the state addressed in Mitchell, *Colonising Egypt;* Amira al-Azhary Sonbol, *The Creation of a Medical Profession in Egypt, 1800–1922* (Syracuse, N.Y.: Syracuse University Press, 1991); Laverne Kuhnke, *Lives at Risk: Public Health in Nineteenth-Century Egypt* (Berkeley: University of California Press, 1990); Nancy Elizabeth Gallagher, *Egypt's Other Wars: Epidemics and the Politics of Public Health* (Syracuse, N.Y.: Syracuse University Press, 1990); and Khaled Fahmy, *All the Pasha's Men: Mehmed 'Ali,*

His Army, and the Making of Modern Egypt (Cambridge: Cambridge University Press, 1997).

A full list of the works translated by Dar al-Alsun can be found in al-Shayyal, *Tarikh al-tarjama*, appendixes 1 and 2.

32. Regarding the body of literature, the most famous of these works is that of al-Jahiz, who lived and worked in Basra and Baghdad in the eighth and ninth centuries C.E. See Charles Pellat, ed., *The Life and Works of Jahiz* trans. D. M. Hanke (Berkeley: University of California Press, 1969).

33. One of the most visible activities of the Napoleonic expedition was surveying. Egypt was constantly subjected to drawing and measuring, such that it could be mapped and "placed." Such activities, combined with the expedition's obsession with the budding science of "Egyptology," served to "locate" Egypt in new spatial and historical frameworks.

34. See al-Shayyal, *Tarikh al-tarjama*, chap. 2.

35. Ibid., 160.

36. Machiavelli's translator was Father Anton Rafa'el Zakhur, one of the first of Mohammad 'Ali's translators. Castera was translated by Jacoraki Argyropoulo. See Bianchi's "Catalogue général des livres Arabes, Persans, et Turcs imprimés à Boulac en Égypte depuis l'introduction de l'imprimerie dans ce pays," in *Nouveau Journal Asiatique* 2 (1843): 24–60.

37. The translator of this last book was Mohammad Moustafa al-Baya'a, who after graduating from Dar al-Alsun worked as an editor of foreign translations. (Al-Tahtawi himself corrected the translation before it was published in Bulaq in 1841.) One of the first men to graduate from Dar al-Alsun, Khalifa Mahmoud, who later served as head of the Bureau of Translations, translated a number of histories from French to Arabic. See Salah Magdi, *Hilyat al-zaman bi manaqib khadim al-watan. Sirat Rifa'a Rafi' 'al-Tahtawi*, ed. Jamal ad-Din al-Shayyal (Cairo: Wizarat al-Thiqafa wal-Irshad al-Qawmi, 1958), 43–54.

38. According to Crabbs, Mohammad 'Ali intended to produce an encyclopedic history of his reign, as well as his memoirs. Apparently he was too distracted by other projects to finish either work. See Crabbs, *The Writing of History*, 68.

39. On the relationship between behavior, progress, and the ultimate construction of ethnicity, see John and Jean L. Camaroff, "Of Toteism and Ethnicity," in *Ethnography and the Historical Imagination* (Boulder, Colo.: Westview Press, 1992).

40. The full title of Depping's text is *Aperçu historique sur les moeurs et coutumes des nations: Contenant le tableau comparé chez les divers peuples anciens et modernes, des usages et des cérémonies concernant l'habitation, la nourriture, l'habillement, les marriages, les funérailles, les jeux, les fêtes, les guerres, les superstitions, les castes, etc.* (Paris: L'Encyclopédie Portative, 1826). On al-Tahtawi as author of his own geographies, see Eve M. Troutt Powell, "From Odyssey to Empire: Mapping Sudan through Egyptian Literature in the Mid-Nineteenth Century," *International Journal of Middle East Studies* 31 (1999): 401–27.

41. Al-Tahtawi, *Qala'id al-mafakhir fi ghara'ib 'aw'id al-awa'il wa al-awakhir* (Cairo: Dar al-Tiba'a, 1833).

42. In Arabic, *bilad al-kufar*. I imagine that this must have been a concession al-Tahtawi made to French; he makes reference to cleanliness and its place both in Islamic law and "that of Moses," using all the honorific phrases traditionally used when mentioning their names, something Depping would not have done. This might also be a case of al-Tahtawi inserting himself as "author."

43. Al-Tahtawi, *Qala'id al-mafakhir*, 20-21.

44. Cited in Anwar Luqa, *Voyageurs et écrivains Égyptiens en France au xix-ième siècle* (Paris: Didier Press, 1970), 62. "Si les Français s'adonnent aux sciences . . . s'ils jouissent d'une vie économique prospère et cultivent des habitudes et des moeurs de plus en plus raffinés, c'est grâce à un régime politique favorable."

45. Al-Tahtawi, *Qala'id al-mafakhir*, 104-5.

46. Geography as the very concrete practice of studying the surface of Egypt was also crucial to many of Mohammad 'Ali's modernization programs, such as the construction of railroads, telegraphs, and irrigation canals. Here I am interested in geography as the more abstract practice of ordering the universe. As Winichakul has suggested, this "abstract" geography becomes more concrete when maps are used to give boundaries to nations once they have been "placed."

47. DWQ, Ahd Isma'il, Ta'lim, Box 12, *Buletin de la societé de géographie à Paris,* Deuxième série, Tome III, 1835: "Enseignement de la géographie en Égypte."

48. *Programmes de l'enseignement primaire, et de l'enseignement secondaire, approuvés par arrêt ministériel No. 849, au date du 16 Septembre 1901.* N.p., n.d.

49. The full title of Malte-Brun's text is a *System of Universal Geography, Containing a Description of all the Empires, Kingdoms, States, and Provinces in the Known World, Being A System of Universal Geography or a Description of All the Parts of the World On a New Plan, According to the Great Natural Divisions of the Globe, Accompanied With Analytical, Synoptical, and Elementary Tables.* In French, the book's complete title is *Précis de la géographie universelle; ou description de toutes les parties du monde sur un plan nouveau* (Brussels: Berthot, Ode et Wodon, 1829). I was unable to use al-Tahtawi's Arabic translation and therefore used an English version. The following passages are taken from James G. Percival's translation (Boston: Samuel Walker, 1834). Al-Tahtawi's Arabic translation of Malte-Brun first appeared in 1838.

50. Conrad Malte-Brun, *System of Universal Geography,* vol. 1, preface, 3.

51. Patrick Wolfe, "History of Imperialism: A Century of Theory, from Marx to Postcolonialism," *The American Historical Review* 102: 2 (1997): 388-420.

52. Malte-Brun, *System of Universal Geography,* vol. 1, 1-2.

53. Ibid., 322. My emphasis.

54. Ibid., preface, 4. My emphasis.

55. Here I wish to draw attention to the activities and interests of state-employed translators in two areas where questions over "modernity" and the role and import of "modern" habits and behavior, especially those pertaining to "the woman question," were central to nationalist debates in the late nineteenth

and early twentieth centuries: Ottoman Istanbul and Qajar Iran. Translations of very similar texts were requisitioned in Iran under the Qajar dynasty, particularly during the reign of Prince 'Abbas Mirza (d. 1833), who was the first Qajar to lead an aggressive program of reform and modernization, not unlike Ottoman reforms and those of Mohammad 'Ali. Some of the books he had translated were later printed and circulated under the reign of Minister Mirza Taqi Khan, or Amir Kabir, who founded Iran's first European-style institution of higher education, Dar al-Founun. Dar al-Founon's press printed both translations and the original compositions of its professors throughout the nineteenth century. Like the texts produced as the result of Dar al-Alsun's efforts, those texts were originally produced for the purposes of training a new military and a new bureaucracy. (The titles I list here are in addition to texts printed on the military sciences, engineering, and medicine.) 'Abbas Mirza translated Voltaire's histories of Charles XII, Catherine the Great, Peter the Great. French literature was translated in abundance, including a number of works by Alexandre Dumas (père) and Molière. Travel literature, both that of Europeans and Persians abroad, comprised a number of the school's productions. (In the period slightly succeeding that of this study, Nasr ad-Din Shah, in whose administration Amir Kabir worked, had four volumes of the journals he wrote while traveling and studying in Europe published). Geographies were translated, such as *Jám-i-Jam* (The world-showing goblet of Jamshíd), which, published around 1850, appears to have been a translation of William Pinnock's *Geography*. The text was translated by 'Abbas Mirza's son, Farhad Mirza. The notion of "world-showing" reappears consistently throughout the nineteenth century, both in translations of geographies and those written by Persians. See Edward Granville Browne, *The Press and Poetry of Modern Persia* (Cambridge: Cambridge University Press, 1914), 154–66.

In *The Emergence of Modern Turkey* (London: Oxford University Press, 1961), Bernard Lewis also notes that one of the more crucial reforms that took place in Istanbul in the 1830s was the creation of a "translation chamber" *(terciime odasi)*, which was used to educate statesmen to serve in Ottoman embassies in London, Paris, and Vienna. The establishment of the chamber did not lead to the establishment of an equivalent to Dar al-Alsun. A full-blown school for administration and the establishment of a school for the training, linguistic and otherwise, of new state bureaucrats did not happen until the opening of the Imperial Ottoman Lycée at Galatasaray in 1868. Nonetheless, Lewis notes that a number of state administrators trained in the *terciime odasi* went on to translate a variety of European texts into Ottoman Turkish. The most noteworthy among them, according to Lewis, was Ahmed Vefik Pasha who, in addition to a long career as ambassador in Paris and as Grand Vezir, wrote a Turkish dictionary and translated a number of Molière's plays into Turkish. He also translated Fénélon's *Adventures of Télémaque,* a text that was also translated by al-Tahtawi and one of the members of Amir Kabir's Dar-al-Fanoun.

I wish to thank Camron Amin for drawing my attention to the activities of translators in Tehran.

56. Georges-Bernard Depping, *Evening Entertainment; or, Delineations of the Manners and Customs of Various Nations, Interspersed with Geographical Notices, Historical and Biographical Anecdotes and Descriptions of in Natural History* (Philadelphia, Pa.: David Hogan, 1817). According to Timothy Mitchell, the book's leitmotif was indolence, as opposed to productivity. I think that Mitchell is correct in noting that the text gives specific, prescriptive formulas for wiping out indolence, and that part of the Egyptian state's program for reform was the creation of more productive Egyptians. Mitchell does not include the book's other agendas, however, not the least of which was this process of assessing modernity through morals and behavior. See Mitchell, *Colonising Egypt*, 104-8.

57. Heyworth-Dunne, *An Introduction to the History of Education in Modern Egypt* (London: Frank Cass, 1968), 104-5.

58. According to Alain Silvera, most of the records from the early missions were destroyed in a fire in the Citadel, which formally housed the state's archives, in 1830. See his "The First Egyptian Student Mission to France under Mohammad 'Ali," in *Modern Egypt: Studies in Politics and Society*, ed. Elie Kedourie and Sylvia G. Haim (London: Frank Kass, 1980), 1-22.

59. Ibid., 8-9.

60. See Rifa'a Rafi' al-Tahtawi, *Takhlis al-ibriz fi-talkhis Pariz*, in *al-'Amal al-kamila li Rifa'a Rafi' al-Tahtawi*, ed. Mohammad 'Imara (Beirut: al-Mu'assasa al-'Arabiyya lil-Dirasa wal-Nashr, 1973), vol. 2, *al-Siyassa wal-wataniyya wal-tarbiyya*, 189.

61. For a fairly detailed account of the students' daily program of study, see al-Tahtawi, *al-'Amal al-kamila*, vol. 2, 189-93.

62. Albert Hourani argues Mohammad 'Ali did not want his students to see much of French life, hence his rather rigorous policy of sequestering them. Silvera argues, however, that the students were, in fact, kept in the public eye as much as possible and were frequently presented to Parisian audiences. See Hourani, *Arabic Thought in the Liberal Age, 1798-1939* (Cambridge: Cambridge University Press, 1962), chap. 4; and Silvera, "The First Egyptian Student Mission."

63. There are numerous biographies on al-Tahtawi. The best discussions of his career in service to the state — as translator, educator, and administrator — are found in Shayyal, *Tarikh al-tarjama*; Magdi, *Hilyat*; and Gilbert Delanoue, *Moralistes et politiques musulmans dans l'Égypte du XIXième siècle*, vol. 2 (Cairo: Institut Français d'Archéologie Orientale, 1982), which contains a considerable bibliography on al-Tahtawi and his various endeavors.

64. On al-'Attar, al-Tahtawi, and "science," see John W. Livingston, "Western Science and Educational Reform in the Thought of Shaykh Rifa'a al-Tahtawi," in *International Journal of Middle East Studies* 28 (1996): 543-64.

65. The text was translated into Turkish in 1839. See Anwar Luqa's translation of the text into French, *L'Or de Paris: Relation de voyage, 1826-1831* (Paris: Sindbad Press, 1988).

66. Delanoue, *Moralistes et politiques*, 388.

67. Al-Tahtawi, *al-'Amal al-kamila*, vol. 2, 4.

68. Allen argues that *Takhlis al-ibriz* was the first in a series of works in which

Arab writers recorded their impressions of Europe. He claims that the subject of the "grand tour" of Europe later served as the trope for a series of novels about the relationship between the East and the West that have appeared over the course of the twentieth century and for autobiographies such as Taha Hussein's famous *al-Ayyam* (The days). See Roger Allen, *The Arabic Novel: An Historical and Critical Introduction* (Syracuse, N.Y.: Syracuse University Press, 1982).

69. Roger Allen, *A Study of Hadith 'Isa Ibn Hisham: Mohammad al-Muwaylihi's View of Egyptian Society during the British Occupation* (Albany, N.Y.: State University of New York, 1974).

While *'Alam al-din* was a fictional account of a trip to Europe, 'Ali Mubarak was later sent to France on a mission in 1867 when he was serving as Isma'il's undersecretary of education. His task was to look at French schools. According to Anwar Luqa, the biggest effects of Mubarak's sojourn in France are reflected in his activities in the Ministry of Public Education. He built the Khedival Library in Cairo along the lines of the Bibliothèque Nationale de Paris, and he was instrumental in writing the Law of 1867, which separated Egypt's schools into primary, secondary, and superior schools. Luqa claims that, like al-Tahtawi, Mubarak acquired the talent for translating while he was in France and also developed a taste for history and geography. See Luqa, *Voyageurs et écrivains Égyptiens en France*, 87–88.

70. Cole, *Colonialism and Revolution*, 38–44; Leon Zolondek, "Al-Tahtawi and Political Freedom," *The Muslim World* 54 (1964): 90–97.

71. Hourani, *Arabic Thought*, chap. 4; 'Awad, *Tarikh al-fikr al-misry*, 268–86; Baha' Tahir, *Ibna' Rifa'a: al-Thaqafa wal-hurriya* (Cairo: Dal al-Hilal, 1993), 31–48.

72. Al-Tahtawi mentions his translations of Depping's work in the second chapter of his third *maqala*, "ahl paris," or "The People of Paris," in which a number of institutions and customs are described. See al-Tahtawi, *al-'Amal al-kamila*, 75.

73. A *parasang* is an ancient Persian unit of distance, roughly 3.5 miles.

74. Al-Tahtawi, *al-'Amal al-kamila*, vol. 2. This is a paraphrasing of pages 63–65. Al-Tahtawi "placed" France in relation to practically every other country in the world. He named the nations and the oceans by which it was surrounded; he named the nations that lay outside Europe and their capitals so that the reader would understand the importance of Paris.

75. Al-Tahtawi admired French architecture and craftsmanship but thought that the materials with which Parisian homes were built were generally bad, especially compared with Cairo. See *al-'Amal al-kamila*, vol. 2, 107–9.

76. Ibid., 107.

77. Ibid., 108.

78. Ibid.

79. Ibid. The prevalence of literacy in France was noticed by numerous Egyptian travelers. Ahmed Zaki, who journeyed to Paris in 1892 and 1900, noted that even drivers knew how to read. To him, the existence of numerous

libraries in Paris was proof of the extent to which the French were literate. See Luqa, *Voyageurs et écrivains Égyptiens en France*, 212.

80. Al-Tahtawi, *al-'Amal al-kamila*, vol. 2, 107–10.

81. Ibid., 113–14.

82. Ibid., 108–9.

83. Ibid., 121.

84. Al-Tahtawi calls the preservation of health "politics" *(siyasat al-siha)*. Ibid., 128–30.

85. Ibid., 169.

86. Ibid., 132.

87. In Arabic: *al-dafatir al-sanawiyya, al-taqwimat al-jadida, wal-zijat al-musahaha.*

88. Al-Tahtawi, *al-'Amal al-kamila*, vol. 2, 172.

89. Ibid., 93.

90. Marsot, *Egypt in the Reign of Mohammad 'Ali*, chap. 7.

91. Janet Abu-Lughod, *Cairo: 1001 Years of the City Victorious* (Princeton: Princeton University Press, 1971), 90–91.

92. Cited in André Raymond, *Cairo*, trans. Willard Wood (Cambridge, Mass.: Harvard University Press, 2000), 301–2.

93. The reason behind the prohibition of *mashrabiyya* is said to have been fire. Some historians have suggested, however that the pasha intended new building styles to mark a new era. Janet Abu-Lughod, *Cairo*, 94.

94. Ibid., 96 and 106; Nihal Tamraz, *Nineteenth-Century Cairene Houses and Palaces* (Cairo: American University in Cairo Press, 1998),5.

95. Tamraz, *Nineteenth-Century Cairene Houses and Palaces*, 1.

96. 'Ali Mubarak, *al-Khitat al-tawfiqiyya al-jadida li misr al-qahira wa muduniha wa biladiha al-qadima wa-al-shahira*, vol. 1 (Cairo: Matba'at Bulaq, 1980), 214–16, cited in Tamraz, *Nineteenth-Century Cairene Houses and Palaces*, 26.

97. Hunter, *Egypt under the Khedives*, 100.

98. Ibid., 99–110.

99. Toledano, "Social and Economic Change in The Long Nineteenth Century," 274–75.

100. Toledano, *State and Society in Mid-Nineteenth-Century Egypt*, 54.

101. Tamraz, *Nineteenth-Century Cairene Houses and Palaces*, 46

102. Isma'il Sarhank, *Haqa'iq al-akhbar 'an duwal al bihar*, vol. 2 (Bulaq: Matba'at al-Amiriyya, 1898), 260, cited in Ibid., 45, 46–47.

103. Valérie Boissier de Gasparin, *Journal d'un voyage au Levant* (Paris: M. Ducloux, 1948), cited in Ibid., 42.

104. Raymond, *Cairo*, 307.

105. Janet Abu-Lughod, *Cairo*, 105.

106. Russell, "Creating the New Woman," 81–85.

107. Abu-Lughod, *Cairo*, 106.

108. Hunter, *Egypt under the Khedives*, 103.

109. Russell, "Creating the New Woman," 33.

110. Cole, *Colonialism and Revolution*, 33–34.

111. Judith E. Tucker, *Women in Nineteenth-Century Egypt* (Cambridge: Cambridge University Press, 1985), 182.

112. See Huda Shaarawi, *Harem Years: The Memoirs of an Egyptian Feminist (1879–1924)*, trans. Margot Badran (New York: The Feminist Press at the City University of New York, 1987), especially pts. 1 and 2. See also Ermine Foat Tugay, *Three Centuries: Family Chronicles of Turkey and Egypt* (Westport, Conn.: Greenwood Press Publishers, 1973), esp. chaps. 8, 11, and 12.

113. Tucker, *Women in Nineteenth-Century Egypt,* 182–83.

114. See ibid.; and Mervat Hatem, "The Politics of Sexuality and Gender in Segregated Patriarchal Systems: The Case of Eighteenth- and Nineteenth-Century Egypt," *Feminist Studies* 12: 2 (1986): 257–59.

115. Hunter, *Egypt under the Khedives,* 102.

116. Russell, "Creating the New Woman."

117. Sandra Naddaf, "Mirrored Images: Rifa'a al-Tahtawi and the West,' in *Alif: Journal of Comparative Poetics* 6 (1986): 73–83. Lane was a British Arabic scholar who became fascinated by Egypt and who traveled there in 1825 to write a book about its peoples and monuments. He later settled in Egypt for a three-year period, during which he wrote an ethnographic study entitled *An Account of the Manners and Customs of the Modern Egyptians* (1836).

118. Ibid., 75.

119. Ibid., 75–76. This translation is Naddaf's.

120. See al-Shayyal, *Tarikh al-tarjama,* pt.3.

Chapter 2: Inside Egypt

1. This is, of course, the argument put forth by Edward Said in *Orientalism* and Timothy Mitchell in *Colonising Egypt.*

2. See chapter 3.

3. Here I am following the lead of Edward Said who, in *The Question of Palestine,* convincingly demonstrates the role that art and literature played in the shaping of colonial policy in Palestine. Said claims that images of Palestine as *empty,* particularly those produced by painters and novelists, were instrumental in the construction of the epithet "A land without a people for a people without a land," which was so instrumental to the construction of Zionist platforms and to British policy in Mandate Palestine (1920–48). See Said, *The Question of Palestine* (New York: Times Books, 1979).

4. Edward William Lane, *An Account of the Manners and Customs of the Modern Egyptians: Written in the Years 1833–1836* (London: L. Nattali and Bond, 1836).

5. Afaf Marsot, "The Revolutionary Gentlewoman," in *Women in the Muslim World,* ed. Lois Beck and Nikki Keddie (Cambridge, Mass.: Harvard University Press, 1978). See also Leila Ahmed, "Western Ethnocentrism and Perceptions of the Harem," in *Feminist Studies* 8: 3 (1982): 521–34; and Judy Mabro, *Veiled Half-Truths: Western Travellers' Perceptions of Middle Eastern Women* (London: I. B. Tauris, 1991).

6. Jean-Marie Carré, *Voyageurs et écrivains français en Égypte,* 2d ed. (Cairo: L'Institut Français d'Archéologie Orientale [hereafter IFAO], 1976).

7. See, for example, Sir John Mandeville, *Mandeville's Travels,* ed. M. C. Seymour (Oxford: Clarendon Press, 1967); and Geoffrey Chaucer, *Canterbury Tales,* selected, translated, and adapted by Barbara Cohen (New York: Lothrop, Lee, and Shepard Books, 1988).

8. See, for example, Mary Wortely Montagu, *The Complete Letters of Lady Mary Wortely Montagu,* ed. Robert Halsband (Oxford: Clarendon Press, 1967). My thoughts on travel literature and the enterprise of knowing "the world outside" of Europe has largely been shaped by work done on South Asia, in particular Ronald Inden's *Imagining India* (London: Basil Blackwell, 1990), which offers an excellent depiction of the ways in which India, as object of inquiry, changed over the centuries. I am also indebted to Thomas R. Metcalf, with whom I took two extremely informative and engaging graduate seminars at the University of California, Berkeley, the topics of which, "Europe and the World Outside" and "Imagining Differences and Similarities," shaped this chapter.

9. Michel Foucault discusses the importance of naming sexual "disease" and depravity in order to categorize it, issue better surveillance over it and, ultimately, control or reform it. See Foucault, *The History of Sexuality,* vol. I, trans. Robert Hurley (New York: Pantheon Books, 1978). Likewise, I wish to suggest that part of the process of colonizing Egypt was naming it as a distinct political, cultural, and territorial entity and assigning to it "national" characteristics that could be similarly controlled or reformed.

10. Abraham Parsons, *Travels in Asia and Africa* (London: Longman, Hurst, Rees, and Olme, 1808), 306.

11. Jean Coppin, *Voyages en Égypte de Jean Coppin, 1638–39 et 1643–66* (Cairo: IFAO, 1976), 290. "Généralement toutes les maisons qui composent la ville ne paraissent pas agréables au dehors, et du côté de la ruë *[sic]* ont les fenestres *[sic]* barrées et l'aspect aussi mélancholique."

12. Le Père Antonius Gonzales, *Le Voyage en Égypte du Père Antonius Gonzales, 1665–1666* (Cairo: IFAO, 1977), 196. "Les maisons des fellahs sont pour la plupart faites de briques séchées au soleil, et d'argile; couvertes en haut, de lattes et planches ou de poutres, sur lesquelles ils étendent . . . des feuilles de palmiers. Là-dessus ils appliquent deux ou trois couches d'argile, qui, sous l'influence du soleil, devient dure comme la pierre et tient durant la vie d'un homme. . . . Les maisons dans les villes sont toutes peintes à la chaux."

13. Riya Salima, *Harems et musulmanes d'Égypte* (Paris: F. Juven, 1900), 6. "Vous voulez pénétrer dans un harem et le connaître parfaitement." Riya Salima was the pseudonym of Madame Rachid-Pasha. Her nationality is unclear, although her "knowledge" of both European and Egyptian homes leads me to believe she was European.

14. This point is also made by Said in *Orientalism.*

15. Salima, *Harems et musulmanes,* 9–10. This quote is taken from the chapter entitled "Intérieur du 'harem.'" What Salima describes here appears to be the

salamlik, where the (male) master of the house received guests, and not the *haremlik*, or women's quarters. While Salima wrote the book as if she was describing her own home to a Western reader, one has to wonder if she simply imagined a visit to a harem. "Entrons . . . dans un de ces harems. . . . Voici l'eunuqe à la porte. . . . Nous voici dans la façaha, grande pièce placée à l'entrée, comme nos vestibules, mais largement aérée et éclairée. De nombreux divans, un guéridon de bois doré, un lustre, quelques petites tables chargées de cendriers et de cigarettes, voilà l'ameublement classique. C'est là qu'on reçoit en été, là que la famille se réunit de préférence. Du reste, les salons ne me semblent pas beaucoup plus luxueux et sont généralement moins vastes."

16. Ibid., 1. "En vous donnant la description de ma maison . . . je devine les suppositions bizarres que vous avez faites."

17. Bayle St. John, *Village Life in Egypt (With Sketches of the Said)* (London: Chapman and Hill, 1853), 136–38.

18. On the relationship between ethnography and teleology, see Johannes Fabian, *Time and the Other: How Anthropology Makes its Object* (New York: Columbia University Press, 1983).

19. See Joan Rees, *Writings on the Nile: Harriet Martineau, Florence Nightingale, Amelia Edwards* (London: Rubicon Press, 1995).

20. See James Stevens Curl, *Egyptomania: The Egyptian Revival. A Recurring Theme in the History of Taste* (Manchester: Manchester University Press, 1992); and Peter France, *The Rape of Egypt* (London: Barrie and Jenkins, 1991).

A brief glance at the *Description* suffices to illustrate the extent to which mapping the inner realm of Egypt's edifices, both ancient and modern, was central to the process through which they were known. Most illustrations are accompanied by detailed floor plans, through which the most inner realms could be accessed. See, for example, *Étape Moderne*, vol. 2, plate 189, "Tours de l'enceinte des Arabes située près du port vieux; vues intérieures." Mosques, churches, palaces — all were finely and accurately mapped out, as were the private homes of the ruling elite.

I wish to thank Darcy Grigsby of the Art History Department at the University of California, Berkeley, for her help with the *Description*. Her suggestions, as well as her interest in this project, were enormously useful. She is not, of course, responsible for any errors or misinterpretations on my part.

21. See E. A. Wallis Budge, *Cook's Handbook for Egypt and the Sudan* (London: Thomas Cook and Son, 1876). See also Piers Brendon, *Thomas Cook: 150 Years of Popular Tourism* (London: Secker and Warburg, 1991).

22. The preface to Budge, *Cook's Handbook*, for example, reads: "This handbook is divided into four parts: Part I contains a series of chapters in which a connected outline of the history of Egypt is given, and accounts of the writing, art, architecture, learning. etc., of the Ancient Egyptians . . . ; a number of important facts about . . . the religion, architecture, etc., of the Mohammadans or Modern Egyptians have also been included." See ibid., iv–v; emphasis mine. The section on the ancient Egyptians was covered in 117 pages, while the "Mohammadan" period occupied ten.

23. William Morton Fullerton, *In Cairo* (London and New York: Macmillan and Co., 1891), 1–2.

24. Robert Smythe Hichens, *Egypt and Its Monuments* (New York: The Century Co., 1908), 14. My emphasis.

25. Amelia Edwards, *A Thousand Miles up the Nile* (London: Longman's, 1877), 17. My emphasis.

26. Karl Baedeker, *Egypt: A Handbook For Travellers* (Leipzig: Baedeker, 1885), 17. My emphasis. See also Sir I. Gardner Wilkinson, *A Handbook for Travellers in Egypt* (London: John Murray, 1858); and *Cook's Tourists' Handbook for Egypt, the Nile and the Desert* (London: Thomas Cook and Son, 1897).

27. Sophia Lane Poole, *The Englishwoman in Egypt: Letters from Cairo Written during a Residence There in 1842, 43, & 44* (London: C. Knight, 1844), 133–35. See also the *Description de l'Égypte, Étape Moderne,* vol. V, plate 13, which shows the French completely engulfed in the inner passages of the Great Pyramid. One of them seems to disappear into its depths; only his legs are visible as he makes his way through its passages.

28. Ibid., 136–37.

29. Ibid., 54–55.

30. Pierre Loti, *Égypte,* trans. W. P. Baines (London: T. W. Laurie, 1909), 11.

31. Jeanne Fahmy-Bey, *l'Égypte Eternelle* (Paris: Renaissance du livre, 1863), 46. "Madame Jeanne" was said to be a Frenchwoman writing under an Egyptian nom de plume.

32. Ibid., 46.

33. Florence Nightingale, *Letters from Egypt: A Journey on the Nile, 1849–1859,* selected and introduced by Anthony Satt (London: Barrie and Jenkins, 1987), 139.

34. Johann Michael Wansleben, *Nouvelle relation en forme de journal, d'un voyage fait en Égypte en 1672 et 1673* (Paris: Chez Estienne Michallet, 1677), 43. "Les femmes du pays sont ordinairement de petite taille, d'un teint brun; toute leur beauté consiste en un oeil vif; leur conversation est fort ennuyeuse, et la manière dont elles sont vestues *[sic]* n'est point du tout agréable. Les femmes des gens de qualité . . . sont bien mieux élévées et plus agréables en toutes manières."

35. Lane, *Manners and Customs,* 195–96.

36. H. G. Cutler and L. W. Yaggy, *Panorama of Nations* (Chicago: Star Publisher's Company, 1892), 28–29.

37. Ibid., 189–90.

38. Gonzales, *Le Voyage en Égypte du Père Antonius Gonzales,* 210.

39. Claude Etienne Savary, *Lettres sur l'Égypte où l'on offre le parallèle des moeurs anciennes et modernes de ses habitants, où l'on décrit l'état, le commerce, l'agriculture, le gouvernement du pays* (Paris: Onfroi, 1785), 164.

40. Lane, *Manners and Customs,* 191. My emphasis.

41. Sir I. Gardner Wilkinson, *Modern Egypt and Thebes. Being a Description of Egypt, Including the Information Required for Travellers in that Country* (London: John Murray, 1843), 228.

42. Lane, *Manners and Customs,* 189. My emphasis.

43. Stanley Lane-Poole, *Cairo: Sketches of its History, Monuments and Social Life* (London: J. S. Virtue and Co., 1892), 10. My emphasis.

44. Mabro, *Veiled Half-Truths*.

45. Charles Dudley Warner, *Mummies and Moslems* (Hartford, Conn.: American Publishing Co., 1876), 50. My emphasis.

46. Gonzales, *Le Voyage en Égypte*, 200. "Les femmes et les filles honnêtes en Égypte . . . ne viennent jamais là où se trouvent des hommes; on ne voit pas non plus dans les rues un homme s'adresser à des femmes ou à des filles . . . Elles circulent dans les rues avec modestie et d'une manière édifiante. Quand des hommes visitent une maison, même si leurs maris se trouvent présents, elles se retirent sans tarder ou couvrent leur visage jusqu'à leur départ."

47. Ibid.

48. Coppin, *Voyages en Égypte*, 119. "Elles sont retirées dans un appartement secret dans les maisons de telle sorte qu'elles ne sont point veuës [sic] de ceux qui y fréquentent."

49. Gonzales, *Le Voyage en Égypte*, 200. "Mais dès qu'elles sortent de leurs maisons, on ne remarque rien de tout cela puisqu'elles son entièrement enveloppées." My emphasis.

50. Coppin, *Voyages en Égypte*, 117–18.

51. Parsons, *Travels in Asia and Africa*, 313.

52. Benoît Maillet, *Description de l'Égypte contenant plusieurs remarques curieuses sur la géographie ancienne et moderne de ce pays, sur ses monuments anciens, sur les moeurs, les coutumes, flora et fauna composée sur les mémoirs de M. de Maillet par M. L'Abbé le Mascrier* (Paris: Chez L. Genneau et J. Rollin, fils, 1735), 114.

53. Sir Frederick Treves, *The Land That is Desolate: An Account of a Tour in Palestine* (London: John Murray, 1913), 52–53.

54. Carsten Neibuhr, *Travels Through Arabia and Other Countries in the East* (Edinburgh: R. Morison and Son, 1792), vol. 1, 118.

55. Carl Benjamin Klunzinger, *Upper Egypt: Its People and Its Products* (London: Blackie, 1878), 40–42.

56. Lane Poole, *Cairo*, 146. My emphasis.

57. Mary Louisa Whately, *Letters from Egypt to Plain Folks at Home* (London: Seeley, 1879), 181.

58. Warner, *Mummies and Moslems*, 294–95. My emphasis.

59. St. John, *Village Life*, 143–44.

60. Charles Perry, *A View of the Levant* (London: T. Woodward, 1743).

61. Claude Etienne Savary, *Lettres sur l'Égypte*, 158. "Les femmes jouent un rôle brillant en Europe. Elles paroiffent [sic] en souveraines sur la scène du monde. Elles régnent sur les moeurs, et décident des événements les plus importants. Souvent le fort des nations est dans leurs mains. En Égypte, quelle différence!! Elles ne s'y montrent que chargées des fers de l'esclavage. Condamnés à la servitude, elles n'ont aucune influence dans les affaires publiques. Leur empire se borne aux murs du harem. C'est là que leurs graces, leurs charmes sont enfevelis [sic]. Confinées au sein de la famille le cercle de leur vie ne s'étend pas au-delà des occupations domestiques."

62. Ibid., 158–59.

63. Ibid., 143.

64. Ibid., 144. "Le veillard le plus âgé tient le sceptre en ses mains."

65. *Travels of Ali Bey [pseud.] in Morocco, Tripoli, Cyprus, Egypt, Syria and Turkey between 1803 and 1807, Written by Ali Bey Himself* (London: Longman, Hurst, Rees, Orme and Brown, 1816), 114.

66. Nassau William Senior, *Conversations and Journals in Egypt and Malta* (London: S. Low, Marston, Searle and Rivington, 1882), vol. 1, 155.

67. Ibid.

68. Ibid., 155.

69. Ibid., 151–53.

70. Ibid., vol. 2, 199.

71. A well-developed body of literature exists on the similar position of both the traveler's gaze and women in South Asia. See, in particular, Chatterjee, *The Nation and Its Fragments*. See also the collection of articles in *South Asia: Journal of South Asian Studies* 14: 1 (1991); and Mani, *Contentious Traditions*. The role of Europeans in reforming Egyptian women through education will be discussed further in chapter 4.

72. For an excellent discussion of representing Egypt at the expositions, see Mitchell, *Colonising Egypt*, chap. 1.

73. Charles Edmond, *L'Égypte à l'exposition universelle de 1867* (Paris: Dentre, 1867), 217.

74. Ibid., p. 214. ("Les deux civilizations mortes des pharoans et des khalifes.") See Zeynep Çelik's *Displaying the Orient: Architecture of Islam at Nineteenth-Century World's Fairs* (Berkeley: University of California Press, 1992) for a more extensive discussion of nineteenth-century expositions and their role in displaying the Orient in the West.

75. The display was commissioned by Isma'il but designed and built by European architects. Frenchman Jacques Drévet designed the Egyptian buildings at the 1867 exposition. See Çelik, *Displaying the Orient,* chap. 3.

76. Ibid., 217. "Le décor dans l'ensemble et dans les plus petits détails, les hommes et les choses, tout nous transporte en Égypte."

77. Ibid., 219–20. "Un escalier en bois, brisé en plusieurs paliers, dans une cage carrée, mène au premier étage et jusque sur la terrasse, où il se termine, nous l'avons dit, en un *lanternon* fait tout entier en moucharabiehs. Nous le quittons pour visiter la galerie supérieur. . . . Les moucharabiehs valent qu'on les examine de près, et elles ne sont pas la partie la moins curieuse de notre construction. Elles ont été toutes détachées de la maison d'Hussein Bey, située au Caire."

78. Ibid., 15. "Elle offre aujourd'hui aux yeux éblouis du monde entier, en miniature et comme condensée en un si petit espace, toute l'Égypte, brillante, splendide, révélant les grandeurs de son passé, les riches promesses de son présent, et laissant à l'opinion publique elle-même le soin d'en tirer des conclusions pour l'avenir." My emphasis.

79. See Fabian, *Time and the Other.*

80. Lata Mani, "Multiple Mediations: Feminist Scholarship in the Age of Multinational Reception," in *Inscriptions* 5 (1989): 18-32. Mani calls this the dominant narrative of colonialism.

Chapter 3: Domesticating Egypt

1. Wilfrid Scawen Blunt, *My Diaries: Being a Personal Narrative of Events, 1888-1914* (London: M. Secker, 1920).

2. Wilfrid Scawen Blunt, *The Future of Islam* (London: Kegan Paul, Trench, 1882).

3. Max Egremont, *The Cousins: The Friendship, Opinions and Activities of Wilfrid Scawen Blunt and George Wyndham* (London: Collins, 1977); and Noel Anthony Lytton (The Earl of Lytton), *Wilfrid Scawen Blunt* (London: Macdonald, 1961).

4. See Sir Edward Malet, *Egypt, 1879-1883,* ed. Lord Sanderson (London: John Murray, 1909), section 2.

5. Wilfrid Scawen Blunt, *A Secret History of the English Occupation of Egypt* (New York: Howard Fertig, 1967), preface of 1895, vii.

6. Cole, *Colonialism and Revolution,* 33.

7. According to Ronald Robinson and John Gallagher, whose now classic account of the British invasion and occupation of Egypt has become the standard interpretation of the events of 1882, the intention of Gladstone's cabinet was simply to "intervene and withdraw." See Robinson and Gallagher, with Alice Denny, *Africa and the Victorians: The Official Mind of Imperialism,* revised ed. (London: Macmillan and Co., 1981), 121.

8. Milner was a journalist until taking up this position in 1884. He later served as Britain's secretary of state for the colonies from 1918 to 1921 and returned to Egypt in that capacity in December 1919. Alfred Milner, *England in Egypt* (London: E. Arnold, 1892), 215.

9. Ehud Toledano, "Social and Economic Change in the 'Long Nineteenth Century,'" 274.

10. F. Robert Hunter, "Egypt under Mohammad 'Ali's Successors," 187.

11. The khedive issued a decree on August 18, 1878, delegating governmental responsibility to the cabinet. P. J. Vatikiotis, *The History of Modern Egypt: From Mohammad Ali to Mubarak* (Baltimore: Johns Hopkins University Press, 1991), 130.

12. For the best discussion of the secret societies, see Cole, *Colonialism and Revolution.*

13. Vatikiotis, *The History of Modern Egypt,* 148.

14. "Lord Dufferin's Scheme," cited in E. W. P. Newman, *Great Britain in Egypt* (London: Cassell, 1928), appendix 1, 284.

15. Lord Granville, cited in Milner, *England in Egypt,* 27. Excerpts from the

Granville Doctrine can be found in J.C. Hurewitz, *Diplomacy in the Near and Middle East, A Documentary Record* (New York: D. Van Nostrand Co., 1956).

16. FO 141/168, Dufferin to Granville, Feb. 14, 1883.

17. PRO 30/20/160, Malet to Granville, Jan. 2, 1882.

18. On the British in Egypt, see also Malet, *Egypt, 1879–1883*; and Afaf Lutfi al-Sayyid Marsot, *Egypt and Cromer: A Study in Anglo-Egyptian Relations* (London: Murray, 1968).

19. Milner, *England in Egypt,* 1.

20. Ibid., xxii.

21. The journal *The Nineteenth Century,* for example, is full of articles in favor of an occupation based on territorial interests. See Edward Dicey, "Our Route to India," *The Nineteenth Century* 1 (1877): 665–86; ibid. 2, "The Future of Egypt," 3–14; and W. E. Gladstone, "Aggression on Egypt and Freedom in the East," ibid., 149–66.

22. See, for example, Blunt, *Secret History.*

23. This was the theory put forth by John Atkinson Hobson in *Imperialism: A Study* (Ann Arbor: University of Michigan Press, 1965); and, somewhat later, conflated with Vladmir Ilich Lenin's *Imperialism, The Highest Stage of Capitalism: A Popular Outline* (New York: International Publishers, 1939).

24. Milner, *England in Egypt,* 416; cited in A. G. Hopkins, "The Victorians and Africa: A Reconsideration of the Occupation of Egypt, 1882," in *Journal of African History* 27 (1986): 363–91, quote 367.

25. See Cole, *Colonialism and Revolution,* esp. his introduction.

26. See also Alexander Schölch, *Egypt for the Egyptians: The Socio-Political Crisis in Egypt, 1878–1882* (London: Ithaca Press, 1981). Roger Owen, in his "Egypt and Europe: From French Expedition to British Occupation," in *Studies in the Theory of Imperialism,* ed. Roger Owen and Bob Sutcliffe (London: Longman, 1972), argues that the causes of the invasion, both British and Egyptian, were multifaceted and reflected the influence of various elements of the population in both countries.

27. Hopkins, "The Victorians and Africa," 381.

28. See Edward Dicey, *England and Egypt* (London: Chapman and Hall, 1881). Dicey was editor of *The Observer* from 1870 to 1889 and a staunch advocate of Egypt's annexation. See also M. E. Chamberlain, "Sir Charles Dilke and the British Intervention in Egypt, 1882: Decision Making in a Nineteenth-Century Cabinet," in *British Journal of International Studies* 2 (1976): 231–45; cited in Hopkins, "The Victorians and Africa."

29. FO 633/87. This file contains the manuscript "Cromer's Situation in Egypt: Lord Cromer's Account," which later became his published text, *Modern Egypt* (London: Macmillan, 1908). The writing of the manuscript was apparently begun in 1895. According to Cromer's notes, much of the manuscript was omitted when *Modern Egypt* went to final publication.

30. See, for example, Peter Mansfield, *The British in Egypt* (New York: Holt, Rhinehart and Wilson, 1971), chap. 1, and Blunt, *Secret History.*

31. Alfred Milner, *Britain's Work in Egypt. By an Englishman in the Egyptian Service* (London: T. Edinburgh and A. Constable Publishers, 1892), 3.

32. Blunt, *Secret History,* 349.

33. FO 141/168, Dufferin to Granville at FO, Nov. 18, 1882.

34. PRO 30/29/126, Dispatch, Gladstone to Granville, Sept. 15, 1882.

35. Wingate later wrote that "a Consul General, a few consuls, and an occasional corespondent of the 'Times' *[sic]* were their only source of information, except for the odd Englishman in the service of Egypt who was sufficiently famous through his exploits to be able to obtain the ear of a Foreign Secretary." Wingate Papers, St. Antony's College, Oxford.

36. FO 141/168, Dufferin to Granville, Nov. 18, 1882.

37. Mansfield, *The British in Egypt,* 8.

38. FO 141/168, Dufferin to Granville, Nov. 18, 1882.

39. Ibid.

40. FO 141/168, Dufferin to Granville, received Feb. 14, 1883.

41. Ibid.

42. FO 141/168, Dufferin to Granville, Nov. 18, 1882.

43. Ibid., Jan. 26, 1883. My emphasis.

44. Regarding his perception of capable leaders, he wrote: "Cherif *[sic]* Pasha . . . may be regarded as the father and prophet of the parliamentary principle." FO/141/168, Dufferin to Granville, Nov. 18, 1882.

45. FO 633/84, ca. 1895. "Cromer's Situation in Egypt: Lord Cromer's Account." My emphasis.

46. Said, *Orientalism,* chap. 2.

47. Boyle was referred to as the "hidden Cromer," able to penetrate Egyptian society and get information in ways others could not. His daughter, Clara Boyle, later wrote, "His power extended even to the innermost parts of their private houses and their families." Clara Asch Boyle, *Boyle of Cairo: A Diplomatist's Adventures in the Middle East* (London: Titus Wilson and Son, 1965), 177.

48. Ibid., 32.

49. Ibid., 43-44.

50. Dicey, "Our Route to India," 674.

51. Cromer, *Modern Egypt,* 56. This was echoed by Dicey in *The Story of the Khedivate* (New York: C. Scribner and Sons, 1902), 50. Dicey frequented Egypt off and on from 1869 to 1899.

The use of *Modern Egypt* as a source about the British occupation and contemporary views of the Egyptians is problematic, for Cromer did not indicate how and when he penned the text in his prefatory comments. His notes on the text contained in the file that holds the original manuscript at the Public Records Office in London indicate that the text was already underway in 1895, but it is impossible to detect if the book was written as a kind of diary or if Cromer recorded his experiences in hindsight. Certain phrases in the text reveal that Cromer wrote the book in Egypt. On page 145, for example, he wrote: "The Centenary of Mehemet Ali's birth has just been celebrated in Egypt." Mohammad 'Ali was born in 1769. Other phrases give no indication of the date on which they were written. At the same time, while Cromer indicates that his purpose in writing the text was to describe the state of things at the outset of the British protectorate state, it is impossible to distinguish between observation and memory. However problematic, the text is full of descriptions of Egypt as degenerate, incapable, immoral, and justifying, if not exonerating, his official policy of open-ended, ambiguous rule, and is thus useful for discussing the problematic structure of "the Egypt question."

52. FO 633/87, from Dispatch 450, Cromer to Granville, appended to chap. 32 of "Cromer's Situation in Egypt: Lord Cromer's Account," n.d. My emphasis.

53. Edward Dicey, "England's Intervention in Egypt," *The Nineteenth Century* 12 (1882): 174.

54. Edward Malet, cited in Cromer, *Modern Egypt,* vol. 1, 181.

55. Dicey, "Our Route to India," 678.

56. Cromer, *Modern Egypt,* vol. 1, 86.

57. Taken from Boyle, *Boyle of Cairo,* 36, "Memorandum on the Background of the Khedival Family."

58. Ibid. This tale appears in most accounts of Isma'il's rule, as well as in travel literature from the period.

59. Milner, *England in Egypt,* 212. My emphasis.

60. Ibid., 176. My emphasis.

61. Ibid., 211.

62. According to historians, the dichotomies of Isma'il's personality "complicated" his rule. Mostyn, for example, says, "Ismail, a nineteenth-century Medici and the founder of modern Egypt, reflected the dichotomies. . . . Perfectly happy to have his finance minister strangled to death in the palace he built for his beloved Eugénie, he posed in Europe as the perfect gentleman." Trevor Mostyn, *Egypt's Belle Epoque: Cairo, 1869–1952* (London: Quartet Books, 1989), 2.

63. Cited in Boyle, *Boyle of Cairo,* 38.

64. Ibid., 36–37.

65. Dicey, "Our Route to India," 674.

66. "According to the gossip of the bazaars, his mother had occupied a menial position in the Viceregal harem, had caught the fancy of Ismail and had given birth to Tewfik." Dicey, *Story of the Khedivate,* 227. Milner, *England in Egypt,* 24–25.

67. FO 141/168, Dufferin to Granville, Feb. 14, 1883.

68. Malet, *Egypt, 1879–1883,* 85.

69. Milner, *England in Egypt,* 135.

70. The British briefly considered putting a European on the Egyptian throne, creating a kind of "Oriental Belgium."

71. FO 633/99, Cromer, "Memorandum on the Present Situation in Egypt," Simla, 1882.

72. Dicey, *Story of the Khedivate,* 229.

73. Blunt, *Secret History,* 96.

74. FO 141/168, Dufferin to Granville, Feb. 14, 1883.

75. Thomas Babington Macaulay, "Minute on Education," in *Sources of Indi-*

an Tradition, vol. 2, ed. William Theodore de Bary (New York: Columbia University Press, 1958), 49.

76. Homi Bhabha, "Of Mimicry and Man: The Ambivalence of Colonial Discourse," in *Tensions of Empire,* ed. Cooper and Stoler, 152–60.

77. Cromer, *Modern Egypt,* vol. 1, 156.

78. Milner, *England in Egypt,* 394, 404.

79. Milner, *Britain's Work in Egypt,* 3.

80. PO 633/5, Cromer to Nubar Pasha, June 15, 1891.

81. Milner Papers, 443, Bodelian Library, Oxford; Dufferin to Granville, Mar. 7, 1883.

82. Cromer, *Modern Egypt,* vol. 2, 528.

83. PRO 30/29/126, Gladstone to Granville, Sept. 15, 1882.

84. Cromer, *Modern Egypt,* vol. 1, 343.

85. Lord Dufferin, cited in George Ambrose Lloyd, *Egypt Since Cromer* (London: Macmillan and Co., 1933), 5.

86. FO 633/87. "Cromer's Situation in Egypt: Lord Cromer's Account," chap. 42, "The Struggle for a Policy."

87. FO 633, Cromer to Granville, Nov. 2, 1883.

88. Cromer, *Modern Egypt,* vol. 2, 154–55.

89. FO 141/168, Dufferin to Granville, Nov. 18, 1882.

90. Stephen Cave, Mar. 23, 1876, cited in Cromer, *Modern Egypt,* vol. 1, 4.

91. Cromer, *Modern Egypt,* vol. 2, 157.

92. Ibid., 525.

93. Ibid., 528. According to Cromer, such idiosyncrasies, coupled with a lack of money available for education, were the primary stumbling blocks to the reform of Egyptian men. This section of *Modern Egypt* was clearly written in or after 1894.

94. Ibid., 538–39.

95. Ibid. My emphasis.

96. Ibid., 524–42.

97. Ibid., 539.

98. Ibid., vol. 1, 158.

99. Edward Dicey, "Our Egyptian Protectorate," in *The Nineteenth Century* 7 (1880): 343.

100. Here my thinking has been influenced by Ashis Nandy whose text *The Intimate Enemy: Loss and Recovery of Self Under Colonialism* (Delhi: Oxford University Press, 1983) argues that the ways in which India was imagined by Britons, as well as the forms of imperial policy there, served to infantilize Indians and to create images of childish helplessness.

101. Cromer, cited in Boyle, *Boyle of Cairo.* My emphasis. Cromer, in fact, claimed that a "relapse" would occur if British supervision were withdrawn. See Cromer, *Modern Egypt,* vol. 1, 155.

102. M. W. Daly, "The British Occupation, 1882–1922," in *The Cambridge History of Egypt,* vol. 2, 242–43.

103. Lord Salisbury cited in Vatikiotis, *The History of Modern Egypt,* 173; PRO 633/7, Cromer to Granville, Jan. 7, 1894.

104. Daly, "The British Occupation," 243.

105. Histories of modern Egypt usually grant Egypt three "fathers": Mohammad 'Ali, Lord Cromer, and Gamal abdel Nasser (1956–71). It is thus usually fatherhood and its concomitant guises, especially patriarchal relationships, that are used to analyze both the colonial mission in Egypt and the nationalists' responses to it.

106. See Said, *Culture and Imperialism.*

107. Beth Baron, "Nationalist Iconography: Egypt as a Woman," in *Rethinking Nationalism in the Arab Middle East* ed. Israel Gershoni and James Jankowski, 105–24 (Princeton: Princeton University Press, 1988).

Chapter 4: The Home, the Classroom, and the Cultivation of Egyptian Nationalism

1. The only monographs on education in Egypt — both precolonial and colonial — to take on the relationship between the state and the inner world of the schoolchild and his morals are Mitchell's *Colonizing Egypt* and Gregory Starrett's *Putting Islam to Work: Education, Politics, and Religious Transformation in Egypt* (Berkeley: University of California Press, 1998).

2. On the role of the state in creating hegemonic discourse through which a dominant nationalism takes shape, see Antonio Gramsci, *Prison Notebooks* (New York: Colombia University Press, 1992), esp. 206–75, "State and Civil Society."

3. The classic text on educational reform in Egypt is James Heyworth-Dunne, *An Introduction to the History of Education in Modern Egypt* (London: Frank Cass, 1968).

4. See ibid., chap. 5.

5. 'Ali Mubarak, *'Alam ad-Din* (Alexandria: Matba'at Jaridat al-Mahrusa, 1882). Cited in ibid., 361.

6. A *waqf* is a land grant used for generating income.

7. DWQ, Majlis al-Wuzara', Nizarat al-Ma'arif, Box A4, Series 2, Ma'arif al-'Umummiyya, 1879, articles 3–6, 9. In addition, the *mudiriyya* schools were entitled to a second, first-degree school for every five thousand inhabitants beyond its initial ten thousand. Cairo and its governorates and towns got a first-degree school for every twenty thousand inhabitants and another for every ten thousand beyond.

8. Ibid., articles 5–6; Heyworth-Dunne, *An Introduction to the History of Education in Modern Egypt,* 364–65.

9. For a less attenuated discussion of the Dar al-'Ulum project and its difficulties, see ibid., esp. 378–80.

10. "Rapport adressé à Son Excellence Monsieur Victor Duray, ministre de l'instruction publique, sur l'état de l'instruction publique en Égypte," Octave

Sachot, Officier d'Académie, Paris, June 1, 1868, 21. DWQ, Ahd Isma'il, Box 12, "Ta'lim." "Lecture, écriture, religion, instruction morale, langue arabe, langue turque [celle-ci pour les filles riches]; les quatre règles de l'arithmétique . . . un peu de géométrie; manière d'élever les enfants et de conserver la santé; la direction et l'art de la cuisine; l'économie domestique; travaux d'aiguille."

11. Ibid., 22.

12. On the school for midwives, started during Mohammad 'Ali's reign, see Tucker, *Women in Nineteenth-Century Egypt;* and Khaled Fahmy, "Women, Medicine, and Power in Nineteenth-Century Egypt," in *Remaking Women,* ed. Lila Abu-Lughod, 35-72.

13. See Maria Fundone, "L'École Syoufieh (1873-1889) une première expérience d'enseignement primaire gouvernemental pour les filles au Caire," (Cairo, IFAO, Colloquium On Social Reform in Egypt, Dec. 1993). Fundone makes an excellent argument about the parallels between the modernity project, in toto, and the goals of the al-Siyufiah project. I disagree with her argument, however, that the creation of schools for middle- and upper-class girls represented the interests of the government alone and did not represent the interests of Egyptians from those classes. The extent to which missionary education, foreign schools, and the employment of foreign tutors had caught on among the financially able reflects changes in taste and expectations for Egyptian girls. On the education of women under Isma'il, see also Baron, *The Women's Awakening in Egypt;* Tucker, *Women in Nineteenth Century Egypt;* and Russell, "Creating the New Woman."

14. DWQ, Majlis al-Wuzara', Nizarat al-Ma'arif, Box A4, Series 27, Ma'arif al-'Umummiyya. Yacoub Artin Pasha, *Memorandum sur l'enseignement des jeunes filles, soumis à S.A. le Khedive Abbas Pacha Helmy,* June 10, 1892 (Cairo, L'Imprimerie Centrale). See also the same series, Box M6, "Note Requesting an Order to Improve what is Necessary at the Saniah School Until the End of 1889," Nov. 18, 1889. Addressed to the board of the Ministry of Education, the note requests money, cloth for the production of clothes, and clothes for the poor students who attended the school.

15. DWQ, Ahd Isma'il, Box 12, "Ta'lim," 35/1, Feb. 9, 1875.

16. Ibid., no dossier number.

17. Heyworth-Dunne, *An Introduction to the History of Education,* 388.

18. The extent to which development of the child's character and the goals of the state was part of the same project was made clear in a report on education written by one of Isma'il's favorite advisors, Dor Bey, who in 1872 wrote that the shaping of national character was "la seule tâche d'un gouvernement vraiment civilisateur, doit donc être de se rendre compte de tous les défauts du caractère populaire. . . . De cette habitude, de ce besoin que nous avons de jeter dans la discussion les principes de notre organisation sociale, naissent la participation du citoyen aux affaires publiques et la vie politique de l'état." See V. Eduard Dor, *L'instruction publique en Égypte* (Paris: Lacroix, 1872), 36.

19. See Girgis Salama, *Tarikh al-ta'lim al-ajnabi fi misr* (Cairo: Nashr al-Rasa'il al-Jama'iyya, 1963).

20. See Rev. Thomas McCague, "History of the Egyptian Mission," Presbyterian Historical Society Archives (hereafter, PHSA), Record Group 192, Box 1, 1.

21. PHSA, Record Group 192, Box 1, Series 2, McCague's Correspondence from the Missions (1854–61). This letter was also printed in the periodical *Watchmen of the Valley* of Cincinnati, Ohio.

22. "The Need of Women in Foreign Fields," *Women's Missionary Magazine* (hereafter, *WMM*) 4: 2 (Sept. 1890), 31.

23. According to Salama, when the Presbyterians did establish a standard curriculum in the first decades of the twentieth century, it included: geography, U.S. history, Arabic, English, and French in addition to *tadbir al-manzil* (home economics, apparently for boys and girls alike), music, and physical education.

24. Mary W. Hogg, "The Khayatt School," *WMM* 7: 1 (Aug. 1893), 4.

25. Ibid., 5.

26. Salama, *Tarikh al-ta'lim al-ajnabi*, 196. In 1897 there were, according to the British annual reports on Egypt and the Sudan, 11,304 students enrolled in the public schools. This number jumped to 19,684 by 1898. See Parliamentary Papers, *Report by Her Majesty's Agent and Consul General on the Finances, Administration and Condition of Egypt and the Sudan in 1898* (London: Harrison and Sons, 1899), 35 (hereafter *Annual Reports*). By 1902, the *Annual Reports* also list the opening of primary and secondary schools by local Muslim and Christian benevolent societies as detracting from the number of students enrolled in the missionary schools.

27. Advertisements for the missionary schools appeared frequently in the press. On October 1, 1885, for example, *al-Muqtataf* ran an ad for the American Mission School in Alexandria. The school distinguished itself from other schools by stating that it taught Arabic in addition to French, English, and Italian. In October 1896, Cairo's American Mission School announced that it was following the standards of the Ministry of Education. It claimed to have both American and Egyptian teachers and to offer instruction to boys and girls, Muslims and Christians.

28. There was no commentary attached to the report that 'Urabi's daughters were enrolled in the school. One has to wonder, however, if the subtext to claiming their presence in the school was that a sound, Protestant education socialized them away from the rebellious activities of their father.

29. See Salama, *Tarikh al-ta'lim al-ajnabi*, chap. 4.

30. Carrie Buchanan, *Educational Work in Egypt* (Pittsburgh, Pa.: Women's General Missionary Society, United Presbyterian Church of North America, n.d.).

31. Rena L. Hogg, *Farida's Dream* (Pittsburgh, Pa.: Women's General Missionary Society, United Presbyterian Church of North America, n.d.), 6–8. "Mohammad . . . could talk of houses and households, but not of home."

32. Rena L. Hogg, "What Missions Have Done for Homelife in Egypt through the Pupils of the Schools," *WMM* 23: 1 (Aug. 1909): 11.

33. Minnehaha Finney, "The Village School and the Home," Finney Papers, PHSA, Record Group 240. Minnehaha Finney was appointed to the Egypt Mission by the Women's Board of Missions in 1894. She taught primarily in

Mansoura, in the Delta, and in Alexandria. She developed a curriculum for girls' schools, introduced the kindergarten to Egypt, and established the Training School for Women. She was a long-time editor of the *Women's Missionary Magazine.*

34. Ibid., 11.

35. Ibid., 14, my emphasis.

36. Carrie Buchanan, *Broadening Horizons in Egypt* (Pittsburgh, Pa.: Printing House of the Women's General Missionary Society, United Presbyterian Church of North American, [c. 1917]), 2–4.

37. Another of the school's graduates, an Egyptian, wrote a text that was used by the missionaries to teach domestic sciences. Buchanan claimed that it was also used by certain government schools.

38. Parliamentary Papers, *Annual Report,* 1905, 571.

39. Thomas Macaulay, "On the Government of India," a speech delivered in the House of Commons on July 10, 1833, from *Critical Historical and Miscellaneous Essays* (New York: Sheldon and Company, 1866), 141.

40. Cromer, *Speeches, 1882–1911* (Edinburgh: R. & R. Clark, 1912), 26.

41. In 1895, for example, certain *kuttabs* were made eligible for state subvention under the stipulation that they not teach English to their students. See Starett, *Putting Islam to Work,* chap. 2.

42. For the best discussion of British educational policies, as well as the practicalities of administration during the years of the occupation, see Mohammad Abu al-Is'ad, *Siyasat al-ta'lim fi misr taht al-ihtilal al-britani (1822–1922)* (Cairo: Matba'at al-Khatab, 1976). Historian 'Abd al-Rahman al-Rafi'i makes reference to the Egyptian educational system in his biography of nationalist leader Mustafa Kamil (1874–1908). Although al-Rafi'i situates the genesis of Kamil's nationalism in the latter's genius, he does allude to the role of education in shaping Kamil's nationalist tendencies. See his *Mustafa Kamil,* 5th ed. (Cairo: Dar al-Ma'arif, 1984), 31–47.

43. All *kuttabs* under government supervision used Arabic. Cromer claimed that European languages were maintained at the secondary level so that Egyptians could be employed by the government and to keep Egyptian students from studying in the missionary schools. See Parliamentary Papers, *Annual Report,* 1906, 109–14.

44. Sir Eldon Gorst, *Autobiographical Notes,* Elizabeth Monroe Collection, St. Antony's, Oxford, cited in Michael Richard Van Vleck, "British Educational Policy in Egypt, 1882–1922" (Ph.D. diss., University of Wisconsin, 1990), 316.

45. Abu al-Is'ad, *Siyasat al-ta'lim.*

46. *Oeuvres du Congrès National Égyptien, tenu à Bruxelles le 22, 23, 24 Septembre 1910* (Bruges: St. Catherine's Press, 1911), 141–49, esp. 144–45.

47. *Al-Waqa'i al-Misriyya,* Sept. 18, 1909, cited in Van Vleck, "British Educational Policy in Egypt," 363.

48. Parliamentary Papers, *Annual Report,* 1904, 71.

49. Ibid., 1905, 84; 1907, 32–33.

50. Ibid., 1911, 51.

51. The class was taught once a week for the first two years of study and then twice a week in the second two years until 1887 when it was taught for four hours a week. See *Program al-durus: al-madaris al-ibtida'iyya (al-daraja al-ula)* (Bulaq: Matba'at al-Ahiliyya, 1885 and 1887).

52. Ibid.

53. *Programmes de l'enseignement primaire et de l'enseignement secondaire approuvés par arrêt ministériel 849 en date du 16 Septembre, 1901*, p. 12. (No place or date of publication information available; found in the Egyptian Ministry of Education's private archives [hereafter EME].)

54. Ibid.

55. In 1897, the syllabus described "social conduct" as 'Lessons given . . . in order to implant in the minds of pupils (1) the benefits to be derived from acting in accordance with the principles of morality and (2) the mutual dependency of individuals upon one another." In 1901, the course description was redefined somewhat to include, in the third year of study, "conduite dans les circonstances ordinaires de la vie" and, in the fourth year, "savoir vivre." See Ministry of Public Instruction, *Syllabus of Secondary Courses of Study* (Cairo, 1897); and *Programmes de l'enseignement primaire et de l'enseignement secondaire approuvés par arrêt ministériel no. 849*, en date du 16 Septembre, 1901.

56. In 1927, a law made it compulsory for every school in Egypt, public or private, to teach *al-tarbiyya al-wataniyya wa al-akhlaq*. Teachers in all schools had to be certified through the Teachers' College, and part of the certification process included getting a degree *(shahada)* in that subject. DWQ, Mahafiz Abdin, "Ta'lim," Box 230, "Compilation of laws which were sent to the *Majlis al Wuzaara'* on primary education and general education," May 9, 1927.

57. Wizarat al-Ma'arif Al-'Umummiyya, *Al-Tahajiya wal-mutala'a*, 9th ed. (Cairo: Matba'at al-Amiriyya, 1916). The 1918 edition of the same book opened with the following sentences (called "useful sentences for the reader"): "You are raised in the Nation's schools," and "Love your nation with a true love." Similar editions, designed purely for the *kuttabs*, included passages from the Qur'an and discussions of prayer and fasting as well as discussions of the nation and the proper domicile. All of the textbooks used in this chapter were found in the small library and archives attached to the Egyptian Ministry of Education.

58. Ibid., 94–98.

59. Sayyid Mohammad Ahad, *Kitab al-tahliyya wal-targhib fil-tarbiyya wal-tahdhib*, 11th ed. (Cairo: Matba'at al-Amiriyya, 1911), 24.

60. Hafith Ibrahim, trans., *Kuttaib fil-tarbiyya al-awaliyya wal-akhlaq: al-juz' al-awal*, 2nd ed. (Bulaq: Matba'at al-Amiriyya, 1913), 10–15. The introduction states that this book was translated from the French when the then-minister of public instruction, Ahmed Hasmet, reviewed all the books written for boys and girls on morals and *tarbiyya*. When he found nothing to his liking on morals, he contacted the French minister of education and translated a goodly number of books used in the French primary and secondary schools into Arabic for use in Egypt.

61. ʿAbd al-ʿAziz Hasan, *Durus al-akhlaq al-maqadara ʿala tulab al-sana al-ula* (Cairo: n.p., 1913), 6.

62. Wizarat al-Maʿarif al-ʿUmummiyya, *al-Mukhtara al-ibtidaʾiyya lil-mutalaʿa al-ʿarabiyya* (Cairo: Matbaʿat al-Amiriyya, 1912.)

63. Parliamentary Papers, *Annual Report*, 1899, 36.

64. Ibid.,1912, 27. This number represented an 8 percent increase over the number of girls enrolled in 1910.

65. DWQ, Mahafiz Abdin, Box 238, "al-Taʿlim." "The Renaissance of Education in Egypt: 1917–1922," written for King Fuad by Minister of Public Education Mohammad Tawfiq Rifaʿat, Aug. 1, 1923, 80. This number had increased to 128 by 1922.

66. An 1888 report by Mohammad Said stated, for example, that the goal of public education was to repair the damage, done both to boys and to girls, by the "veilles domestiques," women who had not had a proper education. Mohammad Said, *De l'Instruction publique en Égypte et des réformes a y introduire* (Cairo: Imprimerie Franco-Egyptiene, 1888) 12. "On doit . . . combattre énergiquement par tous les moyens, les superstitions dont les veilles domestiques de nos maisons cultivent . . . car ses superstitions affaiblessent l'esprit et exerçent toujours une influence fâcheuse dans la vie."

67. Yacoub Artin, *L'Instruction publique en Égypte* (Paris: E. Leroux, 1890), 121.

68. Parliamentary Papers, *Annual Report*, 1902, 56.

69. Ibid., 1904, 77, my emphasis.

70. DWQ, Majlis al-Wuzaraʾ, Nizarat al-Maʿarif, Box 2, "al-Katatib." From the minister of public instruction to the Finance Committee, June 2, 1903, from Ahd Mazloum, president of the council of ministers of the Nizarat al-Maʿarif.

71. Parliamentary Papers, *Annual Report*, 1908, 43–44.

72. Ibid., 1909, 44–46. This represented a 44 percent increase in the number of *kuttabs* for girls from 1905, and a 111 percent increase in the number of girls enrolled. By 1909, there were forty-two graduates of the Bulaq school teaching in different *kuttabs* throughout Egypt.

73. Parliamentary Papers, *Annual Report*, 1905, 88.

74. Ibid., 1907, 34.

75. Ibid., 1905, 88.

76. Ibid., 1906, 92.

77. DWQ, Majlis al-Wuzaraʾ, Nizarat al-Maʿarif, Box A4, Series 143, Maʿarif al-ʿUmummiyya, Law no. 14 of 1916 for the Creation of Superior Primary Schools for Girls *(al-madaris al-awaliyya al-raqiyya lil-banat)*. In 1915, the minister of public education, ʿAdly Yeghen, tried to terminate the examinations for getting a certificate from the primary schools and admitting girls into the secondary schools or the teachers' training school because he thought that the difficulty of passing the examinations was keeping too many girls out of school. He encouraged secondary education for girls as well as teacher training, seeing them as sources for the spread of "l'enseignement de l'économie domestique." He said that "il importe plus haute point que l'éducation des filles qui doit les preparer à la vie sociale et qui peut être si féconde et a bons résultat pour la famille, ne soit

pas détournée de son véritable objet." (It is most important that the education that prepares girls for social life, and that gives rich results for their families, not be deterred.) DWQ, Majlis al-Wuzara', Nizarat al-Ma'arif, Box 23A, May 25, 1915.

78. The best information on what was taught in the government schools in the years preceding the revolution is found in a report entitled "Ministry of Education: Educational Progress in Egypt during the Period of 1882–1922." DWQ, Ahd Isma'il, Box 12, "Ta'lim."

79. Ibid.

80. DWQ, Majlis al-Wuzara', Nizarat al-Ma'arif, Box A4, Series 143, on laws created in 1921 to amend a law written for al-Saniah in 1915 (law no. 27). Mostly those laws address teacher credentials and duration of study; the documents, however, shed light on what was being taught in the schools earlier in the century.

81. DWQ, Mahafiz Abdin, Box 231, "Ta'lim," "The Egyptian University: Administration Council's Plan for the Operation of the University in the year 1911–1912." (No date or place of publication available.)

82. Francis Mikhail, *Al-Tadbir al-manzili al-hadith* (Cairo: Matba'at al-Ma'arif, 1916).

83. Ibid., 4–6.

84. For a lengthier discussion of home economics courses and texts, see Russell, "Creating the New Woman."

85. Francis Mikhail, *al-Nizam al-manzili* (Cairo: Matba'at al-Ma'arif, 1912), 30–35.

86. Hasan, *Durus al-akhlaq*, 6.

87. Mikhail, *Al-Tadbir al-manzili*, 96.

88. *Al-Talba*, issue 1, year 1, Nov. 20, 1908. For a more thorough discussion of the rise of the children's press in Egypt and its seminal period (1893–1910), see Bertrand Millet, *Samir, Sindbad et les Autres: Histoire de la presse enfantine en Égypte* (Cairo: CEDEJ, 1987).

89. On structured play see Omnia Shakry, "Schooled Mothers and Structured Play," in Lila Abu-Lughod, *Remaking Women*, 126–70.

90. Such lessons were accompanied by articles like "Famous Europeans: How They Eat and How They Drink," which appeared in *al-Tarbiyya* in May 1908. It should also be noted that the early editions of *al-Tarbiyya* had illustrated covers that featured neat and disciplined boys playing sports and studying together and girls playing with dolls, practicing needlepoint and other domestic activities, and sitting quietly with their books.

91. *Al-Tarbiyya*, March 1, 1905, 24.

92. The Egyptian press under colonial occupation will be discussed in chapter 6.

93. See also the February 19, 1909, edition of *al-Talba*, 7, which returns to the theme of theater as a means of inculcating nationalism. Hamdi wrote that the nation was in need of a school of morals: "The school that we're talking about is acting. Acting is like a public school of morals . . . from which everyone derives something according to their willingness to learn, and according to the

knowledge that they bring with them. We should make acting the means of spreading the morals and the principles of which the nation is in need."

94. Anthropologist Gregory Starrett makes the extremely compelling point that this kind of pedagogy, in Egypt and elsewhere, reverses children's roles with their parents, such that children end up instructing their parents in the kinds of behaviors required for the new social order. In this way, the hand of the state extends to the home vis-à-vis its schoolchildren. See Starrett, "The Margins of Print: Children's Religious Literature in Egypt," *The Journal of the Royal Anthropological Institute* 2: 1 (1996): 117–140.

95. *Al-Talba*, Nov. 20, 1908, 2–3.

96. Ibid.

97. My thinking here has been largely influenced by Lynn Hunt, *The Family Romance of the French Revolution* (Berkeley: University of California Press, 1992), especially her notion (informed by Freud's *Totem and Taboo*) that the fraternal relationships that are so crucial to the formation of a "democracy" depend on the unseating of the father and the subsequent reform of the familial order.

Chapter 5: Table Talk:
The Home Economics of Nationhood

1. Abbas Kelidar, "The Political Press in Egypt, 1882–1914," in *Contemporary Egypt Through Egyptian Eyes: Essays in Honor of P. J. Vatikiotis*, ed. Charles Tripp (New York and London: Routledge, 1993), 13.

2. Cole, *Colonialism and Revolution*, 106.

3. Ibid., 123.

4. Ibid., 123–24.

5. Kelidar, "The Political Press in Egypt," 4.

6. Ibid., 5.

7. Sannu' himself claimed a circulation of ten thousand. See Cole, *Colonialism and Revolution*, 123; Kelidar, "The Political Press in Egypt," 1–21; and Irene L. Gendzier, *The Practical Visions of Ya'qub Sannu'* (Cambridge, Mass.: Harvard University Press, 1966).

8. John Ninet, "Origins of the National Party in Egypt," *The Nineteenth Century* 13 (1883): 127–28, cited in Cole, *Colonialism and Revolution*, 124.

9. Cole, *Colonialism and Revolution*, 131.

10. For the best discussions of Sannu°'s life and work, see Cole, *Colonialism and Revolution;* and Gendzier, *Practical Visions.*

11. A title given to a minor governing official, *"sheikh al-hara"* can also mean the neighborhood gossip, or the local who knows everything about everybody's business. *"Sheikh al-hara,"* like "the Pharaoh," was one of the nicknames Sannu' gave to Isma'il. *Abu Nazzara Zarqa'*, Sept. 15, 1878. The magazine, from the time of Sannu°'s arrival in Paris through the spring of 1882 had a number of different

names, including *Abu nazzara zarqa' lisan hal al-umma al-misriyya al-hurra* (The man with the blue spectacles: Organ of the free Egyptian nation).

12. Ibid., July 22, 1879. Most of Sannu°'s captions were in Arabic and French; sometimes meanings were quite different from one another. In French the caption reads: "Pharaoh, in order to forget the past, makes himself out to be Lazarus and gives himself over to dancing." My thanks to Amira Sonbol for her help with the captions to these cartoons. She is, of course, not responsible for my interpretations of them.

13. Ibid., June 24, 1879.

14. Ibid., Aug. 19, 1879.

15. An Ottoman royal decree.

16. *Abu Nazzara Zarqa'*, May 12, 1882.

17. Ami Ayalon, *The Press in the Arab Middle East: A History* (Oxford: Oxford University Press, 1995), 51–52.

18. Ibid., 52–53.

19. Ibid., 53.

20. Ibid., 54.

21. Ibid.

22. Ibid., 55.

23. Ibid., 57

24. See Kelidar, "The Political Press in Egypt"; and Vatikiotis, *The History of Modern Egypt*.

25. Russell, "Creating the New Woman," 82, n. 203

26. *Al-Ahram*, Mar. 31, 1883.

27. Ibid., Sept. 23, 1887.

28. Ibid., Sept. 18, 1888.

29. Zeidan was a Syrian emigrant to Egypt. He was a self-taught historian. He is considered by historians to have been instrumental in forging an entente between Muslim conservatives and secular nationalists in the early twentieth century.

30. See *al-Hilal*, Sept. 8, 1900. The column was called "Table Talk" until 1919, at which point it became "The House and the Family." I thank Mona Russell for sharing her research on *al-Hilal* with me.

31. See *al-Ustadh*, Aug. 30 and Nov. 29, 1892.

32. *Al-Ustadh*, Nov. 1, 1892.

33. Ibid.

34. Ibid.

35. *Al-Manar* 6 (1901): 339.

36. During the 1890s, Nimr and Sarruf also printed a daily newspaper, *al-Muqatam*, which was equated with pro-British policy. Its publishers advocated a period of administrative and economic reform overseen by the British as the best path to a sound independence.

37. *Al-Muqtataf*, Jan. 1, 1895, 55.

38. Ibid.

39. Ibid., 56–57. Throughout the 1890s, *al-Muqtataf*'s *tadbir al-manzil* col-

umn ran articles with titles such as "Modernity is Had through the Preservation of Health," "Cleaning Children," "Feeding Children," "Manners and Customs," "Exercise and Rest," "Parties Given at Night, and Those Given During the Day," "*Tarbiyya*," and "Children's Clothing."

40. For a thorough discussion of the women's press in Egypt at the turn of the century, see Baron, *The Women's Awakening in Egypt*. See also Marilyn Booth, *May Her Likes Be Multiplied: Biography and Gender Politics in Egypt* (Berkeley: University of California Press, 2001).

41. *Al-Fatah* 4 (1892): 166. My emphasis.

42. Ibid., 167.

43. *Le Lotus* 1: 1 (Apr. 1901). The journal proved to be very expensive to run, and closed down after only one year.

44. See *Le Lotus* 1: 5 (Aug. 1901): 270–79. The author was S. Nahhas.

45. This journal was the organ of a Muslim beneficent organization, called Jama'iyyat al-Hayah.

46. *Majallat Jama'iyyat al-hayah*, Mar. 1909, 101.

47. For a much less attenuated discussion of consumerism and nationalism, see Russell, "Creating the New Woman."

48. See, for example, *al-Hilal*, Sept. 1, 1896. The same edition ran ads for two new pharmacies, a new brand of soap, and several types of remedies for anemia.

49. An ad for Odol toothpaste dominated the pages of *al-Ahram* in the early months of 1905. Its ads were huge and gave detailed accounts of tooth decay, cavities, and how toothpaste could improve the general health of the mouth. See *al-Ahram*, Jan. 12, 1905. Doans Pills for "backaches caused by kidney disease"; *al-Ahram*, Jan. 15, 1905. The advertisement for pain killers asked the question: "How Can I Be in the Best Health?" "Pilules de Blanchard," which were described as general pain-killing tablets; *al-Ahram*, Jan. 15, 1905. Siroline Roche was described as a syrup for "tightness of the chest, or sinus congestion, or whooping cough." Both "Kona monavon" and "Fer Bravis" were advertised as cures for lethargy; *al-Ahram*, Jan. 5, 1905.

50. *Al-Ahram*, Jan. 10, 1905.

51. On February 4, 1900, "nationalist" tobacco vendors "Sa'ad and Da'ud" ran an ad in *al-Ahram* promoting their new store.

52. *Al-Ahram*, Oct. 15, 1910. It was not uncommon in the first decade of the twentieth century to see clothing stores calling themselves "nationalist" or offering sales to their "nationalist" customers. On February 14, 1900, for example, a certain Mr. Kamoin announced a sale, offering European clothing for men, women, and children for half price to his "nationalist" clientele.

53. The September 9, 1900, issue of *al-Hilal* ran a large ad for a book called *Egypt's Geography*. It carried a large drawing of the Great Pyramid and the Sphinx, surrounded by the armies of the French occupation.

54. *Al-Ahram*, Mar. 6, 1905.

55. For an excellent discussion of home furnishings pitched at "nationalist"

women and the role of education in producing a taste for such items, see Russell, "Creating the New Woman."

56. *Al-Ahram,* Jan. 18, 1905. The ad was accompanied by a drawing of a very European-looking woman standing in front of a fireplace, clutching her aching back.

57. Ibid., Feb. 4, 1900.

58. On September 9, 1896, for example, *al-Hilal* ran an article called "The Corset," (*al-mashdu*), which included detailed diagrams of women's organs and intestines in order to illustrate the harm that could be done by "such binding and squeezing."

59. An ad for *Kitab al-Aghla* ran throughout the month of January 1905 in *al-Ahram.* It was advertised as "the best book on manners and morals."

60. *Al-Ahram,* Mar. 6, 1905.

61. *Al-Liwa'*, Nov. 3, 1902.

62. Juan R. I. Cole, "Feminism, Class and Islam in Turn-of-the-Century Egypt," *International Journal of Middle East Studies* 13 (1981): 387–407.

63. This is the opinion put forth by Mohammad 'Imara, whose edited collection of Amin's work is used in the discussions below.

64. Leila Ahmed claims that more than thirty books and articles appeared in response to *The Liberation of Women* in 1899. See Ahmed, *Women and Gender in Islam,* 162. Nationalist and future founder of the exclusively Egyptian bank, Bank Misr, Tal'at Harb (1876–1941), first came to the attention of the Egyptian reading public when he published a rejoinder to Amin on women's rights, *Tarbiyyat al-Mar'a wal-Hijab* (The *tarbiyya* of women and the hijab). See Mohammad Tal'at Harb, *Tarbiyyat al-Mar'a wal-Hijab,* 2d ed. (Cairo: Matba'at al-Manar, 1914).

65. Indeed, Leila Ahmed has argued that Amin's texts created a "discourse of the veil," in which debates over whether women should be kept veiled constituted intellectuals as either liberal, nationalist, or conservative reactionary. See her *Women and Gender in Islam.*

66. See Samiha Sidhom Peterson, trans., *Qasim Amin: The Liberation of Women. A Document in the History of Egyptian Feminism* (Cairo: The American University in Cairo Press, 1992); and idem, *The New Woman* (Cairo: The American University in Cairo Press, 1995). Because I do not consider "veil" to be a uniformly correct translation of *hijab,* I do not use Sidhom Peterson's translations. All passages from Amin cited below, therefore, are from the translation of the text by Raghda al-'Essawi of the American University of Cairo and myself, completed in 1995. We used Mohammad 'Imara's collection of Amin's works: *Qasim Amin: al-'Amal al-kamila,* 2nd ed. (Cairo: Dar al-Shuruq, 1988).

67. See Lila Abu-Lughod, *Remaking Women.*

68. This was not a trope that was unique to Qasim Amin. A glance at the turn-of-the-century press suffices to show that while some articles on the *hijab* are clearly about the *hijab* as a garment, others very clearly refer to the maintenance of women in isolation and ignorance.

69. Amin's first major contribution to debates over nationalism was with his publication of *Les Égyptiens* in 1894. The text was written in response to an essen-

tialist text about the "nature" of Egyptian society written by a Frenchman, le Duc d'Harcourt, called *L'Égypte et les Égyptiens,* published in 1893. D'Harcourt argued for an Egypt that could be understood in light of its customs, especially those pertaining to women. Amin's response was just as essentialist: In it one finds his first articulations of the role of women in reflecting a nation's modernity.

70. Amin wrote anonymously—the articles were not immediately attributed to him. On the role of *al-Mu'ayyad* in publishing the work of Amin and other reformers, see Abbas Kelidar, "Shaykh 'Ali Yusuf: Egyptian Journalist and Islamic Nationalist," in *Intellectual Life in the Arab East, 1890–1939,* ed. Marwan R. Buheiry (Beirut: Center for Arab and Middle East Studies, the American University of Beirut, 1981), 11–20.

71. Amin's introduction to *"Asbab wa Nata'ij,"* cited in Mohammad 'Imara's edited text *Qasim Amin: al-A'mal al-kamila,* 171. It is important to note that the expression "lifting the curtain," as it is used to discuss the uncovering of the nation's defects, is an expression often used in Amin's texts on women to describe the process of getting women out of isolation and into society. The "curtain" was to be lifted on their ignorance and isolation.

72. Qasim Amin, "The New Woman," trans. Raghda el-'Essawi and Lisa Pollard (unpublished ms. Cairo, 1995), 9.

73. Ibid., 10.

74. Ibid.

75. Ibid.

76. Amin was obviously aware of the kinds of theories about Egyptian development that were the common currency of travel literature. In the final chapter of *The New Woman,* he refutes the "climate" theory, the "geography" theory, and the "religion" theory about Egyptian backwardness.

77. Here, Amin used the expression "forced women out of *hijab.*" Ibid., 14–15.

78. Ibid., 98.

79. Ibid., 10.

80. Ibid., 73–74.

81. Getting men into the domicile to take a greater role in domestic affairs was common to the press from the turn-of-the-century onward.

82. Ibid., 67.

83. Ibid., 88.

84. Ibid., 78.

85. Ibid., 79.

86. Ibid., 80

87. Ibid.

88. On the establishment of political parties in Egypt, see Jamal Mohammad Ahmed, *The Intellectual Origins of Egyptian Nationalism* (London: Oxford University Press, 1960); and Nadav Safran, *Egypt in Search of a Political Community* (Cambridge, Mass.: Harvard University Press, 1961).

89. This is from a speech given by al-Sayyid on May 17, 1908, at the Club of

the People's Party in Cairo, cited in *Discours politques* (Cairo: Imprimerie al-Jaridah, 1909), 5-6.

90. Ahmad Lutfi al-Sayyid, *Safahat matwiyya min tarikh al-haraka al-istiqlaliyya fi Misr* (Cairo: Matba'at al-Muqtataf wa al-Muqatam, 1946), 20-22.

91. *Oeuvres du Congrès National Égyptien*, 103.

92. Ibid., 128-29.

93. Taken from DWQ, Majlis al-Wuzara', Mahafiz Abdin, Box 216, "al-ahzab al-siyasiya," Jan. 19, 1925.

94. *Al-Sufur*, May 21, 1915, 1-2.

95. Ibid.

96. For a discussion of journalists of Amin's era and their creation of new masculinities through discussions of women's issues, see Marilyn Booth, "Women in Islam: Men and the 'Women's Press' in Turn-of-the-Twentieth-Century Egypt," *International Journal of Middle East Studies* 33: 2 (2001): 171-201.

Chapter 6: Reform on Display

1. I hold to the definition of the revolution that includes the period from the end of World War I through the announcement of Egyptian independence on February 28, 1922.

2. This is the interpretation given by most nationalist historians. See, for example, 'Abd al-Rahman al-Rafi'i, *Thawrat 1919: Tarikh misr min sanat 1914 ila sanat 1921*, 4th ed. (Cairo: Dar al-Ma'arif, 1987); and 'Abd al-'Aziz Ramadan, *Tatawwur al-haraka al-wataniyya ul-misriyya min sanat 1918 ila sanat 1936* (Cairo: Dar al-kitab al-'Araby, 1968).

3. Morcos Fahmy, "Reflexions sur le conflit Anglo-Égyptien de Monsieur Morcos Fahmy, avec deux lettres à Sa Hautesse le Sultan et au Genéral Allenby, Haut Comissaire." DWQ, Majlis al-Wuzara', Nizarat al-Ma'arif, Box M13. Taken from a section of the "Réflexions" entitled "Un Protectorat juste et équitable," 40. "Ce n'est qu'un commencement d'émancipation . . . pour permettre à ce prétendu mineur que le serait l'Égypte, de faire, sans trébucher, quelques pas nécessaires et indispensables, pour fortifier ses muscles et l'initier à la marche sûre de l'âge mûr."

4. Egyptian historian 'Abd al-Rahman al-Rafi'i calls the revolution a natural stage in Egypt's history. Al-Rafi'i, *Thawrat 1919*, 66.

5. Fahmy, "Réflexions sur le conflit," 41.

6. PRO FO 141/810/8013, "Propaganda Intercepted by the British," Mar. 27, 1919.

7. PRO FO 141/744/8916, General Army Headquarters, Cairo, Mar. 26, 1919.

8. Mohammad Anis, *Dirasaat fi watha'iq thawrat 1919*, vol. 1 (Cairo: Anglo-Egyptian Bookstore, 1964), 11.

9. Here my thoughts were shaped by Lynn Hunt, *Politics, Culture, and Class*

in the French Revolution (Berkeley: University of California Press, 1984), who illustrates the extent to which French revolutionaries invented the symbols and the rhetoric of their movement only after it began.

10. See, for example, al-Rafi'i, *Thawrat 1919;* and Maurius Deeb, *Party Politics in Egypt: The Wafd and its Rivals, 1919–1939* (London: Ithaca Press, 1979).

11. The word *wafd* means delegation in Arabic.

12. Deeb, *Party Politics in Egypt,* 43.

13. Al-Rafi'i claims that the creation of the Wafd in November 1918 was a main cause of the revolution. *Thawrat 1919,* 84–85.

14. Ellis Goldberg, "Peasants in Revolt — Egypt 1919," *International Journal of Middle Eastern Studies* 24: 2 (1992): 261–80.

15. Joel Beinin and Zachary Lockman, *Workers on the Nile: Nationalism, Communism, Islam, and the Egyptian Working Class, 1882–1954* (Princeton: Princeton University Press, 1987), 89.

16. For the best discussions of the impact of the war on all classes, see al-Rafi'i, *Thawrat 1919;* Ramadan, *Tatawwur al-haraka al-wataniyya al-misriyya* . In English, see Beinin and Lockman, *Workers on the Nile;* John D. McIntrye Jr., *The Boycott of the Milner Mission: A Study in Egyptian Nationalism* (New York: Peter Lang, 1985).

17. Reinhard C. Schulze, "Colonization and Resistance: The Egyptian Peasant Rebellion in 1919," in *Peasants and Politics in the Modern Middle East,* ed. Farhad Kazemi and John Waterbury (Miami: Florida International University Press, 1991), 185.

18. Ibid., 184.

19. For the best discussion of the colonial economy, both prior to and during the war, see Schulze, "Colonization and Resistance."

20. FO 407/186/325, cited in Beinin and Lockman, *Workers on the Nile,* 85.

21. Schulze, "Colonization and Resistance," 184.

22. FO 371/1971, Cheetham to Grey, Dec. 3, 1914, cited in McIntyre, *The Boycott of the Milner Mission,* 9.

23. Afaf Lutfi al-Sayyid Marsot, *Egypt's Liberal Experiment 1922–1936* (Berkeley: University of California Press, 1977), 47. See also Mahmud Zayid, *Egypt's Struggle for Independence* (Beirut: Khayats, 1965). On Sa'ad Zaghlul, his life and influence on the Egyptian political realm, see 'Abd al-Khaliq Lashin, *Sa'ad Zaghlul wa dawruhu fil-siyasa al-misriyya* (Cairo: Maktabat Madbudi, 1975); and 'Abbas Mahmoud al-'Aqqad, *Sa'ad Zaghlul, sira wa tahiyya* (Cairo: Dar al-Shuruq, 1987).

24. Amine Youssef, *Independent Egypt* (London: John Murray, 1940), 32.

25. Milner Papers, Dec. 11, 1919, Bodelian Library, Oxford.

26. Mohammad Sabry, *La Révolution Égyptienne* (Paris: Le Librarie J. Vrin, 1919), 24.

27. From the "Report of the Egyptian Administration Committee," CAB 27/12 (the War Cabinet), cited in McIntyre, *The Boycott of the Milner Mission,* 19.

28. Deeb, *Party Politics in Egypt,* 3.

29. Schulze claims that the experience of World War I promoted the development of a sense of state consciousness in the native elite.

30. Deeb, *Party Politics in Egypt*, 43.

31. Numerous workers' groups went on strike during the revolution, including workers from government and private printing presses, the Cairo electric company, postal and communications workers, taxi and carriage drivers, and government bureaucrats. The role of workers and workers' syndicates in the revolution is covered in Beinin and Lockman, *Workers on the Nile*.

32. Schulze, "Colonization and Resistance," 188–89.

33. For a general account of the events of 1919, see al-Rafiʻi, *Thawrat 1919*. On the role of the peasantry in the demonstrations, see Goldberg, "Peasants in Revolt — Egypt 1919."

34. See Elie Kedourie, "Saʻad Zaghlul and the British," *Middle East Papers no. 2 (St. Antony's Papers, no. 11)*, ed. Albert Hourani (London: Oxford University Press, 1961), 139–60.

35. See esp. Anis, *Dirasaat fi watha'iq 1919*.

36. Deeb, *Party Politics in Egypt*, 43.

37. Anis, *Dirasaat*, 11.

38. Deeb, *Party Politics in Egypt*, 63.

39. Ibid.; Anis, *Dirasaat*, 205–6.

40. Deeb, *Party Politics in Egypt*, 43.

41. FO 141/744/8916, Apr. 21, 1919.

42. Al-Rafiʻi, *Thawrat 1919*, 142.

43. Deeb, *Party Politics in Egypt*, 53.

44. Ibid., 64; al-Rafiʻi, *Thawrat 1919*, 68–69.

45. Anis, *Dirasaat*, 13.

46. Ibid., 10.

47. When Milner arrived in Egypt, he was supplied with an impressive armory of information about Egypt, much of it from British nationals residing in Egypt — agriculturalists, businessmen, and educators. Some information was provided by British officials themselves. Milner reviewed annual budgets and notes on education, the mixed courts, Egyptian politics, and constitutional reform. He had access to treasury memos and notes on the Nile control works and capitulations commissions. He even had texts on Egypt's mentally ill and the number of Egyptians housed in the nation's insane asylums.

48. Fuad was Ismaʻil's son.

49. Deeb, *Party Politics in Egypt*, 55.

50. The problems inherent to the constitution and the difficulties of implementing constitutional rule in Egypt are beyond the scope of this project. For the best accounts of the period between 1922 and 1936, see Marsot, *Egypt's Liberal Experiment*; Selma Botman, *Egypt from Independence to Revolution, 1919–1952* (Syracuse, N.Y.: Syracuse University Press, 1991); and Zaheer Masood Quraishi, *Liberal Nationalism in Egypt: Rise and Fall of the Wafd Party* (Allahabad: Kitab Mahal, 1967).

51. Sabry, *La Révolution Égyptienne*, 28.

52. Thomas Russell Papers, Apr. 13, 1919, St. Antony's College, Oxford.

53. Ayalon, *The Press in the Arab Middle East*, 76–77.

54. Ibid.

55. Milner Papers, Dec. 9, 1919, Bodelian Library, Oxford.

56. Ayalon, *The Press*, 78.

57. Beth Baron, "Nationalist Iconography: Egypt as a Woman," *Rethinking Nationalism in the Arab Middle East*, ed. James Jankowski and Israel Gershoni (New York: Columbia University Press, 1997), 116.

58. *Al-Ahram*, Mar. 18, 1919, 1.

59. Ibid.

60. *Al-Mahrusa*, Mar. 18, 1919, 1.

61. Ibid., Mar. 21, 1919, 1.

62. *Al-Lata'if al-Musawwara*, Dec. 8, 1919. The caption also states that the caricature was created according to an idea submitted by Mustafa Fahmy Mahmoud Effendi of Alexandria, for which he received a prize of one hundred Egyptian piasters.

63. Gouraud and his troops entered Damascus on July 25, 1920.

64. On the role and importance of Egypt as a woman, see also Baron, "Nationalist Iconography: Egypt as a Woman."

65. *Al-Lata'if al Musawwara*, Aug. 20, 1920. According to the magazine's editors, such cartoons were drawn according to ideas submitted by their readers. This one, drawn by Mustafa Fahmy Mahmoud of Alexandria, received a prize of one hundred Egyptian piasters.

66. FO 848/11, Milner to Curzon, Dec. 25, 1919.

67. FO 141/680/9527, June 1919. The owners of the press were Mohammad Ibrahim Abaza and Mohammad Sa'ad. Other pamphlets intercepted from the press were calls to students to attend rallies at al-Azhar.

68. *Al-Lata'if al-Musawwara*, Apr. 3, 1922. The editors' comments were that this cartoon needed no explanation.

69. FO 848/11, Milner to Curzon, Dec. 25, 1919.

70. *Al-Kashkul*, Sept. 10, 1922.

71. *Al-Lata'if al-Musawwara*, Oct. 11, 1920.

72. The phrase *"fil-mish mish"* connotes indefinite postponement of Egypt's independence.

73. *Al-Sufur*, Jan. 17, 1919.

74. *Al-Kashkul*, July 17, 1922.

75. *Al-Muqtataf*, June 1919; *al-Sufur*, June 5, 1919; and *al-Ahram*, Mar. 23, 1919.

76. *Al-Lata'if al-Musawwara*, July 21, 1919.

77. Badran, *Feminists, Islam and Nation*, 80–81.

78. *Al-Lata'if al-Musawwara*, Aug. 27, 1919.

79. See Chapter 5. While the caricature offers a clear critique of Anglo-Egyptian politics, I would suggest that it also makes a statement about European motherhood. It speaks out against rote imitation of Europe and implies that the wholesale acceptance of European customs had dangerous effects.

80. FO 848/12, circular by the students of al-Madrasa al-Uliyya, Dec. 1919. Milner referred to this as a "windy appeal to Egyptians to stand fast in their boycott of the Mission."

81. FO 848/12, folio marked "Precis of other Circulars," January 1920.

82. Ibid.

83. Marilyn Booth, *Bayram al-Tunisi's Egypt: Social Criticism and Narrative Strategies* (Exeter, England: Ithaca Press, 1990).

84. This line can also be read "shook the horns." Horns, in this instance, refer to the cuckold Fuad.

85. Cited in Mohammad al-Tabi'i, *Misr ma qabla al-thawra: Min asrar al-sasah wa al-siyasiyin* (Cairo: Dar-al-Ma'arif, 1978), 87–88.

86. Ibid., 85.

87. Nasim later became an opponent of the Wafd. In June of 1920, his enmity with Sa'ad Zaghlul had not manifested itself.

88. *Al-Lata'if al-Musawwara*, June 1920.

89. Similarly, the split that later developed between 'Adly and Sa'ad Zaghloul was not known at the time that this article was printed. See Anis, *Dirasaat;* and Deeb, *Party Politics in Egypt*.

90. *Al-Lata'if al-Musawwara*, July 19, 1920, 1 and 12. 'Adly was said to be an example of "practical" nationalism.

91. Ibid., Nov. 22, 1920, front page.

92. Ibid., Apr. 28, 1919, 2.

93. See, for example, *al-Sufur*, May 8 and 15, 1919.

94. *Al-Ahram*, Apr. 9, 1919.

95. See, for example, *al-Lata'if al-Musawwara*, Aug. 20, 1919. Mr. Gabriel Yarad, who had a store in Mosqui, announced a sale of men and women's clothing, the proceeds of which he would donate to the Freedom Orphanage.

96. The press was remarkably silent about the origins of Cairo's homeless children, giving no indication of where the children had come from. Were these the children of prostitutes? If so, were they fathered by the British or by Egyptians? Were they the children of war dead? Did the hardships of the war lead parents to abandon or sell their children? (There were numerous articles in the press about the poor who tried to sell their children. Such deeds were, of course, denounced as antinationalist.) Did a drastic rise in the number of children on Cairo and Alexandria's streets cause the great flood of interest in the plight of homeless children? I was not allowed to examine the police reports at Dar al-Watha'iq, hence I cannot contribute any archival materials to clarify such questions.

97. *Al-Ahram*, July 5, 1919. Similar accounts were given in *al-Mu'ayyad, al-Muqatam, al-Watan, Misr, al-Liwa'*, and *Misr al-fatah*.

98. See *al-Lata'if al-Musawwara* from June and July 1919. Also carried in the July issues were photos from other orphanages, particularly one that was established by Syrians and Armenians in Alexandria called Malga'a al-muhagiriin, or the Émigrés Orphanage.

99. This image of the "nation" or constitutional government was rare at the

time of the revolution. It had previously appeared in the press in 1906, when Mustafa Kamil was represented petitioning the French government for Egypt's freedom. The French government is represented in the same sort of Greco-Roman costume. Again upon the occasion of Kamil's funeral, Egypt is depicted in similar attire. See Dar al-Hilal, *Sajil al-hilal al-musawwar, 1892–1992*, vol. 1 (Cairo: Dar al-Hilal, 1992), 80 and 454–55.

100. *Al-Lata'if al-Musawwara*, Jan. 7, 1920.

101. Cited in *al-Lata'if al-Musawwara*, May 19, 1919, 3. The poem was also carried in *al-Ahram, al-Sufur*, and others. Another of Hafith al-Ibrahim's poems, "To Children," was also commonly circulated in the revolutionary press. See also 'Abd-al-Rahman al-Rafi'i, *Shua'ra' al-wataniyya fi misr*, 2d ed. (Cairo: Dar al-Ma'arif, 1966).

102. FO 848/12, Jan. 1920. This was a circular distributed by students for other students during the revolution.

103. Beinin and Lockman call the relationship between the Wafd and the masses during the revolution "a populism couched in paternalistic terms." *Workers on the Nile*, 14.

104. FO 141/810/8013. See, for example, files from Jan. 15, 20, and 23, 1919. "I am told that Saad Zaghloul proposes to hold a 'tea party' at his house at 3:45 p.m. on Friday, January 31st. Invitations have been issued to a large number of persons including all members of the Legislative Assembly."

105. See, for example, *al-Sufur*, May–July 1919, "al-Doktor Ahsan Kamil Bey." *Al-Sufur* also carried fiction glorifying the virtues of the reformed, *effendi* family. See "'Ali wa Samira" ('Ali and Samira), June 18, 1915, and "Umm Pauline" (Pauline's Mother), Feb. 2, 1916.

Conclusion: It's a Girl!

1. *Al-Ahram Weekly*, July 20–26, 1995. This article, edited by Fayza Hassan, was also printed in Arabic in *al-Ahram* on July 20, 1995.

On March 16, 1995, the day on which Egypt celebrated its first national Women's Day, *al-Ahram Weekly* published a similar article, entitled "Women on the Long March." Female revolutionaries were similarly feted for having begun women's entrance into the public sphere. "Egypt," the article claimed, "is celebrating its first national Women's Day, not on 8 March, the date of International Women's day, but on 16 March, in commemoration of the day, in 1919, when Egyptian women took to the streets to march in protest against the British occupation. Safiya Zaghloul . . . and Hoda Sha'rawi, who led the demonstration, were two of the most prominent players in the events of 1919." Rania Khallaf, *al-Ahram Weekly*, March 9–16, 1995, 6. This article did not appear in Arabic in *al-Ahram*.

2. There is no word for "feminism" in Arabic. What is referred to in Western languages as the Egypt feminist movement is, in Arabic, *al-haraka an-nisa'iyya*, or "the women's movement." For an excellent discussion of the various

ways contemporary Egyptian women describe "the movement," see the introduction to Nadje al-Ali's *Secularism, Gender and the State in the Middle East: The Egyptian Women's Movement* (Cambridge: Cambridge University Press, 2000).

3. *Al-Ahram Weekly,* Mar. 9–16, 1995. My emphasis.

4. Baron, *The Women's Awakening in Egypt.*

5. Badran, *Feminists, Islam and Nation.*

6. Ibid., 80–81.

7. See Thomas Philipp, "Feminism and Nationalist Politics in Egypt," in *Women in the Muslim World,* ed. Beck and Keddie (Cambridge, Mass.: Harvard University Press, 1971), 277–94. Al-Ali problematizes the relationship between feminism and nationalism past and present in *Secularism, Gender and the State in the Middle East.*

8. Ahmed, *Women, Gender and Islam.*

9. It is difficult to find a history of modern Egypt that, when it discusses the nationalist and feminist movements, does not begin with a discussion of Qasim Amin or one of his female contemporaries (usually Sha'rawi, Nabawiyya Musa, or Bahithat al-Badiyya). Hanna F. Wissa's *Assiout: The Saga of an Egyptian Family* (Sussex, England: The Book Guild, 1994), for example, takes up the appearance of feminism on the nationalist agenda by saying, "The cause of the emancipation of women was taken up by Mr. Kassem *[sic]* Amin and Mrs. Bahisat al-Badia *[sic]*, but did not reach any satisfactory result. So, when the 1919 Revolution under the leadership of Sa'ad Zaghlul Pasha arose, and women played such an important part in it, a chance was given them to realize their hopes" (196).

10. See Mervat Hatem, "The Pitfalls of the Nationalist Discourses on Citizenship in Egypt," in *Gender and Citizenship in the Middle East,* ed. Suad Joseph (Syracuse, N.Y.: Syracuse University Press, 2000), 33–57.

11. Overviews of the relationship between the women's movement and the 1919 Revolution are included in most texts on the history of modern Egypt. See, for example, Afaf Marsot, *A Short History of Modern Egypt* (Cambridge: Cambridge University Press, 1985); and idem, *Egypt's Liberal Experiment: 1922–1936;* Gabriel Baer, "Social Change in Egypt: 1800–1914" in *Political and Social Change in Modern Egypt,* ed. P. M. Holt (London: Oxford University Press, 1968); and Cole, "Feminism, Class and Islam in Turn-of-the-Century Egypt." On women in the revolutionary demonstrations see Afaf Marsot, "The Revolutionary Gentlewoman"; Thomas Philipp, "Feminism and Nationalist Politics in Egypt"; and al-Rafi'i, *Thawrat 1919.*

12. On the French Revolution, see Mona Ozouf, *Festivals and the French Revolution,* trans. Alan Sheridan (Cambridge Mass.: Harvard University Press, 1988); Maurice Agulhon, *Marianne Into Battle: Republican Imagery and Symbolism in France, 1789–1880,* trans. Janet Lloyd (Cambridge: Cambridge University Press, 1981); Lynn Hunt, *Politics, Culture and Class in the French Revolution* (Berkeley: University of California Press, 1984); Joan B. Landes, *Women and the Public Sphere in the Age of the French Revolution* (Ithaca: Cornell University Press, 1988). On the Chinese Revolution of 1911, see Kazuko Ono, *Chinese Women in a Century of Revolution, 1850–1950,* ed. Joshua A. Fogel, trans. Kathryn Bernhardt (Stan-

ford: Stanford University Press, 1988). On the American Revolution, see Mary Beth Norton, *Liberty's Daughters: The Revolutionary Experience of American Women 1750–1800* (Boston: Little, Brown, 1980); Linda K. Kerber, *Women of the Republic: Intellect and Ideology in Revolutionary America* (Chapel Hill: University of North Carolina Press, 1980); and Joan Hoff Wilson, "The Illusion of Change: Women in the American Revolution," in *The American Revolution: Explorations in the History of American Radicalism,* ed. Alfred Young (DeKalb: Northern Illinois University Press, 1976), 383–446. An excellent overview of the history of women and the public realm is Patricia Hollis, *Women in Public, 1850–1900: Documents of the Victorian Women's Movement* (London: Allen and Unwin, 1979).

13. Here I am working somewhat against the arguments made in the early chapters of Selma Botman's *Engendering Citizenship in Egypt* (New York: Columbia University Press, 1999). While I ultimately agree with Botman that the constitution of 1923 institutionalized patriarchy in Egypt, I suggest that she overlooks the processes of modernization and colonization that brought the constitutional model to the fore.

14. FO 141/748/8822, Mar. 23, 1919. "Il nous importe que le monde entier soit convaincu que la sécurité règne en notre bien-aimé pays . . . qu'il conaisse jusqu'à nos plus intimes secrets."

15. PRO/FO 141/522/9085, Wingate to the Foreign Office, Apr. 18, 1919.

Bibliography

Archives and Papers

EGYPTIAN NATIONAL ARCHIVES (DAR AL-WATHA'IQ AL-QAWMIYYA, DWQ), CAIRO, EGYPT

Ahd Isma'il Collection
Mahafiz Abdin
Majlis al-Wuzara' Collection

PRESBYTERIAN HISTORICAL SOCIETY ARCHIVES, PHILADELPHIA, PENNSYLVANIA

Minnehaha Finney Papers, Record Group 240
Thomas McCague Papers, Record Group 192
Anna Young Thompson Papers, Record Group 141

PUBLIC RECORDS OFFICE (PRO), FOREIGN OFFICE (FO), KEW GARDENS, GREAT BRITAIN

ST. ANTONY'S COLLEGE, OXFORD

Thomas Boyle Papers
Sir Milne Cheetham Papers
Sir Ignatius (Valentine) Chirol Papers
Francis Edwards Papers
Sir Eldon Gorst Papers

Sir Thomas Russell Papers
Sir Ronald Wingate Papers

BODELIAN LIBRARY, OXFORD
Viscount Alfred Milner Papers

Published Sources

CONTEMPORARY PERIODICALS

Abu Nazzara Zarqa' (Man with the blue spectacles; Cairo, 1877; Paris, 1878)
al-Afkar (Thoughts; Cairo, 1900)
al-Ahali (The people; Cairo, 1894)
al-Ahram (The pyramids) and *al-Ahram Weekly* (Cairo, 1876)
Anis al-Jalis (The intimate companion; Alexandria, 1898)
Anis al-talmiz (The students' companion; Cairo, 1898)
al-'Asr al-Jadid (The new era; Alexandria, 1880)
Dalil al-tulab (The students' guide; Cairo, 1902)
al-Fatah (The young woman; Alexandria, 1892)
al-Hilal (The crescent; Cairo, 1892)
al-Jarida (The paper; Cairo, 1907)
al-Kashkul (The scrapbook; Cairo, 1921)
al-Lata'if al-Musawwara (Illustrated niceties; Cairo, 1915)
al-Liwa' (The standard; Cairo, 1900)
Le Lotus (The lotus; Alexandria, 1901)
al-Madrasa (The school; Cairo, 1893)
al-Mahrusa (The divinely protected; Alexandria, 1880)
Majallat jama'iyyat al-hayah (The 'Hayah' Organization; Cairo, 1909)
al-Manar (The lighthouse; Cairo, 1898)
Misr (Egypt; Cairo, 1877)
Misr al-fatah (Egypt the young woman; Alexandria, 1879)
al-Mu'ayyad (The strengthened; Cairo, 1889)
al-Mufid (The informer; Cairo, 1881)
al-Muqatam (Cairo, 1889)
al-Muqtataf (Selections; Cairo, 1896)
al-Nizam (The order; Cairo, 1909)
al-Sufur (Uncovering; Cairo, 1915)
al-Talba (The students; Cairo, 1908)
al-Talmiz (The student; Cairo, 1893)
al-Tankit wal-Tabkit (Mockery and reproach; Alexandria, 1881)
al-Tarbiyya (Childraising; Cairo, 1905)
al-Ustadh (The professor; Cairo, 1892)
Wadi al-Nil (The Valley of the Nile; Cairo, 1866)

al-Watan (The nation; Cairo, 1877)
Women's Missionary Magazine (Pittsburgh, Penn.)

TEXTBOOKS IN ARABIC

Ahad, Sayyid Mohammad. *Kitab al-tahliyya wal-targhib fil-tarbiyya wal-tahdhib.* 11th ed. Cairo: Matba'at al-Amiriyya, 1911.

Ahmad, 'Abd al-Rahman. *al-Mutala'a.* Cairo: Dar al-Kuttub al-Khedwiyya, 1912.

Amin, Ahmed. *al-Akhlaq.* Bulaq: Matba'at al-Amiriyya, 1934.

Fikry, 'Ali. *Adab al-fata.* 8th ed. Cairo: Matba'at al-Ma'arif, 1914.

Gamayyil, Anton. *al-Fatah wal-bayt.* 2nd ed. Cairo: Matba'at al-Ma'arif, 1916.

Hasan, 'Abd al-'Aziz. *Durus al-ahklaq al-maqadara 'ala tulab al-sana al-ula.* Cairo: n.p., 1913.

Hussein, Mohammad Ahmed. *Maqarar al-akhlaq lil-madaris al-ibtida'iyya.* Cairo: Matba'at Dar al-Kuttub, 1929.

Ibrahim, Hafith, trans. *Kuttaib fil-tarbiyya al-awaliyya wa al-akhlaq: al-juz' al-awal.* 2d ed. Bulaq: Matba'at al-Amiriyya, 1913.

Isma'il, 'Abd al-Rahman. *al-Tarbiyya wal-adaab al-ra'iyya.* 8th ed. Bulaq: Matba'at al-Amiriyya, 1911.

Mikhail, Francis. *al-Nizam al-manzili.* Cairo: Matba'at al-Ma'arif, 1912.

———. *al-Tadbir al-manzili al-hadith.* Cairo: Matba'at al-Ma'arif, 1916.

Qumha, Ahmed, and Monsieur Logran. *Kitab al-adkhar.* Bulaq: Matba'at al-Amiriyya, 1914.

Rakha, Mohammad Ahmed, and Mohammad Hamdy. *Kitab al-akhlaq lil-banat.* Cairo: al-Matba'a al-Handasiyya Bil-Mosqui, 1918.

Rushdy, Mohammad. *Tadbir al-'am fil-siha wa al-mard.* Cairo: Matba'at al-'Itimad, 1912.

Sayyid, Mohammad Ahad. *Kitab al-tahliyya wal-targhib fil-tarbiyya wal-tahdhib.* 11th ed. Bulaq: Matba'at al-Amiriyya, 1911.

Wizarat al-Ma'arif al-'Umummiyya. *al-Mukhtara al-ibtida'iyya lil-mutala'a al-'arabiyya.* Bulaq: Matba'at al-Amiriyya, 1912.

———. *al-Tahajiya wal mutala'a.* 9th ed. Bulaq: Matba'at al-Amiriyya, 1916.

Yasmine, Bashir, and Nasr al-Din Hashim. *al-Ma'alumat al-wataniyya.* Cairo: Matba'at Wizarat al-Ma'arif, 1952.

WORKS IN ARABIC, ENGLISH, AND FRENCH

'Abd al-Karim, Ahmad 'Izzat. *Tarikh al-ta'lim fi 'asr Mohammad 'Ali.* Cairo: Maktabat Al-Nahda al-Misriyya, 1938.

Abu al-Is'ad, Mohammad. *Siyasat al-ta'lim fi misr taht al-ihtilal al-britani (1822–1922).* Cairo: Matba'at al-Khatab, 1976.

Abu-Lughod, Janet. *Cairo: 1001 Years of the City Victorious.* Princeton: Princeton University Press, 1971.

Abu-Lughod, Lila, ed. *Remaking Women: Feminism and Modernity in the Middle East.* Princeton: Princeton University Press, 1998.

Adelson, Roger. *London and the Invention of the Middle East: Money, Power, and War* 1902–1922. New Haven: Yale University Press, 1995.

Agulhon, Maurice. *Marianne Into Battle: Republican Imagery and Symbolism in France, 1789–1880.* Trans. Janet Lloyd. Cambridge: Cambridge University Press, 1981.

Ahmed, Jamal Mohammad. *The Intellectual Origins of Egyptian Nationalism.* London: Oxford University Press, 1960.

Ahmed, Leila. "Western Ethnocentrism and Perceptions of the Harem." *Feminist Studies* 8: 3 (1982): 521–34.

——. *Women and Gender in Islam: Historical Roots of a Modern Debate.* New Haven: Yale University Press, 1992.

al-Ali, Nadje. *Secularism, Gender and the State in the Middle East: The Egyptian Women's Movement.* Cambridge: Cambridge University Press, 2000.

Allen, Roger. *The Arabic Novel: An Historical and Critical Introduction.* Syracuse N.Y.: Syracuse University Press, 1982.

——. *A Study of Hadith 'Isa Ibn Hisham: Mohammad al-Muwaylihi's View of Egyptian Society during the British Occupation.* Albany, N.Y.: State University of New York, 1974.

Alloula, Malek. *The Colonial Harem.* Minneapolis: University of Minnesota Press, 1986.

Amin, Qasim. *Les Égyptiens: Réponse à Monsieur le Duc d'Harcourt.* Cairo: Jules Barbier, 1894.

——. *The Liberation of Women. A Document in the History of Egyptian Feminsim.* Trans. Samiha Sidhon Peterson. Cairo: The American University in Cairo Press, 1992.

——. "The New Woman." Trans. Raghda el-'Essawi and Lisa Pollard. Unpublished ms. Cairo, 1995.

——. *The New Woman.* Samiha Sidhon Peterson. The American University in Cairo Press, 1995.

Anderson, Benedict. *Imagined Communities.* Extended ed. London: Verso Press, 1991.

Anis, Mohammad. *Dirasaat fi watha'iq thawrat 1919.* Vol. 1. Cairo: Anglo-Egyptian Bookstore, 1964.

Appadurai, Arjun. *Modernity at Large: Cultural Dimensions of Globalization.* Minneapolis: University of Minnesota Press, 1996.

al-'Aqqad, 'Abbas Mahmoud. *Sa'ad Zaghlul, sira wa tahiyya.* Cairo: Dar al-Shuruq, 1987.

Artin, Yacoub. *L'instruction publique en Égypte.* Paris: E. Leroux, 1890.

'Awad, Louis. *Tarikh al-fikr al-misry al-hadith, min al-hamla al-faransiyya ila 'asr isma'il.* Cairo: Maktabat Madbouli, 1987.

Ayalon, Ami. *The Press in the Arab Middle East: A History.* New York: Oxford University Press, 1995.

Badran, Margot. "Competing Agendas: Feminists, Islam, and the State in Nineteenth- and Twentieth-Century Egypt." In *Women, Islam, and the State,* ed. Deniz Kandiyoti. Philadelphia: Temple University Press, 1991.

————. *Feminists, Islam, and Nation: Gender and the Making of Modern Egypt.* Princeton: Princeton University Press, 1995.

Baedeker, Karl. *Egypt: A Handbook for Travellers.* Leipzig: Baedeker, 1885.

Baer, Gabriel. "Social Change in Egypt: 1800–1914." In *Political and Social Change in Modern Egypt,* ed. P. M. Holt. London: Oxford University Press, 1968.

Baron, Beth. "Mothers, Morality, and Nationalism in Pre-1919 Egypt." In *The Origins of Arab Nationalism,* ed. Rashid Khalidi, 271–88. New York: Columbia University Press, 1991.

————. "Nationalist Iconography: Egypt as a Woman." In *Rethinking Nationalism in the Arab Middle East,* ed. James Jankowski and Israel Gershoni, 105–24. New York: Columbia University Press, 1997.

————. *The Women's Awakening in Egypt: Culture, Society, and the Press.* New Haven: Yale University Press, 1994.

Beinin, Joel, and Zachary Lockman. *Workers on the Nile: Nationalism, Communism, Islam, and the Egyptian Working Class, 1882–1954.* Princeton: Princeton University Press, 1987.

Bhabha, Homi. "Of Mimicry and Man: The Ambivalence of Colonial Discourse." In *Tensions of Empire: Colonial Cultures in a Bourgeois World,* ed. Frederick Cooper and Laura Ann Stoler.Berkeley: University of California Press, 1997.

Bianchi, T. X. "Catalogue général des livres Arabes, Persans, et Turcs imprimés à Boulac en Égypte depuis l'introduction de l'imprimerie dans ce pays." *Nouveau Journal Asiatique* (Paris) 2 (1843).

Blunt, Wilfrid Scawen. *The Future of Islam.* London: Kegan Paul, Trench, 1882.

————. *My Diaries. Being a Personal Narrative of Events, 1888–1914.* London: M. Secker, 1920.

————. *A Secret History of the Occupation of Egypt.* New York: Howard Fertig, 1967.

Booth, Marilyn. *Bayram al-Tunisi's Egypt: Social Criticism and Narrative Strategies.* Exeter, England: Ithaca Press, 1990.

————. *May Her Likes Be Multiplied: Biography and Gender Politics in Egypt.* Berkeley: University of California Press, 2001.

————. "Woman in Islam: Men and the 'Women's Press' in Turn-of-the-Twentieth-Century Egypt." *International Journal of Middle East Studies* 33: 2 (2001): 171–201.

Bordieu, Pierre. *Reproduction in Education and Society.* Trans. Richard Nice. London: Sage Publications, 1977.

Botman, Selma. *Egypt from Independence to Revolution, 1919–1956.* Syracuse, N.Y.: Syracuse University Press, 1991.

————. *Engendering Citizenship in Egypt.* New York: Columbia University Press, 1999.

Boyle, Clara Asch. *Boyle of Cairo: A Diplomatist's Adventures in the Middle East.* London: Titus Wilson and Son, 1965.

Bozdogan, Sibel, and Resat Kasaba, eds. *Rethinking Modernity and National Identity in Turkey.* Seattle: University of Washington Press, 1997.

Brendon, Piers. *Thomas Cook: 150 Years of Popular Tourism.* London: Secker and Warburg, 1991.

Browne, Edward Granville. *The Press and Poetry of Modern Persia.* Cambridge: Cambridge University Press, 1914.

Buchanan, Carrie. *Broadening Horizons in Egypt.* Pittsburgh, Pa.: Printing House of the Women's General Missionary Society, United Presbyterian Church of North America, n.d.

——. *Educational Work in Egypt.* Pittsburgh, Pa.: Printing House of the Women's General Missionary Society, United Presbyterian Church of North America, n.d.

Budge, E. A. Wallis. *Cook's Handbook for Egypt and the Sudan.* London: Thomas Cook and Son, 1876.

Bugler, Caroline. "Innocents Abroad: Nineteenth-Century Artists and Travelers in the Near East and North Africa." In *The Orientalists: Delacroix to Matisse. European Painters in North Africa and the Near East,* ed. Mary Anne Stevens. London: Royal Academy of Arts, 1984.

Burton, Antoinette. "From Child Bride to 'Hindoo Lady': Rukhamabai and the Debate on Sexual Responsibility in Imperial Britain." *The American Historical Review* 103: 4 (1998): 1119–46.

——. "Rules of Thumb: British History and Imperial Culture in Nineteenth- and Twentieth-Century Britain." *Women's History Review* 3: 1 (1994): 483–99.

Butovsky, Avriel. "Reform and Legitimacy: The Egyptian Monarchy." In *Entre reform sociale et mouvement national: Identité et modernisation en Égype, 1882–1962,* ed. Alain Roussillon. Cairo: CEDEJ, 1995.

Carré, Jean-Marie. *Voyageurs et écrivains français en Égypte.* 2nd ed. Cairo: L'Institut Français d'Archéologie Orientale, 1976.

Çelik, Zeynep. *Displaying the Orient: Architecture of Islam at Nineteenth-Century World's Fairs.* Berkeley: University of California Press, 1992.

Chamberlain, M. E. "Sir Charles Dilke and the British Intervention in Egypt, 1882: Decision Making in a Nineteenth-Century Cabinet." *British Journal of International Studies* 2 (1976): 231–45.

Chatterjee, Partha. "Colonialism, Nationalism, and Colonized Women: the Contest in India." *American Ethnologist* 16:4 (1989): 622–33.

——. *The Nation and Its Fragments: Colonial and Postcolonial Histories.* Princeton: Princeton University Press, 1993.

——. "A Religion of Urban Domesticity: Sri Ramakrishna and the Calcutta Middle Class." In *Subaltern Studies 7: Writings on South Asian History and Society,* ed. Partha Chatterjee and Gyanendra Pandey, 40–68. Delhi: Oxford University Press, 1992.

Chaucer, Geoffrey. *Canterbury Tales.* Selected, translated, and adapted by Barbara Cohen. New York: Lothrop, Lee, and Shepard Books, 1988.

Chennels, Ellen. *Recollections of an Egyptian Princess by Her English Governess.* London: W. Blackwood and Sons, 1893.

Chirol, Valentin. *The Egypt Problem*. London: Macmillan and Co., 1902.

Clancy-Smith, Julia, and Frances Gouda, eds. *Domesticating Empire: Race, Gender, and Family Life in French and Dutch Colonialism*. Charlottesville, Va.: University Press of Virginia, 1998.

Cole, Juan R. I. *Colonialism and Revolution in the Middle East: Social and Cultural Origins of Egypt's 'Urabi Movement*. Princeton: Princeton University Press, 1993.

——. "Feminism, Class, and Islam in Turn-of-the-Century Egypt." *International Journal of Middle East Studies* 13 (1981): 387–407.

Comaroff, John, and Jean L. Comaroff. *Ethnography and the Historical Imagination*. Boulder, Colo.: Westview Press, 1992.

Cook's Tourist Handbook for Egypt, the Nile and the Desert. London: Thomas Cook and Son, 1897.

Cooper, Elizabeth. *The Women of Egypt*. London: Hust and Blackett, Ltd., 1914.

Cooper, Frederick, and Ann Laura Stoler, eds. *Tensions of Empire: Colonial Cultures in a Bourgeois World*. Berkeley: University of California Press, 1997.

Coppin, Jean. *Voyages en Égypte de Jean Coppin, 1638–39 et 1643–66*. Cairo: Institut Français d'Archéologie Orientale, 1976.

Crabbs, Jack A., Jr. *The Writing of History in Nineteenth-Century Egypt: A Study in National Transformation*. Cairo: American University of Cairo Press, 1984.

Cromer (Evelyn Baring), Earl of. *Modern Egypt*. London: Macmillan, 1908.

——. *Speeches, 1882–1911*. Edinburgh: R. & R. Clark, 1912.

Curl, James Stevens. *Egyptomania: The Egyptian Revival. A Recurring Theme in the History of Taste*. Manchester: Manchester University Press, 1992.

Cutler, H. G., and L. W. Yaggy. *Panorama of Nations; or, Journeys Among the Families of Man: A Description of Their Homes, Customs, Habits, Employments and Beliefs; Their Cities, Temples, Monuments, Literature and Fine Arts*. Chicago: Star Publishing Company, 1892.

Daly, M. W. "The British Occupation of Egypt." In *The Cambridge History of Egypt*, vol. 2, ed. M. W. Daly, 239–51. Cambridge: Cambridge University Press, 1998.

Daniel, Norman. *Islam, Europe and Empire*. Edinburgh: University of Edinburgh Publications, 1966.

Dar al-Hilal. *Sajil al-hilal al-musawwar min 1892–1992*. Cairo: Dar al-Hilal, 1992.

Davidoff, Leonore, and Catherine Hall. *Family Fortunes: Men and Women of the English Middle Class, 1780–1850*. Chicago: University of Chicago Press, 1987.

Deeb, Maurius. *Party Politics in Egypt: The Wafd and its Rivals, 1919–1939*. London: Ithaca Press, 1979.

Delanoue, Gilbert. *Moralistes et politiques musulmans dans l'Égypte du XIXième siècle*. Cairo: Institut Français d'Archélogie Orientale, 1982.

Depping, Georges-Bernard. *Aperçu historique sur les moeurs et coutumes des nations: Contenant le tableau comparé chez les divers peuples anciens et modernes, des usages et des cérémonies concernant l'habitation, la nourriture, l'habillement, les marriages, les funérailles, les jeux, les fêtes, les guerres, les superstitions, les castes, etc.* Paris: L'Encyclopédie Portative, 1826.

———. *Evening Entertainment, Or Delineations of the Manners and Customs of Various Nations: Interspersed with Geographical Notices, Historical and Biographical Anecdotes, and Descriptions in Natural History*. Philadelphia: David Hogan, 1817.

Dicey, Edward. *England and Egypt*. London: Chapman and Hall, 1881.

———. "England's Intervention in Egypt." *The Nineteenth Century* 12 (1882): 160–74.

———. "The Future of Egypt." *The Nineteenth Century* 2 (1877): 3–14.

———. "Our Egyptian Protectorate." *The Nineteenth Century* 7 (1880).

———. "Our Route to India." *The Nineteenth Century* 1 (1877): 665–86.

———. *The Story of the Khedivate*. New York: C. Scribner and Sons, 1902.

Dor, V. Eduard. *L'Instruction publique en Égypte*. Paris: Lacroix, 1872.

Duben, Alen. "Household Formation in Late Ottoman Istanbul." *International Journal of Middle Eastern Studies* 22 (1990): 419–35.

———. "Turkish Families and Households in Historical Perspective." *Journal of Family History* 10 (1995): 75–97.

Duben, Alen, and Cem Behar. *Istanbul Households: Marriage, Family and Fertility, 1880–1940*. Cambridge: Cambridge University Press, 1991.

Edmond, Charles. *L'Égypte à l'exposition universelle de 1867*. Paris: Dentre, 1867.

Edwards, Amelia. *A Thousand Miles up the Nile*. London: Longmans, 1877.

Egremont, Max. *The Cousins: The Friendship, Opinions and Activities of Wilfrid Scawen Blunt and George Wyndham*. London: Collins, 1977.

Egyptian Ministry of Public Instruction. *Syllabus of Secondary Courses of Study*. Cairo: n.p., 1897.

Fabian, Johannes. *Time and the Other: How Anthropology Makes Its Object*. New York: Columbia University Press, 1983.

Fahmy, Jeanne. *L'Égypte eternelle*. Paris: Renaissance du Livre, 1863.

Fahmy, Khaled. *All the Pasha's Men: Mehmed Ali, his Army, and the Making of Modern Egypt*. Cambridge: Cambridge University Press, 1997.

———. "The Era of Muhammad 'Ali Pasha, 1805–1948." In *The Cambridge History of Egypt, Volume Two. Modern Egypt from 1517 to the End of the Twentieth Century*, ed. M. W. Daly, 139–79. Cambridge: Cambridge University Press, 1998.

———. "Women, Medicine, and Power in Nineteenth-Century Egypt." In *Remaking Women: Feminism and Modernity in the Middle East*, ed. Lila abu-Lughod, 35–72. Princeton: Princeton University Press, 1998.

Fargues, Philippe. "Family and Household in Mid-Nineteenth-Century Cairo." In *Family History in the Middle East: Household, Property, and Gender*, ed. Beshara Doumani, 23–50. Albany, N.Y.: State University of New York Press, 2003.

Fay, Mary Ann. "From Concubines to Capitalists: Women, Property, and Power in Eighteenth-Century Cairo." *Journal of Women's History* 10: 3 (1998): 118–40.

———. "From Warrior Grandees to Domesticated Bourgeoisie: The Transformation of the Elite Egyptian Household into a Western-Style Family." In

Family History in the Middle East: Household, Property, and Gender, ed. Beshara Doumani, 101–18. Albany, N.Y.: State University of New York Press, 2003

Fleischmann, Ellen. *The Nation and Its "New" Women: Feminism, Nationalism, Colonialism, and the Palestinian Women's Movement, 1920–1948.* Berkeley: University of California Press, 2003.

——. "Selective Memory, Gender, and Nationalism: Palestinian Women Leaders of the Mandate Period." *History Workshop Journal* 47 (1999): 141–58.

Fortna, Benjamin C. *Imperial Classroom: Islam, the State and Education in the Late Ottoman Empire.* Oxford: Oxford University Press, 2002.

Foucault, Michel. *Birth of the Clinic: An Archeology of Medical Perception.* Trans. A. M. Sheridan Smith. New York: Pantheon Books, 1973.

——. *Discipline and Punish: The Birth of the Prison.* Trans. A. M. Sheridan Smith. New York: Vantage Books, 1979.

——. *The History of Sexuality,* vol. I. Trans. Robert Hurley. New York: Pantheon Books, 1978.

Fox-Keller, Evelyn. "Baconian Science: The Arts of Mastery and Obedience." In *Reflections on Gender and Science,* ed. Evelyn Fox-Keller. New Haven: Yale University Press, 1985.

France, Peter. *The Rape of Egypt.* London: Barrie and Jenkins, 1991.

Friedland, Roger, and Diedre Boden. *NowHere: Space, Time, and Modernity.* Berkeley: University of California Press, 1994.

Frierson, Elizabeth. "Unimagined Communities: State, Press, and Gender in the Hamidian Era." Ph.D. diss., Princeton University, 1997.

Fullerton, William Morton. *In Cairo.* London and New York: Macmillan and Co., 1891.

Fundone, Maria. "L'école Syoufieh (1873–1889) une première expérience d'enseignement primaire gouvernemental pour les filles au Caire." Cairo: Institut Français de l'Archéologie Orientale, Colloquium on Social Reform in Egypt, December, 1993.

Gallagher, Nancy Elizabeth. *Egypt's Other Wars: Epidemics and the Politics of Public Health.* Syracuse, N.Y.: Syracuse University Press, 1990.

Gasparin, Valérie Boissier de. *Journal d'un voyage au Levant.* Paris: M. Ducloux, 1948.

Gay, Peter. *The Bourgeois Experience, vol. I: Education of the Senses.* London: Oxford University Press, 1985.

Gendzier, Irene. *The Practical Visions of Ya'qub Sannu'.* Cambridge, Mass.: Harvard University Press, 1966.

Gladstone, W. E. "Aggression on Egypt and Freedom in the East." *The Nineteenth Century* 1 (1887): 149–66.

Goçek, Fatima Müge. *Political Cartoons in the Middle East.* Princeton: Marcus Weiner, 1998.

Godlewska, Anne, and Neil Smith. *Geography and Empire.* Oxford: Blackwell Publishers, 1994.

Goldberg, Ellis. "Peasants in Revolt — Egypt 1919." *International Journal of Middle East Studies* 24: 2 (1992): 261–80.

Gonzales, Antonius. *Le Voyage en Égypte du Père Antonius Gonzales, 1665–1666.* Vol. 4. Reprint. Cairo: Institute Français d'Archeologie Orientale, 1977.

Graham-Brown, Sarah. *Images of Women: The Portrayal of Women in the Photography of the Middle East, 1860–1950.* London: Quartert Books, 1988.

Gramsci, Antonio. *Prison Notebooks.* Trans. Joseph A. Buttigieg and Antonio Callari. New York: Colombia University Press, 1992.

Hall, Catherine. "The Sweet Delights of Home." *The History of Private Life.* Vol. 4. Cambridge, Mass: Bellknapp Press, 1990.

Hamouda, Sahar, and Colin Clement, eds. *Victoria College: A History Revealed.* Cairo: American University in Cairo Press, 2002.

Haney, Lynne, and Lisa Pollard, eds. *Families of a New World: Gender, Politics and State Building in Global Context.* New York and London: Routledge Press, 2003.

Hanna, Nelly. *Habiter au Caire aux XVIIième et XVIIIième siècles.* Cairo: Institut Français d'Archéologie Orientale du Caire, 1991.

Harb, Muhamad Tal'at. *Tarbiyyat al-Mar'a wal-hijab.* Cairo: Matba'at al-Manar, 1914.

Hatem, Mervat. "'A'isha Taymur's Tears and the Critique of the Modernist and the Feminist Discourses on Nineteenth-Century Egypt." In *Remaking Women: Feminism and Modernity in the Middle East,* ed. Lila Abu-Lughod, 73–88. Princeton: Princeton University Press, 1998.

———. "The Enduring Alliance of Nationalism and Patriarchy in Muslim Personal Status Laws: The Case of Modern Egypt." *Feminist Issues* 6: 1 (1986): 19–43.

———. "The Pitfalls of the Nationalist Discourses on Citizenship in Egypt." In *Gender and Citizenship in the Middle East,* ed. Suad Joseph, 33–57. Syracuse, N.Y.: Syracuse University Press, 2000.

———. "The Politics of Sexuality and Gender in Segregated Patriarchal Systems: The Case of Eighteenth- and Nineteenth-Century Egypt." *Feminist Studies* 12: 2 (1986): 250–74.

Hathaway, Jane. *The Politics of Households in Ottoman Egypt: The Rise of the Qazdaglis.* Cambridge: Cambridge University Press, 1997.

Heyworth-Dunne, James. *An Introduction to the History of Education in Modern Egypt.* London: Frank Cass, 1968.

Hichens, Robert Smythe. *Egypt and Its Monuments.* New York: The Century Co., 1908.

Hobson, John Atkinson. *Imperialism: A Study.* Ann Arbor: University of Michigan Press, 1965.

Hogg, Rena L. *Farida's Dream.* Pittsburgh, Pa.: Printing House of the Women's General Missionary Society of the United Presbyterian Church of North America, n.d.

Hollis, Patricia. *Women in Public, 1850–1900: Documents of the Victorian Women's Movement.* London: Allen and Unwin, 1979.

Hopkins, A. G. "The Victorians and Africa: A Reconsideration of the Occupation of Egypt, 1882." *Journal of African History* 27 (1986): 363–91.

Hourani, Albert. *Arabic Thought in the Liberal Age, 1798–1939*. Cambridge: Cambridge University Press, 1962.

Hunt, Lynn. *The Family Romance of the French Revolution*. Berkeley: University of California Press, 1992.

———. *Politics, Culture, and Class in the French Revolution*. Berkeley: University of California Press, 1984.

Hunter, F. Robert. *Egypt under the Khedives, 1805–1879: From Household Government to Modern Bureaucracy*. Pittsburgh, Pa.: University of Pittsburgh Press, 1984.

———. "Egypt under the Successors of Muhammad 'Ali." In *The Cambridge History of Egypt, Volume Two. Modern Egypt from 1517 to the End of the Twentieth Century*, ed. M. W. Daly, 180–97. Cambridge: Cambridge University Press, 1998.

Hurewitz, J. C. *Diplomacy in the Near and Middle East: A Documentary Record*. New York: D. Van Nostrand Co., 1956.

Hyam, Ronald. *Empire and Sexuality: The British Experience*. Manchester and New York: Manchester University Press, 1990.

'Imara, Mohammad, ed. *al-'Amal al-kamila li Qasim Amin*. 2d. ed. Cairo: Dar al-Shuruq, 1988.

———. *Rifa'a al-Tahtawi: Za'id al-tatwir fil-'asr al-hadith*. 2d. ed. Cairo: Dar al-Shuruq, 1988.

Inden, Ronald. *Imagining India*. Oxford: Basil Blackwell, 1990.

al-Jahiz. *The Life and Works of Jahiz*. ed. Charles Pellat. Trans. D. M. Hawke. Berkeley: University of California Press, 1969.

Joseph, Suad, ed. *Gender and Citizenship in the Middle East*. New York: Syracuse University Press, 2000.

Joubin, Rebecca. "Creating the Modern Professional Housewife: Scientifically Based Advice Extended to Middle- and Upper-Class Egyptian Women, 1920s–1930s." *Arab Studies Journal* 4: 2 (1996): 19–45.

Kabbani, Rana. *Europe's Myths of Orient*. London: Quartet Books, 1986.

Kandiyoti, Deniz. "Gendering the Modern: On Missing Dimensions in the Study of Turkish Modernity." In *Rethinking Modernity and National Identity in Turkey*, ed. Sibel Bozdogan and Resat Kasaba. Seattle: University of Washington Press, 1997.

———. "Identity and Its Discontents: Women and the Nation." In *Colonial Discourse and Post-Colonial Theory: A Reader*, ed. Patrick Williams and Linda Chrisman, 429–43. New York: Columbia University Press, 1994.

Karl, Rebecca E. "Creating Asia: China in the World at the Beginning of the Twentieth Century." *American Historical Review* 103: 4 (1998): 1096–1118.

———. *Staging the World: Chinese Nationalism at the Turn of the Twentieth Century*. Durham, N.C.: Duke University Press, 2002.

Kedourie, Elie. "Sa'ad Zaghlul and the British." *Middle East Papers no. 2 (St. Antony's Papers, no. 11)*, ed. Albert Hourani. London: Oxford University Press, 1961.

Kelidar, Abbas. "The Political Press in Egypt, 1882–1914." In *Contemporary Egypt through Egyptian Eyes: Essays in Honor of P. J. Vatikiotis,* ed. Charles Tripp, 1–22. New York and London: Routledge Press, 1993.

———. "Shaykh 'Ali Yusuf: Egyptian Journalist and Islamic Nationalist." *In Intellectual Life in the Arab East, 1890–1939,* ed. Marwan R. Buheiry, 11–20. Beirut: Center for Arab and Middle East Studies, the American University of Beirut, 1981.

Kerber, Linda K. *Women of the Republic: Intellect and Ideology in Revolutionary America.* Chapel Hill: University of North Carolina Press, 1980.

Khater, Akram Fouad. *Inventing Home: Emigration, Gender, and the Middle Class in Lebanon, 1870–1920.* Berkeley: University of California Press, 2001.

Khouri, Mounah A. *Poetry and the Making of Modern Egypt (1882–1922).* Leiden: E. J. Brill, 1971.

Klunzinger, C. B. *Upper Egypt: Its People and Its Products.* London: Blackie, 1878.

Koven, Seth, and Sonya Michel, eds. *Mothers of a New World: Maternalist Politics and the Origins of Welfare States.* New York and London: Routledge Press, 1993.

Kuhnke, Laverne. *Lives at Risk: Public Health in Nineteenth-Century Egypt.* Berkeley: University of California Press, 1990.

Kuno, Kenneth M. "Ambiguous Modernization: The Transition to Monogamy in the Khedival House of Egypt." In *Family History in the Middle East: Household, Property, and Gender,* ed. Beshara Doumani, 247–70. Albany, N.Y.: State University of New York Press, 2003.

Lacqueur, Thomas. *Making Sex: Body and Gender from the Greeks to Freud.* Cambridge, Mass.: Harvard University Press, 1990.

Landes, Joan B. *Women and the Public Sphere in the Age of the French Revolution.* Ithaca: Cornell University Press, 1988.

Lane, Edward William. *An Account of the Manners and Customs of the Modern Egyptians: Written in the Years 1833–1836.* London: L. Nattali and Bondi, 1836.

———. *The Thousand and One Nights, Commonly Called, in England, The Arabian Nights' Entertainments.* London: C. Knight, 1839.

Lane-Poole, Stanley. *Cairo: Sketches of its History, Monuments and Social Life.* London: J. S. Virtue, 1898.

Lashin, 'Abd al-Khaliq. *Sa'ad Zaghlul wa dawruhu fil-siyasa al-misriyya.* Cairo: Maktabat Madbouli, 1975.

Lenin, Vladimir Ilich. *Imperialism, the Highest Stage of Capitalism: A Popular Outline.* 1939. Reprint. New York: International Publishers, 1972.

Lewis, Bernard. *The Emergence of Modern Turkey.* London: Oxford University Press, 1961.

———. *The Muslim Discovery of Europe.* New York: W. W. Norton, 1982.

Livingston, John W. "Western Science and Educational Reform in the Thought of Shaykh Rifa'a al-Tahtawi." *International Journal of Middle East Studies* 28 (1996): 543–64.

Lloyd, George Ambrose. *Egypt since Cromer.* London: Macmillan and Co., 1933.

Loti, Pierre. *Égypte.* Trans. W. P. Baines. London: T. W. Laurie, 1909.

Luqa, Anwar. *L'Or de Paris: Relation de voyage, 1826–1831*. Paris: Sinbad Press, 1988.

———. *Voyageurs et écrivains Egyptiens en France au XIXième siècle*. Paris: Didier Press, 1970.

Lytton, Noel Anthony (Earl of). *Wilfrid Scawen Blunt*. London: Macdonald, 1961.

Mabro, Judy. *Veiled Half-Truths: Western Travellers' Perceptions of Middle Eastern Women*. London: I. B. Tauris, 1991.

Macaulay, Thomas Babington. *Critical, Historical and Miscellaneous Essays*. New York: Sheldon and Company, 1866.

———. "Minute on Education" In *Sources of Indian Tradition*, vol. 2, ed. William Theodore de Bary. New York: Columbia University Press, 1958.

Magdi, Salah. *Hilyat al-zaman bi manaqib khadim al-watan. Sirat Rifa'a Rafi' al-Tahtawi*. Ed. Jamal ad-Din al-Shayyal. Cairo: Wizarat al-Thiqafa wa al-Irshad al-Qawmi, 1958.

al-Mahalawi, Hanafi. *Harim muluk misr, min Mohammad 'Ali ila Faruq*. Cairo: Dar al-Amin, 1993.

Maillet, Benoît. *Description de l'Égypte contenant plusieurs rémarques curieuses sur la géographie ancienne et moderne de ce pays, sur ses monuments anciens, sur les moeurs, les coutumes, flora et fauna composée sur les mémoirs de M. de Maillet par M. L'Abbé le Mascrier*. Paris: Chez L. Genneau et J. Rollin, fils, 1735.

Malet, Edward. *Egypt, 1879–1883*. Ed. Lord Sanderson. London: John Murray, 1909.

Malte-Brun, Conrad. *Précis de la géographie universelle; ou description de toutes les parties du monde sur un plan nouveau*. Brussels: Berthot, Ode et Wodon, 1829.

———. *System of Universal Geography, Containing a Description of all the Empires, Kingdoms, States, and Provinces in the Known World, Being A System of Universal Geography or a Description of All the Parts of the World On a New Plan, According to the Great Natural Divisions of the Globe, Accompanied With Analytical, Synoptical, and Elementary Tables*. Trans. James G. Percival. Boston: Samuel Walker, 1834.

Mandeville, John, Sir. *Mandeville's Travels*. Ed. M. C. Seymour. Oxford: Clarendon Press, 1967.

Mani, Lata. *Contentious Traditions: The Debate on Sati in Colonial India*. Berkeley: University of California Press, 1998.

———. "Multiple Mediations: Feminist Scholarship in the Age of Multinational Reception." *Inscriptions* 5 (1989): 18–32.

Mansfield, Peter. *The British in Egypt*. New York: Holt, Rhinehart, and Wilson, 1971.

Marsot, Afaf Lutfi al-Sayyid. *Egypt and Cromer: A Study in Anglo-Egyptian Relations*. London: Murray, 1968.

———. *Egypt in the Reign of Mohammad 'Ali*. Cambridge: Cambridge University Press, 1984.

———. *Egypt's Liberal Experiment, 1922–1936*. Berkeley: University of California Press, 1977.

————. "The Revolutionary Gentlewoman." In *Women in the Muslim World,* ed. L. Beck and N. Keddie, 261–76. Cambridge, Mass: Harvard University Press, 1978.

————. *A Short History of Modern Egypt.* Cambridge: Cambridge University Press, 1985.

————. *Women and Men in Late Eighteenth-Century Egypt.* Austin: The University of Texas Press, 1995.

Mayer, Thomas. *The Changing Past: Egyptian Historiography of the 'Urabi Revolt, 1882–1983.* Gainesville,Fla.: University of Florida Press, 1988.

McIntyre, John D., Jr. *The Boycott of the Milner Mission: A Study in Egyptian Nationalism.* New York: Peter Lang, 1985.

Mernissi, Fatima. *The Veil and the Male Elite: A Feminist Interpretation of Women's Rights in Islam.* Trans., Mary Jo Lakeland. Reading, Mass.: Addison Wesley, 1991.

Millet, Bertrand. *Samir, Sindbad et les Autres: Histoire de la presse enfantine en Égypte.* Cairo: CEDEJ, 1987.

Milner, Alfred. *Britain's Work in Egypt. By an Englishman in the Egyptian Service.* London: T. Edinburgh and A. Constable Publishers, 1892.

————. *England in Egypt.* London: E. Arnold, 1892.

Mitchell, Timothy. *Colonising Egypt.* Cambridge: Cambridge University Press, 1988.

Moi, Toril. *Sexual Textual Politics; Feminist Literary Theory.* London and New York: Methuen Press, 1985.

Montagu, Mary Wortley. *The Complete Letters of Lady Mary Wortely Montagu.* Ed. Robert Halsband. Oxford: Clarendon Press, 1967.

Mostyn, Trevor. *Egypt's Belle Epoque: Cairo, 1869–1952.* London: Quartet Books, 1989.

Mubarak, 'Ali. *'Alam ad-din.* Alexandria: Matba'at Jaridat al-Mahrusa, 1882.

————. *al-Khitat al-tawfiqiyya al-jadida li misr al-qahira wa muduniha wa biladiha al-qadima wa-al-shahira.* Vol. 1. Cairo: Matba'at Bulaq, 1980.

Naddaf, Sandra. "Mirrored Images: Rifa'a al-Tahtawi and the West." *Alif: Journal of Comparative Poetics"* 6 (1986): 73–83.

al-Nagar, Hussein Fawzi. *Sa'ad Zaghlul: al-Za'ama al-ra'iyya.* Cairo: Maktabat Madbouli, 1986.

Nandy, Ashis. *The Intimate Enemy: Loss and Recovery of Self under Colonialism.* Delhi: Oxford University Press, 1983.

Neibuhr, Carsten. *Travels Through Arabia and Other Countries in the East.* Edinburgh: R. Morison and Son, 1792.

Nelson, Cynthia. *Doria Shafik: Egyptian Feminist—A Woman Apart.* Gainesville, Fla.: University Press of Florida, 1996.

Newman, E. W. Polson *Great Britain in Egypt.* London: Cassell, 1928.

Nightingale, Florence. *Letters From Egypt: A Journey on the Nile, 1849–1859.* Selected and introduced by Anthony Satt. London: Barrie and Jenkins, 1987.

Norton, Mary Beth. *Liberty's Daughters: The Revolutionary Experience of American Women 1750–1800.* Boston: Little, Brown, 1980.

Oeuvres du Congrès National Égyptien, tenu à Bruxelles le 22, 23, 24 Septembre 1910. Bruges: St. Catherine's Press, 1911.

Ono, Kazuko. *Chinese Women in a Century of Revolution, 1850–1950.* Ed. Joshua A. Fogel. Trans. Kathryn Bernhardt. Stanford: Stanford University Press, 1988.

Owen, Roger. "Egypt and Europe: From French Expedition to British Occupation." In *Studies in the Theory of Imperialism,* ed. Roger Owen and Bob Sutcliff. London: Longman, 1972.

———. "The Influence of Lord Cromer's Indian Experience on British Policy in Egypt, 1883–1907." In *Middle Eastern Papers no. 4* (St. Antony's Papers no. 17), ed. Albert Hourani. London: Oxford University Press, 1960.

Ozouf, Mona. *Festivals and the French Revolution.* Trans. Alan Sheridan. Cambridge Mass: Harvard University Press, 1988.

Parliamentary Papers. Report by Her Majesty's Agent and Consul General on the Finances, Administration and Condition of Egypt and the Sudan in 1898–1911. London: Harrison and Sons.

Parsons, Abraham. *Travels in Asia and Africa.* London: Longman, Hurst, Rees, and Orme, 1808.

Pateman, Carole. "The Fraternal Social Contract." In *Civil Society and the State: New European Perspectives,* ed. John Keane, 101–28. London: Verso Press, 1988.

———. *The Sexual Contract.* Stanford: Stanford University Press, 1988.

Pederson, Susan. "National Bodies, Unspeakable Acts: The Sexual Politics of Colonial Policy-Making." *The Journal of Modern History 63* (1991): 647–80.

Pelley, Patricia M. *Postcolonial Vietnam: New Histories of the National Past.* Durham, N.C.: Duke University Press, 2002.

Perry, Charles. *A View of the Levant: Particularly of Constantinople, Syria, Egypt and Greece.* London: T. Woodward, 1743.

Philipp, Thomas. "Feminism and Nationalist Politics in Egypt." *Women in the Muslim World,* ed. Lois Beck and Nikki Keddie, 277–94. Cambridge, Mass.: Harvard University Press, 1971.

Pierce, Leslie P. "Beyond Harem Walls: Ottoman Royal Women and the Exercise of Power." *Gendered Domains: Rethinking Public and Private in Women's History,* ed. D. O. Helley and S. M. Reverby, 40–55. Ithaca, N.Y:. Cornell University Press, 1988.

———. *The Imperial Harem, Women and Sovereignty in the Ottoman Empire.* Oxford: Oxford University Press, 1993.

Pollard, Lisa. "The Family Politics of Colonizing and Liberating Egypt, 1882–1919." *Social Politics* 7: 1 (2000): 47–79.

———. "The Habits and Customs of Modernity: State Scholarship, Foreign Travel and the Construction of a New Egyptian Nationalism," *Arab Studies Journal* 7: 2 (1999/2000): 45–74.

———. "Nurturing the Nation: The Family Politics of the 1919 Egyptian Revolution." Ph.D. diss., University of California, Berkeley, 1997.

Poole, Sophia Lane. *The Englishwoman in Egypt: Letters from Cairo, Written During a Residence There in 1842, 43, and 44.* London: C. Knight, 1844.

Poovey, Mary. *Uneven Developments: The Ideological Work of Gender in Mid-Victorian Britain.* Chicago: University of Chicago Press, 1988.

Powell, Eve M. Troutt. *A Different Shade of Colonialism. Egypt, Great Britain, and the Mastery of the Sudan.* Berkeley: University of California Press, 2003.

———. "From Odyssey to Empire: Mapping Sudan through Egyptian Literature in the Mid-Nineteenth Century." *International Journal of Middle East Studies* 31 (1999): 401–27.

Pratt, Mary Louise. *Imperial Eyes: Travel Writing and Transculturation.* New York and London: Routledge, 1992.

Program al-durus: al-Madaris al-ibtida'iyya (al-daraja al-ula). Bulaq: Matba'at al-Ahiliyya, 1885 and 1887.

Programmes de l'enseignement primaire, et de l'enseignement secondaire, approuvés par arrêt ministériel no. 849 en date du 16 Septembre 1901. N.p., n.d.

Quraishi, Zaheer Masood. *Liberal Nationalism in Egypt: Rise and Fall of the Wafd Party.* Allahabad: Kitab Mahal, 1967.

al-Rafi'i, 'Abd al-Rahman. *'Asr Isma'il.* 4th ed. Cairo: Dar al-Ma'arif, 1987.

———. *Mustafa Kamil.* 5th ed. Cairo: Dar al-Ma'arif, 1984.

———. *Shua'ra' al-wataniyya fi misr.* 2d ed. Cairo: Dar al-Ma'arif, 1966.

———. *Thawrat 1919: Tarikh misr min sanat 1914 ila sanat 1921.* 4th ed. Cairo: Dar al-Ma'arif, 1987.

Ramadan, 'Abd al-'Aziz. *Tatawwur al-haraka al-wataniyya al-misriyya min sanat 1918 ila sanat 1936.* Cairo: Dar al-Kitab al-'Araby, 1968.

Ramusack, Barbara N., and Antoinette Burton. "Feminism, Imperialism and Race: A Dialogue Between India and Britain." *Women's History Review* 3: 4 (1994): 469–81.

Raymond, André. *Cairo.* Trans. Willard Wood. Cambridge, Mass.: Harvard University Press, 2000.

———. "Essai de géographie des quartiers de résidence aristocratique au Caire au XVIIIième siècle." *Journal of the Economic and Social History of the Orient* 6 (1963): 58–103.

Rees, Joan. *Writings on the Nile: Harriet Martineau, Florence Nightingale, Amelia Edwards.* London: Rubicon Press, 1995.

Regulations approuvés par le ministre de l'instruction publique pour l'organisation des écoles sous Mohammad 'Ali. Paris, n.d.

Reid, Donald Malcolm. *Whose Pharaohs? Archeology, Museums, and Egyptian National Identity from Napoleon to World War I.* Berkeley: University of California Press, 2002.

Report of Commissioners Appointed by the Board of Foreign Missions of the United Presbyterian Church of North America to Visit the Missions of India and Egypt. Philadelphia, Pennsylvania, 1881.

Ringer, Monica. *Education, Religion and the Discourse of Cultural Reform in Qajar Iran.* Costa Mesa, Calif.: Mazda Publishers, 2001.

Rizq, Younan Labib. "Al-Ahram: A Diwan of Contemporary Life." *Al-Ahram Weekly* (Cairo): 1994, 1995, 1999.

Robinson, Ronald, and John Gallagher, with Alice Denny. *Africa and the Victo-*

rians: The Official Mind of Imperialism. 1961. Reprint. London: Macmillan and Co., 1981.

Roper, Michael, and John Tosh. *Manful Assertions: Masculinities in Britain since 1800.* New York and London: Routledge Press, 1991.

Russell, Mona L. "Creating the New Woman: Consumerism, Education, and National Identity in Egypt, 1863–1922." Ph.D diss., Georgetown University, 1997.

Sabbah, Fatna A. *Woman in the Muslim Unconscious.* Trans. Mary Jo Lakeland. New York: Pergamon Press, 1984.

Sabry, Mohammad. *La Révolution Égyptienne.* Paris: Le Librarie J. Vrin, 1919.

Said, Edward W. *Culture and Imperialism.* New York: Knopf, 1993.

———. *Orientalism.* New York: Vintage Press, 1979.

———. *The Question of Palestine.* New York: Times Books, 1979.

Said, Mohammad. *De l'Instruction publique en Égypte et des réformes a y introduire.* Cairo: Imprimerie Franco-Egyptienne, 1888.

Safran, Nadav. *Egypt in Search of a Political Community: An Analysis of the Intellectual and Political Evolution of Egypt, 1804–1952..* Cambridge, Mass.: Harvard University Press, 1961.

Salama, Girgis. *Tarikh al-ta'lim al-ajnabi fi misr.* Cairo: Nashr al-Rasa'il al-Jama'iyya, 1963.

Salima, Riya (Pseud. of Mme. Rachid-Pasha). *Harems et musulmanes d'Égypte.* Paris: F. Juren, 1900.

Salmoni, Barak A. "Pedagogies of Patriotism: Teaching Socio-Political Community in Turkish and Egyptian Education." Ph.D. Diss., Harvard University, 2002.

Sarhank, Isma'il. *Haqa'iq al-akhbar 'an duwal al bihar.* Vol. 2. Bulaq: Matba'at al-Amiriyya, 1898.

Savary, Claude Etienne. *Lettres sur l'Égypte où l'on offre le parallèle des moeurs anciennes et modernes de ses habitans, où l'on décrit l'état, le commerce, l'agriculture, le gouvernement du pays.* Paris: Onfroi, 1785.

al-Sayyid, Ahmad Lutfi. *Discours politiques.* Cairo, Imprimerie al-Jaridah, 1909.

———. *Safahat matwiyya min tarikh al-haraka al-istiqlaliyya fi Misr.* Cairo: Matba'at al-Muqtataf wa al-Muqatam, 1946.

Sazkar, Tanika. "The Hindu Wife and the Hindu Nation." *Studies in History,* 8: 2 (1992): 213–35.

Schölch, Alexander. *Egypt for the Egyptians: The Socio-Political Crisis in Egypt, 1878–1882.* London: Ithaca Press, 1981.

Schulze, Reinhard C. "Colonization and Resistance: The Egyptian Peasant Rebellion in 1919." In *Peasants and Politics in the Modern Middle East,* ed. Farhad Kazemi and John Waterbury, 171–202. Miami: Florida International University Press, 1991.

Scott, Joan Wallach. *Gender and the Politics of History.* New York: Columbia University Press, 1988.

Senior, Nassau William. *Conversations and Journals in Egypt and Malta in Two Volumes.* London: S. Low, Marston, Searle and Rivington, 1882.

Shaarawi, Huda. *Harem Years: The Memoirs of an Egyptian Feminist (1879–1924)*. Trans. Margot Badran. New York: The Feminist Press at the City University of New York, 1987.

Shakry, Omnia. "Schooled Mothers and Structured Play: Child Rearing in Turn-of-the-Century Egypt." In *Remaking Women: Feminism and Modernity in the Middle East,* ed. Lila Abu-Lughod, 126–70. Princeton: Princeton University Press, 1998.

Sharkey, Heather. *Living With Colonialism: Nationalism and Culture in the Anglo-Egyptian Sudan.* Berkeley: University of California Press, 2003.

al-Shayyal, Jamal al-Din. *Tarikh al-tarjama wal-haraka al-thiqafiyya.* Cairo: Dar al-Fikr al-'Araby, 1951.

Shissler, Holly. *Between Two Empires: Ahmet Agaoglu and the New Turkey.* London: I. B. Tauris, 2003.

Silvera, Alain. "The First Egyptian Student Mission to France under Moham-mad 'Ali." In *Modern Egypt: Studies in Politics and Society,* ed. Elie Kedourie and Sylvia G. Haim, 1–22. London: Frank Kass, 1980.

Sinha, Mrinalini. *Colonial Masculinity: The "Manly Englishman" and the "Effiminate Bengali" in the Late Nineteenth Century.* Manchester and New York: Manchester University Press, 1995.

Sonbol, Amira al-Azhary. *The Creation of a Medical Profession in Egypt, 1800–1922.* Syracuse, N.Y.: Syracuse University Press, 1991.

Spellberg, Denise A. *Politics, Gender, and the Islamic Past: The Legacy of 'A'isha bint Abi Bakr.* New York: Columbia University Press, 1994.

St. John, Bayle. *Village Life in Egypt (With Sketches of the Said).* London: Chap-man and Hall, 1853.

Starrett, Gregory. "The Margins of Print: Children's Religious Literature in Egypt." *The Journal of the Royal Anthropological Institute* 2:1 (1996): 117–40.

———. "Our Children and Our Youth: Religious Education and Political Authority in Mubarak's Egypt." Ph.D diss., Stanford University, 1991.

———. *Putting Islam to Work: Education, Politics, and Religious Transformation in Egypt.* Berkeley: University of California Press, 1998.

Steward, Desmond. *Great Cairo: Mother of the World.* London: Hart-Davis, 1969.

Stoler, Ann Laura. *Carnal Knowledge and Imperial Power. Race and the Intimate in Colonial Rule.* Berkeley: University of California Press, 2002.

al-Tabi'i, Mohammad. *Misr ma qabla al-thawra: Min asrar al-sasah wa al-siyasiyin.* Cairo: Dar al-Ma'arif, 1978.

Tahir, Baha'. *Ibna' Rifa'a: al-thaqafa wal-hurriya.* Cairo: Dal al-Hilal, 1993.

al-Tahtawi, Rifa'a Rafi'. *al-'Amal al-kamila li Rifa'a Rafi' al-Tahtawi.* Ed. Moham-mad 'Imara. Beirut: al-Mu'assasah al-'Arabiyya lil-Dirasa wal-Nashr, 1973.

———. *Qala'id al-mafakhir fi ghara'ib 'aw'id al-awa'il wa al-awakhir.* Cairo: Dar al-Tiba'a, 1833.

Tamraz, Nihal. *Nineteenth-Century Cairene Houses and Palaces.* Cairo: American University in Cairo Press, 1998.

Tang, Xiaobing. *Global Space and the Nationalist Discourse of Modernity: The Historical Thinking of Liang Qichao*. Stanford: Stanford University Press, 1996.

Tawwaf, Cf. *Egypt 1919, Being a Narrative of Certain Incidents of the Rising in Upper Egypt*. Alexandria: Whitehead Morris, 1925.

Thompson, Elizabeth. *Colonial Citizens: Republican Rights, Paternal Privilege, and Gender in French Syria and Lebanon*. New York: Columbia University Press, 2000.

Toledano, Ehud R. "Social and Economic Change in the 'Long Nineteenth Century.'" In *The Cambridge History of Egypt, Volume Two. Modern Egypt from 1517 to the End of the Twentieth Century*, ed. M. W. Daly, 252–84. Cambridge: Cambridge University Press, 1998.

———. *State and Society in Mid-Nineteenth-Century Egypt*. Cambridge: Cambridge University Press, 1990.

Travels of Ali Bey [pseud.] in Morocco, Tripoli, Cyprus, Egypt, Syria and Turkey between 1803 and 1807, Written by Ali Bey Himself. London: Longman, Hurst, Rees, Orme and Brown, 1816.

Treves, Fredrick, Sir. *The Land That is Desolate: An Account of a Tour in Palestine and London*. London: John Murray, 1913.

Tucker, Judith E. *Women in Nineteenth-Century Egypt*. Cambridge: Cambridge University Press, 1985.

Tugay, Ermine Foat. *Three Centuries: Family Chronicles of Turkey and Egypt*. Westport, Conn.: Greenwood Press Publishers, 1973.

Van Vleck, Micheael Richard. "British Educational Policy in Egypt, 1882–1922." Ph.D. diss., the University of Wisconsin, 1990.

Vatikiotis, P. J. *The History of Modern Egypt: From Muhammad Ali to Mubarak*. Baltimore: Johns Hopkins University Press, 1991.

Wansleben, Johann Michel. *Nouvelle relation en forme de journal d'un voyage fait en Égypte*. Paris: Chez Estienne Michallet, 1677.

Warner, Charles Dudley. *Mummies and Moslems*. Hartford, Conn.: American Publishing Co., 1876.

Whately, Mary Louisa. *Letters from Egypt to Plain Folks Back Home*. London: Seeley, 1879.

Wilkinson, Sir I. Gardner. *A Handbook for Travellers in Egypt*. London: John Murray, 1858.

———. *Modern Egypt and Thebes, Being a Description of Egypt, Including the Information Required for Travellers in that Country*. London: John Murray, 1843.

Williams, Patrick, and Linda Chrisman, eds. *Colonial Discourse and Post-Colonial Theory*. New York: Columbia University Press, 1994.

Wilson, Joan Hoff. "The Illusion of Change: Women in the American Revolution." In *The American Revolution: Explorations in the History of American Radicalism*, ed. Alfred Young, 383–446. DeKalb: Northern Illinois University Press, 1976.

Winichakul, Thongchai. *Siam Mapped: A History of the Geo-Body of a Nation*. Honolulu: University of Hawaii Press, 1994.

Wissa, Hanna F. *Assiout: The Saga of an Egyptian Family*. Sussex, England: The Book Guild, 1994.

Wolfe, Patrick. "History of Imperialism: A Century of Theory, from Marx to Postcolonialism." *American Historical Review* 102: 2 (1997): 338–420.

Youssef, Amine. *Independent Egypt*. London: John Murray, 1940.

Zantop, Susanne. *Colonial Fantasies: Conquest, Family, and Nation in Precolonial Germany, 1770–1870*. Durham, N.C.: Duke University Press, 1997.

Zayid, Mahmud Yusuf. *Egypt's Struggle for Independence*. Beirut: Khayats, 1965.

Zolondek, Leon. "Al-Tahtawi and Political Freedom." *The Muslim World* 54 (1964): 90–97.

Index

'Urabists, 75–77, 79, 81–82, 84–85, 134,
142–43, 154
urban education, 103
al-Ustadh (The professor), 143

veiled protectorate, 75, 83, 93–94, 97–99,
171
veiling, 6, 61–63, 96. *See also hijab*
Versailles Peace Conference, 168–69,
173–76
Voltaire, 26, 33, 46, 220–21n55

Wadi al-Nil (The Valley of the Nile), 47,
133
Wafd Party, 163, 168–69, 171–81, 183, 185,
189–90, 193, 195–96, 202, 211, 249nn11,13,
250n29, 252n87, 253n103
Waqf administration, 104–5, 155, 198
waqf moneys, 103, 236n6
Warner, Charles Dudley, 64–65
al-Watan (The nation), 134, 200, 252n97
water pipes, 59
Western imagination: Egyptian pharaonic
past in, 53
Whately, Mary, 64
white slavery, 44, 104–5, 197
widow burning, 3–4
Wilson, Woodrow, 167, 172
Wingate, Reginald, Sir, 172, 211
Winichakul, Thongchai, 216–17n2, 220n46
Wissa, Hanna F., 254n9
woman question, 5–7, 214–15nn18–20;
Dar al-Alsun and, 220–21n55; feminism

and, 207–8; "new woman" debate and,
152–54, 163–65, 246nn64,65,68; 1919
Revolution and, 182, 188–89
women, Egyptian, 5–6; British occupation
and, 96–99; cultivation of nationalism
and, 108, 238n21; education of (*see* education of Egyptian women); in Egyptian press, 143–44; in European travel
literature, 57–69, 71–72; modernity in
Cairo and, 44–45; "new woman"
debate and, 152–65; 1919 Revolution
and, 174, 182–95, 205–11, 251n64
women, French, 37–38
Women's Central Committee (Wafd
Party), 189, 207
Women's Missionary Magazine, 109, 113,
238–39n33
women's press, 7–8, 146–49, 151, 207, 210,
245n40, 246nn56,58
women's work, 109
World War I, 169–78, 195, 249n16,
250n29

Youssef, Amine, 172
Yusuf, 'Ali, 141, 155, 161

Zaghlul, Sa'ad, 117, 119, 131, 141, 163, 171–
77, 183, 185, 195–97, 202–4, 211, 249n23,
252nn87,89, 253n104
Zaghlul, Safia, 131, 195
"Zaghlul Misr," 202–4
Zeidan, Jurji, 140, 142, 150, 244n29
zenana work, 108–9

Compositor:	BookMatters, Berkeley
Indexer:	Sharon Sweeney
Text:	10/13 Galliard
Display:	Galliard
Printer and Binder:	Integrated Book Technology, Inc.